THE LIFE AND TIMES OF HENRY BELLMON

THE LIFE AND TIMES OF HENRY BELLMON

by Henry Bellmon

WITH PAT BELLMON

Council Oak Books   Tulsa

Council Oak Publishing Company, Inc.
Tulsa, OK 74120
© 1992 by Henry Bellmon
All rights reserved
96 95 94 93 92   5 4 3 2 1

ISBN 0-933031-47-5
LC 91-73539
Designed by Carol Haralson

CONTENTS

To Shirley and our daughters Ann, Gail, and Pat,
whose understanding and tolerance made a political career possible;
And to my mother Edith Caskey Bellmon,
whose teaching made public service personally rewarding.

PREFACE

There will never be another Henry Bellmon.

Some will cheer loudly at the mention of that thought. Others, more prescient, will know the truth.

Henry Bellmon defies easy classification. A Richard Nixon ally and confidant, Bellmon supported busing to promote racial integration; a combat-decorated Marine, he voted "to give away the Panama Canal"; the founder of the modern Oklahoma Republican Party, he has consistently opposed formalized prayer in the public schools, while supporting the Equal Rights Amendment and appointing American Civil Liberties Union members to important cabinet positions.

For four exciting, often roller coaster years, 1987 through 1990, I had the privilege of occasionally serving as Henry Bellmon's lawyer, for when I was Attorney General of Oklahoma that is often what he thought I was. I'll never forget the call I received from him before either of us took office. Even though we were strongly committed to different political parties, he wanted to meet with me to enlist my aid for a complicated education matter. I instantly agreed, and off we went.

Over the next few years, the hot lines often rang; the governor and I found ourselves in airplanes negotiating with union and management, touring industrial facilities, conducting round tables and always discussing his incredible career. In one of my favorite summits, the Governor and I met with Governor Bill Clinton and the Arkansas Attorney General to discuss the volatile Illinois River pollution issue. Governor Bellmon, whom some erroneously think of as humorless, got a full briefing from me and my staff on the way to the meeting at Shangri-La Resort in northeastern Oklahoma. The Governor began the summit with, "Welcome to Green Country—and we don't mean the rivers." Later, at the press conference, when asked what Oklahoma would do if no agreement or progress was reached, Bellmon deadpanned, "Well, we have a large National Guard in Oklahoma that needs something to do."

I had always felt that a major problem in Oklahoma was that the various branches of government, and even departments within those branches, refused to work together. So I was committed to try to work with the Governor whenever possible, despite political differences. When you got to Henry Bellmon, it was easy. He was well-informed and wise, but he always listened. He had the general interest of Oklahoma at heart, though many partisan legislators of both parties refused to see that. We even plotted occasionally for one of us to play the bad-guy role to fool those whose superficiality prevented them from seeing the bigger picture. Some legislators came to refer to us as "Henry I and Henry II," but I didn't mind. To know Bellmon well was to trust him, even to the point of confiding personal problems. He listened, cared, and helped.

In times of crisis when a course of immediate action wasn't clear, Henry Bellmon would, more often than not, simply announce that he would just let the adversaries "stew in their own juices." He braised many a foe, seemingly turning up the heat by his unwillingness to lose control. Perhaps the nervous slip of tongue with which an inexperienced emcee once introduced the Governor is sometimes appropriate: Struggling to get both "honorable" and "Henry" out, he blurted, "Ladies and Gentlemen, the ornery Henry Bellmon."

Over his impressive career, this mountain of a man has farmed, fought for his country on the islands of the Pacific, created a modern political party. He has been a governor—indeed, his place in history is assured as he was the first Republican governor of a southern state since the Reconstruction—and a United States senator and then a governor again. He has been a businessman, a manufacturer, a director of one of the finest, most socially responsible major corporations in America. He's been the confidant of presidents and eminent political figures. He's been a proud husband and father, and perhaps above all, he's been a friend— not only to those he knows, but to those he knows about—the poor, the disadvantaged, the oppressed, the uneducated.

This important book is more than kiss and tell, although some of that appears. Herein Henry Bellmon tells the story of how it all occurred (of use to any political candidate or any person interested in this fascinating era of American history) and why it occurred. Here a self-confessed not-very-successful farmer and not-very-dynamic orator shows what happened to make him a sterling example of that great American myth—the American dream. Here this yeoman farmer rises to accept the challenges offered him and succeeds beyond anyone's imagination. Now, unbowed by success, and unconverted by the flirtations of power, he takes his tough hide back to the farm, though he has seen "Paree."

This is a story with some self-defense and some admissions against interest. Throughout it is a story of the courage, humility, intellect, wit, and morality that is Henry Bellmon.

Henry Bellmon doesn't demand that the reader see everything his way. Indeed, I could make the case that Henry Bellmon doesn't care what the reader thinks at all. I do believe he trusts both readers and citizens alike to see why he acted as he did, and after time for reason, he believes they will approve.

There probably will never be another Henry Bellmon. But for the sake of our state and country, I hope I'm wrong. For Henry Bellmon, echoing Burke, has followed the observation he makes in this book that "the politician who tries to follow public opinion rather than lead gets left behind."

ROBERT H. HENRY
Dean, School of Law
Oklahoma City University

Boy, Marine, and Farmer

ABOVE: *Isaac Beniah Caskey and Nancy Eleanor Andrews Caskey with their seven children. Bellmon's mother Edith stands behind her father and his aunt Beth on the front row, far left.*

FACING PAGE, CLOCKWISE: *Edith Caskey married George Delbert Bellmon August 18, 1920. He was a farmer and widower with nine children. Delbert holds Henry, the couple's first son. The students of Penrose School. Henry, a second-grader, is fourth from left front row; younger brother in is fourth from right.*

Bellmon's father, Delbert (third from left) in front of what would become the Bellmon "Home Place."

RIGHT: Henry's high school graduation picture, taken in 1938. He purchased the suit for debate team contests with money raised from the sale of skunk and possum hides. BELOW: In April 1942, Henry went to Oklahoma City to sell a load of pigs and returned a Marine enlistee. This is the twenty-five cent photo he had taken for the Marines.

BELOW: The house as it looked when Henry returned from World War II and began bulldozing work to improve the deteriorating farm.

Henry's favorite photograph of Shirley is this 1945 high school graduation picture. The shy young woman would get a thorough breaking-in to political life. With pots, pans and utensils, Henry's fellow legislators shivareed the newlyweds Oklahoma-style on the House floor.

AT RIGHT: On a rabbit-hunting trip, Henry photographed Shirley along Red Rock Creek in December 1946, shortly after they met.

Henry proposed marriage to Shirley Lee Osborn on their third date. They married six weeks later, January 24, at the First Methodist Church in Billings. A state representative and farmer, he was 25; she was 19.

As she often did, Shirley made these identical dresses for her stair-step daughters. Left to right are Pat, Gail and Ann. The Bellmons had this Christmas photograph taken in 1958; Henry was Noble County Republican chairman.

Henry's favorite Marine photo is this one, taken when he received the Silver Star. It was Henry's resolve during the war— to do whatever he could to find peaceful ways to resolve conflicts—that would soon draw him into public service.

BELOW: After the battle of Iwo Jima, Henry (at left) became executive officer of C Company. Company commander George Hartness is third from left. Shortly after, the Japanese surrendered.

The Boy

My mother, Edith Caskey, had cared for her aged parents and been a school teacher for eighteen years before she married my father when she was thirty-seven years old. My father, George Delbert Bellmon, had already raised a family of seven girls and two boys. His first wife died on Armistice Day 1918, and he and my mother married two years later. I was born September 3, 1921. Mother was eleven years younger than Dad, and she often retold an episode from a then-popular Aunt Het cartoon strip that showed Aunt Het talking across the back fence to a neighbor lady. Aunt Het was saying, "No, there was never any insanity in my family, but I do have an aunt who married a man with nine children."

My mother's family had come to Oklahoma from Iowa before statehood. They made the three-week trip in a covered wagon after loading the farm machinery on a freight car to be moved by rail. The family settled on a farm three miles east of Billings, where the thirteen of them lived for many years before moving to town. The Caskeys were Covenanters, members of a branch of the Reformed Presbyterian Church. They had been devout followers of their faith in Iowa and joined with other local members to form a church in the Billings community. When the church faded away, my mother became a Methodist and served for twenty-five years as superintendent of the Sunday school. In addition to being devoutly religious, members of the Caskey family were talented musicians. I have fond memories of my mother playing the piano and singing in a deep alto voice. Her favorite song was "Whispering Hope" and I imagine, considering the financial circumstances in which she and my father were living, it was a message she frequently needed to hear.

In 1913, after my grandfather's death, my grandmother, my mother,

her sister Beth, and her brothers moved to Kansas City so my mother's brothers, who had formed a musical quartet, could pursue their musical careers. They travelled as members of the Redpath organization on the Chautauqua circuit. When one of the boys died at an early age, his place was taken by another brother and the quartet continued touring until 1916. World War I broke up the quartet and my grandmother, mother, and his sister Beth returned to Billings. As a young woman, my mother taught in rural schools in the Billings community and then in Kansas City. Her salary started at only $35 a month, but even so she saved enough to help purchase her brothers' musical instruments. One of the instruments they bought was a set of portable chimes, said to be one of the few of its kind ever made. The instrument has become a family heirloom.

Mother was a truly remarkable woman. She made many of our clothes and arranged for hand-me-downs from other members of the family in somewhat better financial circumstances. She was a fabulous cook, even though the kitchen was primitive and her range of supplies strictly limited. She planned her baking so she was taking bread out of the oven at the time my brothers and I arrived home after our mile-and-a-quarter walk from school. I still savor the privilege of eating freshly-baked bread thoroughly slathered with fresh country butter. She usually made extra dough which she turned into doughnuts dipped in sugar glaze. Even today I can recall the tastes and smells of her kitchen.

My father was a different type. He was born on June 30, 1874, near Pittsburgh, Kansas, to a coal-mining family. His father used teams of horses to scrape away the overburden and mine coal which was hauled to town and sold to homeowners for heating. At different times, the family operated a small dairy. One of my father's jobs was to drive the milk wagon and sell milk door-to-door. Sales were made to householders who came to the wagon, where my father would pour dippers of milk into whatever containers his customers brought.

When my father was reaching his teenage years, his father decided to take the family west into what was then No Man's Land, later to become the panhandle of Oklahoma. They loaded their belongings onto wagons and drove the livestock. The trail took them down a main street of Wichita, Kansas, which at that time was a small town.

The family located along the Beaver River in what is now Beaver County, Oklahoma. They lived about five years in a dugout and endured some extremely hard times. My father and his father made the living for the family by picking up dried buffalo bones, which abounded on the prairie. These were loaded on wagons and hauled north to Liberal, Kansas, where they were sold to be shipped east and ground into bonemeal. The two of them then loaded freight on the wagons and hauled it back to Beaver City to be used by merchants to stock their stores. This was not unpleasant work during summer, but in winter when the cold winds blew from the north, the trip from Beaver to Liberal was extremely difficult and hazardous. My father told about dismounting from the wagon to walk between the doubletree and one of the horses so he could stay out of the biting cold wind.

About the time my father reached the age of fifteen, in 1889, the government made the decision to divide No Man's Land into 160-acre quarter-sections to be opened for settlement. My father hired on as a cowboy with the Q Half Circle Ranch which was being relocated to Wyoming. His job was to round up the cattle to be driven overland to their new home. He and a partner frequently had to rope renegade animals with two lariats and lead them to the corral between their horses. Dad liked to tell stories about going into prairie dog towns at sundown. The prairie rattlesnakes would be curled up waiting to go into prairie dog holes for the night. He and his partner doubled their lariats and went through the prairie dog towns killing snakes as fast as they could. He also talked about the large hailstorms which sometimes fell across the open prairie. The only protection cowboys had was to unsaddle their horses and hold the saddles over their heads until the hailstones stopped falling.

After a couple of years of riding the range, my father re-joined his family which had returned to Kansas, settling on a farm south of Sedan. At first, he intended to return to school, but he soon found he was a head taller than other members of his class and was years behind academically. He dropped out of school, married, and started a family. They came to Noble County, Oklahoma, in 1897. At the time of the Cherokee Strip Run, in 1893, he had been 19 years old, too young to participate in the land run. But four years later he purchased a relinquishment from one of the homesteaders. He paid $700 for what he later would call the North Place and brought his wife and two young daughters from Kansas to live in a dugout.

They travelled in a covered wagon and as they forded the Arkansas

River near Ark City, my father dug five small cedar trees. He planted them near the dugout on his claim and later moved them to the South Place. Three still live today.

In the third year after he had moved from Kansas, he had broken up some thirty or forty acres of prairie grassland and planted it to wheat. His crop was looking good. One morning a travelling hail insurance salesman came to see him. The salesman tried for a couple of hours to talk my father into taking out a hail insurance policy on the crop. My father declined, but the salesman persisted and continued to try to make the sale until noontime. In the custom of the day, my father invited the man to put up his horse and stay for dinner. The salesman readily agreed. After dinner, they sat and the man again made his pitch to sell hail insurance to my father. Still, Dad resisted. Hail insurance could save the farm if the wheat crop was destroyed in bad weather, the salesman told Dad. A selling point was that the policy went into effect the moment the contract was signed.

After about an hour, the salesman gave up and the men went outdoors. Off to the west, over the fields of ripening wheat, a large, threatening black cloud was rolling in. My father took one look at that cloud, turned to the salesman, and said, "Well, I believe you have convinced me that I should buy hail insurance." The deal was made, the men saddled the salesman's horse, and he rode away. Before he had gone two miles, an intense storm struck and the wheat crop was destroyed by hail. For this my father collected a substantial sum of money which helped him stay on his Oklahoma claim.

After four years, Dad purchased the adjoining farm to the south for $4,000. The South Place, as it was called, had no well for drinking water, but with a four-room frame house located on a well-maintained country road, it was a more desirable place to live. There Dad would raise two families, totalling thirteen children. During the late teens and the roaring twenties, my father prospered. An oil field was discovered that was partially on his land. Unfortunately, the two "Bellmon wells" were not prolific or long-lived. They caused a flurry of prosperity which probably left the family worse off than if it had never happened. It was a cycle that would be repeated in my own case sixty years later.

In addition to production of the oil wells, my father had income as a teamster. He owned about fifty head of horses which were formed into teams of four and hired to do various kinds of oil field work: scraping slush pits, moving boilers, hauling rig timbers and bull wheels, digging cellars, and performing other heavy work. Work in the East Billings field went on for several years but when the rigs finally were built and the wells drilled, the work stopped and my father's days as a teamster were over. At that time he owned five quarter-sections of land, two of them high-priced Kay County quarters east of Tonkawa. (It was there that my mother went to stay with a sister-in-law when I was due to be born.)

As the oil boom fizzled, my father found himself heavily in debt and was forced to turn back the Kay County land to its former owners. Also, he sold one quarter of the Noble County land and tried to hang on to the other two—the North Place and the South Place. He was burdened with a $10,000 "deficiency judgment," calling for payment at ten percent interest. The interest of about a hundred dollars came due each month. With wheat selling for twenty-five cents a bushel and hogs and cattle about four cents a pound and with the low yields we were receiving, there was simply no way the payments could be made. My father was facing foreclosure and bankruptcy.

Built in stages mostly before the turn of the century, our farm house was a t-shaped structure, without electricity, running water or modern-day amenities. Our home was seven miles east and one mile south of Billings on a subsistence farm. We raised chickens and eggs for food. We milked cows, then separated milk into skim milk, which was fed to the pigs, and cream, which was churned into butter to be sold on Saturdays at a nearby country store which provided food to oil field workers. Surplus eggs were sold and the money used to buy staples we could not produce.

In summer we tried to raise a garden, but generally without much success. We usually had cabbages, green beans, tomatoes, lettuce and onions. Any surplus was canned or stored for winter so that we rarely bought vegetables. My father was successful at growing potatoes. Some-times he harvested as many as fifty bushels. These were put in bins in the cellar under the house and one of my weekend jobs was to sort potatoes, removing spoiled ones. He had planted a small orchard and we raised apples. They were abundant, though often of inferior quality. Many were crushed for cider and apple butter.

In addition to raising our food, my father also half-soled our shoes, trimmed our hair, and butchered all the meat we used. Most of this was pork, which could be cured in the smokehouse and used as needed. We kept a sizable flock of chickens which had the run of the barnyard. The hens frequently hid their nests and laid their eggs in out-of-the-way places. One regular evening chore was to gather the eggs so snakes and varmints would not destroy them.

Rural electrification reached our community in 1938. I remember coming home from college for Thanksgiving vacation and finding electricity finally had been turned on. My dad had been concerned that he could not meet the $3 minimum monthly payment and so had insisted on installing the minimum number of light sockets. Even so, I remember how dim the coal oil lights looked in comparison to the bright electric lights. We would not get our first electric refrigerator until after my return from World War II.

We heated the house and cooked with wood-burning stoves. It soon came to be my job to keep the wood box full. This was an onerous task that took the better part of an hour every evening so Mom could keep fires going that night and next day. Keeping the house warm in winter was impossible. Our house sat on a sandstone rock foundation. The rocks were loosely laid and left plenty of space for the wind to whistle through. Small animals and rodents also had easy access to the dry, relatively warm space under our house. The kitchen and living room linoleum puffed up and down and, on cold, windy winter days, allowed much cold air and odor to come into the house. Our upstairs bedrooms were never heated and the north room, where my brother Irvin and I slept, always seemed colder than the inside of an icebox.

Going to bed in winter was a dreaded experience. Irvin and I would wait as long as we could, get as warm as possible by the pot-bellied stove in the living room, dash up the stairs, and jump into bed where we snuggled together until we got a place warm enough to be comfortable. In addition, the windows did not fit too well and many mornings we stepped out of bed onto a floor lightly dusted with new-fallen snow. Our bedroom was also the storage place for the family's winter supply of flour. At harvest time my father always managed to save a fifty-bushel trailerload of wheat which was taken to the flour mill and milled into white flour. Wheat germ was turned into a cereal which we called cream of wheat and bran was brought home and fed to milk cows. The flour was put into hundred-pound sacks which my father carried upstairs and stored on a board platform laid on top of two fifty-five-gallon oil drums. This was designed to keep the mice away from the flour, which it generally did. However, nothing we could do would prevent the flour from becoming infested with weevils, so it was necessary for my mother to sift the flour before using it to make bread or gravy.

One of the greatest problems around our home was the shortage of potable drinking water. My father considered that he had a special gift as a "water witch." Taking a forked limb from a peach tree or, in an emergency, a willow tree, he would walk slowly across the ground and when he felt the limb in his hand begin to pull downward he would be on top of a vein of water. According to Dad, the stronger the pull, the larger the vein and the shallower the well would have to be drilled or dug. He also felt he could follow the vein along to the point where two veins crossed and that would be the ideal spot to locate a well. He gave my brothers and me instructions on how to be a water witch and on many occasions I was convinced I could feel the peach limb being pulled downward no matter how firmly it was grasped.

The fact was that in spite of his assumed powers as a water witch and even though many wells were drilled on our farm, none of them produced water of satisfactory quality in significant quantities. Witching may work where water abounds, but where there's no water a water witch can't help. Even though over the years my father had hand-dug or drilled seven different wells to depths of thirty to forty feet, none of them produced enough water to meet the needs of the family and our livestock during the frequent hot, dry periods.

East of our home in an adjoining pasture there was a high quality water well that never went dry. Since the owner was friendly to my parents, for years we were allowed to haul water from that well to our house for domestic use. This was done in a fifty-five-gallon, galvanized water barrel mounted on a sled which we pulled behind a team of horses or sometimes behind our automobile. Hauling water was a great nuisance, especially in cold or windy weather. We pulled the sled-mounted barrel from our kitchen door along a dusty trail through the pasture to the water well. After removing the cover of the well, we used a bucket attached to the end of a rope to draw up water and pour it through a funnel into the barrel. Since the barrel held fifty-five gallons and the bucket held two gallons, it took a considerable amount of drawing to fill the barrel. On the way home we drove slowly to prevent too much water from sloshing out. In winter we would arrive back at the house with the barrel thoroughly coated with ice. During winter nights, water in the barrel would freeze so it was necessary to keep a crowbar handy to knock a hole in the ice.

Facing the persistent shortage of water caused my mother and our family to be innovative in the way water was used. We all washed in the same bowl of water and all bathed in the same galvanized tubfull. This worked well for the first bather but by the time six people had used the water, it got a little thick. In winter we bathed in the kitchen in front of a hot kitchen stove with the oven door down. Altogether, it was not a terribly unpleasant experience, but it was usually limited to Saturday nights, and the Bellmon boys never objected to the infrequent bathing schedule.

Mother was a great cook and very proud of her boys. When I was old enough to start school, she packed me a fabulous lunch in a gallon lard bucket — the customary lunch pail at the time. At noon I sat on the school house steps eating. Besides sandwiches, there were two pieces of fried chicken and a big slice of my all-time favorite — lemon meringue pie. The pie was wrapped in wax paper which necessitated prolonged licking so none would be wasted. The process attracted a small crowd of detractors who began calling me a "Mamma's Boy." I failed to catch the intended insult at first, because I was justly proud of my mother. Later, I was a little angry. I felt my mother had a right to fix a good lunch if she wanted to. I was never to be much of a conformist.

The school was a one-room school house called Glenrose. It was a mile and a quarter north of our house and, at the time I started, had over forty children in eight grades. Our teacher was a very stern man named G. M. Lemon. How he managed to keep order and conduct anything resembling classes with so many children in so many grades in one room, I'll never understand. The fact is that we did learn a great deal at Glenrose and I've never in any way felt deprived educationally.

G.M. Lemon had a somewhat twisted sense of humor. It was difficult at that time for our family to keep us properly clothed. I sometimes wore shoes to school that had the toes completely worn out. My socks would work out the toes of the shoes and drag along the ground. One day we were playing baseball and I was at bat. G. M. Lemon, who was standing quietly behind me, stuck his foot around in front of mine and put his toe on my sock. When I hit the ball and started to run, I tripped and fell on my face — to gales of laughter from the other kids and the teacher. I never quite forgave him his thoughtlessness.

Partly because I did well as a first-grader and, I suppose, partly because my mother was clerk of the school board, it was decided I should skip second grade. This made my third grade year extremely difficult but I managed to keep up. One reason I suppose was that in a one-room school each class can listen to other classes recite their lessons and some learning goes on by osmosis. I've never regretted skipping a grade in school and even in college finished in seven semesters. For some reason, I never liked going to school and was happy to speed it along and get it over with.

After school was out, my brothers and I quit wearing shoes until cold weather arrived. Going barefoot gives a young boy a sense of freedom that is difficult to achieve otherwise. However, going barefoot around the farm presents certain hazards. My father had a series of strange cures for the swellings that followed when a wound became infected, as was usually the case when a rusty nail penetrated the skin. His favorite was a cow manure poultice which consisted of getting a dab of fresh cow manure, wrapping it in a cloth and tying it around the infected area. This was a long time before antibiotics and may have worked, but to my mind it wasn't worth the ignoble feeling brought on by the greenish yellow stain.

Another remedy was to find a discarded woolen garment, tear it into strips and set a piece on fire. The infected area was then held as near as possible to the smoldering fabric with the assumption that the smoke and heat would effect a cure. The worst was the remedy for sore throat. My father thought there was something therapeutic about skunk oil. One of our jobs when we were skinning skunks we had trapped for their hides was to carve away some of the fat, which was rendered and stored in bottles in the medicine cabinet. When any of us experienced a sore throat, the remedy was to take a woolen sock, saturate it with "skunk oil," and wrap it around our throats. We not only had to sleep with this remedy but wear it to school until our sore throat went away.

Adjoining our farm were other family farmers, most of whom had many children. On Sunday afternoons we frequently got together in the pasture and participated in choose-up-sides baseball games. In summer, we swam in creeks and slush pits around the oil field. Swimming in slush pits was a dangerous business because oil field workers dumped damaged steel cable and other debris into the pits. On many occasions my brothers and I stepped on sharp objects and had to go home for cow manure treatment. Swimming in creeks was safer. It was great fun to swing out over the water on homemade grapevine swings and drop in.

As early as I can remember, my brothers, neighbors and I loved to roam the creek that ran through our place, exploring the wonders of nature and temptations of adolescence. This was a small creek that, so far as I know, was never named. It drained a large area and with spring rains became a raging torrent. We swam in the fast current and floated on whatever kind of buoyant object we could find. Old inner tubes were best. After the spring rain floods abated, we frequently went fishing and usually brought home small catches of sunfish or mudcats. These my mother welcomed, though I suppose cleaning such small fish was tedious. As we grew older we were required to clean our own fish, which took much of the joy out of fishing.

When the hot dry months of summer came, the creeks dried up, and only the few deeper holes held water. These were seined with gunny sacks held open and dragged as rapidly as possible through the water. During this time my brothers and I and the neighbor boys developed a unique method of fishing. We would get into the pools in our bare feet and our birthday clothes and thrash around as violently as we could, stirring up the mud from the bottom of the creek. When the water became so muddy that the fish could not get oxygen, they came to the surface with mouths open and whiskers extended, gasping for air. Our fishing crew would be ready. With stout green clubs we cut from surrounding trees, we would creep up on the fish and hit them a sound lick. We then grabbed the stunned fish and threw them on the bank where one of our colleagues was ready to string them up. Wading barefoot, we sometimes accidentally stepped on the shell of a submerged snapping turtle. Carefully, we would probe with our hands to decide which end was the head and which end was the tail. As soon as we grasped the tail, we would lift the turtle out and throw it squirming and snapping onto the bank where our colleague would put it in a gunny sack. Snapping turtle, while not exactly a delicacy, was edible and was even sought after by some neighbors. At our house, mother tried cooking turtle only once and drew the line on any further experiences with this gourmet delight.

Trapping for civet cats, skunks, and opossum was an adventure we looked forward to each winter. We learned to identify the dens where these animals lived, set traps, and cover them. We ran the traps in early dawn before it was time to do the milking, skinning the animals and stretching the carcasses on a suitably shaped pine board so they would dry and be marketable. It was a great challenge to find a way to remove the odor from my hands after I had skinned a civet cat or skunk before going to school. I don't recall ever being sent home but there were times when my presence was undoubtedly a distraction for the entire class.

After the age of ten, my summer days were spent in the fields working with teams of horses. As soon as the school year was over there were row crops to be cultivated, then came the harvest season with horses pulling binders, then wheat to shock, then bundle wagons at threshing time. After that came plowing, which seemed to take all summer, and finally the hard clods had to be broken up with harrows or discs. By the time school started in the fall it was time to plant winter wheat.

Threshing time was the highlight of our summers in wheat country. It was the exciting culmination of a year's work, the time when rural families received most of the year's income. The Kopps, who lived three miles down the road, were the community threshermen. My brothers and I frequently rotated between sitting on the steam engine near the engineer or in the grain wagon where the rich-looking wheat poured out. Wheat would come in torrents when the measuring device on the threshing machine dumped a bushel into the wagon. It was our job to scoop the wheat around in the wagon to keep it level so the maximum quantity could be hauled to the bins.

Straw piles were like little golden mountains that sprung up in wheat fields after the threshing machine had done its job. In summer they were delightful places for active young boys to play. We could climb high up on the piles, play king of the mountain by pushing off aggressors, or, during times when we felt less combative, simply slide down the slick straw to the ground. In winter, straw piles became sources of forage for the cattle herds and homes for fur-bearing wild animals which we learned to trap and sell and thereby gain some spending money. In fact my first suit of clothes (so I could be a member of the high school debate team) was paid for with skunk skins which I trapped during a Christmas vacation.

Realizing that animal power, mostly horses, was responsible for powering agriculture for centuries, I, nevertheless, experienced no personal sorrow when mechanized equipment began to take over in the late thirties. Horses are among the Creator's most obstinate creatures. During the summer my first job early each morning was to get the horses into the barn, which sometimes meant a vigorous foot race. Then they had to be fed and harnessed, which meant getting stepped on and sometimes nipped. After breakfast the horses were taken to the field, hooked to whatever machine we were using, then worked until noon. Some horses were particularly cussed critters. Inevitably one would deliberately lift a hind foot over the steel chain tug, which would wear the skin off the inside of the leg unless the team was stopped and hooked up properly again. As often as not, the horse would lift up his foot again to get it outside the tug before you could even get the machine started.

We took our drinking water to the field in a half-gallon fruit jar wrapped in a gunny sack which was wet down early in the morning. We usually made a little house of clods to provide shade for the water jug. The water would remain cool for a couple of hours, after which it was tepid to scalding, depending on how hot the day became. The first time we stopped the horses to get a drink of water the horses would learn where the water jug was and invariably would stop at that exact spot every time we came around. My father counted himself as something of a self-taught veterinarian and tried to doctor our animals when they became ill. He had a potion which he called Humphrey's Colic Cure which he kept with him at all times. Sometimes when the teams were brought in at noon and allowed to drink too much water they would be hit with the "colic" which caused them to fall down unconscious. My father's system was to pull out the horse's tongue, put a dose of Humphrey's Colic Cure on it and close the horse's mouth. As often as not, the animal would revive quickly and could work again that afternoon. At noontime we fed the horses their hay and oats and then went to the house for our own meal. After dinner my father always said, "Now we've got to let the horses rest," whereupon we would all stretch out on the living room carpet for a twenty-minute nap. It is a practice I wish I could have followed for the rest of my life.

Along about the time I was a senior in high school, my dad decided tractors had come to stay and he worked out a deal with the local tractor salesman to trade several of our horses in as a down payment on an Allis-Chalmers tractor. The tractor had steel lugs on the wheels and, for its time, was fairly powerful and fast. The first day the tractor was delivered, my father loaded my three brothers and me on the tractor and hitched it to a drag harrow, which he pulled with a length of log chain. He drove to the field to show us how much work the tractor would do compared to the horses it was replacing. After we had made a trip across the field, he made a sharp turn to go back. As he did, one of the steel lugs caught the log chain and began dragging the harrow up on the fenders where my brothers and I were seated. Frightened and unfamiliar with the way the tractor operated, my dad cried out, "Whoa, damn you, whoa." Fortunately, before anyone was hurt the tractor engine overloaded and died. It was quite a problem to unscramble the wreckage but no permanent damage was done.

On our farm, every day began with milking cows. Each of us had to milk three or four. The normal practice was to let the cow's calf suckle at the same time we were milking. We tried to take half the milk and let the calf have half. This meant that while we were milking, the calf would be nursing and butting sharp teeth against the udder. We frequently came away with bleeding knuckles. Some of the foam from the calf's slobber would fall into the bucket of milk. I suppose this did no harm but it certainly made the milk less than palatable for drinking. My father was a "wet-handed milker." He normally squirted some of the milk onto his hands before stroking the udder and this discolored milk also dropped into the pail, adding to its unpalatability. Understandably, I have never cared much for drinking milk. In the wintertime we went out to milk the cows before sunup when frost was on the ground. In the fall before our parents had found the money to buy us new shoes for winter, we would take great delight in getting the cows up and standing on the warm ground where they'd been lying, to give our feet reprieve from the frost.

When my brothers and I were teenagers, I remember many evenings the family spent at the round oak dining table looking over pamphlets ordered from the Union Pacific Railroad. The brightly-colored brochures told glowing stories of free land available in Washington and

Oregon. At that time it seemed hopeless that we would keep the land in Oklahoma and my parents planned that when their creditors foreclosed, they would join the increasing flow of "Okies" being forced by low prices, dry weather, and high interest to leave Oklahoma and try to make a new start on the west coast. In what seemed like an act of God, one day in 1936 an oil lease broker from Perry named H. C. Donahue came to call. He wanted to lease our land for oil. My dad told him that if he would agree to take responsibility for our debts, my father would turn over the land to Donahue or to the oil company or anyone else who would take it. Donahue, who was a compassionate man, declined the offer. He told my dad that he could work out a better deal for him.

Under Donahue's guidance, my father sold Phillips Petroleum Company 240 acres of mineral rights for a twenty-year term. This left my father still owning about eighty acres of mineral rights, and Phillips took an oil lease on that for a period of five years. Donahue then arranged for my father to get a real estate loan from the Federal Land Bank for an amount sufficient to pay off all his creditors and have $800 left over to build a new barn, which we badly needed. Phillips drilled a dry hole on an adjoining farm and then allowed the lease and royalty to lapse.

In addition to the two quarter sections my parents owned, we farmed two quarters which belonged to the Robertson family. The Robertson family had been more fortunate than the Bellmon family in that fourteen good oil wells had been discovered on their land. The wells produced for many years and made the Robertsons quite wealthy. They had previously lived in Nebraska where they owned a hardware store and had bought the Oklahoma land as an investment.

After receiving the wealth from the oil field, the Robertsons moved to Ft. Lauderdale, Florida, where they bought beachfront property and a nice home and started a golf and country club. The Robertsons owned a summer home on Squirrel Lake near Minnesaqua, Wisconsin, and usually made the trip north from Florida through Oklahoma in late spring. It was a great event when they drove up in their nine-passenger Cadillac, bringing many gifts for my brothers and me. In preparation for their visit we swept down the hard-packed dirt yard in front of our house and raked away the pebbles and chicken droppings to make the place as presentable as possible. The Roberstons were ideal landlords in that they never threatened to take away the land, never criticized the amount of rent they were paid and as far as I know were satisfied they were getting a fair deal. The relationship between the Robertson family and the Bellmons lasted for over fifty years, when the land was sold.

The saddest memories of my boyhood concern the death of my brother. Irvin was only a little more than a year younger than I and was a truly outstanding student and athlete. In the summer of 1939, after Irvin had graduated from high school, he planned to attend Oklahoma A&M college. I was already a sophomore, having spent my freshman year there. We went to Stillwater and arranged to rent a room together and share expenses when the fall semester began. To supplement the family income, Irvin hired out on a threshing crew. A few days after our trip to Stillwater, the crew was working on the Lively farm a mile and a half south of our place when a thunderstorm came up. Irvin and two other men took their load of wheat into the Lively barn for shelter and were standing in the doorway watching the rain fall. A bolt of lightning hit the barn and Irvin was killed.

I vividly remember that day. When a car came over the hill from the south on the muddy road, my mother looked out the window, saw it coming and said, "I know something's happened to Irvin." Indeed, the occupants of the car told us that my brother had been killed by lightning. We immediately called the fire department in Perry which brought a resuscitator. My brother George and I tried for some time to give artificial resuscitation, but it did no good. As usual in a farm community when a tragedy occurs, my brother's funeral was huge, with every high school student and many families in attendance. The funeral parade to the Union Cemetery southeast of Billings looked a mile long. The impact on my mother and father was great, though different, as my parents' personalities were different. The men of our family were all sleeping in the upstairs bedrooms and I remember hearing my father twisting and moaning in the night as he tried unsuccessfully to sleep. My mother, who had a deep, abiding Christian faith, felt that even though the tragedy was heartbreaking, some good might come from it.

In spite of his lack of formal education, my father remained something of a philosopher all his life. He frequently gave my brothers and me cogent advice. Many of his "sayings" have stayed with me. One thing he advised us was that when we grew up and started farming on our own we should never hire a man who smoked a pipe or wore a straw hat. Pipe smokers, he said, spent all their time stuffing tobacco in their pipes and trying to keep them lit. Straw hats were a menace because in a high wind they would blow away, frightening the horses and causing the teams to run off, wrecking the machinery and possibly injuring the driver. Another bit of advice which I took literally was his counsel to marry a girl from close to home. He claimed that if a man's wife came from far away she would spend too much of her time and his money going back to visit her mother. This seemed to make sense.

My father had spent most of his life outdoors and had many observations to make about the weather. One that stuck with me was "a morning rain, like an old woman's dance, is soon over." Another of his sayings was "a whistling girl, like a crowing hen, is bound to come to some bad end." This was a reference to the fact that a hormone imbalance can cause a laying hen to act like a rooster. She then stops producing eggs and usually winds up in the stew pot. Perhaps his favorite admonition was that we should all learn to be good listeners. He put it this way: "You ain't a-learnin' nothin' when you're talkin.'" Somewhere along the way my father had learned to play the harmonica and would play and sing for the amusement of our family. He would stomp his foot as he played and then break into song. One of his favorites was "Shake that fat leg Dinah girl, make that big foot jar the ground."

Because my dad never had a chance to get an education and felt handicapped by this, he insisted his children go on to school. Many children in his first family attended colleges or universities during the more economically flush times of his life, and when my brothers and I came along, he wanted us to attend too. However, by the time I finished high school, our family's financial situation was such that I knew I could get little or no help from home. While my dad wanted me to become a lawyer, I felt a much greater interest in farming, so I chose to go to Oklahoma A&M College and study agriculture. A&M was only half as far away as the University of Oklahoma and I believed I would be more comfortable on that campus.

At A&M I enrolled in the school of agriculture, got a room for six dollars a month rent and signed up to take my meals at the so-called Aggie Co-op. About one hundred students had rented a building, hired a cook and manager and shared proportionately in the monthly bills. The bill only came to about $12 a month per customer. Food at the Aggie

Co-op was never fancy but it was nutritionally sound and we got by well on the rations we were served. By the time I'd been eating at the Aggie Co-op a few weeks, an opening for a dishwasher came up and I got the job. From then on, my meals were free.

Prior to that time, I was in economic straits. I had gone to the college with only twenty dollars and that lasted barely time enough to pay one month's rent and one month's meals. As soon as I ran out of money, I came home and sold the sow and nine pigs which I owned as a result of an FFA project. The buyer was a neighbor, Ray Osborn, who later became my father-in-law. The seventy-two dollars he paid me for my livestock, plus the money I earned, saw me through the first semester.

As time between classes allowed, I went regularly to the student employment office and sat and waited to be interviewed. From time to time I picked up small amounts of income from odd jobs, including washing windows on the newly-constructed city library, picking pears off trees that belonged to a lady who wanted the fruit but could not climb the trees, painting the steam lines which ran from the power station to the newly-constructed Gallagher Athletic Hall, and working in the "used feed" department (cleaning out chicken houses) at the College Poultry Farm. In the fall I made a few dollars picking cotton at the Agronomy Farm.

It was at the student employment office that I had my first brush with politics. Many job-seeking students were sitting patiently in the waiting room when Lt. Governor Jim Berry came bustling in with an attractive young female in tow. Without delay, they were ushered into the presence of Mr. Holland, who ran the office. Within a few minutes, the duo emerged all smiles. It was plain the girl had been given a job — something many in the waiting room had been seeking for weeks. I was infuriated at the injustice.

My first-semester roommate was a boy from a neighboring town who went to our church and whom I had known through FFA. He was a very diligent student. We both studied hard, made the Dean's Honor Roll and I was admitted to the freshman honorary scholastic fraternity, Phi Eta Sigma. At the beginning of my second semester I was unexpectedly called to the office of the dean of men. Reference was made to some form I'd filled out during the enrollment process in which I'd indicated I expected no financial support from my family. The assistant dean who was conducting the interview acted very understanding but in a condescending voice explained to me that I had no chance to make it through college and should drop out. My immediate reaction was to think, "I'll show you, you stuffy S.O.B." I went out of the office and back to my struggles. I never knew what precipitated the interview and hope not too many aspiring students left school because of this thoughtless elimination process.

By the time the second semester ended, I not only had a steady job as a dishwasher at the Aggie Co-op, but also was regularly employed in the agronomy soil laboratory, grinding soil samples. For this work, I was paid twenty cents an hour, up to seventeen dollars per month. During one period I was working at three different jobs, including the Daily O'Collegian, where I was supposed to have been paid. Because of the paper's dire economic circumstances the paychecks never came. The last three semesters I was in school, I made beds and cleaned rooms at the Dickman boarding house. This was run by another farm family from Billings which had two attractive daughters. The house was home to about twenty boys and it was a full-time job to keep the floors swept, the trash cans emptied and beds made. The other boys were somewhat tolerant of me and I generally got the job done. As a result of my school employment I brought a little money home, which I hoped to save for the fall semester. This, however, was not to be; my folks needed too many things.

After Irvin's death, I first thought I would not go back to college, but after a few days I began to realize that was a ridiculous reaction. I called the landlady, told her what had happened, and suggested that she find another person to occupy the room with me. I obtained a twenty-five dollar loan from Hal C. Jones, the local banker, a loan I paid off at the end of the school term when my final paychecks came in.

The room was rented to a young man from Minco whom I had not known. He turned out to be a difficult person, a fastidious fellow who, among other things, insisted that his mother boil his shirts. He had plenty of money to spend and liked to regale me with stories of his love life. At first I thought I would move out and leave him alone. After a few weeks, it occurred to me that the situation presented a challenge I should not pass up. I made up my mind to make a friend of this fellow rather than let him know how much I disliked him. The result was that I began to cultivate the relationship and managed it in such a way that we lived together for two semesters. I never again had difficulty in coping with distasteful people. Over the succeeding years I saw my former roommate many times and we retained a friendly relationship.

Since I was facing austere financial circumstances, college social life was not a priority for me. There were many free events, however, including regular dorm dances and musical productions in the college auditorium. Also, on the weekends I was in town, I regularly attended the First Methodist Church and participated in some of the youth activities there. I even tried to sing in the church choir but was soon invited to leave. The Caskey family musical talents passed me by.

At least once or twice a month I hitchhiked the forty miles from college to home, taking my soiled clothes for my mother to wash. I spent the weekend helping around the farm and then hitchhiked back on Sunday afternoon. Going to college under these circumstances meant dedicating every available moment to either working or studying. In the process, it was necessary to develop good work habits and strict discipline in order to keep up the load. I carried as many hours as the college would allow — twenty-two hours one semester. I completed my course work in seven semesters and put college behind me.

Making good use of available time, dealing with difficult personal relations, and managing money were the main lessons I learned in college. Much of the agricultural expertise had to be unlearned since it didn't work in practice.

At this time, events in Europe were very much on the minds of students. Hitler had captured Europe and England was under aerial bombardment, seriously threatened with invasion. Conversations among draft-aged college students frequently turned to whether the United States would be drawn into the war and whether we would be forced to leave school to join the fighting forces. The prevailing attitude was that it was Europe's war, that we had no reason to get involved as we had in World War I and that Hitler was not our problem.

On Sunday, December 7, at the end of my last semester at A&M, news came of the Japanese attack on Pearl Harbor. Our attitudes seemed to change instantly. We suddenly realized that it was not just "Europe's war," but that World War II involved all of us in one way or another. This became especially evident the next day when President Bennett called a convocation of the student body in Gallagher Field House. There, a public address system had been hooked up so we could listen by radio to President Roosevelt when he appeared before a joint session of Congress and asked for a declaration of war against Japan, Italy, and Germany. It was a particularly dramatic moment because all of us knew our lives would be changed forever. Because of the uncertainty, a dark cloud seemed to settle over the campus that afternoon. It was not completely lifted until the end of the draft some thirty years later at the conclusion of the Vietnam War.

Prior to the attack on Pearl Harbor, there had been much grousing in the press about the softness of the generation of young Americans upon whom the country would have to depend for its defense. The media reports had made the German soldiers and the Japanese military appear ten feet tall. For some reason, they chose to make Americans look and feel inferior to our potential enemies and there was some uncertainty that we would measure up to the battlefield tests that were imminent. Once Pearl Harbor occurred, the emphasis shifted and reports of American acts of heroism became frequent. I suppose it was part of some kind of propaganda effort on the part of our government. If it was, it worked well.

In my own case, my college training ended in January a few days after Pearl Harbor at the conclusion of the fall semester. I attempted to get jobs at the Boeing Aircraft factory in Wichita, at Douglas Aircraft plants in Oklahoma City and Tulsa, and at various local places. Since there was very little demand for agronomists and no interest in young men of prime draft age who would be drafted about the time they had completed their on-the-job training, I could not secure work anywhere. I went back to the farm to live with my parents. My father wanted me to apply for a 4-F exemption since he needed help on the farm. There were others in our neighborhood who did this but somehow using this device to evade the war never appealed to me.

It's a little hard to remember or explain why I chose to join the Marine Corps. No member of my family had been in any branch of military service and I knew very little about the Army, Navy, or Marines. I did have some friends at Oklahoma A&M College who had joined the Marines and I suppose I felt I would like to be with them. In addition, I had some vague notion that Marines would be where the action was and if there was to be war, I preferred to be active rather than in some backwater post. One day in April, I hauled a truckload of hogs to the Oklahoma City stockyards and while I was there I went by a Marine recruiting office and filled out the papers. It was necessary to have a photograph attached, so I went to a place where photographs could be had for a quarter, and, wearing my overalls, I had my picture made.

The Marine Corps accepted me for officer candidates school, and since I wanted to help with harvest, I chose to go into the November class. This allowed me to help with the summer work, help get the wheat planted, and then arrive in Quantico, Virginia, on November 2. I'd never been further away from home than Wichita to the north, Oklahoma City to the south and Tulsa to the east. After we had finished the harvest that summer I decided that before I went off to get shot I should see something of the world. My mother and father did not object, so on a bright early July morning, I packed a tin suitcase and hitched a ride with a young man from the neighborhood who worked at the Boeing plant in Wichita. He let me out on the highway near the Boeing factory and I waited there until I could catch a ride.

The first benefactor took me to Belleville, Kansas, where I was let out to be picked up later by two young boys from Inman, Kansas. They were using their family's tractor, combine, and truck to harvest wheat near Sidney, Nebraska. They offered me a job shoveling wheat. The harvest was slow because of untimely wet weather and because the wheat yield was great. After several days, the boys from Inman decided to move on to Redfield, North Dakota. We loaded the tractor on the back of the truck, hitched the headerless combine behind and started north. The header was mounted on a trailer and pulled behind the car. Near Rapid City, South Dakota, the grain wheel of the combine hit a bridge abutment, jerking the axle loose and letting the combine fall to the pavement. Asleep in the front seat of the truck, I woke up to the sensation of the truck rocking violently from side to side as if it would upset at any moment, and to the terrible racket of the combine scraping along the concrete pavement. The momentum carried the machinery down the road for a couple of hundred yards, where the driver finally brought it to a stop. We got out and checked the damage. Looking at me, he said, "Well, our harvest is finished." He suggested I catch a ride, which I quickly did.

At Spearfish, South Dakota, I was standing on the road trying to catch a ride further north when a pickup came by going the other way. The driver saw me, turned around, came back, and stopped. He was the operator of a lumber mill about eight miles east of Devil's Tower, Wyoming. He had a contract for making machine gun ammunition boxes for the U.S. Army and was having trouble keeping a crew to cut the timber, haul the logs, and man the sawmill machinery. He offered me four dollars a day to work as a log skidder. I did not know what a log skidder was but I was willing to find out.

Early next morning, I was taken to the area where trees were being felled. This was a very steep, hilly region with slopes of up to thirty-five percent. The team of horses I was to use were spirited Arabian stallions well-experienced in log skidding. My job was to go into the forest where the lumberjacks had felled the trees, hook the cant hooks into the end of a log, and then drag the log down the hill to the skidway where the trucks would come to take the logs to the sawmill. I struggled to keep up with my experienced instructor as he drove the horses up the steep hill to the area where the trees had been cut down. There, he adroitly fastened the cant hooks to the log and spoke to the horses, which took off at a dead run dragging the bouncing log down the hill. We ran after them. The horses stopped immediately when they got to the skidway and waited for the cant hooks to be released. My instructor then turned the reins over to me and headed back to camp.

Still a little uncertain about what was expected of me, I spoke to the horses and we started up the hill. They went so fast that I was sort of dragged along holding onto the reins and had little opportunity to guide the team. Nevertheless, we came to the appropriate place and I attached the cant hooks to the end of a log. The horses stood patiently waiting for my command. Stupidly, I had chosen a log that was lodged behind a stump and I stood downhill from the log. The instant I spoke to the horses, they jumped to keep from being hit by the log and the log was dislodged. It came crashing downhill and rolled completely over me.

I lay there on the forest floor for awhile getting my senses. My left knee had been knocked out of socket and was cocked at an awkward angle. It hurt like the very devil. Otherwise I was not injured. I suddenly realized I was in a terrible jam. It was unlikely that I would be missed until nightfall. And I wondered if those rough characters I was working with would bother to come looking for me. Even if they did, no one would know where I was. Somehow I had to get myself in condition to make my way back to camp. I began working with my leg, and though it hurt terribly, I finally got the socket back in place and tried to stand up. To my surprise, I could put my weight on my leg and in a little while could hobble down the hill.

The horses had done what they were trained to do. They had taken the log directly to the skidway and were standing, waiting patiently for someone to disengage the cant hooks so they could go back for another log. By this time, I was feeling fairly good, so I disengaged the cant hooks, spoke to the horses, and we went back up the hill and continued skidding logs for the rest of the day. I had no further difficulty remembering to stand on the uphill side of the logs.

After a few days of log-skidding I was promoted to operator of the cut-off saw and went on to do other jobs at the sawmill. I stayed for two weeks, after which I told the boss I was going to move on and wanted to be paid. To my amazement and disgust, he did not pay me the four dollars a day I had signed on for, but rather one dollar a day, after deducting three dollars a day for board and room. Nevertheless, he kindly took me back over the eight miles of logging road to the highway near Devil's Tower, where I stood in the gathering darkness hoping to catch a ride to Moorcroft, Wyoming. For the first and really only time in my life I became intensely homesick and almost changed my direction to hitchhike towards home.

Fortunately, a young man and his twin sisters driving the family pickup offered me a ride. I sat in the back while we bounced over country roads and finally wound up at a schoolhouse out in range country where there was to be a Saturday night dance. Since I was there more or less as a guest of these three people, we sat around and visited while waiting for the dance to begin. My benefactor was also a member of the military and was home on his last weekend before being sent overseas. The girls were friendly and pleasant to be with and we had a good time. After the dance, they took me to Moorcroft, where I got a room in the hotel. The next day, Sunday, I got up and went to church, had something to eat at the hotel, then took my tin suitcase and went out to the highway to catch a ride. After having no luck for several hours, I heard a train whistle. I ran to the station, quickly bought a ticket and got on the train to Cody, Wyoming.

The next morning as I was leaving my motel, I chanced to speak to the family who had the room next door. They asked me where I was going and I told them I was going to hitchhike through Yellowstone National Park. They were also going through the park and invited me to join them. The man was a dentist from Milwaukee travelling with his wife and son, who was a year or two younger than I. For the next two days, I was their guest, touring Yellowstone Park as they paid all the fees, bought all the food, paid for lodging, and generally treated me like a member of the family. At the conclusion of our tour, they left me at Old Faithful, where I fished unsuccessfully for trout in nearby meadow streams, then walked to the west gate and hitchhiked in the direction of Idaho Falls.

At Idaho Falls, I got a job working for a potato farmer. He was attempting to irrigate his crop, but a weed cutter was cleaning the canal channel above his farm and weeds were floating down, blocking the grate to his pump so that it kept running dry. My job was to go to the pump at sundown and stay all night pulling weeds out of the grate around the pump so the water could get in. For someone who's always had trouble staying awake, this was an impossible task. I did everything in my power to keep from falling asleep, but frequently dozed off. The farmer had given me a flashlight which I'd strapped to my head so I could see the weeds I was trying to pull away from the grate. After a few hours, the flashlight dropped from its mooring and I heard a thud as it went through the pump. From then on I worked in the darkness. I was continually fearful that I would get my hands on a poisonous snake while groping around in the weeds. The family gave me a quiet bedroom where I tried without much success to sleep during the day. They had several children who made considerable racket during the daytime. After a week of this, I asked for my pay and left to seek my fortune elsewhere.

At Swan Valley, on the Idaho side of the Teton Mountains, I helped a farmer put up hay for a week, then headed back to Salt Lake City. Coming into Salt Lake, I was given a ride by a Mexican field worker and two women in a dilapidated car. One woman and I sat in the back seat. After awhile she began to take an extraordinary interest in me. The closer we got to Salt Lake, the more her interest was aroused. The group got the notion I was going with them to some kind of social event. I told them I would need to get a hotel room and clean up. They let me out at the front door of a hotel and waited. I hurried through the lobby, out the back door as fast as I could, and away to another hotel. After a day in Salt Lake City, I started hitchhiking again. I hitchhiked through Wyoming and Colorado and stopped in Pampa, Texas, where I visited my half-sister Lida, then hitchhiked home. When I arrived, I still had my tin suitcase, a fairly new shirt, a new pair of khakis, and the same five dollars I'd left with two months earlier.

My hitchhiking trip was an important experience for me, as such adventures were for many young men of my generation. Hitchhiking gave us freedom of movement even though we lacked the means to travel under our own power; it enabled us to get out on our own for the first time and grow up. Each benefactor who stopped to give us a ride became a new acquaintance, and often had an interesting story to tell. The common public attitude of trust and openness which made successful hitchhiking possible seems remarkable now. It is regretable that a series of highly-publicized crimes involving hitchhikers, and a general erosion of trust have reduced the practice to emergencies. All my adult life, up to my later years in the Senate, I would frequently stop and offer a ride to a hitchhiker. Even today, I feel a sense of guilt when I pass a hitchhiker by.

My arrival home coincided closely with fall wheat-planting. I helped my father work the ground, plant the wheat and then was ready to leave for Quantico, Virginia, for Marine Corps training. Arriving at the station in Quantico, I walked across the Marine parade grounds from the depot to the headquarters building. As I passed one of the training areas, I saw several of the candidates practicing bayonet drill. Lunging at each other with sheathed bayonets on their rifles, they appeared to be doing one another great bodily harm. It was a rough introduction to military life for a farm boy who had little concept of what bayonets were all about and little desire to get involved in such activities.

The time in Quantico was extremely valuable and generally pleasant. My biggest problem was that I tended to take long steps and had a difficult time adjusting to the quick Marine Corps cadence. I was usually out of step. When a column of men is marching and one person is out of step, that person is up when the others are down and it gives a bouncing appearance. My drill instructor came to refer to me as "Bouncing Bellmon" and I was afraid of being busted out of the Marines. This ended when we held a forced march of several miles and I wound up at the head of the column right on the heels of our officers who were not burdened with the packs and weapons enlisted men were carrying. The balance of the company was strung out over the distance of a mile or more. After that, there was no more talk of my "bouncing," and I graduated around the middle of the class. About forty percent of those who had enrolled had dropped by the wayside or failed to graduate.

After graduating from reserve officers class, which lasted another ten weeks, I was assigned to the infantry training center at Camp Elliott, California. Another long train ride took me home for one week's leave. During the time I had been at Quantico, I had gained over fifty pounds, (most of it muscle) and was probably in the finest physical condition of my life. My mother hardly recognized me when I returned home but it was obvious she was very proud of her oldest son. As I was leaving the farmhouse to catch the train to California, for the only time in my adult life my mother took me in her arms and kissed me. It was the last time I saw her.

The Marine

"American Devils"

I had requested tank training. My experience with farm machinery would help me, I reasoned, and I had no particular desire to be a rifleman. I wanted no more close-order drill. From Camp Elliott, I was detailed to tank school at Jacques' Farm near San Diego, California. Jacques' Farm was a fairly primitive tent encampment where several hundred Marine trainees were being taught the rudiments of tank operation and battle tactics. After completing the training, new tankers would be assigned to combat units for transport to the Pacific area where the Marines were expanding their island-hopping operations.

Within a relatively short time, I was called to the camp headquarters where I was interviewed by a young captain named Bob. Bob had been a member of the First Marine Division during the attack on Guadalcanal and had been sent back to the states to help form a tank company of the new Fourth Division being organized at Camp Pendleton some forty miles north. Bob told me later he picked me to be a tank platoon leader because he saw me swinging a sledge hammer helping a tank crew repair a broken track. He liked the idea of officers who were not afraid of getting their hands dirty and who were not above working with their men. I suggested to Captain Bob that we choose our company personnel from those whose record books indicated they had been in the 4-H or FFA clubs. This would bring in the farm boys who could probably maintain and operate mechanical equipment with a minimum of problems. He made the selections at least partially on that basis.

After a few additional weeks at Jacques' Farm, the company was moved to Camp Pendleton for several more months' training. As time went on and I came to know Bob better, I began to have misgivings about his choice of me as a company officer. We were as different as two people can be. He was from a wealthy New York City family and his interest was primarily in social events. Feeling extremely uncomfortable and out of place among Bob's friends, I didn't particularly want to travel in these circles, but as a company officer I was frequently pressed into going with him to Los Angeles and Beverly Hills. Another lieutenant was also a socialite and he and Bob always managed to find a reason to get away from camp on weekends. Anytime there was weekend duty to be taken care of that involved one of the tank officers, the assignment was likely to come to me.

By the time we were ordered overseas, it was determined that the tanks used for training were not suitable for battle, so they were to be returned to the Marine supply depot in San Diego. The railroad cars to haul our tanks arrived on Friday and, as could be anticipated, Captain Bob called me into the office and told me it would be my duty to remain with my men in camp over the weekend to load the tanks on flat cars and have them ready for a locomotive to pick up Monday.

I passed word to my platoon members that their weekend leaves were cancelled and on Saturday morning we gathered the twelve training tanks and headed for the railroad. When we reached the Aslito siding five miles north of camp, I was appalled to discover there was no ramp and simply no apparent way to get the tanks from the ground up to the deck of the flat cars. Nearby, we found a supply of new railroad cross-ties which had been unloaded in anticipation of making track repairs. We also discovered that the width of the tank tracks was adequate to allow the tanks to be driven straddling the rails from a road crossing to where the flat cars had been parked. Using the wrenches we had, the brake control wheels which blocked the end of each of the flat cars could be removed.

It was decided that a temporary ramp could be made by stacking the ties at the end of the first flat car and that by removing the railroad brake control wheels, the tanks could be driven from one flat car to another. This made it possible for us to drive the first tank up onto the first flat car, then across the intervening spaces to the end of the train. As the tanks were loaded, however, the ends of the cars began to crumble and considerable damage was done. Then, after the tanks were finally on the cars, no load-binders were available to hold the tanks on the flat cars. We assumed the railroad would take care of this problem. Since we had no chains, boomers, or blocks of any kind, we could do no more. Movement of the tanks from the road to the ramp caused the spikes in the rails to loosen and the rails to fall over. We did our best to straighten the rails and replace the spikes, but without the right tools, our work was less than perfect. Finally, we replaced the brake control wheels on the flat cars and returned the railroad ties. We felt we had done all we could under the circumstances. In any event, we had followed orders. We complimented each other about the system we had improvised. *Semper Fidelis!*

A few days later, I was called to division headquarters where a very irate two-star general confronted me with a series of photographs showing the broken flat car ends, the tipped over rails, and a long line of tanks in various precarious positions about to fall off the flat cars. It turned out that the railroad switch engine had simply hooked onto the flat cars and hauled them the forty miles into San Diego without bothering to check whether or not the tanks were secured. At first the general was beside himself with fury, but as I explained what had happened, the old man became practically congratulatory for our having accomplished the job under such handicaps.

Following another near-tragedy, I had a second run-in with the general. One afternoon, Lieutenant English, who was Third Tank Platoon leader, and I, leader of the Second Platoon, were ordered to move a column of twenty-six tanks from our camp at Pendleton to the boat base at Oceanside. The trip involved crossing a railroad track travelled by the fast San Diego/Los Angeles passenger train. Lieutenant English was at the head of the column in a Jeep and I brought up the rear in another Jeep. We were moving at about ten miles per hour with intervals of seventy-five feet between tanks. At the rear of the column, I could see tanks going over the raised railroad track one after the other like huge grasshoppers. As the fifteenth tank began to cross, the train from San Diego came bearing down from the south. When the engineer saw the column of tanks crossing his track, he slammed on the brakes and almost plowed up the track for about half a mile. Passengers were thrown about, luggage went sailing through the air like missiles, beverages rained over people, and pandemonium ruled.

Our parade of tanks proceeded blissfully unaware of what had happened. I doubt if tank crewmen, who were helmeted and driving under dusty conditions, even knew the train was in the area. At the rear of the column I could see the motionless train when I crossed the track. I did not give the incident a second thought until three or four days later when I was again called into the division commander's office and given the most serious dressing-down I ever received in my life. While I was not at the head of the column, I was the senior officer and therefore responsible for the incident. The general threatened to deduct $300,000 in damages from my salary of $170 per month and mentioned the possibility of personal injury suits by passengers shaken by the abrupt stop. I could see myself in servitude to the U.S. Marine Corps the rest of my life.

No action against me was taken. However, a flashing red signal light with a swinging bell was installed at the railroad crossing. An armed sentry was posted and no person or vehicle was allowed to cross the railroad tracks so long as the light was red and the signal bell was swinging. The signal was automatically activated when a train approached within a mile in either direction. This became one of the least favorite guard stations for the Marines, but it was religiously staffed from that point on.

A problem arose because of a vegetable packing shed located about a mile south of the crossing. Often when growers were shipping vegetables, a train would stop and leave empty cars and pick up loaded ones. The switching of cars sometimes took forty-five minutes and during the whole period, the red light at our crossing would stay on, the signal would swing and the bell would sound, giving the danger warning even though no train was approaching. The sentry was under orders to let no one pass while the red light was on. This became a major harassment because an impatient column of vehicles would form, but Marines could do nothing to change the order or to use common sense.

The whole matter came to a climactic conclusion on a Saturday scheduled for the general's inspection of the tank battalion. The inspection was to begin at 9:30. At 9:15, the general and his driver appeared at the railroad crossing. The light was on and the signal was sounding, so the general, in compliance with his own order, parked his Jeep to wait until the train passed. As luck would have it, the general was kept sitting and fretting at the railroad crossing some forty-five minutes. Half an hour late for inspection, he was thoroughly embarrassed. One of his first actions on Monday was to modify the order so the sentry could at least use common sense in allowing vehicles to cross. This episode has always served as an example to me of how bureaucracies, whether private, governmental, or military, overreact to problems and how ridiculous it is to set regulations in concrete and refuse to allow individuals to use some judgment.

After training, the Fourth Marine Division was loaded aboard ship and sailed west into the Pacific to make landings on the Japanese-held Marshall Islands, Roi and Namur. Our convoy stopped briefly at Lahina Roads, Hawaii, where a few of us took a small boat ashore. At that time Lahina was a small fishing village. It was my first experience on the island of Maui, where we later established our base camp. It was the beginning of a long, pleasant association with one of the world's most beautiful islands.

The landing on Roi and Namur was by far the simplest and least hazardous of any of the four landings our division made. The islands, really small atolls, had been bombed, strafed, and shelled heavily; they were not strongly defended and our division easily overpowered the Japanese defenders. The attack on Roi was finished in one afternoon after which we crossed a causeway and began the assault on Namur. I spent most of the night on Namur sitting in my tank commander's seat catching bits of sleep but feeling far safer than I would have outside the tank in a foxhole.

On Namur, the Marines threw a percussion grenade into a block house and it blew up with an enormous roar. The blast destroyed the munitions storage house, including torpedoes and mines which the Japanese used to rearm their fleet when it operated in that part of the Pacific. The explosion blew a huge hole in the earth and scattered debris over most of the island. A dive bomber pilot who had been flying over that spot radioed that his plane had been blown about one thousand feet straight up. My own platoon captured the block house the Japanese were using for their command headquarters. In it we found the safe and managed to blast it open. Inside was a huge quantity of Japanese currency which to us was simply "play money." For two days after the battle we used it in poker games and wagers of one kind or another. We planned to send quantities home as souvenirs. When word reached division intelligence headquarters that we had captured this Japanese treasure, one of the senior officers came, searched me out and demanded that we turn over every yen in our possession. He claimed the money would be of great value to our intelligence operatives in Japan; that we were incredibly stupid to regard it as worthless. The exchange rate at the time was four yen to the dollar.

On Roi-Namur, the Japanese proved to be brave but poor soldiers. One attacked my tank with what looked like a mine on the end of a long pole. He was quickly machine-gunned down by our bow gunner. Later examination of the corpse showed that the soldier had attacked the tank with a garden hoe! The Japanese defenders had dug long trenches where riflemen were deployed in straight lines. Once our tanks crossed the trenches the soldiers made easy targets for our machine guns and cannons. The Japanese made no effort to surrender and few prisoners were taken. Several times in desperation the Japanese climbed up the sides or backs of our tanks and beat on the turrets and periscopes with clubs. The Marines quickly learned to work with a buddy tank-watching so that any Japanese who climbed on a tank was quickly dispatched by machine gun fire. The bullets did no harm to the Marine tankers protected by thick tank armor.

Walking along the beach, I came upon the body of a Marine major. In pulling the corpse out of the water, I discovered a .45 caliber Colt automatic pistol still in its holster. The gun had rusted badly in the salty water. Since .45's were much sought after, I removed the gun, cleaned it of rust and sand and stored it away in my tank. Later I turned in the .45 I had been issued and carried the found pistol for the balance of the war. I managed to get the contraband back to the states when the war was over.

Perhaps the most gruesome task on the islands was the job of collecting the corpses of dead Japanese. Since bombing, strafing, and shelling had gone on for many days prior to landing, many bodies were in advanced stages of decomposition. Flies and maggots were present in great profusion. The peculiar, sickening odor of decaying human flesh made proximity repulsive. Nevertheless, burial was required. The burial crews did their jobs seemingly without hesitation. Their stomachs must have been made of iron.

After the battle was over and we went aboard ship, there was another huge explosion. The American munitions storage caught fire and burned through most of the night. It was the most sensational display of "fireworks" I've ever seen, with ammunition shells and flares exploding in great arrays of smoke and flame.

The Kawajelein Atoll, of which Roi and Namur were a part, was a beautiful sight to behold. The sand was white, the palm trees deep green; the water was indigo, except where the coral reefs lightened the color to pale blue. The Fourth Marine Division suffered few casualties on Roi and Namur and the whole operation took on more the aura of a pleasant adventure than a dangerous wartime experience.

After the operation there, the fourth tank battalion was put aboard a Landing Ship Tank (LST). Our ship was the command vessel of a group of five LSTs. One of the passengers was the Navy commodore in command of the entire flotilla.

In addition to the five LSTs, one ship was towing a disabled destroyer escort. The two ships were connected by a steel cable several hundred feet long. We made slow ten-knots-per-hour progress during the day. Because of the danger of submarines no lights could be used at night. Every night the cable would go slack and when the ships tightened it would snap in two. All night long our flotilla circled round and round the disabled destroyer escort which floated back in the direction we had travelled during the day.

The trip took twenty-eight days. The flat bottomed LST rolled and twisted and tossed and bucked and heaved. I was seasick every single day. The captain of our ship finally allowed me to sleep under a pup tent on the deck where I was less ill than when I was below decks in the dark, smelly, cramped, noisy sleeping quarters. I woke up every morning with a sea spray coat of salt over my face, hands, and arms. The long days on shipboard permanently cured my seasickness except for extreme cases, but it was a high price to pay. Toward the end of the trip, our food supply ran extremely low. We existed for the last couple of days on dehydrated cabbage and weevily rice. I lost twenty pounds during the trip.

Our commodore became testy and paced the deck for extended periods. On one of his marches, he overheard a Marine use profanity. Immediately an order went over the commodore's signature: "No more swearing." From that time forward, when the commodore made his rounds, he beheld many Marines dutifully reading their Bibles.

Our camp on Maui was primitive by many standards, but compared to our living conditions during the battles it was plush. We had six-man tents with cots and wooden floors, a mess hall, cold water showers, an outdoor movie theater, and an officers' club. We had good liberty and could travel to all parts of the island. We fished in the ocean and hiked into the extinct Haleakala volcanic crater and made friends with civilians, most of whom, ironically, were Japanese. On one occasion I was invited to go wild goat hunting on the backside of the volcano and, on another, partridge hunting on lands owned by a friendly rancher. Except for the continual reminder that we were preparing for another landing on enemy territory, the days on Maui were more a vacation than a wartime experience. I came to love the island and the people.

A school teacher named Clarence Yashioko frequently took members of my platoon and me fishing for red snapper. He usually caught more fish than the rest of us put together. Once I speared a sizable squid which Clarence cooked in its own juice while the animal swirled round and round in the hot pot until it expired. Dr. Tofakugi and his family entertained us in their home on more than one occasion. They taught us how to prepare teriyaki steak and how to use a charcoal cooker. Osami Murayama and the waitresses at the Puueune Club were almost daily companions. Then there was the Japanese woman who ran the "canefield" restaurant where for a dollar, a Marine could get a steak that entirely covered a large dinner plate. For another dollar she would put four really fresh eggs on top of the steak, sunny side up.

Among the haole, or white, people we knew on Maui the most prominent were Lou and Charles Mounce. Charles was the superintendent of Baldwin High School and Lou was a teacher at Maui High, where the Fourth Tank Battalion leased the gymnasium so our men could play basketball. The officers of Company A Fourth Tank Battalion came to be good friends with Lou, Charles, and their two sons, and spent many pleasant evenings as their guests. Through the Mounces, we met many other leading citizens of Maui including the Eby family whose daughter Barbara and I became close friends.

After our retraining and re-equipping on Maui was complete, ships began to arrive at Kahului harbor for the Marines to board for the trip to our next combat destination. Kahului harbor could only load two ships at a time and it took twenty-five or more ships to transport the entire division. The plan was to load two ships and send them to Pearl Harbor where they waited until the rest of the fleet was assembled. Thus, each time we went from Maui to make another landing we got to spend a few days on liberty in Honolulu. Once the ships were loaded, the flotilla with its escort ships sailed west to Saipan in the Marianna Islands about fifteen hundred miles south of Japan.

Landing the tanks on Saipan was accomplished from small landing craft which we had hoped we could get over the reef so we could unload the tanks on the beach. Unfortunately, the water over the reef was usually too shallow for the boats to navigate, so the tanks had to disembark on the reef several hundred yards from shore. As a precaution, the tanks had been equipped with fording kits: metal devices that allowed the air intake and the exhaust to extend several feet up in the air. It was hoped that using these devices the tanks would continue to operate even though they were submerged in sea water, up to eight feet deep for several hundred yards. In most cases the fording kits worked, but unfortunately many of the tanks stalled in the deep water between the reef and the beach and some are still sitting there today, rusting away.

All five of my platoon's tanks made it from the reef to the shore and participated in the battle from the beginning. After we landed, I went to battalion foxhole headquarters to get my assignment. The headquarters at that time was in a shallow hole that had been dug in loose sand. While I was there, a Japanese artillery shell hit in the middle of the hole and the infantry battalion commander was killed. A young captain took charge, gave orders, and prevented chaos.

The invasion of Saipan involved two Marine divisions and one Army division. The Second Marine Division was assigned to attack along the west coast of the island, the Fourth Marine Division attacked up the east coast, and the Army division up the center section. For whatever reason, the Marine divisions made far more rapid progress which left both with long, poorly-defended, exposed flanks.

Initially, the Saipan battle was intense. From behind a ridge, Japanese machine-guns were able to sweep the one road through the swamp between the sea shore and the ridge. Heavy American casualties were taken, particularly by the infantry. One Marine rifleman fell dead in the middle of the narrow road which was being heavily used by tanks and armored amphibian vehicles to ferry troops and supplies to front line positions. Enemy machine gun fire was so intense no Marine could reach the corpse to pull it to a secure place. Drivers of vehicles had no room to pass on either side. Much as they tried to avoid crushing the corpse, one by one, drivers drove over the body grinding it into the dusty, gravely road until by the end of the day hardly a trace remained. Whatever glorified image I still had of war, I lost it that day.

A new corporal had joined my platoon as assistant driver in the tank I used as command tank. A short, dapper braggart from Wyoming, he was steeped in love of the Old West, carried two revolvers on his hips, prided himself in his quick-draw skill, and was full of threats about the carnage he would cause in battle with the "dirty Japs." The corporal was riding as bow gunner in my tank when we hit the beach on Saipan.

We came under immediate artillery and machine-gun fire. The artillery shells were high explosive rounds which point-detonated harmlessly on contact, but made an ominous rattling sound as they struck the tank armor. These loud explosions caused showers of hot sparks and the tank's ventilation system sucked in hot, acrid smoke from the burning gunpowder. The sound and smells of our own machine- and cannon-fire added to the apocalyptic environment inside the tank. It was too much for the corporal; it wasn't at all like the movies. He became deathly ill, vomiting, crying, and begging to return to the ship.

We returned that night to the semi-security of the beach to refuel and rearm. The next day the corporal had a severe headache. The day after it was his back; the day after that, asthma made his breathing labored. He never again went to the front lines and was assigned noncombat duty. He was one of two in my platoon who "cracked up."

The Marine divisions moved rapidly up the coast while the Army division was stalled in the center of the island. On one occasion, the Japanese defenders counterattacked into the exposed flank of the Second Marine Division on the west coast and were stopped barely short of getting into the artillery positions where they could have done great damage. The battle order issued by the commanding general of the Japanese on Saipan to his troops before the counter attack was a dramatic document. A captured Japanese intelligence officer turned over a copy of it to the U.S. Marines who translated it. In part, the General said:

Even though the enemy has occupied only a corner of Saipan, we are dying without avail under the violent shelling and bombing. Whether we attack or whether we stay where we are, there is only death. However, in death there is life. We must utilize this opportunity to exalt true Japanese manhood. I will advance with those who remain to deliver still another blow to the American Devils, and leave my bones on Saipan as a bulwark of the Pacific.

As it says in Senjinkun (Battle Ethics), I will never suffer the disgrace of being taken alive, and I will offer up the courage of my soul and calmly rejoice in living by the eternal principle.

Here I pray with you for the eternal life of the Emperor and the welfare of the country and I advance to seek out the enemy.

Follow me.

According to the Japanese intelligence officer, this message was delivered two hours before the general committed hari-kari.

Perhaps the most dramatic battle I observed took place on the Fourth of July on what came to be called Fourth of July Hill. The Marine battalion to which my tanks were attached was moving forward up a hill late one afternoon when it came under heavy machine gun and mortar fire from the higher elevations. Being a well-trained and experienced combat unit, the infantry took cover, dug in, and waited to pull back under the cover of darkness.

On the next day, which was the Fourth of July, a closely-coordinated assault on Fourth of July Hill began. First, the dive bombers from the aircraft carriers offshore made a series of dive-bombing runs, blasting the hill with high explosives and napalm. Then Navy cruisers and battleships barraged the hill with Naval gun fire. Following that, 155 Howitzers let loose with a fearsome artillery barrage. As a finale, the rocket platoon, led by my good friend and fellow Oklahoman Donald Dickey, came weaving in with their rocket launchers, positioned themselves and blasted the hill with a barrage that, while it could not be aimed accurately, did send an enormous amount of firepower in the form of screaming rockets at the Japanese. As soon as the rocket attack was over, the rocket trucks drove away and the Marine infantry, assisted by tanks, began the attack. As best I could tell, we occupied the hill without a single Marine infantryman losing his life.

The attack on Fourth of July Hill shows how closely coordinated the Marine assault units were. All the elements of an attack were involved, and they all worked together hand-in-glove. The question might be raised as to how much one Marine's life was worth. Probably the hill could have been taken using only small arms fire, mortars and tanks, but many American lives would have been lost. As it was, by using the full force of available firepower, we saved many lives at a cost I'm sure taxpayers were willing to pay.

After the Fourth of July attack, the Japanese defenses seemed to cave in and the Marines moved rapidly up the coast to the northern tip of Saipan. Later I learned that a large number of the defenders and island residents committed suicide by jumping over the cliff into the rocks and surf below, a tragedy which would be repeated a few weeks later on Tinian where my tank platoon was immediately involved. Saipan was a fairly heavily populated island. Many of the residents were farm people who lived in neat homes and cultivated various crops in what amounted to, by American standards, large gardens. These were neatly kept and appeared to be highly productive. As the attack advanced, there was no way to know which of the houses were being used by the Japanese soldiers as machine-gun nests or mortar emplacements. The rule was that the tanks would work over the houses with their cannons and machine guns before the infantry advanced. This drove out any residents still living in the houses. Many of the houses were destroyed. In going through the houses that survived the attack, Marines often found articles which they seized to send home as souvenirs. I suppose under any normal peace-time condition this would be thought of and reported as looting, but to the Marines in battle it seemed totally normal and proper.

Marine tankers learned many valuable lessons on Saipan. At night we were never sure that the areas where we parked after refueling and rearming our tanks were secure from enemy infiltration and artillery barrages. We learned to park our tanks in areas where the soil was deep enough that we could dig trenches, over which we parked our tanks. Then we slept in the trenches to be safe from enemy bombardment. A tank is virtually helpless in the dark when vision is too poor to use cannons or machine guns. Also, we usually parked tanks where many Marines were camped so the tanks could have done great harm to our own troops if they began firing in the dark.

Our system was to dig a trench roughly as long as a tank and the same width as the space between the tank tracks. We then drove the tank over the trench, laid sandbags to the front and rear of the trench under the tank, removed the tank's bottom escape hatch, and were ready for the night. The rule was to keep one sentry on guard in the tank turret with the lid up so he could see anyone approaching from any direction. If an intruder came by, the sentry was to challenge, ask for the password and if the intruder proved to be an enemy, start firing with his small arms to alert the other tank crew members who could help by firing through the spaces between the tank boogie wheels down below. It was an effective system that saved many of our crews' lives when the tanks were hit at night during artillery or mortar barrages.

After twenty-six days of generally intense combat, the island of Saipan was secure. The division took a few days to reorganize and make repairs, then went by small boats across the channel to the sister island of Tinian. Our landing there occurred in the early afternoon with no resistance. Quickly we moved inland. Before nightfall the Marines had established a well-organized and defended beachhead with a mile-long perimeter and a depth of some one thousand yards. Soon after darkness, the Japanese defenders counterattacked fiercely, beginning a fire fight which would last all night. Naval support ships firing parachute flares kept the battlefield brilliantly lighted so Marine marksmen could fire with deadly accuracy.

It was one of my duties as tank platoon leader to go out the next morning after daylight to finish off as many still-active Japanese defenders as we could find. It was a gruesome but necessary task because the fanatic Japanese soldiers, though grievously wounded, would still shoot and kill Marines.

After the Japanese counterattack failed, the invasion of Tinian went relatively smoothly. With tanks leading the infantry by a few hundred feet across the flat terrain, we destroyed machine-gun nests and other defenses and advanced about a mile a day. What we did not realize was that we were driving the remaining defenders and the civilian population of the island ahead of us like a herd of animals. Tinian Island emerged from the ocean in a series of uplifts, creating flat plateaus between steep cliffs, so that the island was like a multi-layered wedding cake. We attacked from one end of the island to the other, driving the population ahead of us until we finally reached the top level; then we started back down from the higher cliffs to the lower cliffs.

On the eleventh day, my tank platoon was out in front of the infantry when we came to the last plateau overlooking the last cliff above the sea.

Below us we could see hundreds and hundreds of people milling around. Knots of people would gather. There would be a powerful explosion and bodies would be blown to bits. Also we could see what appeared to be families going to the edge of the cliff. The parents would take the children by the arms, swing them a couple of times, and throw them over the cliff down into the rocks and pounding surf below. Then the parents would jump over the cliff and fall 200 feet to their deaths. Quickly we contacted regimental headquarters to get Jeep-mounted loudspeakers to the area. These were used by the civilian who had run the island sugar mill to try to talk the people into surrendering. Unfortunately, however, the population believed the propaganda about what evil beings and brutes the Marines were and the suicides continued for hours. Several hundred men, women, and children did surrender, but probably twice as many destroyed themselves during this orgy of hysteria and death.

Our tank company was scheduled to return to Maui on board an LST. The ship came to the beach, let down its ramp, and we drove our tanks, trucks, and Jeeps on board. The ramp was lifted up and the ship backed up and moved off shore a couple of miles where it dropped anchor to await orders. It was then that we discovered there were no cots or bunks for the men to sleep on as we made our way back to civilization. Apparently, the Navy expected us to sleep on the steel decks. After six weeks of combat, the men were in no mood for such treatment. Because of my reputation as a scavenger, Major Bob took me aside and asked me to take a small boat and crew back to shore to get sleeping supplies. Knowing that .45 caliber pistols were standard trading stock, I took an extra, got in the boat, and headed through the darkness back ashore. I could hear the men on the LST grumbling as we left.

Once ashore, I asked around until I found where supplies were being unloaded. As luck would have it, equipment was coming from off ship to set up a field hospital. By passing a .45 to a truck driver, I persuaded him to take a load of army cots to our waiting small boat. There was much relief and rejoicing when we began passing the cots up to the LST.

Before going to Saipan, our tank battalion had been strengthened by a company of larger tanks commanded by a Captain nicknamed Spider Webb. On Saipan, Spider Webb's tank company proved to be ineffective. He could not exercise his command responsibilities, his units were not properly trained to operate in combat, and the men could not maintain their tanks in operating condition. Upon returning to Maui, while he kept his rank of captain, Webb was demoted from tank company commander and given the duty of battalion police officer. This meant he was head of the battalion's trash collection service, a job normally handled by a corporal or sergeant.

To everyone's amazement, within a few weeks Spider Webb was promoted from captain to major. In the Marine system each officer had a number. When your number came up, you were promoted almost without regard for your performance. There seemed to be nothing a person could do to accelerate a promotion and almost nothing bad enough to keep a promotion from happening when your number came up. It was then I decided I wanted nothing to do with the military once the war was over. When I was offered a regular Marine commission, the Spider Webb incident came to mind and I respectfully declined.

The Fourth Division returned to Maui where we were issued new tanks and given replacements for the men lost on Saipan and Tinian where our casualties had been heavy. We didn't know where we'd be sent next but we began training for another operation. The Marine relationship with the Japanese on Maui continued as before. Members of the tank battalion played basketball and frequently engaged Maui High School teams in competition. Also, the Marines held dances at which most of the guests were Japanese girls.

One thing I did not like or understand about life on Maui was the very distinct, strict color line between local whites, or haoles, and orientals. The condition had developed because, as it was said, "White missionaries had come to the island to do good. They stayed and did well." They took over the land, developed it into productive pineapple and sugar cane plantations, and brought in field laborers. Workers from different nationalities were tried — Chinese, Filipinos, Japanese, and Portuguese. All were on the wrong side of the color line because of their worker status. The Japanese proved to be the most productive workers so more were brought in. By the time the Marines arrived in 1944, about seventy percent of the Maui population was Japanese. Naturally, Marine friendships formed across racial and social lines.

It was a wrenching experience to party with our Japanese friends the night before we went aboard ship, travel a few days, make landings on another island, and immediately go about the gory business of trying to kill all the Japanese who were there. It was equally strange then to get back on board ship, return to Maui, and be greeted on the docks by our Japanese friends who were anxious to know how we had fared. The Japanese on Maui had the same aspirations as Americans — they loved their families and homes; they enjoyed good food and good times; they were intelligent and friendly. Something was obviously haywire. As individuals, Japanese and Americans got along famously. The problem seemed to be between our governments. The Marines were in the war not because we wanted to kill or be killed but because we were sent by our governments. The young Japanese we were killing were probably in the same situation. I made up my mind that if I survived the war I would get into government and see if I could improve conditions between governments and between races. I did, and I did: these wartime experiences probably led to my votes in the U.S. Senate thirty years later on such issues as the Panama Canal Treaty, school integration, and civil rights.

The Fourth Marine Division base camp on Maui was on the slopes of Haleakala volcano at a town called Haiku. The elevation was a few hundred feet above sea level and living conditions were ideal so far as temperature and rainfall were concerned. Our tank training area was near the small sugar cane mill town of Puunene a dozen miles away. Puunene was in the valley where temperatures were considerably higher and where rain never fell. Our usual plan of operation was for the tank crews and officers to load on trucks and Jeeps around eight in the morning, drive to the Puunene tank training area, train or perform maintenance until noon, have lunch in the field, train and perform maintenance for another two or three hours then send the men back to camp. The officers would break for the day and retire to the Puunene Athletic Club to swim, play tennis, bowl, or just loaf. The Athletic Club was a facility which one of the sugar companies operated for its executives, and they kindly made it available to tank battalion officers.

Among our personnel was a raw-boned gunnery sergeant named Samuel David Johnson. Sam was from Gray, Oklahoma, where he had worked as an oil field roughneck and driller before joining the Marines. He was one of the most talented people in handling men and equipment I have ever seen. One of the great threats during our next invasion would be land mines. Upon receiving this information, Sam took one of our "maintenance tanks" and rigged it with a "flail" made from the drive shaft and differential of an abandoned truck. The flail was equipped with heavy chains that beat the ground a few feet in front of the tank so enemy mines would be detonated harmlessly and we could pass safely through the mine fields.

When Sam finished his invention, he proudly invited Captain Bob and the rest of the officers to see it. Captain Bob was much taken by this device and bragged about it at every opportunity. Finally word reached the commanding general who insisted on seeing the machine so he could decide whether or not it might be applicable for use in other war theaters. On the day of the general's inspection, Captain Bob took the general in tow, showed him Sam's invention, took full credit for the idea and construction, and received the general's congratulations. The captain never once mentioned Sam's name or even bothered to introduce Sam to the general or his party.

I watched Sam's countenance while this miscarriage of justice proceeded and I have never seen anyone change so quickly from pride to raw fury. That evening, Sam, who to my knowledge had never touched a drop of liquor since he joined the division, got roaring drunk. That night he went to Captain Bob's tent and gave him a cussing that only a veteran oil field roughneck knows how to administer. It was an act of rank insubordination. Captain Bob, and the rest of us who heard and saw what happened, were totally taken aback and did not know how to deal with the situation. After Sam had unburdened himself, he marched unsteadily back to his tent and continued on a drunk which lasted a full week.

When Sam returned to duty, Bob told the other officers he was going to bust him back from gunnery sergeant to corporal. The officers advised Captain Bob to let bygones be bygones and not lay a hand on Sam or disturb him in any way because among the men in the company he was highly regarded. We also told Captain Bob that most of us felt the captain deserved the treatment he received. Sam continued as a gunnery sergeant with a new stature among the men. Eventually the order came that combat units could promote enlisted men to officer rank and the first of our battlefield commissions went to Sam Johnson.

My relations with Captain Bob became strained. I had lost much of my regard for him. Here I was in the same situation I had been with my college roommate earlier. Again, I used it as a challenge to see if I could get along with him and avoid conflict. The system worked again. On one occasion, Captain Bob recommended me to Commanding General Clifton Cates to be the general's aide. The general interviewed me for the position, but told me in order to handle the social duties of an aide I would need an outside income at least equal to my pay. I had no outside income. Instead, I was sending home a hundred dollars each month. I was forced to decline and stay with the tank battalion throughout the Pacific combat.

Though I had many friends on Maui, I spent most evenings in my tent writing letters. I wrote my mother nearly every day. In addition, there was a girlfriend in Oklahoma, two in California, cousins in and out of the service, college friends, brothers, and sometimes I wrote letters to editors. On occasion, I would turn out a dozen handwritten letters in an evening.

Back in Oklahoma World War II had brought on a shortage of teachers. My mother got a job teaching at Banner, a school located a mile and three-quarters south of our house. Our car was old, tires and fuel were hard to get, and my father needed the vehicle, so my mother walked that three-and-a-half-mile round-trip each day. Although I never had the chance to talk with her about her teaching, she wrote me at length about her schoolroom experiences.

During her third year at Banner, it became difficult for my mother to walk that distance and she finally needed medical attention. It was discovered she had leukemia, for which there was no known cure. She spent several months in and out of Wesley Hospital in Wichita. When the Red Cross notified me of my mother's illness, I did not know what leukemia was. When I found out that it was a form of cancer and was almost always fatal, I applied for emergency leave so I could see her again. We were on Maui for retraining and resupply and I felt I should be allowed to go home for a couple of weeks. My request was summarily denied on the grounds that I was an experienced combat officer whose services were essential to the war effort.

After several months of retraining and re-equipping the division, we embarked for the assault on Iwo Jima. En route to Iwo Jima the fleet tied up for a few days offshore Tinian. While I was on board ship anchored in the Tinian Harbor, I received a message from the Red Cross office that I was to call in. I got into one of our tanks, tuned in the Red Cross frequency, and received news of my mother's death over the tank radio. For the only time during the war I sat alone in my tank and sobbed. My demonstration of grief for Mother was short-lived, but her death was an enormous loss to me. Though I hadn't seen her in many months, we had corresponded at least twice a week. Unfortunately, all trace of this correspondence was later lost when my father's house burned during a blizzard on the night my oldest daughter was born in 1948.

While on ship off the coast of Tinian, we could see Tokyo-bound B29s using the airports that had been built by the Sea-Bees on the island we'd taken from the Japanese a few months earlier. The B29s were so heavily loaded with fuel and bombs they barely could lift off the runway. In fact, it seemed that after leaving the runway they would actually lose altitude over the water and fly just above the waves as far as we could see them. As the fuel load diminished, the planes would rise to higher altitude and fly on to Japan where they dropped their bombs.

We were told the island we were going to take, Iwo Jima, was necessary as a base for fighter planes to provide air cover for our bombers over the Japanese islands and also as an emergency landing field for disabled planes on their way back from the bombing missions. In addition to Tinian, the B29s were flying from Saipan and Guam. A heavy air assault on the Japanese home islands was underway and would continue for many, many months.

The naval fleet carrying the Fourth and Fifth Marine Divisions approached Iwo Jima mid-morning on a brisk, clear sparkling day in February. I remember how vividly blue the sky and ocean were and how Iwo stood out like a black jewel mounted in a brilliant azure setting. Some jewel!

During the morning before the landing on Iwo Jima, U.S. bombers flew over the island at high altitudes. Even so, we could see Japanese anti-aircraft shells bursting near the airplanes. We watched as the planes bombed the island. To our astonishment, many of the bombs fell uselessly into the sea. The pilots couldn't even hit the island with their bombs. It was an ominous sign. The Marines had been told repeatedly that the small island of Iwo Jima had been under constant bombing and shelling attacks for over seventy days and that there were likely to be few Japanese survivors left on the island. After watching anti-aircraft fire and seeing the planes miss the entire island and drop their bombs in the water, Marines knew these claims by the Air Force and Navy were somewhat exaggerated. I remember thinking about the stacks of white crosses piled on the docks while we were loading our ship at Kahului harbor. I had not previously realized the thoroughness with which invasions were planned. The thought struck me that we would need a lot of crosses on Iwo.

Just before we made the landing on Iwo Jima, I was standing on the bow of our ship watching the panorama unfold. I became involved, as sometimes happened under these circumstances, in a lengthy philosophical conversation with Corporal Darrell Davis, a young member of my tank platoon. We talked about the circumstances which led to the outbreak of World War II. We felt the problem was with governments that had followed policies leading to confrontation and war. Davis agreed that wiser policies might have prevented the outbreak of hostilities which now brought thousands of young men from both countries into armed combat on a useless, desolate island no one ever heard of before. Within hours Darrell Davis lost his life on Iwo Jima.

Tanks were landed on Iwo from medium-sized landing craft — LSMs, Landing Ships Medium. Each of these ships held five tanks and was equipped with a ramp so the ship could go straight to the beach, drop the ramp and the tanks could be driven onto land. The LSM which carried my platoon was hit several times by coastal defense guns before it could get its ramp down. Luckily, we got off the ship and onto the island before the ship started to sink.

After landing, the immediate problem for tanks was to get off the beach. There had been a storm, and a wave-cut terrace some four feet high had been created all along the beach. The tanks could not climb over the terrace. I took my tank platoon down the beach until we found a place where a bulldozer had made a passage through the wave-cut terrace and we could get up to the action.

There was plenty of action. The Japanese were making an all-out effort to stop the Marines on the beach where we were totally exposed and had little opportunity to find cover. My own tank hit a mine which broke the track. Machine gun, small arms, and artillery fire were so intense we could not disembark from the tank to make repairs. The result was our tank became a stationary pill box located squarely in front of a jumble of wrecked airplanes in which the Japanese had hidden several machine guns.

During that first long afternoon, anytime we saw movement around the wrecked airplanes that indicated Japanese activity, we would carefully aim and fire our 75-millimeter cannon or our machine guns with deadly effect. When this happened, the coastal defense guns and artillery located in the cliff to our right would open up on us. Fortunately, they were firing high-explosive, point-detonating shells, none of which penetrated our tank armor. (We did have the unpleasant problem of smoke and sparks flying about inside our tank.)

That first afternoon on Iwo Jima was my most intense combat of the war. The carnage around our tank is impossible to describe. Lt. Col. Haas, our infantry battalion commander, was killed a few feet behind our tank. Dozens of other Marines fell dead in all directions. The area around our tank became a no man's land deserted by the living. Not until after dark could we get out of the tank and find our way to where some others were bivouacked for the night. We dug in with them and I spent the night with my Maui tent mate, Joe Dever. Early the next morning, we returned to our disabled tank to repair the track. Digging in the volcanic ash under the broken track, we discovered a 250-pound Japanese bomb. The mine which only broke the tank track had been planted to detonate the bomb which would have totally destroyed the tank and crew. Loose volcanic ash had served as a cushion and saved us.

The battle was particularly intense between the first and second airfields on Iwo Jima. It became a deadly combat zone where, before it was all over, the bodies of the dead lay so closely together you could almost have stepped from one corpse to another. Our tanks were sent to see if we could clear out the pill boxes and make it possible for the advance to continue.

The tank I was in advanced for several hundred yards before we came under fire from a Japanese anti-tank gun. The projectiles hit the side of our tank, penetrated the armor and set the tank on fire. One of the projectiles went through the chest of the gunner, who was sitting between my legs as I was perched in the tank commander's seat, and another tore the leg off the gunner who was sitting to my left. Not knowing who was still alive and who was injured, I gave the order to abandon the burning tank . When the driver, the bow gunner, and I got on the ground, on the side away from where the projectiles were coming, we realized that two of our tank members were still inside. Quickly I climbed back on the tank, discovered that the assistant gunner was dead and pulled the badly injured gunner out of the tank. I helped him down to the ground, and there we survivors crouched as the tank burned and the anti-tank fire flew. During this time, several other projectiles struck the tank, luckily without causing further injury. We managed to get a corpsman and a stretcher and the four of us carried the injured crewman across the several hundred yards of no man's land to the safety of our own lines. The Japanese anti-tank gunner fired several rounds at our group. Each projectile went wide of the mark, but made a ferocious sound as it passed by. By the time we reached our lines, we were all so exhausted we could not speak. I was covered with so much gore from the body of the dead crewman that the corpsman mistook me for one of the injured.

The injured gunner was immediately taken aboard a hospital ship where his leg was amputated. (He later became a postmaster in Nebraska.) In a worse tragedy, another tank in my command was blown apart by a mine attached to a large bomb, killing all five crew members. The battle cost many more American casualties before Iwo Jima was secure.

I have frequently wondered why our American military commanders chose to attack Iwo Jima, probably the most heavily defended island in the whole Japanese network. A few miles away was Chi Chi Jima, an island of similar size with ample room for airfields, virtually unfortified. Since Americans had complete control of the sea and the air it always has seemed to me it was an enormous waste of human lives to land on a heavily defended island rather than stranding the Japanese on Iwo and starving them into submission. My conclusion is that our military experts overestimated the effectiveness of the bombing and naval gunfire shelling which preceded the landing. Had the high brass seen the bombs miss the island and fall into the sea, had they realized that the loose volcanic ash with which Iwo was covered cushioned the impact of bombs which did hit, perhaps other plans would have been made.

One of the problems may have been the macho image the Marines had of themselves. A story which went the rounds on our ship during the return trip to Maui may explain the reasoning of high military authority during war time. The story told of a Marine general who was in the bathroom one morning shaving while his aide was reading him the early morning news. The aide looked up at the general and said, "You know General, our division has had the record for suffering the highest level of casualties of any division during the war." The general said, "Yes I know that." Whereupon the aide said, "Well we now have lost the record because the First Division has suffered greater casualties on the island of Peleliu. They now have the record." The general laid down his razor, slammed his fist into his hand, glared at the aide and said, "By God they won't have it long!"

Perhaps this kind of attitude was behind the decision to land on Iwo Jima. At any rate, there was a frightful loss of lives both for Americans and Japanese. It was also a foretaste of what would have happened had the atomic bomb not been used and Americans been forced to make landings on the Japanese home islands. Many are critical of President Harry Truman and his decision to use atomic weapons at Hiroshima and Nagasaki, but Marines who were survivors of other Pacific battles and who were facing the necessity to fight on the Japanese home islands were not among Truman's critics. While tank crews suffered fewer casualties than front-line infantry units, our losses were heavy. Of the thirty-two men in my platoon when we left the states, only nine remained after the Iwo Jima invasion. Two had been returned to the states for officer training and two had "cracked up," ten were badly injured, and nine were killed in combat.

The sector assigned to the Fourth Division had been cleared by the twenty-third day of the invasion. Major Bob, in his usual boisterous, bragging way, went to Division headquarters and proceeded to tell the brass what a great job his tanks had done. This caused the commanding general to assign us to assist the Third Division in clearing the remaining sector. Major Bob came back proudly to the camp and announced I was to take my tank crews and lead the way into this area unknown to us to come to the assistance of our less battle-proficient brethren. I was furious. We believed our part of the Iwo Jima battle was over. We had lost many of our crew members and morale was low. We had already cleaned our tanks and were mentally unprepared for further combat. Nevertheless, I had no choice, so I ordered my men to mount up and we headed back into the war.

We were given the radio frequencies of the Third Division and as we approached the battlefront, I began to pick up transmission of an infantry company commander speaking in a deep southern accent, talking to his troops. I immediately recognized the voice as that of Bill Johnstone, a friend who had graduated in the same reserve officers class at Quantico. When I butted in, Bill guided me to a foxhole he was using for a command post and we spent some time in pleasant reminiscing. Then Bill and I went forward to reconnoiter the area to see whether or not it was possible for our tanks to give assistance to the Third Marines, who were operating in terrain much rougher and more difficult than we had been accustomed to. As I was sitting in a foxhole, a Japanese gunner took dead aim at me and fired a round that passed harmlessly through the clothing between my chest and my arm.

We could not be of any assistance to the Third Division. In fact, they could not even use their own tanks. After two or three hours of idleness on the front, I turned our tanks around and we went back to camp where I proceeded to give Major Bob a piece of my mind about butting into something that was none of his damn business, almost getting some of us killed. Major Bob was too eager for praise and glory, and his reputation for this had spread beyond our company. When we returned to Maui, there was what almost amounted to an insurrection. The major was booted upward to battalion headquarters and I was made company executive officer. I continued in that position until the war was over, when I returned to the states. Iwo Jima, however, was the last combat for the Fourth Division.

Major Bob had been my commanding officer throughout the active part of World War II. Interestingly, there was never any real split between him and myself. We continued to have high regard for each other, and as the years have passed, some of my bitterness toward him has mellowed. Major Bob settled in California after the war and he stops to see me when his travels bring him to Oklahoma, or to Washington when I was in the Senate.

After Bob was promoted away from our company, George Hartness was moved into the company commander position of Company C and I was transferred from A Company as platoon leader to C Company, where I was company executive officer. It was a nothing position. My job with George was primarily to see that after social occasions, which became fairly frequent on Maui, George was transported safely to his quarters and put in bed. In one of our conversations, George told me that when I went back to the United States, I should run for public office because, due to my personal habits, no one would ever criticize my conduct. I did not take him seriously.

On Maui, we began training for what we later understood to be a landing on the Japanese home island of Kyushu. One night in early September, I was assigned duty as officer of the guard. The officer of the guard's job was to keep order in camp and to make unannounced rounds to each of the sentries to be sure they were awake, alert, and responding to the challenges. It frequently fell to the officer of the guard to break up fights and put down any unusual conduct that might transpire on his watch. Around four in the morning, I had just come back from making an early morning round of the sentries and had stretched out on a cot to rest when I heard a commotion near the division communication center further up the hill from our guard tent. I thought immediately, "Oh hell, another fight," and got up, put on my shoes, and started up the hill. As I went along in the dim light, I could hear voices that did not sound angry at all. After a few moments, I heard the message, "The Japanese have surrendered. The Japanese have surrendered. The war is over."

An indescribable feeling of relief and excitement swept over me. Other members of the Fourth Division were quickly awakened and soon the rumor that the Japanese had offered to surrender was confirmed. The tension, fear, and weariness began to fall away. I returned to the guard tent to await developments. They weren't long in coming.

One of the jobs of the officer of the guard was to lock up the officer's club at 11 p.m. and send the revelers home. This had been done. After the rumor of peace was confirmed, officers began to approach me to open the club. Since it was four in the morning, not even daylight, and since the orders were that the club not open until 11 a.m., I declined to give them the key. It wasn't long until the colonel came in, stretched out his hand, looked me in the eye, and demanded, "Give me the goddamn key." Of course I complied and the revelry began.

For those of us who did not drink, the celebration consisted of going to the Puunene Club, where we swam, played tennis, and feasted on some of Osami Murayama's, or "Mom's," good food. We were at the Puunene Club on September third, my birthday, when the formal peace-signing ceremony was scheduled to be held in Tokyo harbor aboard the battleship Missouri. Though Mom had religiously prohibited us from ever going into her kitchen, on this day she broke her own rule. She came to the tennis court and swimming pool where several of us were relaxing and invited us to come into her kitchen to listen to the radio as reports of the peace-signing were broadcast. We somewhat uncomfortably took the seats which she had arranged and listened in silence as the reports came in.

Mom was standing behind me and I heard a sound which caused me to turn around and look at her. She was quietly sobbing and trying to avoid being noticed. I never knew if she was crying because her country had been defeated, because she was happy to see the war over, or because she was sad, realizing that within a few days her Marine friends would be leaving, perhaps never to be seen again.

The Farmer

"Marry a Girl from Close to Home"

When I returned to the farm from World War II, my dad had suffered serious financial reverses, partially due to my mother's long and costly illness. There was no Medicaid or Medicare and health insurance was not available. At seventy-one years of age, he was not as aggressive in his farming operation as he once had been. My dad really never had made the psychological shift from horse-power days to mechanization. As a result, the farm operation was a shambles. One of my tasks was to get an enterprise going that would use our land and other assets and bring in enough regular income. It was a challenge to give up the steady Marine Corps pay and get by from harvest to harvest.

With GI Bill benefits open to me, my dad, again, encouraged me to enter law school. I probably would have been smart to take his advice. Because of unpleasant memories of Marine commanding officers, I never considered going to work under a boss. I had been bossed enough to last the rest of my life. While I knew the hardships farming held, I also knew of the personal freedom farmers have and that was all-important to me.

When the war was over, there was a huge amount of surplus government property for sale which veterans were given first preference to purchase. I planned to start a small construction company using war surplus machinery. This would provide a steady income yet leave me free to farm as seasonal work required. My first purchase was a Caterpillar R-4 cable-controlled bulldozer, which I found at the Denison Dam in Texas. It was sitting in a long line of machines and I chose it because it was priced at $1,370 and I had about $2,000 saved from wartime service. I had my terminal leave pay, my vacation pay, and money I'd saved during the war by buying a $50 war bond each month. The additional $100 per month I had sent to the bank in Billings had been used by my father to help defray my mother's hospital bills. I had been somewhat disappointed to return and find that all $2,600 I had sent home was gone. Luckily, my habit of saving impressed the local banker. Normally not a warm-hearted man, he looked with favor upon my request for a loan.

Government regulations required that surplus equipment not be operated or moved until paid for. I had to buy the machine where it was, as it was. The bulldozer I selected looked good, had low hours on the engine meter and as far as I could tell was in first class condition. After making the purchase, I borrowed my father's farm truck, a 1939 one-and-one-half-ton Ford, and drove to Denison to bring the bulldozer back to the farm, a distance of two hundred miles. It was necessary to strip as much equipment from the machine as possible to lighten the load for the small truck. After stripping away the blade, the cable winch, and overhead frame, I tried to start the dozer and drive it onto the loading dock. I quickly discovered a mechanical breakdown had locked the transmission and final drive. It was impossible to even move the machine under its own power. It had to be lifted by a crane onto the truck. I started home very apprehensive that I had bought myself a lemon.

As I came down old Highway 77 through the Arbuckle Mountains, I was forced to drive the old, wheezing, badly-overloaded truck in low gear very slowly down the grades because I could not hold the truck back with the brakes. The road was crooked and there was a considerable amount of traffic. When I finally negotiated the steep, winding road, I came to Davis, where I stopped for gasoline. To my horror, I found that all but two of the right front wheel lug bolt nuts had worked completely loose and the remaining two were barely in place. Had these nuts come loose a few miles further back, the truck would have gone out of control and I would have plunged over the side or had the dozer in the front seat with me. I replaced the nuts and made it home the next day with no further incident.

I took the dozer to the Caterpillar dealer in Enid. The former operator had been very careless about running the government equipment. By the time the tractor was out of the shop, I had spent most of the remaining $600 in my savings account. Luckily, there was unlimited soil conservation work to do around Billings, building farm ponds, clearing trees, draining land, and building terraces and waterways. As I was badly in need of jobs to earn money, I started working the tractor too cheaply. I charged $6 an hour and even though this seemed like a large amount of money after military pay, it was inadequate to keep the machine in repair, buy fuel, pay for insurance, and provide anything like a living wage for me. I soon went up to $7.50 per hour and this made things a little better.

When work was heavy, I often worked long hours. I had learned to sleep sitting up in my tank, so it was no problem to shut the dozer down for an hour or two, get rested up, and go back to work. During cold weather, I would crawl under the tractor where the warmth would keep me comfortable until the machinery cooled down. By then I would be rested and ready to go again for a few more hours.

When work for others was slack, I used the tractor to do our farm work. For several years, we pulled our farm implements with bulldozers. My brother George had also been in the Marine Corps. He was a tank commander and later received a field promotion to second lieutenant. He became a platoon leader in the Sixth Division and had been involved in the invasion of Okinawa. His division was sent to China and Japan to participate in occupation activities, then he returned home in May of 1946.

Our father owned two quarter sections of land and intended to leave one to his first family and the other to his second family. He volunteered he would be willing to sell the old home place to George and me for $12,000. He would use $6,000 to pay off the existing loan against the half section and to give our brother Randall $2,000. He would also give George and myself $2,000 which would make it possible for us to borrow the $8,000 we needed. It was a pleasing and generous offer which gave the two of us the opportunity to own land.

George and I became partners in the bulldozing business. Using a bank loan, we bought an Army surplus six-by-four truck to move the bulldozer, so we were no longer forced to drive it from job to job. We also bought a Jeep and, later, second and third bulldozers. We hired cat skinners, including our youngest brother Randall, to drive the bulldozers. The business came to be fairly profitable. We used the money we earned with the dozers to keep the farming operation going, to buy other equipment, and, ultimately, land. As we acquired land, we used the dozers to build terraces and livestock ponds, fill ditches, clear trees, and make other improvements.

My entry into the Republican party came under curious circumstances. When I turned 21, I was overseas. Without asking my preference, my dad, true to his strong political views, went to the county seat, registered me as a Republican and sent me the papers to sign. Up to that time I had paid little attention to party politics except for listening to my dad and other old-timers argue about Franklin Roosevelt and the New Deal. My dad was a staunch Kansas Republican who detested Roosevelt and probably couldn't wait to get his oldest son properly identified with the party of his (Dad's) choice.

Toward the end of the war, I had received a letter from my good friend Robert McCubbins. Bob had been an outstanding high school athlete and was recruited to play football at Oklahoma A&M. His back had been injured in one of the games. After months of treatment and recuperation, Bob had switched from engineering at A&M college to law school at Oklahoma University. While in law school, he filed for the state legislature and was elected from Noble County in 1944. I wrote from overseas to congratulate him. About the time I returned from the service, Bob decided to resign his position in the state legislature and accept an appointment as Noble County attorney. He remembered my letter and my interest in politics. He came to me and suggested that, due to my wartime experience, I should consider running for his legislative seat. The thought was attractive and I readily consented. My brother George agreed to look after our bulldozing and farming business while I was involved in political activities.

I served one term in the legislature and was defeated when I ran for reelection. My defeat came largely because I declined to campaign. I felt I'd done a good job and the voters would naturally want to send me back. I learned many valuable lessons from this experience, most importantly that it's absolutely mandatory for a candidate to let the voters know he or she wants to win. Voters must be asked for their votes.

Also, my brief stint in the legislature convinced me that politics was not a good way to make a living and that those who succeeded were those who had some sort of financial independence. In 1947, Oklahoma legislators were paid $6 a day when in session. I was living in a one-room apartment in Oklahoma City four days a week. The room cost $6 a day so that all other expenses had to be borne from other income. I determined that before I ever ran for political office again, I would devote myself to farming and contracting with the objective of getting far enough ahead so I could hold office without being worried where the next meal was coming from.

In spite of long hours, pressure to meet payrolls, need to repair breakdowns and the urgency of farm work, I refused to work on Sundays except for necessary chores. Due to my mother's influence, Sundays were "the Lord's day," to be kept holy. Sunday was for rest and for going to church. I attended the Billings Methodist Church. The congregation was not large and I soon began to take notice of a strikingly beautiful young girl. She was tall and slender with large, soulful eyes and long, raven hair. I was still somewhat shy and she seemed very young. I learned that her name was Shirley Osborn, that her father was the neighbor who had bought my pigs when I needed money to stay in college, and that she worked in the local drugstore after one year at college. She was nineteen; I was twenty-five. She had grown up while I was away during the war.

One Sunday after the worship service, I discovered a flat tire on my old car. By coincidence, Shirley came by and I asked her to give me a ride to the filling station so I could get the flat fixed. She readily agreed. On the way, I asked to take her to the movies. She accepted. We both hated movies; still do. We had three dates during the first week of our acquaintance. She made it easy for my shyness to dissolve. On the third date I asked her to marry me and she said yes. I was ecstatic! I wanted to get married right then but she insisted on a regular church ceremony. The four weeks it took to get ready for the wedding was the longest period of my life. We were married January 24, 1947.

Our backgrounds were strikingly similar: raised on farms six miles apart; products of rural, one-room schools; graduates of Billings High School; Oklahoma A&M students; Methodist up-bringings. Both families pioneered in settling Oklahoma's Cherokee Strip, land taken from the Cherokee Indians and opened in the great land run of 1893. My father's admonition to marry a girl from close to home had stood me in good stead.

I had been elected to the state legislature in November. The session began the second Thursday in January. I rode back and forth to Oklahoma City and shared a desk in the House chambers with another new member, Bert McClean from Tonkawa. I purchased the wedding ring during the week before the wedding and absent-mindedly left it in my desk in the House chamber. On the way home, driving alone, I realized what I had done. Thinking to keep my thoughtlessness from Shirley, I stopped in Perry and bought a second ring. My would-be friend found the forgotten ring in my desk and, thinking to befriend me, brought it to the wedding and handed it to Shirley. In doing so, he inadvertently handed her a club which she used effectively for the next forty years, as in, "Yeah, he couldn't even remember to bring the ring to his own wedding."

Our rapid romance and quick wedding caused the local tongues to wag. One spinster even marked her calendar to see when our first child would be born. The blessed event occurred fourteen months after the wedding. Shirley deserves full credit for the propriety.

Since I was a member of the legislature at the time of our marriage, we spent our first several months together dividing our time between our one room in a private house on Fifteenth Street near the state capitol and our small apartment above the grocery store in Billings. We slept in a bed propped up by bricks that tumbled over at inopportune times. Shirley was somewhat shy around other members of the legislature. But she was an attractive girl and soon became popular with those she knew, especially my friend Bert McClean. Bert, who was something of a practical joker, arranged for us to be shivareed on the House floor. Bert enlisted the cooperation of several members who brought pots and pans and other noise makers. Banging and shouting, they paraded around the House floor while Shirley was brought down from the fifth floor visitor's gallery and introduced. All the attention was difficult for Shirley, but she graciously went along with the commotion. It was good training for a future First Lady.

After a few weeks, Shirley became a member of the legislative wives group called the Ohyahoma Club. There were many other young wives and their association made the time go more quickly. There were frequent evening events, most of them hosted by a lobbyist, and Shirley and I attended several of these.

After the session was over, we happily returned to the farm to get ready for wheat harvest. My father and brothers had moved to the Robertson Place to make our old farm house available for Shirley and me to set up housekeeping. At the time we moved in, we had a major clean-up job to do. The house had been "bachelor quarters" since my mother had died some three years earlier. My dad was a true squirrel, saving everything from old magazines to discarded clothes. In addition, he was an absolute patsy for patent medicine salesmen. Among other loads of trash, we hauled away a pickup load of bottles of unused remedies for aches and pains. The experience gave both Shirley and me a revulsion for useless medication.

Except for installation of electricity, the turn-of-the-century house was still pretty much the way it had been built: no indoor plumbing, no convenient, reliable source of household water, and no all-weather road. I marvel that a nineteen-year-old girl was willing to start housekeeping under such conditions. We would not get running water until after our three girls were born. When we were married, Shirley weighed less than a hundred pounds, wore her coal black hair long, and looked even younger than her nineteen years. It was not at all unusual for a stranger to come to the door and ask, "Is your daddy home?"

Some of our first experiences on the farm had to do with wheat harvest. In wheat country in those times it was customary for the wife of the farmer to provide food for the harvest crews. Shirley proved to be a fine cook and well up to her responsibilities. Of course the days were long and the work was dusty and hard but we found our lives together to be highly satisfying.

Shirley was not particularly happy when she became pregnant a few months after our marriage. She felt she deserved a few more years of "freedom," and, though we were in the process of trying to make our farm house more modern to accommodate a family, we still had a long way to go. Like many of our neighbors, Shirley chose to travel to Enid for medical care and made the forty-plus-mile trip on a regular basis. In March, along about the time the baby was due, she had a regularly scheduled appointment with her doctor, and I decided to go to Enid with her.

The morning dawned bright and clear with no apparent threat of a change in the weather. I did the chores and we leisurely made preparations for the drive to Enid. By the time we reached Billings en route, the clouds had rolled in and light snow was falling. After taking care of our business there, we headed west on Highway 15. We'd driven only a mile or two when a strong wind came up and the road began to drift full of snow. As we plowed through the drifts, the snow would pile up on our old car's engine where it would melt, causing the engine to die. We had great difficulty making it through the drifts and by the time we'd gone seven miles west, we were unable to go further.

I turned the car into a farmhouse driveway and Shirley and I ran through the blizzard to the farmhouse door. The farmer and his wife were inside where they had a warm fire and were happy to see us. When they found we were on our way to Enid to see the doctor, they immediately began to anticipate that a baby might be born in their living room. Their phone was working so we called Shirley's dad, who had a brand new Pontiac for which the snow drifts were not an obstacle. He and Shirley's mother came, picked us up, and we once again headed west toward Enid.

Two miles west of the farmhouse, we turned south on Highway 74, which, since it was a north-south highway, had not drifted full of snow. When we turned west again onto Highway 64, we fell in behind a snow plow and, while the going was slow, we drove to Enid without any further problem. Shirley kept the appointment with the doctor, who insisted on putting her in the hospital since the baby's arrival appeared imminent.

Shirley's dad and I had flocks of breeding ewes and March was the time for lambing. We both felt the need to return home to look after our sheep. The Osborns' new car could navigate the snowy highways all the way back to Billings, where we turned off on a country road. We drove about three miles before the drifts became so deep that we could go no further. At that point, Shirley's dad and I left the car and started walking across the fields toward the Osborn home, still three miles away. Neither of us was adequately dressed for walking in a blizzard. The wind was from the north, and luckily we were headed in a generally southeasterly direction so the wind was at our backs. Still, we were terribly cold. The wind whipped the snow up our pants legs and down our shirt sleeves so we were totally miserable. Snow would melt and run down our legs into our shoes. Blinding snow blew into our eyes, up our nostrils. I was truly afraid of losing my way and freezing to death. We finally made it to the home of Maude Hawkins, who lived on one of the places we farmed. She took us in, let us warm ourselves by the stove before we started walking the remaining mile to the Osborn home. Part of the way was on the south side of tree-lined Bunch Creek where we could stay out of the wind. After a total of about three hours, we made it to the Osborn home. There was no way I could go the remaining six miles to our farm, so I spent the night with Shirley's dad.

My father was living in the Robertson house. He was alone on the night of the blizzard and to keep warm, built a hot coal fire in the pot-bellied stove that served as the source of heat for the house. In the glow of the warmth from the stove, he became drowsy and went to sleep. By the time he woke up, the fire had become extremely hot, and the stovepipe was red hot into the flue. The excessive heat set the house on fire and by the time he realized what was happening, it was burning all around him. He escaped but was unable to save any of his belongings, not even his automobile, which was parked south of the house. He walked through the blizzard to the neighbors' house and spent the rest of the night.

The next day, our daughter Patricia was born at the hospital in Enid. Shirley's mother called with the good news. I was extremely happy to know that Shirley and the baby were well but not at all sure that I was ready for the duties of fatherhood. A few days later Shirley's dad and I went to Enid to bring mother and baby home. I remember driving through openings in snow drifts that were as high as the top of the car.

Shirley and I quickly adjusted to having a new member of the family. I was fully occupied with tending livestock, operating the bulldozers, looking after the farming operation, and trying to make our old farm-house more livable. Shirley was amazingly adept at developing the skills of motherhood even under the difficult circumstances of living in a farmhouse without running water and indoor plumbing.

When Patricia was only a few weeks old, she developed a high fever and we took her back to the doctor who discovered she was suffering from a serious ear infection. She was given antibiotics and her fever quickly went down and she recovered. However, about a month later the infection returned and she was again taken to the doctor. Over the next fifteen months, Pat got an ear infection almost monthly, and several times it was so serious that she had to be hospitalized. Finally, the doctor removed her tonsils and adenoids and the infections stopped.

A few months later, Shirley noticed that when Pat tried to run, she would fall down. She was again taken to the doctor who discovered that one of her legs was an inch shorter than the other. He quickly determined that on one occasion when she was ill with her ears she had also suffered from polio, a dreaded disease at the time. It had reached epidemic levels in our community and claimed the lives of several children, leaving others crippled for life. A leg brace was prescribed for Pat to wear at night. At first it was a real struggle for Shirley to install the device, because Pat resisted. But after awhile it came to be routine and no matter what we were doing or how late we might come home, the leg brace had to be installed. To Shirley's credit, she never missed performing this duty even one night for the fifteen months the brace was in use. At the end of the time, Pat's legs were both normal and no other evidence of polio remained. We shared the relief other parents felt when a polio vaccine was developed which has eliminated this disease from much of the world.

Two more baby girls, Gail and Ann, would join our family over the next four years. The circumstances surrounding their births were not as dramatic as we had experienced when Pat arrived. Our girls are different but generally highly compatible. Pat became a nominally accomplished pianist and a professional writer. During our years in Washington, she wrote feature stories for the *Washington Star* and later for the *Tulsa Tribune.* Gail is the sensitive one, much involved with community and church affairs as well as assisting in the operation of a direct mail firm in Enid where she lives with her son and husband, a lawyer. Ann is the rambunctious one with a strong practical turn as far as business is concerned. Her husband is a personnel director for a company near Baltimore, Maryland, where they live with their two sons. Once when Ann was four, she rode to town with me in the wheat truck. Shirley had given her a quarter to buy some thread at the local variety store. While I was unloading the wheat, Ann charged the thread and used the quarter to buy penny candies. When we returned home, she proceeded to sell the candies to her sisters for a nickel each.

Throughout the girls' childhood, Shirley served as a traditional mother. She was on hand when the girls came home from school, transported them to music lessons, served as a 4-H Club leader, taught the girls to cook and sew, and was generally there when a parent was needed. This was fortunate because I was often away on political activities of one kind or another. We always tried to be together for supper but even this was sometimes difficult. Shirley loved to sew and somehow found time to make most of the girls' clothes. She enjoyed making them identical dresses and seemed to revel in the comments made by admirers who enjoyed seeing our three stair-step daughters identically attired.

At the time I came back from the war, I decided, based on studies of animal husbandry at O.S.U., to go into the sheep business. Dr. Hilton Briggs, one of my instructors, contended that the ideal combination for north central Oklahoma was a wheat and sheep farm because sheep utilize winter wheat pasture better than any other ruminant. Besides growing muscle, sheep turn the wheat's protein into wool as well. I went to the Farm Security Administration, now the Farmers Home Administration, and applied for a farm operating loan.

At the time I went into the business, our old farm buildings were badly run down. Every roof leaked and had I known then what I found out within a few short months, I never would have bought the first ewe and tried to make a sheep farm out of a unit that was much better suited for cattle. Initially, our wheat fields were not fenced for sheep so it was necessary for me to stay in the fields with the sheep all day or, at most, to be absent only brief periods of not more than an hour. In the morning, I would have breakfast, do the necessary chores and then take the sheep to the fields of winter wheat. The grazing period lasted from the first of November to the first of March.

On cold or disagreeable days I drove a vehicle to the field and sat inside watching the sheep to keep them from straying to neighbors' land. I carried a rifle and sometimes shot stray dogs, though I never was able to shoot a coyote. I spent most of my time in the car reading. I was a Sunday school teacher, so a good deal of what I read was church literature and the Bible. Unfortunately, I was not as faithful a sheep herder as I should have been and our sheep frequently strayed. They often got quite a distance from home before we discovered they were missing and set out on the difficult task of bringing them back home. Finally I devised a system of building temporary fences held up by portable posts. These worked reasonably well, but it was a great deal of work to repeatedly put up a fence, then take it down and move it to another pasture where the grazing was better.

In late November of 1945, I bought two hundred ewes from a man who had a farm south of Fairview. He was a first-class salesman but, I later learned, not a first-class sheep grower. He assured me all the ewes were bred. In fact, many were not pregnant and those that were dropped their lambs from the day I brought them home until the heat of the next summer, which meant the late lambs did not grow well and did not bring a good price when they were sold. Fortunately for me, Shirley's father was also in the sheep business, so she understood sheep. She was good at bottle-feeding orphan lambs and was patient when, during lambing season, I would crawl out of bed for two or three hours to go to the sheep pens to help ewes and their lambs. She also understood when I purchased an astronomical amount of sheep fence from Sears and undertook to pay for it on a monthly basis.

After my first bad experience with a breeding flock, I shifted to feeder lambs. I would buy South Texas sheep through the National Livestock Commission Company and Credit Corporation in Oklahoma City. The commission company charged me a dollar a head down payment and I took delivery after they were weaned in Texas. They arrived when winter wheat pasture was ready for grazing. Normally, we would shear the lambs soon after they arrived. The wool provided money for the down payments on the lambs. The sheep grew better during the warm weeks of early fall without their wool. The shearing operation was of great interest to our girls, who often served as wool trampers. They'd climb into the big wool sacks and tramp the wool down as the shearers threw it on top of them. Our largest feeder lamb operation was about a thousand head. They were purchased for $12 per head and usually sold for $20 to $25 per head. Sometimes the wool brought $3 or $4 more from each lamb. Coyotes and stray dogs were a problem with the feeder lamb operation, so we always brought the sheep into the corral at night. The lamb-driving excursions provided many happy hours for myself and our daughters. Usually, we would drive the lambs from a car or pickup with the help of sheep dogs. We passed the time singing songs or telling each other tales of current happenings.

The year 1956 was dry and disastrous. If my creditors had gotten their heads together they would have decided I was bankrupt and forced me out of business. By the end of the year we had not paid our gasoline bill, we were in debt at the lumber yard, and were facing winter with absolutely no resources to defray living costs. The federal government had approved an emergency loan program for areas of the country hit by the drought. Since our area was included, the county supervisor for the Farm Security Administration fixed me up with a $5,000 loan. I bought 325 lambs at a cost of $10 each. When they were delivered, I immediately had them sheared and we received about $3 a head for the wool. That provided us $1,000 to get through the winter. The balance of the $5,000 was used to buy calves. The fall and spring proved to be ideal for wheat pasture and our small flock did well. The market recovered so that when I sold sheep in the spring, I received $25 per head. This was one of the most profitable livestock enterprises I ever undertook. Perseverance pays off in farming as in most things.

The lessons I learned in dealing with sheep were later helpful in dealing with people. It was interesting to watch a new shipment of feeder lambs arrive at our farm. The lambs had spent their entire lives with their mothers who led them to find feed, water, salt, and shelter. When weaning time came, the lambs were sold and shipped several hundred miles to new and strange surroundings. Lacking knowledgeable leaders, the lambs simply milled around in a circle, each looking to the other for direction. After a few hours, one lamb would dart out of the group and run off by himself. When the flock did not follow, he darted back into the flock. Leadership developed when a particularly wise lamb stepped out from the flock only a few steps and waited for the others to follow. If they did, he moved slowly toward his objective and the flock followed. I noticed that when a shepherd attempted to drive a flock around an obstacle, it was impossible to apply pressure on the stubborn animals at the front of the group. He could beat or abuse the ones at the back, but these were not the ones causing the difficulty. The trouble-makers at the front seemed to get by scott-free unless those at the rear began to push ahead in concert so they could overrun the cowards. That is often the way it happens in the political process.

Even though I was raising some calves, sheep continued to be our primary livestock until the time I was elected Republican state chairman. I doubt that over the long haul sheep were as profitable as cattle might have been, but under the circumstances, the decision to raise sheep was a good one. It did not take as much money to handle sheep, our girls could help much more around a sheep farm than a cattle farm, and I enjoyed working with sheep more than cattle.

One of the first things I did after returning from service in World War

II was to call upon my favorite college professor, Dr. Horace J. Harper at A&M. During our first conversation, Dr. Harper told me that if I was going to be a successful farmer, it was necessary to get my priorities straight. He said the first thing any farmer needed to do when he sold his crop was to set aside ten percent of the income to put back into the land as fertilizer. He told me that as a new farmer I would have demands for everything. But before I bought new linoleum for the kitchen or a new appliance or new clothes for the babies or new machinery or an automobile, I had to take care of the land by putting back the fertility which the crops had removed. I took the good professor seriously.

The first wheat crop I planted was in the fall of 1945. Unfortunately, it was a wet fall, so through September and October little field work could be done. I leased a farm that had been tilled by another person who had decided he did not wish to farm the land. He sold me his lease for $120. My first crop from the place was a disaster. The green bugs (aphids) ate most of the crop and weeds took the rest. I was able to harvest only about the quantity I had planted as seed. Luckily, I had insured the wheat with the federal crop insurance plan and collected $2,000 insurance money, which I needed to put out another crop.

In the meantime, I had begun the bulldozer business. When the crop failed in 1946, I talked to the landowner about building terraces to protect the land and he was delighted. During the summer I bought a new grain drill equipped with a fertilizer attachment. But I soon found there was no place to buy fertilizer in our area. In order to get fertilizer, I became a fertilizer dealer for the White Diamond Fertilizer Company of North Little Rock, Arkansas. The company agreed to ship me a carload of twenty percent super phosphate which I applied to my wheat crop that fall. This was a tedious process because the material was powder and attracted moisture. Since it was moist, it built up and kept breaking the mechanism that fed the fertilizer out of the drill. When one of these feeds broke, I had to dig out the fertilizer and make repairs before proceeding. The acid in the fertilizer made scratches or abrasions painful.

By the fall of 1946, George and I were farming the land our father owned and land Dad had long-rented from the Robertson family. Planting five hundred acres of wheat put a considerable strain on our finances. However, we got it all planted and fertilized. By next spring our fertilized wheat began to grow much more rapidly, was dark green, looked far healthier, and showed greater promise than our neighbors' fields of wheat that had not been fertilized. Different neighbors asked about our wheat and insisted on inspecting it. We showed them rows of wheat that were only half as large as adjoining rows. This was the result of the fertilizer feed breaking. The rows that did receive fertilizer were far healthier than the unfertilized rows, which appeared sickly and similar to the neighbors' wheat. At harvest, our wheat yielded twenty-six bushels to the acre, which was more than double the yield of the neighbors' wheat. Immediately, our neighbors wanted to buy fertilizer from us. I took orders for several freight car loads and sold it at cost. I had no interest in remaining a dealer but was interested in seeing others use fertilizer so a dealership could be established. In two years the Hayton Grain Company in Billings began to handle fertilizer and I went out of the business.

G.T. Weber was the president and principal owner of the First National Bank in Perry. I had been doing business there and one day went to ask to borrow money to buy a second tractor. I explained that the tractor I had was too small; that it took too long to work the land; that, as a result, I could not get my farming done in a timely manner. Mr. Weber was appalled at the notion that any farmer needed two tractors. He looked at me, snorted, and said, "You already have one tractor." Then he denied my application for a loan.

On another occasion, when the demand for wheat was good I rented as much land as I could find, over-planted wheat on maize land, and, by working long hours and putting wheat in under less than perfect conditions, managed to get more than nine hundred acres planted. Luckily, that was a year when wheat did extremely well, so my share of the harvest was something like 20,000 bushels. I had hired four combines to cut my wheat and because every other farmer had a good crop, the elevators filled rapidly. We were well ahead of the other farmers, but before we could get all the wheat to the elevator in Billings, it was full. I called the Red Rock elevator, where harvest was later, and they agreed to take wheat from me. As a result, I wound up with about the same amount of wheat in both elevators.

As soon as harvest was finished, I went to Billings and sold the wheat there. I took the check, which was for over $16,000, to the First National Bank in Perry to pay on notes and harvesting expenses. Weber was elated to see me with such a large check. I did not tell him this was only half of my crop. A few days later the market went up and I sold the wheat in the Red Rock elevator and again went to Weber with another $16,000 check. Weber was dumbfounded to see a young farmer with such a huge amount of money. He sat and looked at the check and said that my income that year was as much as some people make in their whole lives. I felt rich. I paid every bill I owed and bought a new Model U Minneapolis Moline tractor. I have never felt quite as rich since.

As time went on, G.T. Weber reached retirement age and decided to sell his interest in the bank. He was determined to clean up his loans and called me in and said he wanted me to pay the bank everything I owed. This attitude was directly in contrast to previous years when he had been eager to make loans. My crop had been bad, livestock prices were low, and wheat prices were not particularly good. I was panic-stricken because there was no way I could pay off without selling everything and going out of business. The Security Bank of Ponca City finally took over my loan. Later I paid off the Security loan and returned to Perry after the bank changed ownership. G.T. Weber lived into his nineties. I think he got some pride and satisfaction out of the help he gave me. I don't think he knew how close he came to putting me out of the farming business.

Over the years, wheat has continued to be our principle crop. We have expanded the wheat acreage to some 1,100 acres, though roughly 300 acres is grazed off with cattle and not harvested. During my political years, it was necessary to work with cattle rather than sheep since cattle do not require constant personal attention.

When the Korean War broke out, I was still a captain in the Marine reserves and my brother George was a first lieutenant. The Marines called up the first lieutenants and George was ordered to active duty. We both assumed he would be sent immediately to Korea. I also expected to be called to active duty any day. We worked out an agreement as to what the land and equipment we owned was worth. Since we were equal partners, we agreed that if anything should happen to either of us, the other could purchase the full operation for $13,500. George was stationed first at Fort Knox, Kentucky, and later at New River, North Carolina. At New River he made many friends and came to like the country a great deal. After he had been there a few months, he found a piece of land he wanted to buy, near Pantego. He came back to Oklahoma and asked me to buy his share of our farm.

I managed to get the necessary money and bought him out. He went back to North Carolina and bought three hundred acres of timber and farm land. Unfortunately, the farm George purchased turned out to be too small to justify the purchase of necessary equipment and to return a reasonable living. George took other work to allow him to keep his land. He worked in sales barns as a part-time helper for the local USDA land office while he continued to farm and clear land for cultivation. After a few years, George leased his land to other farmers and took a job as a county supervisor for the Agricultural Stabilization and Conservation Service. He was stationed at Hertford, North Carolina, where he continued to work and live for several years.

About the time I bought George's part of the farm, we had an extremely dry winter and most of the shallow farm ponds dried up. There was a considerable amount of oil drilling activity in the community and various oil companies came to see me about buying drilling water. With our bulldozer we had built a large pond on one of our farms and it was one of the few in the area that still had abundant water. I agreed to sell water to the oil drillers, on the condition they would let me haul it to them in my own truck. They agreed and I bought a large water tank, mounted it on our farm truck, and started hauling water to oil wells being drilled five miles west of where we lived. Luckily, the wells produced oil. The company then agreed to contract me to haul oil from the wells to the pipeline tank farm.

As harvest time came, I had more than I could do so I sold the oil hauling business to my brother Randall. I also worked out a deal to sell him the bulldozers since I was so involved with farming that I could no longer do justice to the bulldozing operation. I sold the whole business to him with no money down with the agreement that he would make monthly payments. Unfortunately, these payments were never made. Later he was called to military service and I took the dozers back and ran them a few months before finding a buyer. I was glad to be rid of the bulldozers. They were a headache to keep going and though they had provided an essential source of income in the early, tough years, they proved to be less profitable than it would appear on the surface. The old bulldozers required constant, costly repair. And, unlike land or livestock, which usually appreciates in value, machinery depreciates.

Following the fire that destroyed the house where he was living on the east Robertson place, Dad moved to an old but still livable house on the Garrett Place. From there, he continued to handle livestock on a small scale and helped me with the farming as best he could. My dad had always liked raising hogs and he continued to handle a few pigs, even to the end. He also kept a small herd of cattle in the pasture on the one farm he still owned. It fell to me to help him with his animals and with putting up hay for his cows. On the last day of his life, he and I hauled hay in the morning. He drove the pickup and I loaded the heavy bales in the truck bed. We then hauled the hay to an old school house he had bought and moved on the place to store hay for feeding during the winter. Carpenters were busily installing a new roof on the Garrett Place house. I took my dad home so he could fix his lunch, and then went on to our place. Shortly after lunch, I received a phone call from one of the carpenters, who said my dad wasn't feeling well. I quickly went to see him and found him stretched out on the couch. I called an ambulance, but he died of a heart attack before he reached the hospital.

In his seventy-nine years, Dad had lived an exciting life, beginning with his birth to a coal miner's family in Pittsburg, Kansas, including his youth as a cowboy in No Man's Land, pioneering as a settler in the newly-opened Cherokee Strip, fathering thirteen children, working as an oilfield teamster, and settling down to farm on a moderate scale for some forty years, including the drought and Depression of the thirties. He never accumulated significant wealth but he lived an independent and generally satisfactory life.

One of the problems wheat farmers have is finding a source of income during the long periods between annual harvests. In our case, the sheep helped; but even so there were long gaps when there was no income. To help cover our growing family needs on a regular basis, I built a poultry house and went into the business of producing eggs for hatcheries. When the girls were old enough, they frequently helped with gathering and processing the eggs. The processing consisted of washing, candling, and casing the eggs for delivery to the hatchery. For reasons I do not understand, the roosters, which paid no attention to me, attacked Shirley and the girls viciously. It was a fearsome task for the little girls, carrying baskets of eggs, to walk through the chicken house knowing that at any moment a rooster might attack them, scattering eggs and feathers every which way.

Finally, to get away from that problem, we dispensed with broiler-type chickens and began raising Leghorns, which produced infertile market eggs and did not require the attention of roosters. These eggs were sold to hospitals, restaurants, and nursing homes. We even had the officers club at Vance Air Base in Enid as a customer. The weekly egg income covered living costs and made it possible to purchase a few luxuries. Egg checks bought our first six-place setting of sterling silver and a Magnavox stereo, which turned out to be a lemon.

Blacksnakes and bullsnakes dote on hen eggs. Also, the dark recesses of nests make cozy resting places for reptiles to snooze after gorging themselves on forbidden "hen fruits." Since the eggs needed to be gathered several times daily to prevent breakage, Shirley and the girls often did this chore. On more than one occasion I would be summoned to the hen house by shrieks after one of my helpers had put her hand into a nest expecting eggs, only to find a snake.

Even with snakes around, our hen house was not rat proof. With abundant feed and water always available and with deep, warm litter to burrow into, the rodent population built up rapidly. Poisoning was out because of the hens. I stocked up on .22 caliber shot shells and began paying regular nightly visits to the hen house where I would switch on the lights and blast away at rodents stuffing themselves on laying mash at the feeders.

After reducing the rat population in the hen house, I decided to use the same tactic in the hog pen where about one hundred barrows and gilts were being fattened. The hog feeder was a wooden affair mounted on four-by-four skids. I attached a magnetic flashlight to the breech of my .22 automatic and quietly approached the hog pen. A few feet before I reached the feeder, I stopped and switched on the flashlight. Rats were jammed into the feeding slots and paid me no attention until I began blasting away. For a time, the rats seemed not to comprehend what was happening; then, in a panic, they scurried away. Dozens took refuge under the hog feeder between the skids.

Even though I was wearing new overalls and a hog pen is not exactly a preferred place to lie down, I went to the front of the feeder and prostrated myself so I could look under the feeder. The rats were climbing all over each other, their beady eyes glowing and their whiskered noses twitching in anxiety. I began firing the .22. Again, the rats panicked, several running straight at where I was lying in the pig waste. As I tried to raise up, the front of my overalls gaped open and a large rat ran into the opening, down my belly, across my crotch, clawed its way through the tight space between my leg and my pants, out over my muddy shoe and away. The shrieks Shirley and the girls gave out during unexpected encounters with snakes were mild in comparison to my utterances that night. I hate rats.

When we first started the chicken business, we bought our laying mash in hundred-pound sacks from the Bisagno hatchery in Perry. The cotton sacks were printed in colorful patterns which farm wives used to make many garments. Shirley and our girls were adept at selecting chicken feed sacks that they made into attractive clothes. As the size of our chicken enterprise grew, the number of sacks we accumulated outstripped the need for clothing. Sacks could be redeemed for twenty-five cents each, so it became a source of spending money for the girls. We were in the egg business for probably ten years. It was good experience for all of us, though everyone in the family developed a distinct dislike for eggs and as far as I know, none of us eats them regularly even to the present day.

Our exit from the egg business was due to economic reasons brought on by what local producers felt was unfair competition. While it was costing fifty cents a dozen to produce eggs, a few stores regularly ran specials on eggs: three dozen for $1. These loss-leader products were reportedly furnished by an out-of-state, vertically integrated egg grower who could set the Oklahoma price by bringing in a small load of eggs every few days to be sold at a loss. By absorbing their small deficit, the out-of-state supplier could set local prices at uneconomic low levels, rapidly drive local producers out of business, and take over the market. At least that's what our Oklahoma Egg Producers Association believed. After I was elected governor, I tried to get the anti-trust division of the Justice Department involved, but failed.

Another of the enterprises we undertook to help with farm income was raising turkeys. For five years, we started turkey poults in the spring and raised them to maturity for sale on the Thanksgiving market. I learned many times not to give turkeys credit for any intelligence whatsoever. On one occasion, I remember being in the turkey pens, filling the feeders and leaving an empty five-gallon bucket behind. When I returned in just a few moments, the bucket was totally filled with young turkeys, yeeping loudly. When I poured them out, there were about a hundred dead ones underneath, trampled by the ones on top. Evidently, one little turkey had jumped in the bucket to see what was there and immediately a hundred others had followed suit.

Another time I parked a Ford tractor in the turkey pen and left it while I did some chores. When I returned, the keys were missing. All I could figure out was that some turkey had jumped up on the tractor, pulled the keys out, and swallowed them.

The turkeys were also the bane of Shirley's existence. The way our farm yard was arranged, the turkey pen was between our house and the trash cans. It was therefore necessary for Shirley to pass through the turkey pen when she carried out the trash. When the turkeys began to reach maturity, inevitably the toms would attack Shirley as she walked through their domain.

The turkey enterprise proved to be profitable and fit in well with other farm work. However, during the fifth year, I began to suffer a painful itch on many parts of my body. A doctor determined the problem was an allergy to turkey feathers. He gave me calcium shots, which controlled the itch. When that year's turkey crop was sold the itch went away completely. That was the end of our turkey business.

When the trucks came to load the last crop of turkeys, one of the workers was a black man. We had about 2,200 heavy turkeys to load. It took several hours of hard work to catch all the birds, overcome their resistance and cram them into shipping crates. Since the trucks were to be weighed on the grain elevator scales at Perry, I went with them that far. When the weighing was over, I invited the group to have supper with me at a local restaurant. When we walked in the front door, to my amazement, the proprietor told the black man he would have to eat in the kitchen. There were no black people living in the Billings community, so this was my first encounter with overt racial discrimination and segregation in Oklahoma. Even though I had seen two water fountains in the courthouse in Perry — one for blacks and one for whites — I had not realized how strongly the color lines were observed even in Noble County. Both Shirley's and my families came from Kansas where integration had long been accepted, so this experience at the restaurant was a real shock to me and started me thinking seriously again about race relations in Oklahoma.

In rural areas, farmers have a saying: "I don't want to be rich. All I want to do is own all the land that 'joins me." I suppose over the years I've been affected by something of that syndrome and have bought land as it came up for sale so long as it joined me. However, there are a couple of other reasons for buying land if you're a politician. Since politicians, of necessity, spend most of their time away from home attending meetings or working at their jobs, a politician who farms has to rely heavily upon hired helpers. It is difficult then for the farmer-politician to rent land because, understandably, land owners much prefer leasing to farmers who are personally on the job rather than those who are absentee operators.

A politician also needs some kind of backup job. In the Marines, we were taught that if, during battle, a group of men were huddled together in a foxhole and the enemy lobbed a grenade into the midst of them, there were probably two seconds for someone to smother the grenade with his body to keep it from killing the entire group. This happened on several occasions in the Pacific invasions and several Marines made the ultimate sacrifice to save their buddies. A similar situation can arise in politics when a highly controversial but essential decision must be made. Sometimes the politician will be called upon to cast a needed and essential vote on a crucial issue, knowing that it's the end of his political career. The votes on Panama, school integration, and the action I took in education reform came close to being those kinds of situations. I learned early on that a successful political career demands that a politician have a sense of security so he can take the risks of acting on needed but unpopular issues and still have a way to make a living in case of defeat at the next election. Some politicians have family wealth or professional careers to sustain them. The farm has always filled that need in my case.

For this reason, as fast as the equity in our land went up, it was remortgaged to buy additional acreage. During the 1970's this proved to be a wise policy since land values escalated rapidly. But during the 1980's, land prices came down as fast as they'd gone up earlier. This put many farmers, including the Bellmons, in a serious financial bind.

Over the years, I frequently talked in glowing terms about the beauty of the island of Maui and how pleasant a place it was to live. I finally talked myself into a corner and Shirley and the girls made me promise to take them to visit Maui at some future date. In checking into the matter, we discovered that the cost of travel was only half as much for children under twelve as it was for adults. We therefore determined to try to make a trip to Maui in the winter before Pat had her twelfth birthday in March. We rationalized our planned extravagance by saying we were spending our cigarette and whiskey money on a trip to Hawaii instead. Every member of the family pitched in to try to save money to make the trip. The girls saved the quarters they earned from selling empty chicken feed sacks, I borrowed what I could against our small insurance policies, we saved money that would have been spent for birthday and Christmas presents, and Shirley saved what she could salvage from the egg money after paying for groceries and other monthly bills. Also, I received a small inheritance from my mother's family when the old homestead finally sold.

When school turned out for Thanksgiving in 1959, Shirley and the girls and I loaded into our car and drove to California where we left the car with relatives and boarded the U.S.S. Matsonia for the trip to the Hawaiian islands. The Mounces and other of my World War II friends were happy to see us after an absence of some fifteen years.

With the help of Lou and Charles Mounce, we had arranged to lease a house and car for six weeks. The house was situated on the western slope of Haleakala volcano and located in the Kealaho school district where the girls attended classes during the period between Thanksgiving and Christmas. One thing the girls never adjusted to was the fact that at Kealaho every student seemed to be from a Catholic family. When the school day opened with prayer, all the other children said their rosaries while our girls felt left out. That was the beginning of my concern about the propriety of prayer in school. Our girls were among the few white, or haole, children in the Kealaho school. Most were Asians, Hawaiians, or Portuguese. Nevertheless, while the girls were aware of the racial differences, there was little tension and no discrimination. The discovery that there are nice people from other races and cultures was helpful to our girls who had spent their lives in an all-white rural community. Their best friend at school was Koalani Han, whose mother was Hawaiian and father was Korean. Koalani would later come to Oklahoma to help with the first governor's campaign.

One of the World War II acquaintances I was particularly interested in locating was Osami "Mom" Murayama. In asking around, I discovered, to my delight, that Mom was working as a housekeeper for a family that lived not more than two hundred yards down the mountainside from our house. Without advance notice, I decided to walk down the path to see if I could locate Mom. As I approached the house where I'd been told she was working, I happened to look over the garden fence to see a person stooped over weeding the vegetables. Thinking to ask about Mom's whereabouts, I quietly opened the garden gate and walked to where the stooped-over person was busily weeding. Noticing a resemblance, I spoke quietly, "Mom?" She jerked her head up, looked at me, and though we had not seen each other in fifteen years, instantly used my Marine Corps name, "Hank." We embraced and spent several minutes reminiscing about our experiences together in the now-distant days of World War II. The years had been good to Mom.

Many changes had occurred in Maui since the end of World War II. Probably most dramatic was the abolition of the color line. No longer were the Japanese, Chinese, Filipino, Hawaiian, and Portuguese expected to sit in the back of the buses and in the upper balcony at the theaters. Also, the country club, the swimming pool, tennis courts, and golf courses were opened to all races, as were all the professions. Most political offices were held by orientals, since they were racially predominant. Once they began to participate actively in the political process, their votes were overwhelming Life on the island seemed much more vibrant and healthy. Elimination of the enormous waste of human resources which had resulted from the old color line had enriched the island in innumerable ways.

The good impressions which Maui residents received of Marines in World War II lingered. Wherever we went, when people found out I was a former Fourth Marine Division officer, they poured out their friendship and generosity. During our seven-week absence, the farm was well managed by our helper and no great catastrophes occurred. The experience helped remind me in later years that my presence on the farm at all times was not essential.

After some twelve years, Shirley and I finally decided that fixing up our circa 1895 farm house was an impossibility. Even though we had installed running water from a new lake, improved the heating system, repaired the roof, filled in around the foundation to keep out the wind and the varmints, covered the old floors with masonite and carpeting, replaced the plaster with sheetrock, and built kitchen shelves and closets, the house was still not suitable for our family. We decided that somehow we were going to build a new home.

Our opportunity came when the federal government created the soil bank program. We planted grass on a hundred acres of marginal wheat land on a farm we'd bought and put in the soil bank. The annual payment would be enough to retire the $13,000 loan, which we felt was enough to build our new house. We immediately began saving material from any source we could find. Interstate 35 was being built nearby and one of the bridge contractors had a large supply of leftover reinforcing bars which we bought at a bargain price. Also, the grocery store where we had first had our small apartment burned and we bought the bricks which Shirley and the girls spent many hours cleaning. We tore down abandoned barns in the neighborhood, salvaging the lumber to be used for studs and sheeting. We cut walnut trees along the creek and had the lumber dried to use for paneling and cabinet work.

Our biggest break came when we enticed Bob Malcolm, a relative who lived near Wichita, to be our builder. Bob was an accomplished carpenter who had built homes in the Wichita area and had connections with wholesale suppliers. He, his wife, Helen, who was my cousin, and their three daughters moved to Billings while our new home was built. Bob was a meticulous carpenter who took great pride in his work. The construction of our new house required about a year. Though I was away most of the time serving as Republican state chairman, I helped with the cement work and, when I could, in other ways. The two main things I got credit for were installing a bathroom mirror on which I tightened the screws too much, causing the mirror to crack, and helping saw the mantlepiece, on which I miscalculated and caused a gap where the logs come together.

We completed the new house on Halloween 1961. Shirley and the girls moved out of our old house and into the new one on a weekend I was away. I remember being somewhat shocked to drive up to the old farm house and find it abandoned. I sheepishly reported to the new home, feeling as if I'd shirked my duty.

Even though I've spent over twenty years in elective public office, I've always considered myself a farmer and counted my political activities as an avocation. During the time I've been in office, the farming operation has given me a close tie to the realities of the real world. It's always been very relaxing to leave the pressures of political life behind and spend a weekend or a holiday helping with the wheat planting, working cattle, or helping with the field work, haying, or harvest.

It's easy to put the cares of office behind me once I get to the farm and I've always come back to the office at the beginning of the week fully refreshed after a weekend at home. The physical exercise that comes from farming keeps me in shape, since I've never developed a dependable physical exercise regime.

The farm has served as an anchor for both Shirley and me throughout our years in public service, both in Oklahoma and in Washington. On many occasions, including Christmas, Memorial Day, and summer vacations, the whole family gathers at the farm. The grandchildren particularly seem to enjoy the great outdoors. My sons-in-law like hunting and fishing, and it gives us a reason to spend some time together. The eight-acre lake next to the house is a good fishing hole and, in winter, a sanctuary for some fifteen hundred giant Canadian geese, which feed on the winter wheat and spend their days and nights on the lake. They are beautiful birds, graceful in flight, though sometimes noisy enough to keep us awake nights.

As a financial enterprise, the farm has not been greatly successful, partly due to my miscalculation on the trend of land values and lack of hands-on management. The place has not been profitable except under the unusual circumstances of the 1970s. It is my hope now that I am out of public office I again can begin to earn higher income, retire some of the debt, and hold on to at least some of the land.

Politician, Candidate, and Governor

TOP: *A two-party tea party. After Shirley sewed his pockets shut so Henry wouldn't bury his fists in them, he learned to stand in front of a chair to occupy his hands.*
BELOW: *The official Campaign Kickoff at Billings High School. Left to right are Martin Garber, newly-appo[in]ted chairman of the state Highway Commission, Henry, Montana Governor Tim Babcock, (from Billings, Mont[ana]) Shirley and Henry's youngest brother Randall.*

mer President Eisenhower came to Oklahoma to boost the campaigns of Bellmon and U.S. Senate candidate
yden Crawford, but Eisenhower forgot to mention them in his speech. After taking his seat, he remembered
got up to make the plug. Henry's youngest daughter Ann poses too.

The hometown headquarters was managed by Henry's aunt Beth Zimmerman, in Bellmon Belle dress at right. Shirley's mother, Laurine Osborn, is also standing.

BELOW:
The Bellmon Belles called door-to-door on businesses in every county, campaigning for Henry Bellmon.

*ABOVE: The newly sworn-in governor signs autographs in the Blue Room at the state capitol.
AT LEFT: Koalani Han, a friend of Gail's the family had met in Hawaii, joined the campaign and sometimes performed the hula dance at rallies. Here she is photographed with (left to right) Pat, Gail, Ann and Shirley at the Rush Springs Melon Festival.*

Returning from the Nation*
Governor's Conference in L*
Angeles the last year of his *
term as governor, 1966.
BELOW: The family—hap*
the end of the campaign, ele*
night 1959 in Oklahoma C*

The Politician

"There's as Much Harmony Among Oklahoma Democratic Leaders as in a Sack Full of Cats Being Hauled to the River"

O f all the people I have known in politics, John Tyler had the greatest influence on my activities. Single-handedly, he made me state Republican chairman; he was the first to seriously identify me as a potential candidate for governor, and his financial support was timely and significant. The Tyler family owned major interests in the Dewey-Portland Cement Plant at Dewey, the Union National Bank in Bartlesville and other investments, including a large ranch in Washington County called "Blue Ribbon." On his own, John had gone into the personal finance business. At the time, his operations had spread into many states and he was highly successful. He enjoyed politics as an avocation, was a heavy and regular contributor and, in 1958, was elected Republican state chairman, a hopeless, payless, thankless job that only a political martyr would take.

As state chairman, John devoted a great deal of his personal time, resources, and energy to the job. He was terse with people and not particularly popular with party workers, but he was a successful organizer because of his dedication to politics and because he brought in many new, badly needed ideas. Prior to the 1958 campaign, I was elected Noble County chairman. Our small county carried on one of the most vigorous campaigns in its history. We invited state chairman Tyler to a party function in Perry at the Methodist Church. He was pleased by what he saw that night and from that point on our relationship grew warmer and warmer.

After our return in January 1959 from our family sojourn to Maui, farming had become a little dull. Things had begun to fit together so that it was not quite as great a struggle as when we started our farm fourteen years earlier. One day, I was sitting in our kitchen after doing the morning chores when the telephone rang. It was John Tyler, who asked me if I was interested in becoming Republican state chairman. The idea had never crossed my mind. He asked Shirley and me to drive to Oklahoma City to talk over the matter with him. John had decided to relinquish the party chairmanship to become a candidate for national committeeman. As Shirley and I drove along, we discussed the possibility and agreed that it would be a sacrifice, but we both felt it was an experience we should undertake.

My election to the state chairmanship in 1960 was literally maneuvered by Tyler. He arranged for me to appear at several Republican district conventions and made it obvious that so far as he was concerned, I was to be his successor.

At the district meeting at Roman Nose Lodge at Watonga, a local party leader named Hod Tolbert decided I was not a satisfactory candidate for chairman and announced he would oppose me. Hod's analysis was probably right because at that time I was clearly a greenhorn so far as state politics were concerned. That year, the Republican state convention was held in Oklahoma City, and most of the delegates were domiciled in the Skirvin Hotel. The night before the convention, Hod went from room to room partying and announcing how soundly he was going to thrash me. The next day Tolbert didn't show up on the convention floor and his name was never entered in the race for chairman. With no opposition, I was elected, or, more accurately, anointed by John Tyler to be state chairman. John ran successfully for national committeeman later in the year and was available to guide me as I learned the political ropes.

Soon after I was elected, John and his wife Margaret invited Shirley, the girls, and me to Bartlesville for Sunday lunch. We were absolutely awed by the size of the Tyler mansion and the warmth of the Tyler family. When he was in Oklahoma City, John would come to the state committee office and help me with the daily functions such as writing press releases, helping with decisions in making appointments, and, in general, serving as a "chairman of the board." Often, the days when John was in the office would end with the two of us eating dinner at the Tower Club. John was not the type to throw his weight around. He was the "available Jones" who would do whatever he was asked to do to the best of his ability and who would make suggestions if he felt he had something to contribute. All in all, our working relationship was nearly ideal and we built an immense personal regard for each other, though our backgrounds were probably as different as they could be.

After my election as governor, John Tyler did not in any way try to move in or take over. He was intensely proud that a Republican had been elected for the first time in state history. He seemed to have unbounded confidence in my ability to handle the job. I knew that anytime I needed his counsel, support, or advice, it would be forthcoming.

At the time I was elected Republican state chairman, the principal function of the party was to disperse U.S. Postal patronage. The Republican state committee was operating from a three-room suite on the eighth floor of the Hightower Building in Oklahoma City. The office was staffed by one person, Peggy, a young woman who served as secretary and who handled routine correspondence relating to post office appointments without too much input from the state chairman. Peggy was an extremely urbane young woman. Her husband was a senior at O.U. medical school and she considered herself far more sophisticated and proficient than the country bumpkin who had been chosen state chairman. I had never worked before with a secretary, never dictated correspondence, never written a press release, and never dealt extensively with people on the telephone. There is no question that my efforts to handle these new means of communication left a great deal to be desired. Unfortunately, Peggy was not the type to help a novice learn ways to be effective. Working with her was torture for me. When I attempted to dictate letters to her, she would sit back in her chair and laugh at my clumsy efforts. When I talked on the phone Peggy would sit at her desk and laugh at the way I handled people.

During this time, I was sometimes writing four or five press releases a day. I would go to the office early every morning, read the newspapers, and prepare press releases attacking or criticizing something the Democratic governor or legislative leaders had done. There were plenty of obvious and deserving targets. In the southern states during the hundred years between the Civil War and 1960, the electoral contests were basically between Democrats. Republicans were out of favor. Without serious Republican opposition, the Democratic party broke into personality cults. In Oklahoma, there were Edmondson Democrats, Gary Democrats, Monroney Democrats, Kerr Democrats, and many others.

During the time I served as state chairman, fighting among Democrats in Oklahoma became so intense that U.S. Senator Bob Kerr was forced to schedule a "harmony meeting." When it was over, I put out a press release saying, "There's as much harmony among Oklahoma Democratic leaders as in a sack full of cats being hauled to the river."

In the process of delivering press releases to the UPI office, I had become well acquainted with Joe Carter. As one of the youngest and newest members of the UPI staff, he seemed to catch the off-hour assignments and also was generally on duty weekends and holidays when I had press releases to distribute. I found those were usually slow news times and that press releases which on other days would wind up in the trash can would be given prominent space if issued on those days. Since my only experience with the press had been as a student reporter during my college days, I had a great deal to learn. Joe took me under his wing and began to help me with my press release writing. He was a flamboyant writer who tipped me off to matters he felt might be worthy of comment and which might get printed if the comment could be attributed to the Republican state chairman. Our cordial relationship developed into a mutually beneficial arrangement whereby Joe got his news and I got the coverage the party needed to show it was an active force in Oklahoma politics. Having my name in the news so frequently was also a major political asset.

The relationship between Peggy and me grew worse. She continued to be a special friend and favorite of John Tyler's, who was as sophisticated and urbane as she was. But rather than being any help to me, she increasingly became a liability. It was a great relief when, after the conclusion of the school term in May, her husband was graduated from medical school and they moved to the West Coast for his internship.

After an unhappy experience with a replacement secretary hired through an employment agency, I became wary of ever again hiring political staff unless they had previously demonstrated their loyalty and their dedication to me personally or to the Republican party. This rule has been followed since then with few exceptions. In most other cases where we have departed from the rule, the results have either been disastrous or disappointing.

Jeannette Baxter, a woman about my age who lived in the Village and who was a neighbor and friend of several active Republicans, was recommended for the secretarial position. She came to the Hightower Building with her husband, Jerry, to be interviewed. She was a loyal Republican, had been active in party activities, and was well skilled in secretarial work. I hired her immediately. Jeannette performed extremely well under trying conditions through the balance of the 1960 presidential campaign. When the election was over and the decision was made to reduce the size of our office and staff to hold down expenses, she stayed. We moved to a small office on Twenty-Third Street, a low-rent area. Those were lean times for the party. There were weeks when we received no income and on occasion we could not pay Jeannette the salary she had earned. She stayed on through those times, helped get the party organization back in shape, and proved to be able, loyal, and diligent in discharging her responsibilities. She was also a highly proficient secretary who could handle the duties of the office with very little guidance from the state chairman.

In addition, Jeannette did much to bolster my self-confidence. It was her suggestion after the campaign that the two of us enroll in a Dale Carnegie course. It helped us considerably in our dealings with people, but did little to help my speaking skills. Jeannette continued to serve throughout the period of party reorganization. She had a particularly important role in hosting the Republican national committee meeting in Oklahoma City and was generally the strong right arm of the state chairman. We developed a close working relationship and my confidence in and regard for her was virtually unbounded.

After the party reorganization work had succeeded and after the bank account had been built back up, we closed the small office on Twenty-Third and moved into larger quarters at 1300 North Broadway in the Kirkpatrick building. This building was owned by oil man and loyal Republican John Kirkpatrick, one of Oklahoma City's most generous philanthropists. He made quality office space available to us at a nominal charge and was generally supportive in the on-going efforts to build the party.

Prior to my selection as Republican state chairman, the Oklahoma Republican Party had focused mainly on national elections. We could be thought of as a "presidential party" because most of the effort was focused on carrying the state for the president, and were very successful in that effort. Since statehood, however, the Republican party in Oklahoma had never captured the governorship. Twice we'd come within 16,000 votes, but in the 1958 governor's campaign, the Democrats won by a vote of four to one, and Democratic party leaders proudly proclaimed the permanent demise of the Republican party.

Another handicap to effective Republican party political work was the way the party raised and spent money. At the time I became state party chairman, the system of handling Republican state finances was extraordinary. One of the previous state chairmen had proved to be a dishonest scoundrel who had squandered party resources and on one occasion had taken his secretary for a lengthy stay in San Francisco at party expense. As a result, heavy contributors to the party, most of them Tulsans, had established a "finance office" on the thirteenth floor of the Mid-Continent building in Tulsa. Jay Walker was the leader of the Tulsa Republican Finance Committee. Originator, owner, and operator of National Tank Company, he employed seven hundred people in Sand Springs where oil field tanks, separators, heaters, and other types of equipment were manufactured for the domestic and international petroleum industry. Jay started from a modest background and became highly successful in business. He developed an interest in government and politics and devoted much of his time and money to the support of the Republican party and its candidates.

Jay was a huge man whose size gave him an aura of power, influence, and generosity. In my experience with him, he lived up to this description. He was probably one of the least articulate people I have known. He rarely had anything to say at any of the finance luncheons held to raise money or report on party activities except to stand up and hand over his own check and perhaps utter some open or veiled threat to others who were slow to fall in line. The man assigned by Jay Walker to run the Tulsa finance office was one of his employees, John Thomas. John was about my age, had an extremely good opinion of himself, and was blessed with a genteel, southern, aristocratic background. The first time I went to the Tulsa finance office and met John Thomas it became evident that the Tulsa office was Thomas's domain and was in no way subject to the control of the state chairman. John Thomas, and not the state chairman, seemed to be the real power in Oklahoma Republican politics.

At the time I became chairman, when funds were needed it was the practice to call a small number of contributors together in Tulsa. At these meetings the arm would be put on these people to ante up. Often, sums approaching $100,000 could be raised at one or more such luncheons. Each month, the state chairman would figure out what money would be required to operate the state organization for the next thirty days. He would calculate how much was needed to pay rent, salaries, postage, stationery, campaign activity costs and to buy paraphernalia. These items were totaled and included in a letter titled "Check Request," which was sent to the Tulsa finance office for approval by John Thomas. Any items Thomas felt were justified were included in a check sent back to the state office for deposit in the state party checking account. Items he felt were unjustified were simply stricken. As far as he was concerned, that settled the matter.

The fact that John Thomas lived in an apolitical, rarified atmosphere, held no elected or appointed party post, and was totally out of communication with Republican activities and opportunities across the state simply made no difference. The fact that he had the confidence of Jay Walker and thirty or forty of the big givers in Tulsa County gave him all the backing he needed to control party finances, and thereby, party activities. John continually catered to these individuals because he knew the source of his authority. He had control of the money and he ruled the party on their behalf. Unfortunately, the party rulers were out of touch with those they sought to govern. As I became more and more aware of the situation, I made up my mind that the Tulsa finance office had to be shut down, that the base for the party's financial support had to be broadened. I decided that if I continued as state chairman, John Thomas was going to have to leave the scene and that control of the party would be shifted to the hands of its duly elected officers.

After the 1960 election, after we had reorganized the party, and after I had been reelected to serve as state chairman for two more years, I told John Tyler of my plan to close the Tulsa finance office. Tyler was appalled by the thought and told me that if we undertook to close the office, we would lose the support of our principle financial backers in the Tulsa area. I told him that, nevertheless, I was going to close the office. I felt we could broaden the party financial base and that one reason the party had not been more successful in the past was that the decisions which really determined our course of action were being made by the representative of a small number of individuals who were out of touch with political realities of much of the state. Finally, Tyler agreed that the Tulsa office should be closed and that control of party finances should be vested in a state budget committee which would be broadly representative of party leadership from all sections of the state.

We then decided that the way to go about closing the office was to go to Jay Walker and tell him our plan and try to get his agreement and support. John Tyler was apprehensive because he felt certain we would alienate Jay and through him lose the support of our other major financial backers in Tulsa. A meeting with Jay Walker was arranged, but when Tyler and I arrived at Jay's offices in Sand Springs, we found he had gone across the street for his morning coffee break. We decided to go to the restaurant. Mr. Walker was seated — more accurately, wedged — into a booth. John and I placed ourselves in the same booth, across from Jay. Because of his size and the difficulty he had sitting in such a narrow place, we were literally sitting nose to nose as we talked.

John left it up to me to broach the subject and explain the problem. As I talked, John's face broke out in a sweat, but Jay was seemingly nodding his head in agreement. When I got to the point of telling him we planned to close the Tulsa finance office, he slammed his hand down on the table and said, "Hell, that's a wonderful idea. I wonder why we didn't think of doing that a long time ago." It is impossible to describe the feeling of relief John Tyler and I felt at Jay's reaction.

After our conversation with Jay, John dispatched me to the Tulsa office to break the news to John Thomas. Jay had told us he needed John back in his business. He felt Thomas had been devoting too much time to the Republican finance effort. When I went into the office and told John and the secretary that the office was going to be closed, it was as if an earthquake hit the place. Thomas had no idea that I would have the temerity to attack his fortress and the support of both John Tyler and Jay Walker; he absolutely refused to accept my decision. He put up a fight, but to no avail. The office was shut down, the finance account was moved to Oklahoma City, the budget committee began to function, and from that point on the state chairman and the elected representatives of the party have made the spending decisions. In a real sense, that was the birth of a broad-based, campaign-oriented Republican party in Oklahoma. Whatever success the party has had since 1960 can be attributed partly to this broadening of the party's base. So far as John Thomas is concerned, he did go back to National Tank Company and after a few weeks of rupture, our relationship was at least partially restored. He was helpful to me during my campaign for governor and following my election.

During my 1962 governor's campaign, Jay Walker was by far the most generous contributor. I do not have a precise number but as I recall, Jay's contributions had totalled up to more than $15,000. With this much contribution coming from one individual, I was more than slightly concerned Jay might feel that he owned a piece of the governor's office. Therefore, I was apprehensive about what he might demand and how I might react. Several months went by after my election before Jay even bothered to telephone the governor's office. I would see him from time to time at events in Tulsa, but nothing even approaching business was ever brought up. I attempted to appoint John Thomas to the Pardon and Parole Board but Jay turned this down because he did not want "criminals hanging around my place asking for favors."

Finally, one day when I came into the office, I was handed a note that Jay Walker had called. It was with great apprehension that I returned the call. I was certain he was now going to ask for a favor of some kind. I was correct. Jay had called to express his interest in the "humane slaughter" bill which had that day cleared the legislature and which would shortly be on my desk for signature. Jay explained to me that his wife had been one of those most active in pushing for passage of this legislation and he called to express his hope that I would look carefully at the bill and sign it. The bill was something that needed to be done anyway and, of course, I would have signed it regardless of Jay's call. It was extraordinary that, after all the years of service and after the thousands of dollars of contributions Jay had made to the party and to my campaign, this was the only request that he ever made of Oklahoma's first Republican governor. Jay was simply interested in seeing that the state was well governed as was the case with the vast majority of supporters.

Jay died while I was in office and control of his company passed into the hands of a national conglomerate. From that point on so far as I know there has never been a significant level of political participation on the part of company executives. It seems to me that a self-made person like Jay Walker feels both a greater debt to the free enterprise system and a greater responsibility to support the government and make it work than do the "hired guns" who are sent to run the subsidiaries of national companies. Old tigers like Jay Walker, Bill Skelly, Bailey Vincent, B. B. Blair, and others — narrow and overly assertive as they sometimes seem to be — still had a basic love of country and confidence in the worth and rightness of the political system that compelled them to devote a generous portion of their time and resources to making the governing system work. I don't find this feeling now among professional corporate executives, who seem to owe their loyalties and their abilities to the home office. The transfer of ownership and control of local businesses out of the hands of individual owners into the control of the large corporations has resulted in serious erosion of the political financial base in Oklahoma and I am sure in many other states. It is a great loss to the political system and is one of the changes that seems to be eroding the support of political activity in the country. This is a gap that political action committees were created to fill.

Following my election as state chairman in 1960, I undertook to check into the condition of the party at the county level. To my amazement and chagrin, I found there were sixteen counties in Oklahoma where no Republican county organization existed whatsoever. These were basically strong Democratic areas with only a small number of registered Republicans. Many of those who were registered with our party had no desire to be identified as Republicans — in many cases because they felt it would hurt their businesses or careers. As one of my first responsibilities, I undertook the task of going into each of those counties where the party was not organized, locating someone who was qualified to serve as party chairman, and convincing him to take on the task.

In a one-party state like Oklahoma, there is a tendency for most citizens who want a voice in government to register with the majority party even though they vote their true preference in a general election. This leaves the minority party with a perplexing mixture of ultra-loyal, dedicated party members and some community misfits, many of whom go out of their way to be offensive. It was my job to identify and recruit Republican leadership from the former and avoid the latter. In many cases, this was a difficult job. It was first necessary to find out who the registered Republicans were and then identify those who had been willing to take party responsibilities in the past. From those individuals

I got other names of prospective party officials and made contact with them.

Defeatism among traditional party leaders plagued Republicans in many areas of the state. A typical experience was the visit I paid on a Republican banker in Jay, county seat of Delaware County. I arrived at the bank about ten in the morning and presented myself to the secretary. I was kept waiting an hour. Then I was ushered into the banker's presence, not even offered a seat but given a lecture. "Young man," the banker said, "I have lived in Delaware County all my life and I know these Democrats. The more you stir them up the worse you will get beat. The thing for you to do is turn around, walk out that door, get into your car, leave Delaware County, and don't come back." I ignored this lecture, of course, and I did succeed in finding a Delaware County Republican chairman. In the 1962 governor's race, we came close to carrying the county.

A unique situation existed in Coal County, where the largest store was owned by the Hudson family who were listed among some thirty-five registered Republicans. When I approached the Hudsons, I expected I would get the usual turn-down; that they did not want to be identified with the party because it would hurt their business. To my surprise, I got exactly the opposite response. The senior member of the Hudson family told me he was very proud to be registered as a Republican and even wanted his customers to know this fact because it helped his business. The Democratic party was prone to intramural personality fights and he wished to stay above the fray. Anytime the Democratic party approached him for a contribution or to support one of their candidates, he told them he was Republican and had no reason to get involved. One of the Hudsons took the position as county chairman and served well.

The last county to be organized was Tillman County in the far southwest corner where Democratic domination was particularly strong. I went there determined to stay until I could find someone who agreed to become a working county chairman. The county had only a handful of registered Republicans and these were largely intimidated by their Democratic opponents. In fact there had been no effective party organization for many years. Following the leads I'd been given, I went from one Republican sympathizer to another trying to find someone willing to stand up and take the party chairmanship. I was finally referred to a farmer named Beatty Patterson who lived several miles east of the small town of Manitou. He was virtually my last prospect.

I arrived at the Patterson homestead at about eleven o'clock and found Mrs. Patterson busy ironing and tending the noon meal, cooking on the stove. When I told her who I was and asked for Beatty, she suggested I remain until he came in for lunch since he was cutting hay in a field that would have been difficult for me to reach. For the next hour Mrs. Patterson and I got acquainted while she did the family ironing, fixed the noon meal, and set an extra plate on the table for lunch. It must have been something of a surprise to find a strange person sitting in the kitchen talking to his wife when Beatty came in dusty and dirty from the hayfield. We struck up a conversation and a friendship which lasted thirty years. During lunch we talked about what the job of county chairman entailed. Probably as much to get rid of me and get back to the hay field as any other reason, Beatty agreed to serve and became an effective county chairman, handling the job with skill and dedication. In later years I appointed Beatty to a state agriculture committee where he served with distinction.

At the time I became Republican state chairman in April 1960, I discovered from John Thomas that the party had about $16,000 in the bank, that we had continual on-going expenses, that we were beginning to gear up for the campaign, and that no organized effort was being made at either the state or county level to bring in additional money. It was plain that unless the money we had was used to bring in more revenue, the party would be out of business in two or three months. John Thomas suggested hiring a professional fund-raising organization and turning over the responsibility for filling the party treasury and broadening the base of party financial support to them. We contacted Burrell Associates of Kansas City and a meeting was arranged with their representative to discuss the party's problem. A decision was made quickly to carry on a full-scale professional fund drive for the party in Tulsa County where most of the money was coming from at that time. The time was relatively short and advice was that it would not be effective to undertake a statewide fund drive. The Burrell Associates proposed to send down an account executive, and, using virtually all of our $16,000 for expenses and fees, they felt that something more than $150,000 could be raised in six to eight weeks.

Our assigned account executive was Drew Mason, a young man from Iowa. A former dairy farmer, he disliked the monotony of farm life and had gone into the fund-raising business. Drew Mason's coming to Oklahoma and our association together probably had as much to do with my political fortunes as any other single event. While we are different types of individuals, we worked together well from the beginning and developed a high degree of mutual respect and trust.

Drew's approach to fund raising and to politics was strictly professional. He insisted on activities being thoroughly and carefully organized, and those who worked with him had to follow the same policy, even volunteers who were concerned about their regular activities and prone to let fund-raising slide or to do things on a catch-as-catch-can basis. Drew structured his fund-raising organization along military lines with generals, colonels, captains, and troops. His theory was that each individual could be expected to contact not more than ten others so the need for careful organization and participation by a large number of individuals was great. He insisted that we find the right person (the general) to head the drive. As the hired professional, Drew kept as low a profile as possible. In reality, the Mason contribution was to give the party a goal and a carefully structured organizational plan. He provided the drive necessary to get as many individuals as possible to live up to the responsibility they had voluntarily assumed.

The fund drive which Drew carried on in Tulsa County was singularly successful. It finally brought in about $160,000. This money was used to pay the full expenses for the 1960 campaign, including expenses for the state organization, the Nixon-for-President efforts in Oklahoma, and expenses for state legislative and congressional candidates. We gave $20,000 to each of four congressional candidates and $300 to $500 to each legislative candidate. This contribution made these individuals feel good toward the state organization and toward the state chairman, which did me no harm in later years.

Drew's stay in Oklahoma terminated with the conclusion of the fund-raising effort. After the election and after John Tyler and I decided to develop an on-going program for the party, we decided to repeat the Tulsa fund-raising drive in Oklahoma County and a few other of the more populous counties. Also, since the Tulsa drive had cost the party $16,000 for two months of professional services, we figured that a better approach would be to try to hire Drew Mason as a full-time party executive director with fund raising as his major responsibility.

By good fortune, Drew's sister and brother-in-law had moved to Tulsa and when we approached Drew about coming to work in Oklahoma, he accepted. I believe that if other members of his family had not been in the state, he might have declined. At any rate, he did come on the party payroll and from that point on our finances were kept in reasonably good shape. His efforts were part of the GOP Countdown that put together both the financial undergirding and the organizational structure for my successful 1962 governor's race. No longer did a few wealthy and generous Tulsans finance and control the Republican party in Oklahoma.

When I resigned as Republican state chairman to enter the governor's race, Drew continued as party executive director under new chairman Forrest Beall. They did not develop the mutual understanding and respect Drew and I had enjoyed. After a few months, Drew told me he was going to leave his position. He wanted to come on the governor's campaign staff and provide the same organizational and financial support he had furnished in his party post. At first, I was reluctant to have Drew leave his position because I felt party people might feel I hired him away. However, in checking with Beall, I found he had no objection, so an arrangement with Drew was worked out. This proved to be another fortunate development in my political career.

The Republican National Convention in 1960 was held under unusual circumstances so far as Oklahoma participation was concerned. Our state convention had been held early in the year and our delegates had all been selected and pledged to Richard Nixon. After our convention, a Goldwater groundswell began and by the time the national convention convened in Chicago, our delegates, including the state chairman, were deluged with telegrams demanding we nominate Barry Goldwater. I received several hundred of these telegrams though they were totally meaningless since the decision had been made months before. Nevertheless, there was intense interest in the convention on the part of Oklahomans who wanted a right to be heard. Many of these were among our party's most stalwart financial backers and tended to be from the conservative wing of the party.

I had never been to a Republican National Convention and felt a little insecure at the enormity of my duties and the stress which was building up between the Goldwater and Nixon factions of the party. The Nixon people were firmly in control, though the Goldwater group was not at all pleased with the way the party had gone about choosing its delegates. Increasingly, I leaned upon Connie Brand, national committeewoman from Oklahoma, for assistance after we arrived in Chicago and had difficult decisions to make as to which Oklahomans would receive tickets to the convention. Admittance was by ticket only and there was a great scramble for admission.

Connie was being challenged at the convention by Dorcas Kelly for her position on the national committee. Connie dearly loved being national committeewoman but was nervous about being defeated if she sought reelection. She worried incessantly and tried to nail down the delegates to get a nose count on how she would come out if a contest were held. As the week wore on, Connie became almost paranoid. She increasingly stayed in her room where nervous friends continually fed her insecurity. From time to time I would be summoned and asked for information or instructed what to do on her behalf. At the same time, I was having frequent conversations with Dorcas Kelly and her son Tracy. The decision came down to two votes.

One of these two was a man who had come to the convention alone and taken up with a woman he met at a bar. We hardly saw him thereafter until he came to my room and demanded his two tickets so he and his new friend could enter the convention hall. Tickets were hard to get and were greatly in demand, especially by large contributors — several of whom showed up unannounced. Since the man was by himself, Connie and I had withheld one of his tickets to use for another Oklahoman. That extra ticket was like pure gold for Connie and me because we used convention tickets as favors for those whose support the party needed. The man continued to demand the convention ticket for his girlfriend. Connie and I continued to refuse to give it to him even as the contest between Dorcas and Connie hung heavily on this man's vote. I avoided him because every time we met he would make a scene. The scrap over the ticket finally came to a head when he and I were closeted in the same elevator. To my amazement, he did not bring up the ticket controversy during our ride together. When we arrived at the hotel lobby I asked him if he wanted the ticket and to my surprise, he said, "Hell, no.

I wouldn't be seen dead with that bitch."

The other needed vote depended upon Bailey Vincent, former Republican national committeeman, who had not shown up in Chicago. Bailey was still in Tulsa and felt he could not leave due to a serious family problem. Connie felt Bailey was firmly in her corner and did everything she could to get him to come to Chicago. She also used her influence on me to make certain Bailey would appear at the crucial moment. The evening before the vote for national committeewoman, Connie became so apprehensive she decided to withdraw from the race. Doug McKeever, a lawyer from Enid, and I went to her room where a bitter exchange occurred between Doug, Connie, myself, and Theo Klockman, who was with her. But there was no way she would stay in the race.

Doug and I held a midnight strategy session at which we finally decided that since Dorcas was going to become the national committeewoman in any event, we needed to make the best of the situation. The principal opposition to Dorcas Kelly had come from the financial contributors in the party who felt the Kelly family had received many party favors but never had been as generous in their financial support of the party as their station in life or the party favors provided them justified. Doug and I decided we could disarm most of Dorcas's opponents if we could get from the Kelly family a sizable contribution in advance of the time Dorcas was nominated and elected.

At about 3 a.m. we called Tracy Kelly into a suite of rooms which had been reserved for an Oklahoman who didn't show up at the convention and told him the situation. We explained that his mother was to be chosen as the next national committeewoman and that we felt it would make her position more tenable if the family would agree to a substantial financial contribution. He agreed and when delegates met next morning to choose the national committee members, criticisms that the Kellys were not substantial contributors could not hold water.

That ended Connie Brand's active participation. I was sorry to see her go because even though she was not closely in tune with the thinking of the majority of people, she was an energetic person who added a certain flair and style to party functions.

Our new national committeewoman was a colorful character. She had been a nurse in the Creek County oil fields; had married an older, prominent banker; had borne five sons, and entered politics as an avocation after her family was raised. She dressed colorfully, leaning heavily to bright purple. She was always jovial, no matter what crowd she was in. Her hats were her trademark, and as time went on she paid more and more attention to them, favoring hats that featured elephants, the Republican party symbol. The more and larger the elephants, the better she liked the hat. It came to be something of a game to speculate about the size and shape of the next Dorcas Kelly hat.

As far as I could tell, Dorcas was basically interested in the social side of politics. Her family idolized Dorcas and gave her great moral support so that she could attend party meetings whenever and wherever they were held. In her own way she made a contribution to the party — mostly as a convention-goer. She served many years as Oklahoma's Republican national committeewoman and gained considerable national attention through her propensity for unusual millinery.

One of the people I have been associated with in politics over the longest period of time is Clyde Wheeler. Clyde is from Laverne, Oklahoma, and was a school teacher before joining Congressman Page Belcher's Washington staff. Clyde left the Belcher staff after several years, spending some time at the U.S. Department of Agriculture before going to the White House where he was one of President Eisenhower's assistants. While I was state chairman, Clyde and I had many contacts and we developed a strong personal friendship as well as a mutual respect for each other's political interests. Our relationship deepened considerably during the race he made for Congress in the sixth district.

At the time of filing in 1960, Republicans were unable to field a congressional candidate for the new sixth district even though these western and southwestern counties had a sufficient number of Republican voters to give a Republican candidate an outside chance of winning. As chairman, I finally prevailed on Alice Frye, a young woman from Oklahoma City, to file. (This was legal, since under Oklahoma law, a candidate is not required to be a resident of the district.) We wanted a candidate to avoid a blank space on the ballot.

A bitter Democratic primary fight developed between Victor Wickersham and Toby Morris. It was clear that the two sides could not repair their differences and that the loser would likely help a respectable Republican candidate after the primary was over. We began to look hard for a serious Republican candidate. Also, the Democrats nominated Jack

Kennedy for president. Clyde Wheeler realized his days in the White House were over regardless of whether Nixon or Kennedy won. After the formal nomination of Alice Frye, Oklahoma law allowed a brief period of time when she could resign. A replacement candidate would then be chosen by Republican party officials. When I contacted Clyde about making this race, he expressed immediate interest. Then began one of the most complicated series of negotiations in which I have ever been involved.

Page Belcher was not too interested in having another Republican congressman in Washington with him. He liked being Mr. Oklahoma Republican in Washington. By the time I arrived in Chicago for the Republican National Convention, Clyde was set to run for Congress. A job had been arranged for him to fall back on with the Sunray-DX oil company in Tulsa in case his race was unsuccessful. When Page found out about these arrangements, he immediately called the president of Sunray-DX and knocked the whole project in the head. Belcher's story was that he was doing Wheeler a favor because if Wheeler left the White House he could go to work directly for DX and be effective as a political advisor, whereas if he ran for Congress and lost, his effectiveness would be destroyed. I did not agree with that position and while Wheeler did not defend himself in discussion with Belcher, in private he did not agree with the congressman either.

A serious schism opened between Belcher and myself. As I tried to persuade Clyde and his future employer of the wisdom of Clyde's candidacy, Belcher did everything he could to keep Wheeler from running. Clyde was tossed back and forth between Sunray Oil, Page, and me for several days before he finally made the decision to return to Oklahoma and enter the race. I met Clyde at the airport and drove pell-mell to Clinton where sixth congressional district party officials were meeting in Pop Hicks's cafe to choose the new nominee to fill the vacancy created by the withdrawal of Alice Frye. There were many details to be handled. We had to get a filing fee, make certain papers were filled out properly, then return them to the state election board before closing time. Fortunately, it all came together and Clyde entered the race. Though he was a late entry, he carried on a highly effective campaign. His sisters joined together to form the "Wheeler Belles," an effective group which inspired us to form the Bellmon Belles for my gubernatorial campaign.

As testimony to the power of the press, after Wheeler had returned to Oklahoma for only a few weeks and had barely gotten his campaign off the ground, the Daily Oklahoman ran an Otis Sullivant column about Clyde Wheeler and his service in Washington. The lead of the column was that Clyde Wheeler had been a "minor Washington bureaucrat," and that his campaign was not catching on. While this may have been Otis Sullivant's honest opinion, the facts were far different. Clyde Wheeler had been an important player in the Eisenhower White House as well as having served in the Department of Agriculture and as Page Belcher's administrative assistant. He had a good grasp of Washington's ways, had many personal contacts with the power brokers in that city, and his campaign was catching on rapidly. This was shown when the votes were counted on election day and Wheeler won narrowly. The Otis Sullivant column set his campaign back several days and slowed down financial contributions. Otherwise, Wheeler probably would have won by a large margin.

Wheeler won the election by some 250 votes. Wickersham called for a recount. I was sent to Caddo County to make sure that the Wheeler interests were protected during the recount process. Under Oklahoma law, after an election has been held, the votes are to be stored in metal ballot boxes, secured by three separate locks. Each member of the county election board, two Democrats and one Republican, is supposed to have custody of one key so the ballot boxes cannot be opened except in the presence of all three election board members. When I arrived in Anadarko, county seat of Caddo County, I discovered to my amazement that the ballot boxes had been stored in a basement vault. There were eight keys to the vault lock — one of them in the custody of the county treasurer, who kept records in the vault and who had also served as Victor Wickersham's Caddo County campaign manager. She kept several keys in a desk drawer in her office so her deputies could go to the vault as the need arose. Another key to the vault was kept hanging in the janitor's office in the boiler room so maintenance personnel could enter the vault to clean it. The keys to all locks for the ballot boxes were stored in a cigar box which was sitting on one of the ballot boxes. Therefore, anyone from the treasurer's office or any janitorial staff who had access to the vault keys could enter the room, unlock the ballot boxes, and work as much mischief as he or she chose.

As the recount proceeded, it was obvious something like that had happened because many ballots were simply marked for both candidates. Apparently, someone had taken out Wheeler ballots and marked them also for Wichersham thus making it impossible for the recounting committee to know what the voters' intentions had been. Wheeler lost many votes in Caddo County which helped cost him the election by a recount. There was nothing I could do to prevent this miscarriage of justice. The experience made me painfully aware of the need for "ballot security" in future races. The problem arose because of the failure of the Republican county election board member to demand custody of one set of keys. When it was over, Wheeler was the loser by seventy-six votes. I am convinced that Clyde was counted out illegally.

In the 1963 scrap over Congressional redistricting, Clyde and I got crosswise over the issue. He sided with Page Belcher in favor of a plan which would serve the interests of Oklahoma's incumbent Congressmen but which, in my judgement, was a disservice to the voters. As a Washington lobbyist, however, Clyde earned the respect of those who worked with him, and our own relationship was soon restored to a high level of cooperation and mutual trust.

As state chairman I soon found that anytime I scheduled a committee meeting for evening, it quickly dissolved into a drinking party and very little business could be accomplished. I therefore began to schedule meetings in morning or early afternoon to avoid situations where alcohol was present. If something extremely controversial was to be taken up, however, we would purposely schedule a meeting following a reception and dinner. Most members of the state executive committee could not focus on serious business by the time the meeting came to order and it was easy for me to prevail. In such a situation we put across the idea of a GOP Countdown. It's debatable whether or not the committee would have agreed to go along with such a scheme had it been presented when members were cold sober, since the countdown was planned as a means to identify new leadership to replace much of the dead wood in the party, including many state committee members.

The GOP Countdown grew out of our success in Oklahoma in the 1960 Nixon campaign. After that experience, we believed that Oklahoma voters, even though registered five to one as Democrats, would vote for Republicans if properly motivated. With John Kennedy installed as president, we also realized that the former postal patronage work of the Republican organization in Oklahoma would no longer be necessary because patronage had shifted into the control of the Democratic administration. This left us two courses of action. One was to close the Republican state office, terminate our small staff and wait in limbo for roughly eighteen months until the beginning of the next election campaign cycle. John Tyler and I disliked this option, for we feared the party and its budding new leadership would atrophy.

The other option was to conduct an organizational activity that would give the party reason to continue operating a headquarters and build the organization for the governor's race in 1962. John Tyler and I decided the latter course of action was wisest. The big Nixon vote we'd received in Oklahoma, plus the growing unpopularity of the incumbent Edmondson administration would give Republicans an excellent chance to capture the governorship if we were properly prepared. We decided we needed the services of a public relations agency. We needed assurance from our major financial contributors that they would provide funding to get us started since the party had used all its resources in support of our candidates and in the Nixon campaign.

Clyde Wheeler was brought into the discussions. The agency we chose was the Beall Agency, which had handled the Wheeler for Congress campaign and whose offices were in Oklahoma City. The proprietor of the firm was Vernon Beall, a staunch Republican. The young man assigned to the Republican account was Warren K. "Doc" Jordan. Jordan had also worked with the Wheeler campaign. We were delighted when Beall agreed to let Jordan handle the state Republican account. Working with Doc, we put together the "GOP Countdown to Victory." This program included ten steps which began almost immediately. One evening, John Tyler and I went with the countdown proposal in hand to Tulsa to meet with a group of about forty of the state's staunchest Republican financial supporters. We raised $19,000 in pledges to support the countdown program on the basis that we would solicit and raise funds statewide.

Before long, we found that our choice of the Beall Agency was a mistake since their costs were more than we could stand and their contribution to the success of the countdown was minimal. In addition, they were doing nothing to help us with fund raising which had to proceed before the bills could be paid. Then, totally to my surprise, Jordan severed his relationship with Beall. The first I knew of it was when he moved into an office in the Kirkpatrick building across the hall from the state GOP headquarters. Jordan told me that one of the reasons he left was that Beall was over-charging us. By this time, the Beall Agency had run up a large bill against the Republican party. John Tyler and I personally signed a note for $10,000 in order to pay off and terminate our relations with the agency. I then arranged for Doc Jordan to handle the state party account for $400 a month. The new association with Doc Jordan helped the party and helped Jordan get his fledgling advertising agency underway.

Countdown objectives included a statewide county-by-county fund-raising drive, a re-registration drive to encourage registered Democrats who voted Republican to change parties, development of a registered voters list for every county, the identification of precinct voting patterns so the next candidates would know where to focus their efforts better, candidate recruitment, and candidate training schools. Defying over fifty years of state history, we even went so far as to plan a victory celebration for when we won the governorship two years hence.

After I first had been elected state chairman, one of our immediate duties had been to secure as many candidates as possible for Congress and the state legislature. Tyler had already appointed Representative Joe Musgrave of Tulsa as chairman of the Candidate Recruitment Commit-tee. Since filing opened Monday following the convention where the party had chosen new leadership, the three of us spent the entire week on the phone pleading with different individuals, whose names we barely knew, to run for office. It was a pitiful and useless activity because many of the people we persuaded to file had very little interest in running and virtually no opportunity of success. Many of them were advanced in years and few had any standing in their communities, an essential for a successful political effort. As part of the countdown, we planned to change this old system of reorganizing the party at the beginning of the campaign season. Precinct meetings and the state convention, where party officers were elected, were scheduled for April in the off-election year, thus giving the new organization twelve months to prepare for campaign activities.

Part of the GOP Countdown included the creation of a Countdown

Taskforce in counties where the regular organization did not wish to be involved. Our purpose here was to identify those county Republican officials whose interest had been in dispensing patronage and set the stage to replace them with individuals interested in winning elections — what the organization should have been about all along.

Unfortunately, over the years when postal patronage had been one of the party's chief purposes, many counties had elected county organizations that were not particularly concerned with winning campaigns. The worst case was a southeastern county where the county chairman was a bulk gasoline dealer for an oil company, the county vice chairman was his secretary, the state committeeman was his truck driver, and the state committeewoman was the chairman's wife. That county, which had many small towns with post offices and rural mail carriers, had not bothered to have a county Republican convention for years. The four party functionaries simply met and reelected themselves. When vacancies occurred in postal positions, the county chairman hand-picked the new employee. It appeared that he was literally selling the jobs for cash. As state chairman, I went into the county and scheduled a Republican county convention which was attended by a considerable number of registered Republicans. The offending county pseudo-organization did not bother to appear. When the convention was over, the party had new, campaign-oriented leadership.

After the Countdown program had been in process for about a year, county and state conventions were held and the party was reorganized from top to bottom. A large number of our older county party officials voluntarily gave up their positions or were replaced by GOP Countdown Taskforce members who had demonstrated an interest in organization and shown some talent for party-building. In many cases the old hands were happy to step aside and let the new, younger, and more aggressive leaders take charge. But some resisted since they still hoped for the return of the time when they would have postal patronage to dispense. About two-thirds of the members of the Republican state committee also were replaced when the reorganization occurred in April of 1961. Most of the new people who assumed party responsibilities had been recruited through the Countdown and had developed considerable organizational expertise as a result of Countdown activities.

I was elected for another two-year term as state chairman and proceeded with the Countdown activities until I resigned to run for governor in February 1962. The net result of the Countdown was that for the first time in many years Oklahoma had an active, aggressive Republican organization in every county, and I had a good grasp of the issues in every community of the state. It was upon this foundation that our successful governor's campaign was launched.

John Tyler, my political mentor, never expected or received anything even remotely resembling financial advantage from his political work nor did he in any way receive the kind of honor and attention which he genuinely deserved. Once after I was governor, he did receive a favor which helped make all his work worthwhile. I had scheduled a 2:30 p.m. meeting of Oklahoma's World's Fair Commission which was made up of three of the state's most prominent business leaders — Dean McGee, Walt Helmerich, and Boots Adams. They had agreed to raise funds so Oklahoma could have a prominent exhibit at the 1964 New York World's Fair. We felt a display of our state's water resources would help erase our "Dust Bowl" image which was impeding economic growth.

In Bartlesville at that time, Boots Adams, president of Phillips Petroleum, was reigning czar of the city. He was the type of individual who threw his weight around and bulldozed anyone who got in his way. At 2 p.m. the day Boots Adams and the World's Fair Commission was due in the governor's office, John Tyler happened to drop by for one of his unannounced, casual visits. When he looked at the schedule and saw that the three World's Fair commissioners had an appointment, he came in and told me to leave the office. I asked him what was going on and he said, "Don't ask questions, just get out of here because I am going to take over your office." I did as I was told and later discovered that Tyler got a newspaper, took off his shoes, put his feet on the governor's desk, leaned back in the governor's chair, and was sitting there reading a newspaper when Boots Adams walked in for the meeting with the governor.

Helping elect a Republican governor so John could be sitting in the governor's chair with his feet propped up on the governor's desk to greet Boots Adams must have given Tyler great satisfaction. It was almost reward enough for all the work he had done in building the Oklahoma Republican party.

The Candidate

"Tax More to Afford the Waste, Graft, and Corruption"

The first time someone mentioned my running for governor was long before I even had become Noble County Republican chairman. One Sunday afternoon when Shirley's uncle Harley Harreld of Oklahoma City was visiting us at the farm, we talked politics and he told me he felt I should consider running for governor. Harley's brother, John W. Harreld, had been the state's first Republican U.S. senator, serving from 1920 to 1926. Harley told me he considered the governor's job a position from which the proper person could render a great service to the state. Harley was a staunch Republican, raised in Kentucky. I think his comment was based more on his deep dislike of the Democratic administration than on recognition of any ability or talent I possessed. Nevertheless, the conversation stuck in my mind and I thought of it often as years went by.

The second suggestion that I run for governor came from John Tyler in June 1961. I had been Republican state chairman for a year and several months. It was about 6 p.m. and I was in the office trying to finish some details when John called and invited me to supper with him at the Tower Club. The conversation began in a strange way. He asked me whether or not there were any family problems between Shirley and myself. I was startled that he would ask such a personal question and was quick to reassure him that there were no problems that I knew about. He then went on to tell me that he was impressed with my political ability and felt I was the ideal person to be the Republican candidate for governor in 1962.

A little startled, I was convinced John's imbibing had blunted his generally good political judgement. The conversation concluded on the theme that I should go about my business of serving as Republican state chairman and not make any overt efforts to become a candidate. However, John wanted me to realize that among Oklahoma Republicans, he felt I was the one who could come closest to being elected. He pledged me his support in case I decided to make the race.

By late fall of 1961, two things had become obvious. First, incumbent Democratic Governor J. Howard Edmondson was growing increasingly unpopular. And secondly, the Republican party had no formidable candidate to challenge the Democratic nominee in 1962. By October, John and I had begun to discuss seriously the possibility of my becoming a candidate. In November, John invited Shirley and me to his home in Bartlesville where the decision was made that I should run.

I was distraught at the thought because I did not feel I could be elected. It seemed incomprehensible to me that in Oklahoma, where registered Republicans were outnumbered five to one, voters would consider electing as the first Republican governor a candidate who had been a partisan Republican state chairman and who often had been critical of the sacred cows of the Democratic party. Bob Kerr and members of the legislature, as well as the governor, had been frequent targets of my critical press releases. I knew full well that my abilities as a candidate were extremely limited. I was not a good public speaker. In addition, there was nothing in my background that could convince anyone I had the qualifications to serve as governor. I had not been particularly successful at farming, had no business career to point to, was not trained or qualified by education for the governor's position, and had no reputation for achievement of any consequence.

I sincerely felt it was possible for a Republican to be elected governor, but I thought it would probably happen when we had a prominent candidate such as O.U. football coach Bud Wilkinson, some outstanding business person, or perhaps a prominent educator who was willing to make the race. On the other hand, having gone through the Countdown experience, I knew we had an excellent organization and that unless someone the group knew and believed in offered himself for the race, the whole thing was going to come unstuck.

Most distressing was the fact that by now, I had completely exhausted what little financial reserve Shirley and I had accumulated. My first year of service as Republican state chairman had been without financial compensation except for the meager $100-a-month expense allowance the party provided. The out-of-pocket travel expenses of the office ran at least $100 per week and frequently more. My family's living expenses were another $100 a week. On top of that, I had to hire help to run the farm, which was costing me another $100 per week. I was running behind well over $1,000 every month while I served as state chairman and this soon took what little cash we had.

By the time the governor's race developed, it was absolutely necessary for me to get at least expense money from the campaign fund. An arrangement was worked out so that I took $600 per month to pay the expenses of campaign travel and whatever other living expenses were required. Even so, while I never sat down and figured it out exactly, I am convinced that had I lost the race, I would have had to sell the farm in order to pay my debts. I suspected this would be so before I got into the governor's race. It was a frightening prospect, because if I ran and lost, we would likely lose our new house and the family would be plunged into really desperate economic conditions.

I was equally distressed about the time the campaign would take away from my family. The girls were approaching their teen years and I felt a real responsibility to be available to them at this time. I knew that the race for governor would keep me continually on the road, and while I had very little concept of what the governor's job would be like, I felt it would amount to an almost total separation for the next several years.

I felt trapped but decided to run. John Tyler gave me the first campaign contribution, $3,000. The only other significant contribution I received during the primary was one of $1,000 from Dave Bartlett, a prominent Tulsa oil operator and loyal Republican. Dave was the brother of Dewey, who later became Oklahoma's second Republican governor and a U.S. senator. Prior to announcing, the only other people with whom I discussed the matter were Shirley and the girls, Drew Mason, Doc Jordan, who was chosen to handle advertising, and Forrest Beall, who had been selected to take my place as Republican state chairman.

Soon after I announced for governor, John Tyler recommended we engage the services of Steve Shadegg to help plan strategy for the campaign. Steve had gained his reputation as a Republican campaign consultant from his handling of Barry Goldwater's campaign in Arizona.

He proved to be a thoughtful man far more prone to listen than talk. When he did have something to say it was usually worth listening to.

Shadegg began by asking me why I wanted to be governor and somewhat put me on the spot. I had not thought through why I wanted the job. I was not even sure I did want the job at that point. I was running primarily because I felt that otherwise the Republicans would not have a strong candidate and I truly felt the state needed the advantages a competitive two-party system would bring. In the three days of discussions with Shadegg, campaign issues developed and I began to see more clearly some of the things that could be accomplished by a Republican in the governor's office.

Shadegg had a theory about how political campaigns are won. He felt that, more than television ads, bumper stickers, fence straddlers, billboards, newspaper ads, radio spots, or any other paid advertising, voters liked to get their political information from associates they respected who had had some direct contact with the candidate. Steve's theory was that this effective personal campaigning works like leaven in the body politic and that if the candidate can have some direct contact with at least one percent of the voters the leaven will spread widely enough to have a major impact on the outcome on election day.

Also, Shadegg eloquently made the point that candidates are not required to persuade all fifty-one percent of the vote. He took the position that even in a heavily Democratic state like Oklahoma, a respectable Republican candidate was assured of getting thirty-five to forty percent of the vote. This meant that through the candidates' efforts and through the support of the organization, if the other eleven percent of the votes could be delivered at the polls, victory would result. Steve pointed out that if you took five and a half percent off the Democratic candidate's tally and added those votes to the Republican side, that made a total of eleven percent difference, which was the margin for victory. In discussions with Steve, I became convinced that it was easily possible for a hard-working candidate who could make a good impression on small groups to contact enough voters directly or indirectly to make a five percent impact. The governor's campaign was planned and carried out with that goal.

When I resigned the chairman's job to begin the campaign, I asked Jeannette Baxter to come with me as my secretary. She agreed and again went through the arduous job of organizing and staffing a political office. This time the office was in a building on Britton Road near

Oklahoma City. Jeannette scheduled what we called "two-party tea parties." We wanted it to be plain that even though I was a Republican, our principal objective was to bring the benefits of competitive two-party government to the state. Our pitch was that with the competition from two parties, each side, in order to win, would be forced to put forth its best candidates. Jeannette collected names of the guests and saw to it that personal letters over my signature went to all those who attended. She handled all other details of the campaign during the early stages. In addition, she took care of probably ninety-five percent of the correspondence, relying on me to dictate only those few letters which required a personal touch.

When Drew Mason gave up his position at the state headquarters and joined us, he assumed many of the duties and responsibilities Jeannette had been handling. Drew Mason's title was organizational director, but for all practical purposes he served as campaign manager. He was responsible for staffing, budgeting, payroll, direct mail, coordinating activities with the advertising agency, arranging for the loan of cars, credit cards, and all the other support which 1960-era political candidates relied upon. He handled his duties with energy, enthusiasm, skill, and diplomacy. There was not the slightest negative publicity and the campaign's success was in a considerable degree due to his contributions. Drew and his secretary Helen Lawson had talents for "scrounging." I use this term in its best possible connotation since what they did was to get individuals to provide support in unusual ways. For instance, Helen was able, through contacts she had, to borrow typewriters and office machines that the campaign could not afford to purchase. She rounded up stamps, envelopes, stationery, office furniture, and similar items. Drew found cars, office space, and other essential support. They seemed to get personal pleasure out of their success and, of course, this was of great value to the campaign effort since funds were always limited. Drew and Helen were the backbone of the organization, tireless workers, and poured themselves into political efforts. To them, political activity was high adventure and fun. They brought in large numbers of volunteers, keeping them properly motivated and directed. These volunteers turned out an immense volume of work.

As activities picked up and the size of the organization grew, we moved the headquarters downtown to the basement of the old Sears building near the Biltmore Hotel. This building was owned by the Weitzenhoffer family who had contacted Drew and offered the space at a price we could afford. No qualified person wanted the jobs of campaign manager or press secretary because they all seemed to feel the race was hopeless. Finally, more or less in desperation, I settled on Wayne Mackey, who was working for the *Oklahoma City Times*. Wayne and I had been schoolmates at Billings High School, where he was one year behind me. Though he was a registered Democrat and we had not been particularly close friends, I hoped I could convince Wayne to do the job. Somewhat to my surprise, he agreed — on the condition that I talk to the publisher and make certain that if he handled the campaign for me and we lost, he would have a job waiting. Publisher Ed Gaylord, who was totally dedicated to the defeat of my opponent Bill Atkinson, agreed. In the summer, Wayne Mackey came aboard as my campaign manager and press secretary. In many ways, this proved to be one of our best decisions. But it also gave us a handicap that could have destroyed the campaign.

Wayne was a genius in handling both campaign issues and news. He could develop newspaper stories where most of us didn't know news existed. I was instructed to call him twice a day, no matter where I was, and give him a blow-by-blow account of what had happened during the previous few hours. One of the stories that came from these conversations happened in the town of Gracemont. I had been campaigning in this small hamlet. At the end of the short main street, there was a small building where the local blacksmith plied his trade. I went into the blacksmith's shop and found the smithy down on his knees repairing a broken mowing machine. To impress the old gentleman, I took the acetylene torch from him and proceeded to complete the welding he had been doing. The old man was quite pleased to find we shared a common skill and I suppose was persuaded to vote for me, although I never will know that for sure. Later, when I talked with Mackey, I told him about this experience and he wrote a clever news story about how I had taken time out from my campaign to repair a farmer's mowing machine. The story received excellent statewide coverage.

One weekend late in the campaign, our furnace at home quit working. This was a considerable nuisance and took some time to repair. Again when I talked to Mackey, I told him about the furnace and he managed to get a headline about how a candidate had spent his Sunday afternoon overhauling his furnace. These kinds of stories conveyed a common touch and generated rapport with many voters who faced similar mundane tasks. The stories got a great deal more attention than the usual political accusations and charges. This was a tremendous boon to me. Wayne Mackey deserves immense credit for his ability to sift kernels out of the political campaign chaff.

Another great contribution Wayne Mackey made was his successful effort to keep me from launching into criticisms of the Welfare Department and the earmarking of sales taxes. Many of us felt we needed a positive issue, but Mackey's position was that all we needed to do was repeat former Governor Raymond Gary's "No New Tax" theme over and over again. There was one very lengthy and heated debate between Mackey, myself, and other members of the campaign organization when Mackey was the only one who felt we should stay with the "No New Tax" theme and avoid other issues. Gradually, as the argument went on, I became convinced that Wayne was right and we continued to use the "No New Tax" slogan, with Raymond Gary's knowledge and consent, to the end.

The problem with Wayne was that he absolutely could not handle liquor. He became extremely talkative and aggressive as soon as he imbibed even a small quantity of alcohol. The situation got so bad by September that I called Wayne into my office and fired him. I told him exactly what the problem was and thought I had his agreement that the connection should be ended. I had no idea what I would do for a campaign manager, but it seemed Mackey had come to be far more a liability than an asset. This was done on Sunday. By Wednesday Mackey insisted on talking to me again. The interview was arranged and Mackey came in very contrite and apologetic. He told me he had not touched a drop of liquor since our conversation, that he had his drinking problem under control, and that he felt he should be given a second chance.

I felt our long-time friendship should be honored, and I had no other candidate in mind, so I allowed Wayne to go back to work as campaign manager and press secretary. For a few days he seemed able to handle himself, but within two weeks he was back to his old habits. By then it was very late in the campaign to make a change. I discussed the matter with Drew, Hubert Gragg, and others and finally we worked out a system. A member of the campaign staff would pick up Mackey at his home early every morning, stay with him every minute of the day, and take him home when the day was over, no matter how late it was. Thus they could help keep him away from the bottle or if he did imbibe, keep him from conducting himself in a way that could have brought the campaign to a disastrous crash. Mackey continued to have the same sharp political instincts he had displayed earlier and major credit for the success of the campaign is due him.

Another reason for the success of the governor's campaign was that Doc Jordan and I had developed a close personal working relationship over the months before I became a candidate. Also, fortunately, to use Connie Brand's term, our "chemistry mixed well." Jordan had abilities and perspectives I lacked. In the past, Oklahoma Republicans had waited until late in the campaign before making an arrangement with an advertising agency. Often the party would go to an agency with a sum of money and say "buy us some political ads." By getting Jordan into the campaign even before there was a campaign, we used his skills to develop issues and campaign materials. He made many public relations contributions at important times and had a hand in planning activities which generated free publicity. It was with Jordan's assistance that the campaign was announced on Lincoln's birthday. By using his agency and the services of a friendly television news reporter, we pre-filmed the announcement of my candidacy and got it into the hands of every television station a couple of days ahead of the actual announcement. This was a bit of a coup and I am not sure a candidate for governor had ever used this device before.

The campaign was a new experience for both Jordan and myself. We spent countless hours trying to figure out clever ways to catch people's attention and make the best possible use of our advertising funds. The total amount of money used in the governor's campaign was about $340,000. For his services, Jordan received fifteen percent of the cost of paid advertising. He never made a charge for the personal time he spent counseling me before or after the advertising campaign began. Throughout the governor's campaign, as well as, to a lesser extent, in campaigns which followed, Jordan functioned as part of the campaign advisory team. He felt completely free to make comments and recommendations in fields far outside the scope of advertising.

No matter how well political campaigns are planned and no matter how dedicated the candidate and volunteers are, little can happen without money. John Tyler said it best: "Money may not be the most important part of a political campaign, but it must come before anything that is important can happen." I had been fortunate in securing the services of Ben Whitehill in Tulsa as our state fund-raising chairman. The campaign never faltered for lack of money. Ben was a respected member of the business and social community with contacts in other parts of the state. Fund-raising events were scheduled regularly whenever and wherever a sponsor could be found. The money came in as needed. We made no deals, though some were offered.

Early in the campaign, I was asked by a state legislator from Tulsa to agree to a meeting with some of his "contacts." It sounded a little mysterious to me, but I agreed. The meeting was arranged in the Cameron Building where the legislator had his office. When I arrived at the building, the legislator met me in the lobby and told me that we were not going to his office, but rather to a room in the basement. Again, I was a little mystified, but went along. When we reached the basement room, I was surprised to find two ominous-looking individuals. While I'd had no contact with hoods, these two looked like they came straight from Central Casting. They were short, swarthy men dressed in blue serge suits. Each was smoking a big cigar and had a large diamond stick pin in his tie. They asked the legislator and me to sit down, which we did, and the meeting got off to an uncomfortable start. As the discussion continued, it occurred to me that these two were sizing me up, trying to make up their minds whether I was a serious candidate for governor. Apparently, they were finally satisfied and made me a proposition.

They explained that one of the issues we would be facing in the next legislature was a state liquor franchise bill. They said they represented the distillers and were very interested in this legislation since it would put an end to the cut-throat competition that was going on between the various dealers who represented the distillers in the state. After describing the importance of the bill for them and, in their judgement, for the state, they proposed that if I were elected governor and would agree to sign the bill, they would provide me $325,000 for campaign expenses and would give it to me in cash, right then. They said I did not need to discuss the franchise issue during the campaign, only agree that if the bill got through the legislature that I would sign it. Even though I was relatively new to campaigning, I was not about to fall for a scheme like that. I explained to the pair that we were having no trouble raising campaign funds (which was true) and that I would look at their legislation on its merits when and if it came to my desk.

Hubert Gragg became fund-raising chairman for Oklahoma County. Hubert was a storybook business success. He began as a rodeo performer in west Texas then went into the pipeline construction business soon after World War II. He also developed the Gragg gas field in northwest Arkansas. As a result of his business success, Hubert built a large home northwest of Edmond. This was a beautiful place set along the bank of a creek. The trees were wired with lights so that the house resembled a castle at night when all the lights were turned on. His contacts with contractors, people in oil and gas production, real estate, and banking made him a highly successful fund-raiser in Oklahoma County where Republican fund-raising is generally tough. Hubert made other contributions to the campaign as well. He made office space available in a building he owned on Britton Road and allowed us use of business machines and secretarial assistance. He also made available to Shirley and me on an as-needed basis, an apartment he had built adjacent to his garage. This was an excellent arrangement because Shirley and I could come and go at our convenience, have privacy and be spared the cost of an apartment or hotel room. An accomplished cook, Hubert would frequently fix breakfast for his entire family and his guests. Hubert was also a help late in the campaign with Wayne Mackey. He spent many days escorting Wayne to the office, working with him and seeing to it that he was returned to his home. I have no idea how Hubert handled Mackey, but he did it with perfection and in so doing made a great contribution to my election.

About half a mile south and a quarter mile east of the Gragg home was the site then-Governor Howard Edmondson had selected for building his new home. As neighbors, Hubert and Howard had become relatively close friends and Hubert became a good source of information about the Edmondson family. The things he told me were not confidences, but rather information to help me know Governor Edmondson and understand him better.

One of the fund-raising events that Hubert arranged was held at a country cabin near Yukon owned by John Kirkpatrick. I had officed in the Kirkpatrick oil company building while I was Republican state chairman. About thirty of Oklahoma City's leading citizens were in attendance at the barbecue at which I stood up and made a statement and responded to questions. One contribution we received at that event was $200 from Ed Gaylord. This was the first tangible evidence of support from the publishing family who owned the state's largest newspaper as well as WKY radio and television stations.

In Oklahoma at that time, the political climate generated interesting fund-raising scenarios. An architectural and engineering firm, Hudgens, Thompson, and Ball, had been very big in Democratic politics and had received a lion's share of contracts from state institutions. The firm was resented by competing engineering and architectural firms, many of whom were helping me with the understanding that the state contracts would be more equitably shared should I become governor. About a week before the election, to our great surprise, Hudgens, Thompson and Ball mailed a check for $5,000 to Hubert Gragg for use in my campaign. Apparently, they had been backing Bill Atkinson but had become concerned that the state was about to elect its first Republican governor. To buy some insurance, they decided to give me an unsolicited contribution. Hubert brought the check to me and asked what should be done. I felt there was no way we could accept the money because an obligation was clearly implied and because other engineering firms would feel double-crossed. We returned the check. To our amazement, within a short time the firm deposited the returned check in my campaign account in the local bank. By now, it was very near election day. When Hubert told me this, I was furious. I suggested we buy a cashier's check and send the money back again. Hubert had another idea. He suggested we go ahead and make out a check, date it at the current time, and then hold it. If I won the election, we would send it back and if I lost, we would tear it up. I agreed and the matter was handled that way.

After I became a candidate and after Jordan had assumed advertising responsibility for the campaign, we had several lengthy conversations about how the campaign should be run and about how Jordan's efforts would be most effective. It was during one of these conversations that Jordan gave me some fatherly advice. He suggested I begin wearing long socks because he felt it was unsightly for a political candidate, who often sat at the head table where the tablecloths might not go to the floor, to have his pants legs hiked up so that the bare skin above his socks showed. Jordan brought along several pairs of long socks and insisted that from that point on I wear them. I took Jordan's advice but unfortunately the socks he brought were so tight over the calves of my legs that they caused a thrombosis to develop which almost took me out of the campaign. When this happened, I ceased wearing the socks and settled for mid-calf length which seemed to solve Jordan's problem without causing any physical danger to me.

When I first had begun making public appearances as Republican state chairman, I was extremely uncomfortable and uneasy on my feet. Due to my discomfort, I formed the habit of pushing my hands down into my coat pockets when I stood before crowds to speak, along with several other problems. Shirley, put out with me because of my awkwardness, took the initiative of sewing my suit coat pockets shut. She didn't tell me she'd done this. I discovered her mischief in the middle of a speech to the Bartlesville Republican Women's Club. I had just begun my talk, and I tried to put my hands in my pockets. Shirley was in the crowd and could hardly keep from laughing as I struggled to find a place for my hands and finally gave up. She made her point. I succeeded in making my speech without jamming my hands in my pockets and the crowd was able to concentrate on what I was saying without being distracted by what I was doing with my hands.

As the campaign for governor developed, I took speech lessons from Mary Gray Thompson in Oklahoma City who advised me to hold a pencil in one hand or arrange to stand behind a chair and put my hands on the chair so they would rest naturally.

My fledgling efforts as a candidate for governor were somewhat pitiful. I was not then nor have I become a gifted speaker. I did, however, learn some successful ways to deal with crowds. For instance, I had the impression that civic club audiences wanted to hear about issues, wanted information about governmental activities, or were interested in having the speaker criticize public officials for their shortcomings. My efforts to talk to groups on that basis had always failed painfully. For a civic club meeting in Stroud, I decided to take a different tack. I prepared by reading some of Will Rogers's writings. While I knew I could never be another Will Rogers, I hoped to generate support for my cause by entertaining crowds rather than trying to inform them. To my amazement the response was both friendly and supportive. From that point on when I talked to civic groups, I tried to limit the heavier part of my talk to not more than five or six minutes and spend the rest of the time on what I hoped would be entertaining comments.

Another case in point arose at a banquet in the small town of Sasakwa in Seminole County, a strong Democratic area. For years, the Sasakwa FFA had sponsored a father and son banquet. Over time, this had come to be a large event often attracting as many as seven hundred participants from nearby towns as well as statewide political candidates. An invitation to speak at the Sasakwa banquet came to be regarded as a mark of arrival for politicians. The banquet's master of ceremonies for many years was Frank Streetman, a local grocer who referred to himself as "Mayor of Sasakwa." He was gifted with a quick and cutting wit and had the ability to puncture political egos. His performance regularly outshone that of any speaker on the program. The crowd came as much to hear and see him as for any other reason. Normally those politicians invited were all Democrats. It was largely due to the intervention of my friend Archie Stout that I was invited and, as far as I know, I was the first Republican ever given the opportunity to participate in the Sasakwa dinner. I accepted with fear and trembling. I was concerned that I could not compete adequately with the accomplished Democratic politicians on the program.

When the big night arrived, practically all the politicians of statewide notoriety were on hand. Several Democratic candidates for governor were present as were members of Congress, members of the state legislature, and even U. S. Senator Mike Monroney, who was principal speaker. As time drew near for my introduction, I became almost panic-stricken until I hit upon the notion of bragging on the crowd. I began my four-minute talk by recalling for the FFA members present the experience I had in the U. S. Marines when we chose members of our tank company by selecting former members of the FFA. I told what fine fighters and brave Marines they became. Since I was limited to four minutes, I spent practically the entire time telling them how great country people were. I was interrupted many times by applause, to the point that I finally asked them to please hold the applause so I could finish my remarks before my time was up. When I finished, I received a standing ovation. Then, the main speaker, U.S. Senator Mike Monroney, paid me the ultimate compliment by referring time after time to things I had said and agreeing with my comments, which had nothing to do with issues but everything to do with politics. It was that evening I decided I could make the grade as a political candidate in competition with others. Also, I came to the conclusion that Senator Mike Monroney was not ten feet tall and that I could compete with him on the stump, if the need ever arose.

Organizing a statewide campaign for Governor is a major undertaking and a good preparation for putting together an administration in the event of success on election day. Steve Shadegg had recommended I make a list of individuals I had known in various activities in all parts of the state including my relatives and Shirley's, the party leaders with whom I'd been working as state chairman, friends from the Marine Corps, and acquaintances of any kind — everybody I'd known at Oklahoma State University, in Farm Bureau, in business, and in church work. Once this was done we had a contact in every sizable town in the state from which to start building our organization. Using this list of personal acquaintances as hosts, we organized a series of two-party tea parties. Shirley and I made a swing across the state and attended tea parties in the home of an acquaintance in every sizable town in each county. The invitations to these meetings were sent by my hosts, who invited their friends and associates. Had the invitations come from the candidate, it's likely the events would have been ignored wholesale. But by using my friends who invited their friends, good attendance generally was achieved.

A regular system was developed for the conduct of these meetings. Traveling with a "break-away man," we would deliberately arrive at the place of the meeting, usually a private residence, a few minutes after the appointed time. I found if I arrived early and started shaking hands while people were still arriving, I was apt to introduce myself more than once to the same individual. This clearly was not good politics, so we began arriving after the crowd had assembled. I could start around the room and meet people in the order they were seated or standing. There is a right and wrong way for a political candidate to meet people. I found for me that the best system is to step in front of the person, shake hands, state my name, "I'm Henry Bellmon. I'm running for governor. What's your name?" and wait, looking the person right in the eye until he or she answers. Then I say, "I need your help" and continue looking at the person until some response is given. When I acknowledge the response, I then move on to the next person. In that brief encounter a good chemistry starts to develop if the person is at all inclined to be friendly.

After walking completely around the room and greeting any new-comers who might have arrived, I would get the attention of the group and start talking. I learned to stand behind a chair so I would have some place for my hands. The content of the talk was not issues or criticism of opponents but rather personal information about my family, about my business experiences, about the kinds of community leadership projects I had been involved with, and general information that helped people feel they knew me better. After fifteen minutes of talking, I would open the meeting for questions. When I'd had a chance to answer questions for about thirty minutes, and before the crowd's interest began to wane, our break-away man was instructed to stand up and say to the group, "Ladies and gentlemen, Henry's obviously having a great time and he'd rather be here than any place else, but we have a schedule to keep and we have another group waiting." This gave me the excuse to say my goodbyes and take my leave before the meeting lost its edge.

After travelling around the state the first time with one meeting in each town, we had time to go back to the more populous swing counties for a second round of tea parties. The hosts or hostesses were selected from swing precincts of larger swing counties since we knew this was where the candidate's impact would be greatest. We tried to avoid spending all our time with the country club set since a majority of those folks were probably going to vote Republican anyway. We tried to go into the middle-income areas where previous history had shown elections could swing either way. During the months of March through early June, we attended hundreds of tea parties in every county of the state. On a typical busy day, Shirley, the break-away man, and I would arrive in a town in time for a seven o'clock breakfast with members of the business community. This meeting would include a short speech and question-and-answer period.

On one such occasion, Bob Breeden, a newspaper owner and state senator from Pawnee County, arranged a breakfast in Ralston. The girls, Shirley, and I had spent the night before in Billings. The breakfast was at 7:30 and Ralston is more than an hour's drive from Billings. Bob met us and was very sad to say that practically no one had shown up. Besides

Bob there was the county chairman and vice chairman and two constituents. Other than that, the room was empty. It was a disappointing but not unusual experience. Bob and I were sitting at a table near a window eating our food when Bob looked up the street and saw a man approaching. He told me that the man was the county's most notorious Democrat and he was undoubtedly coming to the meeting to needle me. Knowing what to expect, I got up from the table, went to the front door of the restaurant, shook hands with the man, and welcomed him to breakfast. He immediately launched into a tirade against Republicans. He made a great point about President Hoover and how hard times had been during the "Hoover Depression." He told of the trouble he had paying his taxes, the rent, buying groceries, keeping his car repaired; about how he had lost money in his business. He wound up saying, "I will never forget the holes I had in my clothes during the Depression under that last Republican, President Hoover."

I'd tried to keep my cool, but this was the last straw. "I'll tell you what," I said to the man, "if you'll come back to the men's room, I'll take off my shirt and show you the holes I got in my hide during World War II under Democratic President Roosevelt." Bob Breeden roared with laughter; the man turned around and left. Bob said it was the first time he'd ever seen anyone get the best of this fellow in a political argument. The event assured me that I could compete in hand-to-hand political combat.

After an early-morning breakfast, we would make calls on the local newspaper, leaving a press kit with family photographs. If possible, we would visit a radio station hoping to be allowed on the air for an interview. The tea parties started at 9:30 or 10, so there was time for two before lunch. At lunchtime I usually managed to get an invitation to a civic club luncheon. That seemed the best use of the noontime hour, even though most business people then were not interested in being identified with a Republican gubernatorial candidate because they felt it was bad for business. After the civic club luncheon, tea parties were scheduled to begin at two, three, and four o'clock. During the dinner hour we usually tried to meet with local Republican organization officials and give them a report on how the campaign was going. By seven we were back to the tea party schedule, this time with couples, since men were home for the evening. We usually managed two tea parties in the evening before collapsing into bed or driving to the next town to be ready for breakfast next morning.

It was an arduous schedule and sometimes I struggled to keep from reacting to questions in a mechanical manner. After four days on the road, we would return to the state headquarters in Oklahoma City to catch up on mail, attend to fund raising and deal with whatever organizational problems had come up. Shirley and I usually tried to be at the farm on weekends, or at least on Sundays.

Prior to the beginning of the tea parties, we held a series of meetings with a hand-picked group of knowledgeable, strong, loyal Bellmon supporters. At these meetings we insisted that participants ask all the mean, impossible questions they could contrive. A tape recording was made of the sessions. I went over the transcript carefully to be sure what was said was defensible, accurate, understandable, and as inoffensive as possible. A second meeting was scheduled and we went through the same routine. By the time we'd done this a third time there was literally no question that anyone could think of that I hadn't already confronted and learned how to deal with in a satisfactory manner. This made it possible for me to go to tea parties and face groups without much concern about surprises. As time went on and the tea parties continued, I became thoroughly adept at dealing with the usual questions and even local issues that I had not known about beforehand.

At each tea party, Shirley would follow me around the room with a sheet of paper on which the guests were urged to write their names, telephone numbers, and addresses. This information was sent to our state campaign headquarters where Jeannette Baxter and her crew wrote and promptly mailed personal letters to each individual. The letter said in effect, "It was a great pleasure to meet you at Mrs. Brown's home in Hugo. I enjoyed our conversation and look forward to seeing you again when I'm back in your area." We would add some tidbit about how the campaign was going and say that we would keep in touch. These names were added to a master mailing list and from that point forward we sent out a Bellmon campaign letter at least once a month to those who had attended the tea parties. From these lists many valuable contacts were made. We built a statewide fund-raising organization, selected people for county campaign coordinators, identified future appointees, and, most importantly, located women who could be recruited for the Bellmon

Belles. Of all the campaign activities that went on in that 1962 campaign, I've long contended that the activities of the Bellmon Belles were the most effective.

During the tea-party phase of the campaign, I discovered there were many women willing to involve themselves in a cause in which they believed. Many of these were elderly ladies, although a great number were young women with families. Shirley designed an inexpensive red, white, and blue outfit which could be manufactured and sold, along with a hat and a large Bellmon Belle button, for five dollars. This made it possible for women of virtually any income level to be members of the Bellmon Belle organization. There were probably one thousand Bellmon Belles in 1962. The Belles became highly active in the campaign. They worked in headquarters, campaigned through neighborhoods, created and staffed parade floats, made telephone calls, talked to their neighbors, and contributed an enormous amount of "people-power" to get out the vote on election day. Even now, over twenty-five years later, many women come up to me in crowds and proudly announce they were one of the original Bellmon Belles and that they still have their costumes hanging in their closets. I believe they're as proud of their contributions as I am grateful.

Once school was out and our girls were home for the summer, we changed the format from two-party tea parties to unannounced visits to the smaller communities in all parts of the state. We'd found by then that if I announced in advance I was coming to a community for a visit, the local Republican leaders would take me under control and insist that I call on all the loyal Republicans in the area. This was almost entirely a waste of time since those Republicans were likely to be for me anyway. In addition, particularly in the southern counties, many Republican leaders made a game of insulting Democrats. I'd long-since learned this was no way to make friends and win votes. Therefore, we developed a campaign schedule that would take us from small town to small town, unannounced, for three or four days a week, giving me a chance to meet as many voters as possible in towns where we had generally not scheduled meetings earlier.

The format for these visits was roughly this: Shirley and the girls would let me out of the station wagon at the newspaper office, if there was one. I would deliver a press kit to the publisher and answer his questions. I would then start down the main street, going into each business, introducing myself and shaking hands with as many people as I could. Meanwhile, Shirley and the girls campaigned down both sides of the streets in residential areas. When we'd covered the town, we met up on the main street and moved on to the next location.

During this process, I learned several valuable lessons about campaigning in small towns. One was that if you intend to campaign in a beer hall or pool hall, it's better to start at the back of the room and move rapidly toward the front. If you start at the front and move to the back and then try to leave, you find yourself mired in many time-consuming arguments that produce much heat and no light. But by starting at the back of the room and moving rapidly toward the front door, the candidate can stay ahead of the "recognition wave." It usually takes a little time for the realization of who the candidate is to soak in and by that time you're out the front door and down the street. Also, it is a mistake to stay too long in the same town because if you do, you'll soon be meeting the person you met in the drugstore a second time in the grocery store and introducing yourself all over again. This makes for a certain amount of ridicule or, at least, disappointment and dislike for a candidate who can't remember meeting a voter for fifteen minutes.

It never pays to argue with contentious voters. If someone wants an argument, the best thing to do is walk on, because there's slim chance of changing the contentious voter's mind. When I ran for governor, Hayden Crawford, a former U.S. attorney who had made a respectable showing in his attempt to unseat U.S. Senator Bob Kerr in 1960, was running against Senator Mike Monroney. Our campaign styles were entirely different. Crawford was an eloquent, intense, opinionated candidate. I struck a much lower key. One day when we were campaigning together in Shawnee, Crawford and I started hand-shaking from the same point at the same time. My system was to meet people, shake hands, ask their names, ask for their votes, and move on. If someone wished to argue, I broke it off and went on, trying to meet as many voters as possible. If anyone raised an issue with Crawford, he was more than willing to debate. On this day, after perhaps half an hour, I realized he was nowhere near me. I looked around and discovered he was still standing on the street corner some two blocks back, arguing with a citizen. He may have persuaded that one person to come to his point of view, but in the meantime, he had missed the opportunity to meet several dozen others who might have voted for him had they had the chance to see him face-to-face.

By this time, Koalani Han, a young girl Gail's age from Maui, Hawaii, had joined our campaign organization. She had become friendly with our girls during the time we spent there in 1959 and came to Oklahoma because she was interested in seeing how a political campaign was run. She was attractive, accomplished at hula dancing, and added a lot to the interest of the campaign organization.

While I was making my way down the small town main street, Shirley would take the station wagon into a residential neighborhood and park at the end of a street. The girls would get out of the car and go in pairs down each side of the street, knocking on doors as they went from house to house. When someone came to the door, one girl would hand them a campaign brochure, saying, "Please vote for my daddy." The other would say, "He's a good man." As soon as possible, they would move on to the next house. The family phase of the campaign went on all summer. We travelled as a group to all parts of the state and as nearly as I could tell, made a good impression wherever we went. It was an inexpensive way to campaign and probably the best use we could have made of the time since there was no interest in large meetings during the heat of the summer and during the time when children were home and needed the attention of their parents.

During the campaign, Shirley again dressed the girls identically — always in red, white, and blue. The travelling for her was challenging because she not only had to follow a difficult schedule, but also had to keep all three of the girls laundered, ironed, combed, clean, and happy. Though they got physically tired, the girls never rebelled nor seemed to tire of campaigning. Not old enough to vote themselves, they were often called upon to explain to adults in one-party, Democratic, "Little Dixie" Oklahoma that the primary and runoff were over, but the general election was still ahead.

When I determined to run for governor, I discussed with my aunt Beth Zimmerman, who lived in Billings, the possibility of opening a hometown headquarters. She agreed to make arrangements and run the operation. Because of her interest in my political fortunes and the excellent standing as well as broad acquaintance she had with Billings people, we got an enormous amount of work done through this small and inexpensive operation. The headquarters was established in an empty bank building, and much of our direct mail was prepared by volunteers and mailed through the Billings post office. Toward the end of the campaign when wheat had been planted and farmers were not especially busy, there were several caravans of campaigners who left Billings and went in different directions across the state putting up fence straddlers and distributing literature. These were all volunteers who used their own vehicles and paid their own expenses.

We held the official kickoff in September in Billings. As principal speaker, we invited Governor Tim Babcock of Montana, whose hometown was Billings, Montana. The event was singularly successful. Probably three thousand people from across the state showed up, making one of the biggest crowds Billings had ever seen. It was held on the school grounds with folding chairs for the crowd, a truck bed for speakers, live country music, and barbecue. The campaign song, to the tune of "Yessir, That's My Baby," was introduced at the kickoff. Recorded by professional singers, it used the line "Get the facts: no new tax." At subsequent rallies, bands played the song over and over again and Wayne Mackey insisted I hit the "No New Tax" theme every speech I made.

The "No New Tax" slogan was carried through in all billboards, brochures, newspaper advertising, and everything else that was used in the Elect Bellmon effort, including a series of ads especially drawn up for each county in the state. These ads showed precisely how much more tax the citizens of each county would be forced to pay in the event my opponent Bill Atkinson was elected and the sales tax was increased, as he proposed. It was a deadly attack. Soon, my opponent began to feel the heat and steered away from his new tax platform by accusing me of having a secret plan to raise taxes. At one point, it appeared that even Atkinson had lost his taste for the new tax issue and began to show signs that he was going to drop it. In discussing the matter with Wayne Mackey, it was decided I should make a public statement projecting that Atkinson would change his position on the tax increase proposal. This was done and immediately it put Atkinson in the position of having to reaffirm his support for a tax increase, thus locking him in that position.

Early in the campaign, Doc had insisted we buy a full showing of billboards for the state. This required the outlay of something in excess of $40,000—money we did not have at that time. Ben Whitehill became convinced the billboard program was necessary and put up the money. He agreed he would not ask to get his money back until later in the campaign when funds usually come in generously but so late it is difficult to use them wisely. I vigorously opposed the billboard program because I thought it would be money wasted. I lost the argument and the billboard contract was signed. Then a great controversy developed over what should go on the billboards — particularly, which photograph. This decision had to be made well in advance of the posting date. Doc and Shirley became distraught as I turned down one photograph after another. Finally, more or less in desperation, Jordan met me at the Norman airport with a half dozen pictures and insisted I choose one. I did and then was thoroughly ridiculed because it was one of those I had turned down earlier. When the billboards were posted early in September, we felt a distinct lift in the campaign. It was as if the billboards proved I was a serious contender. Doc was right. Billboards did help.

Soon after, I was on the program for the Association of University Women in Ponca City. I shared the platform with my opponent Bill Atkinson, who had been refusing to make joint appearances with me for several weeks. But that evening he kept the commitment. Atkinson's billboards also had been erected recently. He had used a full color photograph that made him look years younger than he was. I began my remarks by reminding Bill that I had not seen him for some time and that he was looking well. I said, "Bill, you look almost as good as your billboard and those billboards look to me like a million dollars." Bill was extremely sensitive about being categorized as a millionaire and the jab seemed to cut. He was thoroughly thrown off base for the rest of the evening and that was the last joint appearance he accepted.

There had been earlier joint appearances which gave me a considerable amount of personal pleasure. I had no real dislike for Bill, but it was a great pleasure to try to get under his skin. The first time this happened was inadvertent. The event was a joint appearance between Raymond Gary, Bill Atkinson, and myself on Channel Eight television in Tulsa. We were to be asked questions by four reporters from the Tulsa area during a half-hour program. I was seated between Raymond and Bill, who had been at each other's throats and who seemed determined to destroy one another in their efforts to win the runoff.

During the questioning, Phil Dessauer, a respected political writer for the *Tulsa World* which was supporting Bill Atkinson, asked a question something like, "Bill, you are making a major plank of your campaign platform the proposal to add an additional one-cent sales tax." Phil went on to say that "our present governor, Howard Edmondson, has made the same proposal to the state legislature and they have refused to go along and raise the tax the way he wants. My question is, how will you pay the costs of running state government if the legislature treats you the same way they have treated Governor Edmondson and refuses to go along with your proposal to increase the sales tax?"

Bill took a long moment, appeared to be in deep thought and then profoundly said words to this effect, "Well, if the legislature refuses to go along and raise the sales tax the way I propose, then we'll get busy and eliminate the *waste, graft, and corruption* in government and we'll run the state on the money we have." I couldn't believe my ears. The statement was reported widely. I quoted this Atkinson *faux pas* frequently, especially to his face during joint campaign appearances. I would say "Bill wants to raise your taxes so he can pay for waste, graft, and corruption." It always had the effect of totally devastating Bill and kept him on the defensive every time we met.

On another occasion, Bill Atkinson and I were invited along with many other candidates to share the platform at the Tulsa fairgrounds on a "Good Roads and Streets" meeting. The evening was extremely hot, the humidity was high, the meeting was long and proved to be distressingly uncomfortable. All candidates were seated on the platform under bright lights and as the evening went on the situation became intolerable. Finally, I noticed that in front of the podium was a tray filled with glasses of ice water. I became so thirsty I could hardly stand it and finally, during a break in the program, I went forward to get a glass of water. As I approached the tray, the idea struck that it was going to seem extremely awkward if I stood there and drank a glass of water when obviously everyone else on the stage was as thirsty as I was. Therefore, I picked up the tray and went from one candidate to another serving them a drink of water. The television cameras picked up the scene; flash bulbs popped. Reporters interviewed me later and I told them I had worked my way through college serving tables and it seemed like the natural thing to do.

My act of humanitarianism became the subject of newspaper stories about the meeting.

The next morning, Bill and I were scheduled to make a joint appearance before the Associated Press editors at Lake Murray Lodge near Ardmore. I spent the night in Tulsa and flew to Ardmore the next morning in a small airplane. As frequently happened, we arrived a few minutes late. Bill was sitting smugly with the host editor at the head table. He was very pleased with himself that he had beaten me there and chided me for being late. Bill was introduced first and proceeded to give me a considerable lashing. When it was my turn, I said as many kind things about Bill as I felt I could and then told the crowd that Bill and I had appeared in Tulsa the night before. I apologized for being late and pointed out that Bill had beaten me to the lodge. I then said that the only reason Bill got there ahead of me was that he travelled in a Cadillac and I drove a Chevrolet. This absolutely infuriated him and he insisted on taking the microphone away from me and explaining he had not come down in a Cadillac. The incident showed how sensitive Bill was about his wealth and how unable he was to take any kind of kidding. The crowd enjoyed the combat.

During the Democratic primary, it was generally expected that former Governor Raymond Gary would be renominated. Many of my supporters and friends who had thoroughly disliked Gary, pressed me to jump into the Democratic fray and criticize the former governor. This seemed to me a serious mistake because, first of all, the field was large so no one could be sure who would win. Secondly, it seemed to make no sense to get into somebody else's political battle. Throughout the Democratic primary and the runoff, I refused to say one word that could be taken as criticism of any Democratic candidate. My motive was purely selfish. I hoped that some of those who lost might find it possible to join and help me in the general election. It was later a great frustration to Bill Atkinson when he tried to drive a wedge between Raymond Gary and me and could not find a single place where I had said something critical of Raymond Gary. This helped me a great deal to get on good terms with Raymond and to get general election support from his supporters, who helped a great deal in the southern, heavily Democratic counties.

After the run-off, in which Atkinson defeated Gary by 449 votes, the Bellmon For Governor headquarters was besieged by ex-Gary supporters furious at Atkinson and concerned they be in favor with the new administration. Even though they were all Democrats, they were willing to support a Republican to get even with Atkinson and to try and preserve whatever favor they might have expected from another Gary administration. There were many who came to see me that day. Practically all told me that Raymond Gary had promised certain jobs or personal favors and that if I agreed to these conditions, they would do all they could to help me beat Atkinson. Whether or not Gary knew of all the "promises" he was supposed to have made, I will never know. As the day wore on and I listened to more and more of the deals being offered, the picture began to grow increasingly clear. If I were to agree to these illegal propositions, even if I won the election, Raymond Gary and not Henry Bellmon would be in power in the state because his friends would be running the agencies. If I was going to knock myself out to win the race, the last thing I wanted to do was have so many obligations I could not be governor in fact as well as in name.

I responded to all who came that I would appreciate their support but I was not making deals with anyone. When that word became generally known, we heard little more from the Gary troops. However, there were two or three who came to help us with no strings attached. Among these was Merlin Cooper. Merlin was an old-time political pro. He knew where a lot of bodies in the Democratic party were buried and had a good line of communication with the Gary organization, especially in the southern counties. Merlin had what I took to be a high level of political savvy. As the campaign went on, Merlin emerged as my "break away" man. This is one of the most important jobs in a campaign. It requires someone who can understand when enough and not too much has been said, then make the break-away statement in a plausible and forceful way giving the impression that the candidate would much rather stay where he is and that he is being dragged kicking and screaming away from his friends. Cooper, a large, almost burly man, was a master at the job. He never hesitated to charge into any situation and did a great job of keeping me on schedule. People tended to get sore at him but never at the candidate.

When Atkinson won the nomination, I felt it was absolutely essential for me to go immediately into the southern counties and appeal to Gary supporters. I had scheduled a four-day series of meetings in Tulsa but I called the county chairmen there and cancelled the meetings. The Tulsans were furious and more or less opted out of the campaign as a result, a serious loss. However, it seemed to me that I had to go into the southern counties at a time when there was such intense feeling among the Gary supporters to let them know I was interested in their friendship and support.

One of the first towns we stopped in on our swing through Little Dixie after the runoff was Purcell in McClain County. I looked upon it as completely hostile territory. We drove cautiously up the main street and parked the car in front of a bank. I intended to go into the bank and down to the newspaper office run by former speaker of the House and Democratic wheelhorse Jim Nance, while Shirley and the girls did their campaigning in the residential areas. The minute I stepped onto the street, before Shirley could drive away, someone recognized me and a friendly group began to gather. Soon someone was leading me literally by the hand into the bank to meet with some of the city fathers. Shirley and the girls stayed with me and we received an amazingly warm reception. After shaking hands up and down main street and through the banks, one of the bankers took me into the back room and told me he felt there was a good chance I could carry McClain County. He told me how to go about it and suggested he immediately arrange a session with the terribly bitter Gary forces. They seemed to feel Gary had been "done wrong" and wanted revenge.

The banker arranged a meeting with A.B. Green, a petroleum products wholesaler appointed by Governor Gary to the highway commission. By the time I reached his office, several people, including the local state representative, a Democrat, were already gathered. We had what amounted to a pep rally in which these men all swore they wanted to help me and keep Atkinson from becoming governor. As the meeting was about to break up, A.B. Green reached in his pocket and took out ten $100 bills, which he handed me. He told me there would be more where those came from. It was the first sizable campaign contribution I had received under that kind of circumstance. Obviously, the Gary people were serious and the opportunity for getting support for a Republican candidate from among the Democratic voters in the southern counties was far more real than had ever been the case in past elections.

Another of the Gary people, a Democratic county chairman, made an interesting contribution. He made a recording in his strong southern accent saying in effect: "I'm a Democratic county chairman. I'm here today campaigning for my good friend Bill Atkinson. You know, those Republicans have nominated a dumb farmer to be governor. You folks know we can't allow any farmer to get in the governor's office." Most of the prospective listeners were farmers or rural people. "I want to tell you a few things Bill will do for you when he becomes the next governor of Oklahoma. Take these dinky little schools scattered all over the county. First thing Bill will do is close them all down and we'll just have one big school for the whole county." Closing rural schools was a hot issue and political poison in southern Oklahoma. "Of course this means your kids will have to ride a school bus for an hour, morning and evening, but this won't matter because you've got good roads here." This was sure to anger the crowds since most of the roads were poor and people were furious that they'd not been given the attention they truly felt they deserved. "Then there's this matter of the sales tax. Now there are some who don't like the idea of a fifty percent increase in your sales tax. But this won't hurt you much and it won't hurt either that the tax is not going to the old folks." Since many of the southern counties had high welfare caseloads supported by the present two percent sales tax, this was also a sensitive point.

The chairman, on his own, hired several sound trucks and sent them from town to town on weekends when rural people came to trade and talk. After the sound track had played the recording it would drive to the next town, play music to attract a crowd, and then play the record. There's no telling how much damage this performance did to the Atkinson campaign or how much it helped my race. It would have to fall in the "dirty tricks" category, but in the political climate which existed following the Gary-Atkinson race, the chairman no doubt felt it was clearly in order. I was unaware of this activity until well after the campaign, though I seriously doubt I would have intervened had I been given the opportunity.

Following the campaign kickoff, we planned a rally at least once a week — sometimes twice a week. The idea was that we would attempt to show we could draw crowds in all parts of the state and keep the initiative. Bill Atkinson was being supported by incumbent Governor Howard Edmondson; therefore, our campaign could be run against the

Edmondson record as well as the Atkinson plan to raise the sales tax. We started each rally with a barbecue and band music and wound up with political speeches from various candidates running on the Republican ticket. The evening would end with my remarks. Experience showed that normally only people already solidly committed to the candidate attended rallies. A few political enemies attended to report or harass. So before each rally, letters went to all those we had met at tea parties and every person who had any connection with the campaign. We generated good crowds on most occasions and gave the impression that Bellmon had a large following in all parts of the state.

The nearest disaster in the campaign happened at a rally when President Eisenhower visited the state — theoretically, in my behalf. I was particularly insistent that he do this because I felt nothing could help my campaign more. I was a relatively unheard-of country boy with little or no experience in government, running against a five-to-one Democratic registration in a state that had never elected a Republican governor. Ike was the most popular man in the country. For him to visit and say a good word would mean a great deal. President Eisenhower agreed to come, probably through the urging of Bryce Harlow, who was his close adviser and my good friend. His appearance took place at the Oklahoma City airport in October. U.S. Senate candidate Hayden Crawford and I were on the platform when the former president's plane landed. President Eisenhower was in good form and pleased the crowd, but he completely forgot to mention either Hayden Crawford or me until he had finished his speech and sat down. Then, he suddenly realized his omission and stood up to tell the crowd why he had really come. I never knew whether his manner of handling our endorsement was effective or whether it really had any effect at all. Over the years I have come to doubt the ability of one political figure to transfer support to another, but at least President Eisenhower tried and I was grateful.

We made several swings into the southern counties. When I first began campaigning in Little Dixie, the solidly Democratic southern region of Oklahoma near the Red River, a lot of Republicans felt it was a total waste of time. My feeling is that candidates willing to write off a sizable section of the electorate are giving their opponent an advantage which often leads to defeat. The support I was getting from the Gary forces caused me to feel good about the prospects for a sizable vote out of the southern counties and I did everything I knew to enhance my chances there. I felt this was an area of great opportunity because every vote I got there was likely to count twice. It would be one I got and one Bill Atkinson lost.

During one of these sojourns into the southern counties, WKY-TV sent a reporter who filmed and tape recorded me on the streets as I campaigned person-to-person. The same reporter later went into the south with Bill Atkinson and did the same with him. The station ran the two reports back to back in a program aired shortly before election day. It was called "Duel in Little Dixie." My campaign staff and I went to the Baxter home to watch the program. The photographer had attached a microphone to my shirt and followed with the camera, taking close-ups of various people I met in Valiant, Broken Bow, Poteau, and Wilburton. I was surprised at the way I lapsed into the local vernacular. I was wearing a western hat, an open shirt, and trying hard to be as country as I could. This came fairly naturally, but the southern accent I seemed to have picked up surprised me. I'm sure this way of speaking was acceptable to southern Oklahomans, but it sounded corny when played over Oklahoma City and Tulsa television.

By contrast, Bill Atkinson was very much a big shot in his appearances. He travelled in a big car, frequently with police escort. He seemed to be condescending and showed little rapport with the people he met. He handed out a cartoon he had drawn of me as a puppet sitting on publisher E.K. Gaylord's lap with Mr. Gaylord manipulating me from behind. To Bill Atkinson, who had a hatred of the Gaylords, this had a great deal of meaning, but I doubt many of the southerners knew or cared who Mr. Gaylord was. I was surprised and, frankly, pleased at the miserable impression Bill was making. But I was not pleased with the look of my own campaign on the statewide television hook-up. I was concerned that in Tulsa, Oklahoma City, and Republican areas of the state I looked too much like a hick. Practically everyone else in the room who saw "Duel in Little Dixie" was elated and felt the television show was a real break.

After reflecting on the matter, I came to the conclusion that a Republican candidate in Oklahoma was helped by a rural image. Both our large cities and many smaller ones tend to be Republican, but it is not enough just to carry the cities. A great proportion of the vote is rural and small town. Unless these voters feel some identity with the candidate, they are unlikely to break from their traditional Democratic voting pattern. Bill Atkinson, by coming off as a rich city slicker, failed to appeal to either Republican city voters or Democratic rural voters. I felt better about my chances of success. When the votes were counted election night, I won by 77,000 votes. We carried Raymond Gary's home county, Marshall County, by sixty-one percent of the vote. I also ran better than a Republican gubernatorial candidate ever had in other "Little Dixie" counties.

One of the brightest spots in the campaign was the O.S.U. homecoming parade. Marilyn Heath, head of the Payne County Bellmon Belles, had the responsibility of organizing my activities in Stillwater on homecoming day. The most important feature for me was the Bellmon Belle float. It had been built and decorated by the Belles who had dressed in their red, white, and blue striped uniforms to ride on the float. There wasn't room for all to ride, so many walked along each side. As we came to the entry point into the parade route, we passed the convertible where Bill Atkinson was waiting to take his place. I stopped to shake hands and exchange a few pleasantries with him as I always tried to do. As we were shaking hands, Bill looked at the float and all the women who were with me and in a rather good-natured way said, "This proves you're outspending me in the campaign. I can't afford to hire that many campaign workers." Of course every single one of the Bellmon Belles were volunteers. In fact, each had paid five dollars for her outfit. If Bill was having to pay whatever workers he got, there was not as much enthusiasm for his election effort as there was for mine. Nothing that happened in the whole campaign gave me a greater boost in morale.

It was impossible to get crowds to come to campaign rallies in the southern counties. Even those citizens who planned to vote Republican, did not want it known. To reach voters, we planned bus tours for Fridays and Saturdays. Campaign workers would arrange to park a flat-bed truck on the main street in a strategic place. We hired country-western singer Merle Lindsay and a small band for $1,000 a day. Travelling in a bus, they would drive into town, unpack their musical instruments and sound equipment, climb onto the truck, and as quickly as they could get their sound system operational, strike up the music.

Shirley and I would arrive in town a few minutes after Merle and the boys had started playing. As quietly as possible, I moved through the crowd, shaking hands and introducing myself, and passing out campaign literature. Shirley did the same. After Merle had played a few minutes and given the crowd a chance to assemble, he introduced me without too much extravagance and gave me a chance to make my remarks. While I was talking, Merle and his musicians would disassemble their equipment, pack it into the bus, and move on to the next town. The speeches I made were intended more as an introduction to the crowd to lessen misgivings about Republicans than to try to sell any particular political philosophy or my position on issues. The one issue I did use was the "No New Tax" theme, a real crowd-pleaser. It was totally compatible with my personal viewpoint since I felt we could save money by eliminating the "waste, graft, and corruption" built up during 50 years of one-party rule. I could use the theme in good conscience.

In every town I concluded my remarks by telling a story about a farmer who had a cow he wanted to sell. He ran an ad in the newspaper and advertised the cow for sale, whereupon several potential buyers came to look her over. One of the buyers began asking the farmer a lot of questions. He asked how much milk the cow would give. He asked about the percentage of butter fat in the milk. He also asked questions about the length of the cow's lactations and about her pedigree. Finally, the farmer became upset with the whole business, looked at the buyer, and said, "Now mister, she doesn't have a pedigree and I can't answer all these questions. I don't keep a careful record on this cow. She's just a cow my wife and I and our family have kept to produce the milk and butter we need. But I'll tell you one thing. She's a good, honest, hard-working cow and she'll give you all the milk she's got." I went on to say that I would make the state a good, honest, hard-working governor and would give the job everything I had. I believe this story helped make the point as well as anything I could have done. (The reporters who frequently travelled with the campaign became so sick of this story they would put their fingers in their ears when I started to tell it.)

When we were lucky, we arrived in a town when there was a celebration. Also on occasion we would make our stop at the community livestock sale barn where a large number of livestock producers normally came for the weekly auction. On most occasions we drew at least fifty people and sometimes the crowds were larger. This was fairly substantial considering the fact that the towns were small, that politics, particularly

Republican politics, was not the most popular endeavor, and considering I was a newcomer and not exactly a spellbinder. The use of Merle Lindsay and his band, and the device of going into town and talking to the crowds already on the street, proved to be good campaign techniques. The last several weekends of the campaign were spent this way. As a candidate for governor I was willing to go into all parts of the state to meet anyone who was interested and to make myself available for whatever comments or questions were raised. These appearances helped me get elected.

In preparation for the last week of the campaign, we put together a campaign reserve fund of $100,000, money raised through $2,000 notes signed by fifty of our major campaign contributors. The plan was that if my opponent came out with a last-minute charge which we needed to answer, this money would be used to buy ads and set the record straight. The understanding with our supporters was that we would only use the money if an emergency arose. Also, it was agreed that if the money was used and I lost, the notes would be paid by the signers. If we used the money and won, we would hold a fund-raiser and pay back the $100,000.

As feared, on the Thursday before the election (the last day to get ads in the weeklies and some county daily newspapers), my opponent came out with large ads accusing me of having a secret plan to raise the property tax. The whole thing was ridiculous since the state of Oklahoma collects no property tax. State government had no property tax of any kind in force since Bill Murray had caused the repeal of these taxes back in the Depression when people were losing their homes and farms to the tax collector. The only property taxes in Oklahoma are voted locally by the citizens and are used to support schools and local units of government. The charge was made by someone who claimed to have been present at a secret meeting where I supposedly had revealed the plan. Nevertheless, it seemed to our campaign strategists that we needed to counter the charges.

A plane was sent to pick me up late at night in Altus where I had been campaigning. It took me to Oklahoma City and when I arrived at the television studio at two in the morning Doc Jordan and Wayne Mackey were waiting. We put together television spots that were to be run during the weekend. I made the statement that I was positively opposed to any tax increase of any kind and that as governor, I would veto any tax which the legislature might pass. This proved to be a serious overreaction to the charges and my commitment was one which plagued me all the years I served as governor. Despite my discomfort, however, the state certainly was not hurt by this position. Being locked in against a tax increase made it easier to resist the pressures from special interest groups to increase spending.

On election night, the returns from Midwest City, Bill Atkinson's home town, were slow in being reported. There were some 30,000 votes involved and Wayne Mackey absolutely refused to allow me to claim victory until those returns were received. His concern was that Bill Atkinson had such control in that city and over the political structure there that those boxes were likely to be stuffed with Atkinson ballots and that our early lead would be wiped out. He was not even willing for me to declare that we had won when our margin was greater than the total number of votes expected from Atkinson's hometown. He seemed concerned that Oklahoma's fragile election laws might allow a repeat of the Duvall County vote count scandal in Texas. The result was that it wasn't until 11 p.m. that I claimed victory and started the promised round of visits to television and radio stations in Oklahoma City, then made the two-hour drive to Tulsa where I had agreed to the same procedure. In the final count, we beat Bill Atkinson 392,316 votes to 315,357 votes.

It was six the morning after the election when Shirley and I entered the old Biltmore Hotel where we had a suite. We had been up all day and all night. I was met in the lobby by our Democrat county chairman friend who said he wanted to talk to me right then. He took one of our suitcases from me and we got in the elevator together and went to our suite. Since she was exhausted, Shirley immediately went into the bedroom and went to bed.

Before our conversation began, the chairman had me kneel beside the couch in the living room of the suite where he delivered an eloquent Southern Baptist prayer. I was having a terrible time keeping my eyes open while he explained to me that in each of the previous Democratic administrations, the governor had appointed an "insurance adviser." The idea was that the state of Oklahoma bought large insurance policies for its various operations such as the Turnpike Authority, the Grand River Dam Authority, the university dormitories, and other facilities upon which the state owed money. The job of the insurance adviser was to parcel out insurance business to various friends of the governor. The practice in the industry, he explained, was that each insurance agent charged the same price for the insurance coverage. Therefore, it made no difference so far as the state's monetary interests were concerned which agent got the business. Each agent charged twenty-five percent commission for his service. The county chairman's proposal was that he be selected as my insurance adviser. As insurance adviser, he would require each agent to kick back ten percent of the cost of the insurance and he would keep five percent. The other five percent would be put in a special account which he would open for me at a bank in Dallas. It would be a nice nest egg for me when my term of office was over.

It was 6 a.m. I had just been prayed over by a good friend and a Southern Baptist and my head was not working well. At any rate, while I did not agree, I did not immediately and out-of-hand decline the proposition. The chairman left and I heard nothing more over the busy weeks ahead. In fact, I forgot the conversation by the time I went through all the preliminaries leading to the inauguration. To my suprise, on the day following the inauguration, the chairman moved into the "vault" across from the governor's office and established himself as the governor's insurance adviser. When Drew Mason heard what was going on, he came to ask me whether or not I had authorized the chairman to undertake this activity. At the time, I vaguely recalled the early-morning conversation and it took a little while for it all to be explained to me.

After discussion with Drew, we decided to handle purchase of the state's insurance policies by competitive bids through central purchasing. The adviser's operation never got off the ground. Many insurance agents were furious when we announced our plan to ask for competitive bids on insurance policies. Some refused to participate, but many were pleased with the new, open system. It was discovered that the amount of money the state had been paying for insurance was considerably higher than the going competitive rate. The policy covering the electrical power generation equipment of the Grand River Dam Authority was around $80,000 per year. We were able, through central purchasing, to buy the same policy for less than half that amount.

It soon developed that insurance costs were not all the same. Often a dozen or more agents would bid for the same policy. The savings on all the insurance quickly amounted to well over $100,000 a year and the quality of the service also was increased significantly. Obviously there was slack in the way the state had handled its insurance business and the chairman had intended to skim off the cream for his own benefit and that of the governor. Had this been undertaken, I would not have survived very long in the governor's position. Being morally wrong and illegal, such an arrangement would have left me vulnerable to blackmail. His disenfranchisement as insurance adviser ruptured my relationship with the chairman. The last I heard of him he was tending bar at a private club in Oklahoma City. One of the most colorful political types I encountered, he was effective in his way, but his type of political operation had outlived its usefulness and acceptance in the state.

I had entered into Republican state politics with no thought of running for any office, particularly not the office of governor. My entry into the race had come after I'd spent two years helping reorganize and build the party so that it could provide meaningful support for its candidates and develop a realistic platform upon which candidates could run. I'd gotten into the governor's race feeling that, having built up this organization, the party deserved a candidate who would work hard and who would give volunteers a cause to rally around. About a week before the election, I had begun to feel we had a real chance of winning. This feeling was reinforced when Bill Atkinson made his last-minute charge that I had a secret plan to raise taxes and attracted little attention.

On election day, our family went to a restaurant for dinner and on the way back from campaign headquarters were caught in a rain storm. I told Shirley and the girls we were going to win the election and that it would change our lives forever. My suggestion to them was that we do everything possible to continue as a normal family and that we remember that this was a temporary situation, that in four years we would be back on the farm again.

After having been so long on the campaign trail, winning seemed an anti-climax. There was great jubilation in our headquarters and we realized that my election marked an historic turn in Oklahoma politics. I was somewhat apprehensive as to whether I could handle the job since I was the only state-wide elected Republican and both houses of the legislature were heavily Democratic. It would be a lonely four years! I did have a sense of history. Being the first Republican governor in Oklahoma or in any southern state since the Civil War would make me something of a national figure. At the same time, I realized that my first job was to take care of my responsibilities as governor of the state. There was a big job ahead.

I remember wishing that my mother and father could have been alive to see what had happened to their oldest son. On the other hand, neither of them had much interest in politics so they might not have been greatly impressed. Probably they would have preferred to see me become a successful farmer, "a man out standing in his field."

The Governor

"Forgive, but Remember"

T he campaign for governor had begun without my having any serious thought or hope of winning. Election night, the realiza tion that we had won swept over me. It seemed a ludicrous notion that a farmer from Noble County, who had been a highly partisan state Republican chairman in a five-to-one Democratic state, had become Oklahoma's first Republican governor. I had made no preparation for assuming the office. All our efforts had been directed toward winning the election. Suddenly, I knew we had a tremendous responsibility on our hands.

Among other immediate efforts to prepare for taking over the office was a trip to Madill for an in-depth talk with former Governor Raymond Gary. Raymond's organization had been supportive during the campaign and I had gained considerable respect for him and for his judgment. I told the former governor I felt a need for counsel. He spent a couple of hours offering advice about how the governor's office should be organized, about the various personalities I would have to deal with in the state legislature, and about his experiences as they might relate to my own. Two bits of his advice were especially sound.

First, he told me that no matter how well the governor does his job, no matter how hard he tries to avoid controversy, and no matter how wise or well-intentioned his decisions, times come when things simply refuse to go right. The danger is that by reading and listening to the adverse publicity, a governor is likely to become short-tempered and react in anger, making matters worse. Governor Gary said when things went sour, he simply put the unread newspapers in the trash can for a week or so and turned off the television and radio. If a governor refuses to fight back, the controversy quickly dies out. I've taken his advice on many occasions and found it to be valuable. Another piece of advice Gary offered had to do with selection of appointees. He reminded me that the governor had responsibility for choosing literally hundreds of people to serve on boards and commissions, as well as in his official family. He contended that the ability to choose competent, qualified, dedicated people is the greatest talent and the greatest need a governor has. He then added that "anytime you're forced to choose between brilliance and loyalty, choose loyalty." Again, I have found this advice to be valid.

Soon after the election, I also began meeting with Bob Kerr. Senior U.S. senator from Oklahoma, chairman of the Senate Finance Committee, and by far the greatest power in Oklahoma politics, Kerr was someone I had criticized publicly when I was Republican state chairman. Now I knew I would need to work with him harmoniously and closely. I was troubled about how to go about mending fences with him and finally hit upon the idea of asking Congressman Page Belcher, a friend to both of us, to arrange a meeting. The meeting took place in Bob Kerr's suite at the Mayo Hotel in Tulsa in mid-November. When Page and I went in, Bob was seated on a couch along the west wall. His assistant took a seat along the south wall and Belcher and I sat on a divan along the east wall. Page undertook to break the ice. He began by telling me what a tremendous person Senator Bob Kerr was, what a good friend he was, and how effective he had been in Washington working for Oklahoma. He then began to build me up by giving Bob Kerr a spiel about our association. The senator became impatient, cleared his throat, and Page took that as a signal to put an end to the introduction.

Bob got right to the point. "Now young feller," he said, "I don't know much about you but you are in the same position now that I was in when I was elected governor back in 1942. Up to that time no one in Oklahoma had heard much about Bob Kerr and probably cared less. However, I did put on a strong campaign and won the election for governor. After the votes were counted and I was assured of the office, I went around the state to pay my respects and thank those who had helped me in the campaign. One of the people I went to see was an old gentleman who published the newspaper at Guthrie. I went into his office and, with my hat in my hand, sat down and thanked him for what he had done. The old man was busy and I didn't want to take much of his time so after I had paid my respects I got up and started to leave. At this point, the old publisher turned to me and said, 'Bob, sit down a minute. I want to talk to you before you go.' I took a seat. The old man looked at me and said, 'Bob, I am a lot older than you are and I have seen a lot of things happen that you might have difficulty understanding. I just want to tell you one conclusion I have reached over these past seventy years.'

"I asked, 'What is that?'

"The old man said, 'Well, I am convinced that in this life you don't often get a royal flush, but when you get one, by God, play it for all it's worth.'"

At this point, Bob turned to me and said, "Now, young man, I am telling you the same thing. You are holding a royal flush in Oklahoma government. I don't know whether you have any political talent or not. I have been around the political arena long enough to know that political talent is the rarest gift of God. I know that it is extremely scarce in this country at this time. We need all that's available, whether it comes from Republicans or Democrats or any place else. If it turns out you do have talent and if you'll use it for the good of the state, I'll help you every way I can."

I was startled and immensely pleased. It appeared that Senator Bob Kerr was eager to work with me in a non-partisan way to advance the development of the state. He went on to tell about things he felt we could accomplish working together. During the next few weeks we had three meetings in Oklahoma City. Among other things, he told me his plan for the Talimena Drive; brought me up to date on developments, planned and underway, for the McClellan-Kerr Waterway, and told me about potential coal developments and other economic possibilities for the state. Perhaps most helpful were the tips he gave me on how to deal with Speaker J.D. McCarty and other leaders of the state legislature. He pledged his help in seeing that we had a cooperative relationship with the legislature so that my legislative program could be moved along in an orderly way. Senator Kerr was interested in working across party lines to get results for our state. It was a shock to me when, about the middle of December, news came that the senator had suffered a serious heart attack. And I was extremely saddened when, on the first day of January, 1963, he suffered another heart attack and died. The minister who conducted Bob Kerr's funeral service gave an eloquent eulogy, saying "a giant oak of the forest has fallen." Those familiar with the work of Senator Kerr would agree.

Both as a candidate and later as governor, I found one of the greatest responsibilities and most difficult decisions made by a public official is the choice of a personal staff. There is simply no way for a candidate or a governor personally to take care of the myriad of details that routinely arise. The ability to locate and attract individuals who are intelligent, loyal, dedicated, and possess a modicum of political sensitivity as well as empathy with fellow human beings is the difference between succeeding and failing in public office.

The first person I put on the payroll after election was Jeannette Baxter. As secretary in party headquarters, she had been a great asset. In addition to secretarial duties and managing the office in the early days, she recruited and hired additional staff and served as a confidante and judge of trial balloons. Jeannette had demonstrated her loyalty by her willingness to handle any job that came along and to work anytime I could find time for office work. This frequently meant weekends, sometimes late evening hours, and even working without pay when party funds had been low. Naturally, she was as proud of the victory as anyone and was more than glad to join the staff. When we undertook to arrive at a proper salary, however, I made a mistake I have regretted ever since. Jeannette felt she had made as much of a contribution to my political success and to my election as governor as anyone else. Certainly she was right. She also felt the work she had done in the campaign was of at least equal importance to the work done by anyone else and that the same would be true in the governor's office. Therefore, she felt that her salary should be equal to that of other top members of the staff.

The problem was that Governor Edmondson's secretary had been paid about $600 a month. There was the feeling this salary may have been supplemented by other income but so far as records were concerned, the salary of the governor's secretary was in that range. I offered Jeannette $600 per month, but male members of the staff were to be paid $1,000 to $1,200. Rightly, she was furious. I was oversensitive to the criticism the state's first Republican governor would get if he paid his secretary $1,000 a month or more and I was too cowardly to pay her what she was worth. I finally persuaded her to come to work at the $600 level. There is no defense for my decision. This was long before the time of equal pay for equal work, but I missed the opportunity to break new ground and help end the attitude of discrimination which had long maintained women's pay should not be equal to men's. Jeannette's office was next to mine and she served as traffic cop for what transpired in the governor's office. More than that, she came to rule the roost around the office and probably was somewhat resented by other members of the staff. She was a highly competent secretary and generally a dependable political adviser. She also had excellent judgment in choosing others for the clerical staff. There is no question that Jeannette's loyalty and professional support was essential in the success of the governor's race and the success of the office operation. I strongly regret I was not courageous enough to pay her what she was worth.

In the governor's office, Drew Mason's duties were those of an administrative assistant or chief of staff. Helen Lawson worked with him in this capacity. Of course, the responsibilities of the governor's job were far greater than either of us had faced in any of our previous positions. Drew rose to the occasion and met the responsibility with good grace and high spirits. As probably always happens in a new administration, we were set upon by a large number of individuals who felt they had made a contribution to the campaign and therefore were entitled to favors of one kind or another. Many of these individuals wanted jobs, some of them wanted appointments to boards and commissions, and some wanted favors of other kinds. Whether out of cowardice or convenience, I frequently put upon Drew the job of telling people they could not have what they wanted. The result was that Drew soon became the nay-sayer of the office, which made him highly unpopular with both party functionaries and members of the legislature. It got so bad that Drew came to my office one day and told me he had wrecked his reputation, that I either was going to have to replace him or let him say yes to people on occasion. His wisdom was obvious, so from that point on Drew put out at least some of the good news as well as the bad.

As Oklahoma state government was then structured, there were more than two hundred agencies that, in theory, reported directly to the governor. It was the responsibility of the governor to fill vacancies on those boards when terms of current members expired. A large black book was kept of these positions and the names and addresses of the members then serving. It was Drew's responsibility to watch over this book, determine when terms were expiring, and suggest possible names of appointees. This became an extremely heavy burden. Because of the thoroughness of the records kept by Drew and Helen, we had a large reservoir of supporters to choose from, and once confirmed by the state Senate our appointees served well. We did have one or two cases where individuals did not live up to our expectations or where they were guilty of malfeasance. Considering the number of appointments we were required to make, our record was good. Unfortunately, even though the governor had no way of knowing what the agencies were doing, anytime anything went sour the press immediately assumed the governor was to blame. This caused great difficulty, but we never found a good way of achieving full and constant accountability. The existence of so many independent boards and commissions made up of hold-over appointees makes the job of Oklahoma's governor extremely frustrating.

After my election, I realized I needed a legislative assistant who had a good rapport with the Democrats and yet whose loyalty to me would be beyond question. I settled on Floyd Carrier from the town of Carrier named after members of his family who were pioneers in the area. He had served twenty-four years as a Republican state senator from Garfield County but had retired and was living in his hometown where he was in the propane and grocery business. Floyd took some convincing but finally decided to take the job if Chris Horton, who had been his assistant in the Senate, could be hired as his secretary. Chris was agreeable. She and Floyd came onto the staff the day after inauguration. Floyd and I agreed that anytime he wanted to see me, he could walk directly into my office and no matter what I was doing I would talk to him. We developed a system to promote good relationships with legislators with Floyd the architect of the operation.

The way the governor's office was arranged, most visitors came through the glass front doors where they would be received by a receptionist and led down a long narrow hallway to the governor's office when the time for the appointment arrived. Legislators were encouraged to use another door, which led first through an outer office over which Chris presided with great diplomacy and warmth. Behind this was Floyd's office. The governor's office was adjacent. The standing rule was that no matter who was in the governor's office, if a legislator came with a problem to discuss, Floyd was to bring me into his office and I would talk to the member immediately. This gave legislators easy and immediate contact with the governor so the problem of communications, which apparently had been poor in the past, did not erupt.

Unfortunately, some legislators refused to take the initiative and complained that the governor rarely saw them. To avoid this problem, Chris scheduled meetings with various groups and members of the legislature from time to time, to try to narrow the communications gap. As time went on, I began to recognize in Chris several outstanding talents. She was totally unflappable. No matter what the crisis, Chris kept a cool head and found an orderly way to deal with the problem. No matter how irate or unreasonable a legislator might be coming into her office, she poured oil on the troubled waters and kept the situation from erupting into confrontation.

While serving as my legislative assistant, Floyd helped me raise some $20,000 used in the 1964 legislative campaign in Oklahoma. This money was contributed by various friends who felt it essential for the governor to have a good working relationship with the legislature. The money was taken by Floyd Carrier personally to legislative candidates, some Democrats, many of them in leadership positions with whom he had and wanted to maintain good working relationships. Generally, less than $500 was contributed for each of their campaigns. Some was given to Republicans as well. While we certainly owned no legislators, the fact that we were bipartisan enough to support Democrats financially certainly did us no harm. The good relationships Floyd developed with his clients greatly helped us in our efforts to move legislation we wanted and stop legislation we opposed. Under the law that was in effect at the time, no account was made of this money but Floyd told me he kept a record and if I ever wanted to see it, it would be available. I never asked. Floyd also maintained good relationships with all the Democrats who held elective state offices. He was the kind of person people would take into their confidence and, so far as I know, he never betrayed them. He was a high-minded public servant and I believe whatever success we had with the legislature was largely due to the work and reputation of Floyd Carrier.

In 1962, considerable racial agitation existed in Oklahoma City. Charlton Heston, the actor, had come to Oklahoma City and joined a march for the desegregation of restaurants and public facilities. I had been invited to participate in this march but declined, feeling my participation would result in a great disaffection among white voters and probably wouldn't do that much good among black voters. I explained to my black friends I felt I could help them as governor but that unless I could win the election, I would not be in a position to do anything. After my election, I talked to Drew Mason about the fact that we were going to be pressing for desegregation of both state- and privately-owned facilities and that the best way to make our point was to desegregate our own office. I asked Drew to start looking for black staff members to quietly make the point that we were going to require other state agencies to follow a de-segregation hiring and admission policy.

Drew identified a young black woman, Beulah Ponder, who at that time was employed by the state insurance fund. Drew arranged for Beulah to come to my office, and I was immediately impressed. She came to work soon after my inauguration. Beulah was generally assigned receptionist duties. In those pre-integration days, it was undoubtedly a shock to many to walk into the Oklahoma governor's office and find a black woman at the front desk. Beulah's approach to racial problems was definitely low-key, but she also was determined that her race move ahead on the basis of each individual's ability and that progress not be held back because of prejudice. She frequently took notes at meetings and often advised me on the course of action I should take on racial matters. On her own initiative, she arranged for meetings between myself and black educators in the Oklahoma City school system. She also arranged for me to visit some of the schools, including those her children attended. During those conversations and visits, I became totally convinced that the black children of Oklahoma City were not getting anything like a fair or equal education. These experiences did more than anything to convince me to take the pro-integration position I later took in the U.S. Senate when the forced-busing issue was decided.

Beulah continued as a member of my staff throughout the four years I served as governor and is still a warm friend today. The choice of Beulah to come on the governor's staff was probably one of the better decisions Drew and I made. She was a truly talented and dedicated person who, had it not been for the inferior education she had received in Oklahoma's segregated system, would probably have been qualified for major responsibility in government or the private sector. As it was, all she needed was a break. The waste of human resources which discrimination has caused in lives of women and minorities is incalculable. It's a burden which neither this society nor any other can afford to bear.

When I was putting together the staff to serve in the governor's office, I had a difficult time convincing an able lawyer to give up his practice and join my forces. The problem was that the top salary I could pay a lawyer was $12,000. To me this seemed like a lot of money, but a capable lawyer could earn much more in private practice. Dale Cook had been legal counsel of the state Republican party when I was state chairman. Previously a county attorney in Logan County and an assistant U.S. attorney, he and I developed a good working relationship and after my election he was one of the first I contacted to join the governor's staff. Cook was doing well in a law firm and was not interested. His refusal was a considerable blow since I felt it should be an honor for any loyal party member to serve in the state's first Republican administration. After making an effort to fill this position with other candidates, I still preferred Cook, so I went to him and pleaded. Finally, after great effort and much persuasion, I talked him into giving up his law partnership and becoming legal counsel on the governor's staff.

Dale was a real asset. He had the ability to deal with difficult people or situations in an inoffensive way. He was especially effective with members of the legislature and through his diplomatic talents we avoided confrontation with Attorney General Charles Nesbitt. Nesbitt was openly ambitious to become governor and working with him on controversial matters was clearly out of the question. Dale found among the Nesbitt assistants a man named "Judge" Monroe. He developed a working relationship with Monroe so that when we needed an attorney general's opinion, we usually could get it without great difficulty.

Dale also had the responsibility of reading and passing judgment on the worthiness of bills which came to the governor's desk for signature. He was particularly effective in pointing out deficiencies and flaws and in giving me the pros and cons on the legislation before I made a decision whether to sign or veto. Occasionally when there was a backlog of legislation, Dale and I would closet ourselves in an out-of-the-way place for several hours while he went through one bill after another offering explanations. We would then make up our minds whether or not a bill should be approved. Often Dale would write the message to the legislature explaining our position. There were many occasions when Dale found flaws in bills the legislature had missed. Often these bills were recalled and sent back to committee or to the authors to have the matter straightened out before the decision to approve or disapprove was made. The legislators trusted him and accepted his counsel in good faith.

Dale's working habits were somewhat frustrating to me. He was a night person and absolutely refused to come to work before nine or nine-thirty in the morning. Then he would want to work late in the evening when I was exhausted and more than ready to go home. He had another quality which proved to be a great source of irritation to me. His inclination was to be a fault-finder. He would never propose a solution to a problem on his own, and no matter what course of action was recommended, Dale could find numerous reasons the solution would not work. If Dale's counsel had been taken literally, we would have sat around in the governor's office wringing our hands and doing nothing because every avenue open to us was beset by pitfalls. Finally, I had to decide on a course of action and say "Dammit Dale, this is what we are going to do." From that point on Cook would do his best to make it happen. Soon, however, it became clear that Dale's posture of being the "no man" was of great value. Once I'd listened to his objections and decided which course of action to follow, I could safely conclude that no one else could mount an objection Dale had not thought of already. Therefore, asking his opinion, while it was almost certain to produce a negative reaction, was a valuable preparation for the criticism that often came from reporters, legislators, or others. In fact, in each position I've held since then I've diligently tried to add a "no man," a fault-finder, to the staff so all objections to an issue could be considered before a decision was made.

Dale Cook stayed with me through both the first and second biannual legislative sessions. At the end of the 1965 session, Dale came to me and said, "Now governor, I have been with you for two and a half years and most of your needs for my services are over. I have served at great financial sacrifice to the point that we have had to make our children give up piano lessons and other frills. My wife has gone to work clerking in a Montgomery Ward store. I absolutely must get out of here and back where I can make more money." He said his income over the last two years was less than half of what it was over a similar period in the past.

I was extremely sad to see him go, but I felt the biggest demand for his services had passed and understood he could not continue to work at great financial sacrifice.

At the time he left the governor's office, he told me he had always had an ambition to be a federal judge and while he realized there was no way governors were involved in those appointments, if the occasion ever arose when I could help him, he would be eternally grateful. At the time I had no thought of running for the U.S. Senate, but as things worked out I did help Dale achieve his lifetime ambition. No promise had been made, but there was no question in my mind that Cook was well-qualified to handle the federal judge's position and there is no question I felt a debt of gratitude to him.

Later, during the time I was considering naming Dale for the judge-ship, I was in the offices of Byron Boone, an attorney and the publisher of the *Tulsa World*. He asked me who I was considering for judge and I told him in confidence my preference would be Dale Cook. After I left Boone's office, I went into the office of Phil Dessauer, an old friend who was a *World* editorial writer. I was visiting with him when Boone sent a messenger for me. The messenger took me back to Boone's office where Boone was on the telephone with Judge Fred Daugherty of the western district of the Oklahoma federal court. Boone handed the phone to me and said Daugherty had something he wanted to tell me about Dale Cook. I was petrified that Daugherty was going to object to the appointment, but the message was precisely the opposite. Daugherty told me he had known Dale since Dale was in the U.S. attorney's office, that Dale had frequently been in the Daugherty court and that he felt Dale would make an excellent judge. Naturally this information was most welcome since Daugherty was one of the most respected judges in the country. His endorsement also meant a great deal to Byron Boone. There was no negative press about the Cook appointment even though at the time I had been concerned that many would look upon the appointment as political favoritism. This turned out to be another case where a politician should go ahead and do the thing he feels is right and not be too concerned about the short-range consequences.

After my inauguration, Shirley assumed the duties of First Lady with great charm. Our first official duty was to dance the first dance at the governor's ball. Shirley had designed and made her inaugural gown, probably the only Oklahoma governor's wife ever to be her own designer and dressmaker. The entire capitol building was jammed with people from top to bottom. Since it was the first time a Republican had been elected governor of Oklahoma, we invited the public to come to the ball because we wanted to make the point that ours would be an open administration and that the capitol belonged to all the people.

Life in the mansion was fairly relaxed and pleasant for the Bellmon family. There was little concern about security for the governor. Our "guards" were college students who basically answered the telephone and the door bell. They also served as baby-sitters and big brothers for our girls. At that time it was possible for anyone to drive in off the street, come to the front door of the mansion, and ask to see the governor. There were no locked gates, no sentries, no television sentry cameras. When I walked to work early in the mornings, I frequently saw neighborhood boys on the mansion grounds picking purple plums. This would all change after the Vietnam era.

One of our principal family undertakings was to host a series of dinners for groups of legislators. Since the mansion dining room would accommodate only twelve guests at a time, it was necessary to hold fifteen of these dinners during the legislative session. Shirley and one helper did the cooking and the girls served. They were happy events and probably did much to cement relations with the legislators, most of whom were Democrats who tended to be suspicious of the state's first Republican governor. Another of our undertakings was to plan open houses for campaign supporters and Republican organization leaders from across the state. These were planned to invite supporters from a few counties at a time so that each guest would have an opportunity to visit with the governor and first family. The first events were well attended and seemed to be quite popular, but as time went on attendance dropped until they were hardly worth the effort. Then we began to open the mansion to the public on a regular basis, a practice that has been continued to the present.

While we lived in the mansion, the girls attended public schools. They refused to be taken to school in the limousine. On the rare occasions the limousine had to be used, they insisted on being let out two blocks from school so they could walk the rest of the way and avoid an ostentatious arrival. Pat took piano lessons from the dean of the school of music at Oklahoma City University, Gail took voice lessons, and Ann studied ballet under Yvonne Chouteau. Shirley became a leader in the Oklahoma County 4-H club organization where she made many new friends. We travelled to governors' conferences in cities around the country and frequently the girls went with us. On one occasion, Ann, who was ten, was photographed dancing with Vice President Hubert Humphrey. The picture was carried in many national newspapers.

Even though I'd worked for the *Daily O'Collegian* as a reporter during my final three semesters at A&M, I was not fully prepared for the enormous role newspaper, radio, and television people play in state government. I counted myself a competent reporter, had used those skills vigorously as Republican state chairman to crank out innumerable press releases, and had a more than passing acquaintance with the many reporters who worked the capitol beat in Oklahoma City. I believed most of them were pleased I had won the election and we started the term with a friendly relationship.

Shirley and I decided that since neither of us drank and had never served alcoholic beverages in our home, we would continue following that policy while we lived in the governor's mansion. At a news conference early after our election, Shirley joined me and we announced to a crest-fallen group of reporters that there would be no liquor served in the governor's house as long as we lived there. Since Oklahoma had only recently legalized the sale of liquor and, from reports, my predecessor had been fairly generous in disbursing alcoholic beverages, the news corps was visibly disappointed. I looked at them and said, "Cheer up, we'll keep plenty of cold milk in the ice box." Immediately, I was written up as a *buttermilk* drinker even though I detest the stuff. From that day forward on innumerable occasions proud restauranteurs have presented me with large quantities of buttermilk which they expected me to consume before their eyes. For the next twenty years this reputation stayed with me. This is only one example of the enormous ability reporters have to create an image of a public official even though that image may be inaccurate.

In an effort to maintain good relations with the press and make certain information about the administration available, I agreed to hold six news conferences a week. These were scheduled on Monday, Wednesday, and Friday at 10 a.m. and 2 p.m. This was intended to treat both the a.m. and p.m. papers equally and, though it was a serious drain on the governor's time and energy, we maintained that schedule during the four years I served in office. The effect of so much exposure to the media proved the accuracy of the old saying "familiarity breeds contempt." Several reporters developed techniques to get me to say things that conformed to stories they already planned to write before the news conference began. It took considerable coaching on the part of press secretary Bob Haught to prepare me for these six-times-a-week ordeals.

Otis Sullivant was an employee (I intentionally avoid the word "reporter") of *The Daily Oklahoman*. A political commentator, he wrote a column called "The Observer," which appeared frequently. As early as the mid-1940s, he was recognized as dean of the Oklahoma political press corps. He still held this vaunted position when I entered state politics. Through the years as an outsider I enjoyed reading his columns because he was super-critical of the political powers in the state. Not knowing what was going on behind the scenes, I felt Otis's criticisms were well put, and it's possible that his influence had something to do with my political involvement. I first began to know Otis personally after my election as Republican state chairman. We developed as close a friendship as is possible between a politician and a newsman.

Otis, who was in his late fifties at the time I was state chairman, put on the appearance and mannerisms of a super-cynic. He tried never to smile. He was unwilling to take any statement from a politician at face value and looked for dishonest, self-serving, or unethical motives. As a result of his dealings with state politicians over the years, he trusted no one and felt it was his job to keep the public constantly alert to the real or presumed misdeeds of their elected representatives. To a degree, the Sullivant attitude was helpful to the state. However, his super-cynicism had the counterbalancing effect of weakening public confidence in the honest, hard-working, dedicated officials who are the vast majority in government. Because he wrote so cynically of every politician and never seemed to write anything constructive even about those who took their responsibilities seriously, Oklahomans, including myself, got the impression that everyone in government was rotten to the core.

Otis paid little attention to me during my state chairmanship. He apparently considered the Republican party of little consequence in the real world of governing Oklahoma. However, after I resigned and started campaigning for the governor's job, he did on one occasion during the primary pay me the honor of mentioning my name. As planned, there was little news being generated by our efforts during the primary, so I was surprised, as well as awed and frightened, when Jeannette Baxter came into my small office one morning and told me Otis Sullivant was waiting to see me. I had no choice but to invite him in. He was dressed as usual in an ill-fitting, tweed suit. Also as usual, he had his reporter's note-pad doubled over and stuck in one coat pocket. His posture was slouched and he looked the part of an oversized gnome. With a great show of seriousness and concern, Sullivant took the one seat available, pulled out the note-pad, unfolded it on his knee, licked his pencil, gave me a cold stare, and asked, "Young man, what makes you think you're smart enough to be governor?"

His question absolutely threw me. After I sat in dumbfounded silence for what seemed like an endless time, Sullivant laughed, folded his pad, put it back in his pocket, and said, "Bellmon, I have been around the capitol now for some thirty-five years. I have seen many governors come and go. I have seen good ones and bad ones, honest ones and crooked ones, smart ones and dumb ones. I am convinced of one thing and that is that *you don't have to be smart to be governor!*"

After I shared a relieved chuckle with him, Sullivant continued. He was convinced that the pitfall which wrecked most governors was that during the campaign they are out across the state meeting people from all walks of life and generally listening to what they had to say. However, as quickly as the campaign is over, the only people who come to see the governor are those who want something, are mad about something or are endeavoring to butter him up so they can gain some advantage. Others are bitter about some injustice or failure of government and have come to criticize. He said that most governors quickly lose contact with the majority of normal citizens who go about their daily lives doing their jobs, raising their families, paying their bills, and giving little attention to government.

Sullivant's contention was that for a governor to do a good job, he needs to make a particular effort to keep in contact with rank-and-file citizens on a regular basis. His suggestion to me was that "if lightning should strike" and I won (and he made it plain he didn't expect this to happen), I should plan at least once every two or three weeks to put on my overalls, get in my pickup, and go back and sit for a couple of hours at a community sale, courthouse, or somehow get out and talk and listen to the rank-and-file citizens who are going about their daily lives. He felt that by keeping in touch with these people a politician could retain a proper perspective and keep from being overly caught up in the artificiality of high public office.

I took his recommendation literally and the so-called "Main Street Meetings" were an outgrowth of this advice. For these, we set up "Capitol for a Day" in towns away from Oklahoma City and I listened to people. Not only as governor, but in other political endeavors, I have tried to remember his counsel. After I became governor, Otis felt he merited special consideration as far as the governor's office was concerned. John Tyler described the situation best when he said that the Sullivant notion of a gubernatorial news conference was that Otis should be walking out of the governor's office with his note-pad in his pocket already full of quotes when the other reporters arrived for the conference to begin. As governor, I could not deal with Otis on anything even approaching a preferential basis. As months went on, this irritated Otis. In addition, I often felt that because he and I had something of a friendship, Sullivant felt he needed to lean over backwards to bring me down to size to compensate for any personal warmth he might feel toward me. A kind of game developed between us. After Otis wrote one of his devastating stories about the governor, he would ask me if I had read the article. Invariably, I would deny I had seen it, which would usually cause a chuckle because he knew there was no way a politician could avoid reading "The Observer" every time it appeared.

In 1965 I was scheduled to go to Las Vegas to attend a meeting of the executive committee of the National Governors' Conference. We were taking a National Guard plane with a capacity of one hundred passengers. Knowing that Otis usually spent at least part of his vacation at the gaming tables in Las Vegas, I invited him to make the trip with us. Otis declined with a snort, saying, "Hell! Going to Las Vegas with Henry Bellmon would be about as much fun as kissing your sister."

When a fight broke out over the state chairmanship soon after my election, Otis was critical of my involvement. When the scrap was finally over and the candidate I backed had won, at serious loss to me of support among Republicans, I called Otis on a Sunday morning and asked him how badly he felt I had been hurt by the adventure. He said that, while I had picked up considerable scar tissue, if I avoided any evidence of vengeance against those who had opposed me and treated them magnanimously he felt I could put the party back together and retain a fairly solid base of support among Republican leaders. Taking his advice, I leaned over backwards to appoint those who had been in the other camp to positions which I felt they could fill in my administration. His advice worked reasonably well but there remained a lasting schism. The wounds have never completely healed and I continued to have problems with right-wing elements in the party throughout my political career.

In spite of my problems with him, I feel Otis Sullivant had a positive influence on Oklahoma government. I remember during the Bartlett-Moore governor's race when it looked as if Preston Moore was going to win, how reassuring it was to realize that reporters, including Otis, would be watching the new governor as closely as they had been watching me for four years. I realized clearly the vital role a vigorous, skeptical, free press plays in a representative form of government. It is only the fact that competent reporters see and hear everything that goes on in government and duly report not only the events but their interpretation of these events that makes it possible for citizens to know whether their government is serving them ill or well. In my judgment, not only Otis but other reporters would do the governmental process a service if they could somehow figure out a more balanced way of reporting not only the misdeeds but the constructive things public officials accomplish. Reporters would have far more balance if they could at sometime during their career participate personally in a political campaign or as a member of an administration. They would then have the more balanced perspective they need to judge accurately and honestly the performance of officials against a reasonable norm, rather than the impossible standard of pious perfection they now seem to apply.

Ray Parr was another talented and respected political writer for *The Daily Oklahoman*. In addition to his straight reporting, Ray wrote a Sunday column called "Parr for the Course." It was one of the most skillful and humorous bits of political satire I have ever read. In effect, he was the Oklahoma Art Buchwald, though in some ways he was more gifted than even the national columnist. Following my election as governor, Ray became my favorite among the capitol press corps. His questions were usually penetrating, his writing was accurate and fair. Ray had a strange affection for colorful, though incompetent, politicians. Probably it was largely due to the columns he wrote that Senator Joe Bailey Cobb became a prominent state political figure. Ray, who had a paunchy physique much like Joe Bailey Cobb's, even went so far as to take the Cobb role in the annual Press Association gridiron. His imitation of Cobb was often the highlight of the evening. Unfortunately, Ray made a folk hero out of a politician whose personal qualities were not worthy of the notoriety — and the political support — he received as a result of Ray's talents. The outcome was that Joe Bailey Cobb became a frequent name on the state ballot and even won election to statewide office.

Through the years, Ray Parr gave me sound, well-intentioned advice from time to time. I cannot recall ever having been misquoted by Ray or ever having had a confidence violated by him. He was skillful, experienced enough to be objective, and yet had a strong sense of fairness and good humor. For the good of the political system in the state and country, there need to be more reporters like Ray Parr.

During the 1964 Southern Governors' Conference, Governor Frank Clements of Tennessee told a story on himself in relation to the fairness of the press. After enduring what he considered bad press for several months, he decided to confront the reporters with the evidence of the unfair and biased reporting they had been doing about his administration. For two hours he carefully went through clippings, setting aside those he felt were unfair. Then he gave up and put the clippings back in his briefcase. After examining all the news stories, he discovered that there were more times when the press erred in writing favorably than unfairly. The memory of this story helps to keep my blood pressure down when some news person seems to be after a hunk of my hide.

One of the first people who came to see me after my election was Harry Bailey, director of the Oklahoma Turnpike Authority. Of the people I have met in my political activities, he was one of the most interesting and difficult to understand. Bailey became director after the legislature authorized construction of the Turner Turnpike in 1947. A controversial figure, he was generally regarded as a wheeler-dealer who ran over those who got in his way. When I ran for governor, I came close to making the construction of the Southwestern Turnpike a campaign issue. Many in the campaign organization felt illegal activities were taking place in connection with that project. We hired an investigator to look into the matter and on his recommendaticn and the urging of Wayne Mackey we avoided launching an attack on the turnpike operations.

As a new governor, I had very little concept of how the Turnpike Authority operated and assumed Harry Bailey was someone I could fire. I quickly learned this was not the case. Harry Bailey was in fact hired by the bond holders as the managing engineer. Bond buyers who had invested millions in the project insisted, quite properly, that they had the right to employ an engineer to make certain turnpike construction, management, and maintenance were carried on professionally, that the money was wisely and honestly spent, and that the projects were managed in such a way as to guarantee investors every reasonable possibility of getting their money back, with interest. He did not work for the state and his tenure in office was in no way dependent upon the whim of the governor or the legislature.

Harry Bailey's first visit to me in the governor's office occurred late one evening, giving me my first opportunity to size up this man. Up to that point, I looked upon Bailey as a deadly political enemy, and I fully intended to remove him from office. He turned out to be a heavy, almost squat man with a big cigar, raspy voice, and all the exterior qualities of a ward-heeling politician. He came on strong, was quite profane, and, even when trying to be polite, was thoroughly obnoxious. The conversation that evening made me realize I was likely to be stuck with this man for as long as I was governor. On the spot, I decided to work with him rather than waste time in pointless antagonisms. After working with Harry Bailey a few months, I found he had done a remarkably good job for his employers. In fact, there has never been an Oklahoma turnpike scandal and the program has continued in strong financial condition.

One of the things Harry Bailey had come to tell me was that he wanted the attorney for the Turnpike Authority removed. The man apparently was taking a high fee, which was okay with Harry. However, Harry felt that much of the Authority's legal work was not being dealt with professionally or promptly. He told me that even though the Turnpike Authority members were all Democrats, he felt there were enough votes to remove the attorney if the governor so recommended. He suggested I fire the attorney immediately. He also gave me names of those on the Authority who he felt needed to be replaced and others he felt were doing a good job. While it was the governor's prerogative to remove Authority members, I questioned whether the legislature would allow me to make the changes. Bailey assured me he would work with Senate President Pro Tempore Roy Boecher and J.D. McCarty, speaker, to be sure that whatever changes I wanted were accomplished.

One of the most tense meetings I ever attended was my first meeting with the Turnpike Authority, called soon after these conversations with Harry Bailey. We met in the old turnpike building at Fourth and Walnut. I came into the meeting, a newly elected, highly insecure, Republican governor. I faced a Turnpike Authority totally made up of political opposites and headed by Harry Bailey, thought of as one of my toughest, most partisan opponents. The attorney and his son were present, as well as a fairly large contingent from the capitol press corps. At an appropriate time in the meeting, I brought up the fact that I felt the Authority should make arrangements for new legal counsel. I expected to suffer a humiliating defeat, but, to my amazement, the Authority voted almost unanimously in support of my proposition.

The attorney made an impassioned plea that he, a loyal Democrat, should not be removed since this would allow a Republican governor to bring in his own lawyer. The board stayed with me (or with Bailey) and the attorney was replaced by Doug McKeever, a lawyer I recommended from Enid. Doug had been a prominent Republican serving as state chairman as well as Republican nominee for the U.S. Senate against Mike Monroney in 1952. The turnpike attorney job paid $18,000 a year and required probably not more than two or three days a week of an attorney's time. It was obviously a great plum. The Authority may have had some misgivings about Doug but they appeared to be so eager to make a change that they probably would have taken anyone I recommended. This was one of my first and easiest victories as governor and it was all orchestrated by Harry Bailey. My success with the Turnpike Authority helped my credibility as governor, and I began to think well of Bailey in spite of my earlier misgivings.

As months went on, I came to have a high regard for Bailey's competence as an engineer and as a turnpike manager, as well as for his skill as a political operator. The Southwest Turnpike, later named the H.E. Bailey, was under construction. He was extremely tough on what were called section engineers, those private firms engaged to design and oversee construction of short sections of turnpike. It was Bailey's job to make certain they did their design work properly and watched the contractors closely enough to keep the construction work on schedule and on budget in spite of storms, labor disagreements, supply difficulties, or any other problem that might arise. Bailey prided himself on his ability to write scathing letters to any section engineer who allowed work to fall behind schedule. Copies of those letters were circulated among Turnpike Authority members, employees, and anyone else Bailey thought might enjoy his vituperative comments about the performance of different people and various jobs. It became somewhat of a joke among turnpike members to discuss the tough way Bailey dealt with other engineers. Frankly, if I had been some of those engineers, I believe I would have had a load of wet concrete dumped on his head.

About a year after I became governor, Harry Bailey suffered a massive and near-fatal heart attack. He had become badly overweight and was a chain smoker of strong cigars. We were apprehensive about his welfare but he pulled through in good shape. After he had been in the hospital for awhile and was out of intensive care, doctors decided he could have visitors. Dale Cook and I went late one afternoon to pay him a visit. We found Harry propped up in bed looking pale. He was without the usual cigar and was several pounds lighter. We began by exchanging a few pleasantries. To my absolute astonishment, tough old Harry Bailey broke down and sobbed like a child for several minutes. It became impossible to talk with him and finally, in a state of great embarrassment, Dale and I backed out of the room and left. I did not understand Harry's behavior and for the first time became interested in Harry Bailey as a person.

Asking around, I learned several things. In the first place, the gruff, hard-boiled exterior which Bailey exhibited was a facade he used to cover up what really was a soft and sentimental personality. In addition, I discovered that Harry Bailey was not a graduate engineer. He had learned engineering in the school of hard knocks and was practicing engineering in Oklahoma at the time the engineer licensing law was passed. He was grandfathered under the law and probably did not feel truly competent as an engineer. This may have been the reason he was rough in his treatment of other engineers and contemptuous of those who had professional degrees.

After additional time in the hospital, Harry was allowed to return to his home across south from Twin Hills Country Club in northeastern Oklahoma City. At that time, the Turnpike Authority had a considerable volume of business to transact and it was necessary on different occasions for me to go to his home to sign papers or discuss turnpike matters since he was unable to come to my office. My visits to Harry Bailey's home usually took place early in the morning before I went to the office. Frequently, I was met by Mrs. Bailey, who was a pleasant, mild-mannered, attractive woman — totally opposite from the demeanor Harry Bailey exhibited. Usually, Harry would be in the backyard feeding his animals. He had built a home against an undeveloped creek and over the years had encouraged wild animals to trust him. He brought ears of white corn from his farm near Arkansas City and hand-shelled grains off the cob to hand feed his animal friends. I would sit by the picture window in his living room and see Harry Bailey, this hard-boiled old wheeler-dealer, out in the yard, frequently down on his knees, handing grains of corn to squirrels, quail, wild song birds, and even rabbits. His wife told me that Harry also had a system for keeping peace among his animal friends. When one animal became aggressive toward others, he would trap it, take it far into the woods, and turn it loose, hoping it would stay in a different environment and not return to bother other members of his wild family.

One time when Harry and I had taken care of turnpike business, he asked me if I was going to the upcoming 1964 Republican National Convention in San Francisco. I told him I was. He said that he knew I was not rich, that I had no money left over from the governor's campaign, that I had not maintained a political slush fund and, therefore, he wanted to know how I was going to pay the cost of going to the convention. I assured him I would pay my costs out of my salary. He said this was a great injustice, that I should not be expected to pay the heavy costs that would be incurred. At this point he reached in his desk and took out a thick envelope. He explained it was cash which I could use as I saw fit to defray costs of the San Francisco trip. He told me that no one knew about the money but him, that there was no record made, and that no one would ever know. I looked at the envelope for a moment and was greatly torn about what to do. I did not want to hurt the old man's feelings, but

I knew I could not take the money because to do so would have given him a club to use over me. This I could not allow. In addition, I had made a big thing about not taking any kind of contributions or gifts after the election in an effort to help establish the honesty of the governor's office which had been seriously impaired by the actions of my predecessors.

As gently as I could, I laid the envelope back on his desk and tried to explain there was no way in light of my no-gifts policy that I could accept the money. I told him I appreciated his thoughtfulness and generosity, but under the circumstances I had to decline. Bailey appeared to be quite perturbed and even dismayed by my rejection. But he did not seem to take it as a personal insult, as I feared he would. He finally kept the money and I think the incident strengthened our relationship.

The real payoff of my relationship with Harry Bailey came well toward the end of my term in office. He saved me from a public political brawl that would have permanently ruptured my relationship with Dewey Bartlett, my successor as governor and later a colleague in the U.S. Senate. The Turnpike Authority had been trying for several months to work out a plan to refinance existing Oklahoma turnpikes and in the process generate sufficient funds to build new toll roads from Henrietta to Hugo, Tulsa to Muskogee and Webbers Falls. We also hoped to start the process of building a turnpike from Tulsa to I-35 in the direction of Enid. Unfortunately, each time we were about ready to get the turnpike refinancing program off the ground, the bond market would turn against us, interest rates would go up, and the sale of bonds would become impractical. Bailey watched over the developments like an eagle and worked with Jim Abrams of Allen and Company and O.V. Cecil of Merrill Lynch, who had handled previous turnpike financing. We wanted to be ready to move when market conditions were right. The appropriate conditions developed about the time of the 1966 elections and we sold the bonds.

As news became public that the bond transaction was about to go through, the Republican nominee for governor, Dewey Bartlett, got into the act. He said that regardless of what the governor and the Turnpike Authority did, his administration would take a new look into turnpike matters after he was in office. This infuriated Harry Bailey who went after Bartlett hammer and tong and came to my defense publicly in no uncertain terms. The result was a breakdown in the relationship between

Bartlett and Bailey, but it did a great deal to help me with the public who otherwise might have felt something was irregular about the bond transactions. The bond sale became a major issue in my U.S. Senate campaign two years later. By explaining what went on, Bailey helped me considerably.

One of the great problems about turnpike financing is that it is done through revenue bonds. As governor, I had tried diligently to convince the legislature that we should put the full faith and credit of the state behind the turnpike bonds, thus reducing the interest rate. Issuing general obligation bonds would have reduced the interest by perhaps one-and-a-half percentage points and saved the state millions of dollars over the bond payout period. Since the turnpikes were earning far more income than was needed to retire the debt, the state would be taking little risk. It also would have done away with what is called the bond discount. The discount covered the fees which the bond salesmen, engineers, and attorneys must have in order to prepare the bonds for sale, make necessary estimates of revenue, do the construction cost projections, and handle actual sale of the bonds to investors. Many felt the discount was something the governor or others put into their pockets. It was impossible to adequately explain this to many people. U.S. Senator Mike Monroney tried to make the matter an issue during the 1968 Senate campaign and indirectly charged me with pocketing the millions of dollars of discounts which were paid. Actually, members of the Turnpike Authority never saw any of the discount.

I would have preferred to see the bonds handled as general obligations of the state because under those conditions they could have been auctioned off at the lowest interest rate available and no discount would have been paid. It would have been necessary for the legislature to appropriate money for the engineering, legal fees, and costs of sale. This they refused to do. It also would have been necessary for the citizens of Oklahoma to approve the bond sale in an election.

Regrettably, after the turnpike bond sale had been finalized and after all was set for the roads to be built, including the availability of some $19,000,000 to start the Tulsa to I-35 route, Governor-elect Bartlett still persisted in his opposition. I could never figure out whether his opposition was due to an intense dislike for Harry Bailey, his distrust for the turnpike operation, jealousy or resentment of me, or some other reason.

During his time in office no additional turnpikes were authorized or constructed and the potential Tulsa-to-I-35 project languished. After Bartlett left office and Governor David Hall came in, the Tulsa-to-I-35 road was fully financed and built, though by that time the cost had gone up by some $20,000,000.

In preparation for selling the turnpike bonds, Harry Bailey, Turnpike Authority chairman Marvin Millard, and I decided it would be a good stroke to invite Jim Abrams and O.V. Cecil, our bond people from New York, down for a social occasion and briefing on the progress we'd made with the turnpike system. The briefing occurred one afternoon and was followed by a fancy dinner in the Beacon Club on the top floor of the First National Bank building in Oklahoma City. It was the first time I'd ever encountered escargot, but I managed the snails without incident.

Plans had been made to take Jim Abrams goose shooting near the Great Salt Plains refuge the next morning and then to go to the Cooper Ranch near Fort Supply for lunch and quail hunting. Jim was a typical Wall Street financier, accustomed to plush surroundings and a genteel lifestyle. After dinner, Doug McKeever and I drove with Abrams to Enid, arriving at the old Youngblood Hotel a little before midnight. We left wake-up calls and at four the next morning we arose, dressed, had a light breakfast, and headed for the goose blind near the Salt Plains Wildlife Refuge north of the town of Jet.

It was a cold December morning with a strong wind out of the north. We arrived at the crude, unheated blind in the pre-dawn darkness and took our positions inside to wait for the promised flights of wild geese. Unfortunately, the blind opened to the north and the wind blew gusts of fine sand in our faces, making it both unpleasant and difficult to see. The blind was located near the refuge and we could hear the geese calling from their resting places on Salt Plains Lake. The morning wore on and on. We got colder and colder, suffered more and more from the sand-blast, but the geese absolutely refused to cooperate. In fact, during our four hours in the blind, nary a goose appeared on the horizon.

Arrangements had been made for the governor's airplane, a twenty-year-old Twin Beach tail-dragger, to pick us up at Keggelman airstrip nearby. This was a strip which Air Force pilots from Vance Air Field used for practice landings. About nine o'clock, we finally gave up the goose hunt, loaded into a patrol car, and were driven to the waiting airplane.

The day had become overcast and as we headed west towards Fort Supply, the ceiling dropped lower and lower. By the time our plane approached the Woodward airport near the Cooper ranch, we were flying at rooftop height. Even though the airport was only about six miles further west, visibility became so bad we simply could not go on. The pilot turned the plane around and flew back east some forty miles to Waynoka which had a usable airport. When we arrived in the vicinity of Waynoka, the pilot attempted to throttle back the engines in preparation for landing. At that point, one of the engines "ran away." The pilot was rattled. We heard him shouting on the radio that the governor's plane was about to crash and calling the local fire department to send a fire engine to the airport. Looking out the window of the plane, Jim Abrams and I were very perturbed to see a fire engine coming down the road with its red light flashing brightly, followed by about thirty pickups. Local residents had heard the news and either wanted to help or were coming to see the excitement when the governor's airplane crashed. Our plane circled around and around. Finally, I suggested to the pilot that he simply shut off the runaway engine and go ahead and land with one. This was done without incident, to the disappointment of some spectators I'm sure. Both Abrams and I were considerably relieved to be on solid ground. I never flew in that plane or with that pilot again. A new plane was purchased for the next governor.

We called a highway patrol car to drive us the fifty or so miles to the Cooper Ranch near Fort Supply. When the patrol car arrived it turned out to be one assigned the task of weighing trucks on the highway. The trunk of the patrol car was filled with scales, so Jim Abrams and I had to sit in the back seat of the patrol car and hold our luggage on our laps all the way to Fort Supply. Things were becoming a little strained between us. At the Cooper Ranch an incredible feast had been arranged. The Cooper family operated a large ranch with several full-time cowhands. To cook for the crew of cowboys they had employed two German women who were delighted with the opportunity to prepare a meal for the governor and a New York visitor. There were at least twenty different dishes of specialty foods, all of them prepared to perfection. The scrumptious meal was the one bright spot of the day.

After lunch, I was scheduled to attend a meeting and make a talk to the staff and clients of the mental hospital at Fort Supply. Jim Abrams and the others were to go quail hunting. Jim changed out of his goose-hunting clothes into his quail-hunting clothes, the same suede leather outfit he wore for fox-hunting in Virginia. Unfortunately, the suede was no match for the sagebrush and brambles which he had to traverse in search of quail, and by the end of the day Jim's expensive outfit was in shreds. The absolute low point of the day occurred during the afternoon when a wild turkey suddenly flew up near Jim. He took aim and brought the bird down with one shot. Turkey season had been over for three weeks and he'd killed a bird out of season. The Turnpike Authority paid his fine.

All in all, the trip was a total disaster. I assumed it might have soured our chances of selling the turnpike bonds and raising the money we needed to expand our turnpike system. This feeling was put to rest a few days later when I got a letter from Jim Abrams. The letter said, curtly, "Fix up your goddam airplane." The envelope contained assorted rubber bands and paper clips.

When Dale Cook told me he wanted to leave the governor's staff for financial reasons, he said he wanted to try to start his own law practice and that it would be a great help to him if I could work it out for him to replace Doug McKeever as the Turnpike Authority attorney. I called Harry Bailey in and told him what I wanted to do and he disagreed. He was highly pleased with the services of Doug McKeever. Then, either directly or indirectly, Doug found out about the plan and objected strongly. Finally, after some weeks of uncomfortable negotiations, Harry hit upon a solution. Since we were well along toward refinancing the turnpikes, he was certain the New York bond counsel would need an Oklahoma representative. He felt he could convince them Dale Cook could do the job. I passed word on to Dale who agreed and on his own worked out an arrangement with Bailey and the bond counsel. I never knew and do not want to know how much Dale Cook was paid. But whatever he got from the New York bond counsel made it possible for him to leave the governor's staff, start his own law firm, and succeed.

As the New York bond counsel's representative in Oklahoma, Dale was instrumental in obtaining the Oklahoma Supreme Court approval of the contract for refinancing the turnpikes. The date for the sale was set for a Monday. The plan was that over the weekend the sale would be advertised in the necessary legal publications. Late Friday afternoon, a turnpike opponent filed an action in the district court of Creek County challenging the legality of our bond debenture. Dale, through personal contacts with members of the Oklahoma State Supreme Court, went into action. Late Friday afternoon, he got a sufficient number of members of the Supreme Court in from a golf course in Tulsa where they were holding a State Bar Association meeting. They convened an extraordinary session of the court. The Supreme Court took original jurisdiction of the challenge which had been filed and threw it out of court so that the bond sale could proceed as proposed on Monday. That one action alone probably saved the turnpike refinancing effort and undoubtedly saved the bond underwriters far more than the fee the bond counsel had paid Dale Cook.

In spite of my respect for Harry Bailey, I was ever mindful of the fact that he was someone who looked out for Number One. And in his mind Harry Bailey was Number One. At one turnpike meeting a contract for the so-called section engineers was brought up for approval. It was a lengthy document and I had not seen it before the meeting began and probably would not have had time to read it even if I had. I thumbed through it quietly, turned to Doug McKeever, and asked, "Is this all right?" Doug nodded that it was. The member across the table from me was John Kilpatrick, who had been serving on the Turnpike Authority under appointment by Howard Edmondson and who, on Harry Bailey's recommendation, I had not replaced. John, who had been over this same contract in previous years, turned to page seven and read it quickly. Well-concealed in the language was a provision which would have given Harry Bailey's engineering firm an exclusive contract to do all the engineering for all future turnpike construction in Oklahoma. Harry was trying to slip this through without anyone knowing what was going on. Apparently he had tried it before and Kilpatrick knew where to look for this tricky language. John immediately raised the point. I looked at the language and was appalled at what Bailey was trying to do. The Turnpike Authority voted unanimously to remove the language from the document and Harry Bailey, though he was angry, continued to do his job as the representative of the bond holders, policing the other section engineers. I am thoroughly convinced that had I accepted Bailey's earlier offer of largess by taking the cash he had offered for expenses at the San Francisco convention, he would have maneuvered me into the position of having to approve this engineering contract. This one instance more than justified the "no gifts" policy. It also helped me decide against taking honoraria while serving years later in the U.S. Senate.

The no-gifts policy paid off another time. During the governor's campaign, Boots Adams, chairman and chief executive officer of the Phillips Petroleum Company, had not been visible in support of my campaign. I had the distinct impression he was lukewarm towards me at best. However, shortly after the election, Boots Adams called to congratulate me. During the conversation he mentioned his impression that the campaign had been especially arduous and that probably my family and I were exhausted. He said he had a fine winter home in Ft. Lauderdale, Florida, where he kept a domestic staff year-round. Also, he owned a boat and kept a crew on call. He offered to send the company's jet to pick up the Bellmon family and take us to Ft. Lauderdale for a two-week vacation at his winter home. Naturally, it was a tempting offer, but having made the commitment not to take gifts, I immediately thanked him and declined.

Many months later, Frank Lyons, who was state highway director, called for an appointment. I asked him what he wanted to talk about and he said it was a highway project. I reminded Frank I had created a bipartisan highway commission and had left highway decisions in their hands to keep politics out of the highway system. In the previous administration, it was alleged that bridges and roads had often been traded to legislators for votes. I told Frank I did not want to hear about his project. He replied, "You need to hear about this one." So I told him to come over. Frank brought a map showing Highway 75 that ran north of Bartlesville to Dewey. About two miles north of Bartlesville there is another highway called Highway 75D that runs a mile west, a mile north and a mile east. He pointed out that at the northwest corner of Highway 75D was Boots Adams's home and that Boots had begun to pressure the highway department to get this three-mile section of Highway 75D, which really amounted to a private drive, resurfaced at state expense. I told Frank to decline the request.

My good relationship with Harry Bailey continued over the years. When I ran for the U.S. Senate in 1968, Harry's efforts probably produced more campaign contributions than the efforts of any other individual. He seemed to have a personal animosity toward Senator Mike

Monroney because he had been critical of our turnpike construction program. Bailey went all out to see that Mike was retired from the Senate. His opposition to Monroney was true to Bailey's character: he supported those he liked and fought bitterly and effectively against those he disliked. Harry Bailey insisted on making all the campaign contributions to me face-to-face so that I would be certain to know where the money came from. As badly as we needed money, I hated to go to Harry and receive the checks, but I always did and so far as I know, there was nothing wrong, either legally or ethically, about what he was doing.

I do not know how much money he got from those who had held contracts for engineering or construction of turnpikes, from suppliers of materials, or from others who respected him and looked to him for political advice. There was no way I could do favors for these people as a U.S. senator; the contributions were more a vote of thanks for past support of the turnpike program. Perhaps $15,000 to $20,000 came in through Harry and it was very helpful to me in my U.S. Senate election effort.

After the election, Harry Bailey became our most prolific and persistent correspondent. It turned out that aside from our agreement on turnpike programs, Harry and I had not much in common so far as the philosophy of government was concerned. His approach to federal policies, I felt, was narrow, callous toward many groups of society, and thoroughly unworkable from a practical or political standpoint. His letters came so often that even though I generally dictated a reply, I waited until several accumulated and answered them all at once. Gradually, our relationship deteriorated and I do not believe Harry participated in the 1974 Senate campaign.

Another thing that grew out of my association with Harry Bailey was a great dislike for the Internal Revenue Service. The IRS took after Harry Bailey in what I felt was a politically inspired attack. They kept him in court and forced him to pay large sums for legal and accounting services over trivial irregularities in his income tax. The result of this experience caused me to introduce an amendment into a tax reform bill giving taxpayers authority to recover from the federal government costs of attorney fees in case they challenge the decision of the IRS successfully and win in court. This provision became law. It was obvious to me that if the IRS chooses to do so, it can virtually destroy an innocent citizen or business person. It was my hope to reduce this excessive power.

When Harry Bailey died, he was widely lauded in accounts of his life for his work as an engineer and as the "father of the Oklahoma Turnpike System." These tributes were well-deserved. His complicated makeup embodied the essential qualities necessary for the success of a program as complex and as controversial as the Oklahoma Turnpike System.

Probably of all the people I have known in government, state Welfare Director Lloyd Rader was the most complex, most controversial, most self-confident, and most difficult to work with. My relationship with him was a lesson in the way things in government are done.

When I was a candidate for governor, a mutual friend, Martin Garber, who had worked with Rader during the Eisenhower administration, became concerned I was going to attack the welfare program. At his insistence, I attended a meeting he had arranged with Rader. It took place about five-thirty in the afternoon in Rader's cluttered, crowded office in the Jim Thorpe Building. Lloyd's office was on the upper floor and it was obvious the facilities were totally inadequate. Rader and Garber spent four hours explaining in detail the function and financing of the state's welfare programs. They gave me far more information than I could absorb or retain, but I began to feel respect and even admiration for Rader replacing the suspicion I had harbored about him.

After my election, I began to put together a state budget. To my horror, I discovered that my predecessor and the legislature had appropriated all available funds plus $13.5 million against what was called the "unanticipated surplus." After these bills were paid, there was going to be virtually no new money available to begin operation of a new fiscal year. I was either going to be forced to use the same unanticipated surplus gimmick or present an extremely austere budget. At that time, teachers were advocating strongly for a pay increase and there were the usual pressures for more dollars for highways, mental health, higher education, and all the rest. The suspicion had long been circulated in political circles that, due to his monopoly on the earmarked sales tax, Lloyd Rader had built up a substantial surplus. I decided to go see Lloyd and try to find out whether or not his agency had a surplus and whether or not it might be available for allocation to other agencies.

Lloyd's department had been moved to the new Sequoyah building. I went to see him and we had another four-hour conversation. Someone said that if you asked Lloyd Rader the time of day, he would explain how to build a clock. That was the experience I had with him, not once, but time after time. That afternoon, he went through his agency's complicated finances in great detail. Mr. Rader felt it necessary for the welfare department to have enough money in the bank at the end of every payment cycle to pay at least one additional month's checks to welfare recipients in case the federal matching funds were late or for some reason unavailable. However, he also had another significant amount he was holding for other contingencies. I came away with the feeling there was something like $13,000,000 the welfare department could readily give up without hampering its operation and drew the conclusion that there was a possibility of getting part of it to alleviate the state's severe economic crunch.

At the next day's news conference, I made this announcement. The reporters were delighted because they felt I was wrong. They raced to Rader's office expecting him to deny the existence of these funds and in this way put the governor-elect in an extremely embarrassing situation. To their amazement, Lloyd protected me. When reporters confronted Lloyd with my pronouncement, he was careful not to contradict what I had said, though later he told me he was absolutely appalled at the revelation I had made. He did not agree with me but he was diplomatic enough to avoid the kind of confrontation which might have doomed my administration to an early failure. The result of the flap over the so-called "welfare surplus" was that $11,000,000 of welfare funds were made available to other state programs. We appropriated $4,000,000 to be used for welfare-related activities carried on by other departments. In addition, two state schools, the School for the Blind and the School for the Deaf, and the mental retardation program were transferred to the welfare department.

The mental retardation program had been an orphan. There was the feeling that mental health and mental retardation could be dealt with in the same way. The result was that our so-called "schools for the mentally retarded" were warehouses for hundreds of mentally retarded people. I visited those "schools" and found large concrete block storehouse-like buildings reeking with the smell of urine, with one bunk jammed in as close as possible to the next, an overworked staff simply trying to keep individuals fed and clean. It was one of the most sickening sights I have ever seen and I made up my mind to try to change the situation. With Lloyd's help, the legislature was convinced mental retardation should be separate from mental health because the problems and solutions were different. At the time the transfer was made, there was a backlog of 1,500 applications from families attempting to get children into state schools for the mentally retarded, but there was no room. The waiting period was nearly three years. Governor Howard Edmondson had recognized the problem and his administration had provided funding to build the new Hissom Center in Sand Springs, under construction when my term began. Under Lloyd's guidance, additional funding was provided existing state schools for the mentally retarded. Using matching funds which Lloyd secured from the federal government, state school residents were evaluated and those who could be trained were kept in state schools; those not trainable were transferred to private, smaller nursing homes. As a result, the long waiting period to get a mentally retarded child in a state school was shortened to the few days the admission process required.

During the scrap over the budget and the mental retardation program, I came to understand Rader's legislative technique. His idea was not to pass a bill by a simple majority but to get every single legislator to support every proposal he brought forth. While he did not always succeed, use of patronage and political favors made certain that when Lloyd Rader brought forth legislation, it would become law. He was careful to obtain support and early participation of key legislators and I never knew him to fail in a legislative fight.

After the legislature adjourned and the mental retardation transition began, troubles erupted at the Hissom Center. Either the contractors, engineers, and architects the Edmondson administration had engaged didn't cooperate with each other or they were incompetent. For instance, electrical lines were put underground before ditches for water lines and plumbing were dug. Frequently the ditching machines cut through electrical transmission lines which then had to be replaced. The sewage treatment plant was a concrete structure below ground level with pumps, electrical motors, and controls. Over the months after it was built, but before it was put into regular use, water seeped in and completely filled the building. The mechanical equipment was submerged for a considerable length of time. The whole thing had to be replaced. The design of the buildings was worked out by individuals who seemed to have little knowledge of the behavior of the mentally retarded. While the buildings were attractive, they were not practical. For instance, glass windows were installed at the floor level. This made it easy for children to kick the glass until it broke, often with injury to the child. Heating ducts were put in the floor. Children would stand over the ducts to feel the warm air but this caused them to relieve themselves so that the cottages began to smell like outhouses. In addition, there were many structural problems which had to be remedied. Rather than stir up a big fuss and bring on law suits, Lloyd simply took a substantial amount of money out of other operating funds and made necessary repairs and renovations at Hissom.

Lloyd Rader brought crisis after crisis to my attention. In fact, it seemed that every dealing I had with Lloyd was a crisis. During this time, Lloyd had a proclivity for coming to my office about 5:30 p.m. and staying to discuss problems until late at night. I usually went to the office about 6 a.m. and by 6 p.m., I was ready to go home. It was a terrific struggle for me to stay alert while he described his problems in minute detail. I had the same experience when he called on the phone late in the day. It was a struggle to keep from falling asleep, and I am not sure I always succeeded. I finally started going to his office for meetings so that when I had all I could absorb, I could give excuses and go home.

After Lloyd worked it out so I could have the money from his funds to help with the state budget, it became difficult for me to decline any of his requests. In fact, he frequently reminded me (well past my term as governor) of his support. Over the years, I believe he got his money's worth — and then some. One of the first things Lloyd came to me about was the appointment of the members of his board. The State Welfare Commission was a constitutional board with members serving nine-year terms. They were removed only for cause. The commission hired the director. In effect, Lloyd Rader could stay in office as long as his commission wanted him. This put him out of reach of the governor, which was probably a good thing. Naturally, the appointment of board members was of vital interest to Lloyd.

The first time I realized how obligated Lloyd felt I was over the $11,000,000 transfer was when the term of his first board member expired. I had planned to change members of the commission because I felt he needed more Republican influences. (The chairman of the board, an Edmondson appointee, was a Republican.) Also, I felt the welfare programs had become somewhat incestuous and needed new ideas. After I started discussing the matter with Lloyd, it became obvious that no change would be tolerated. I reappointed the old member only after Lloyd agreed that when other vacancies occurred, he would welcome the appointment of some Republicans. When I was elected governor, I had not promised people jobs. Rader had dealt with many governors and expected me to put the arm on him for certain jobs. When this did not happen, Lloyd finally came and asked me if I was not going to ask for patronage. When I told him I was not, he asked me to find him a couple of people to fill specific jobs. I placed two people with him who turned out to be some of his favorite employees. From that point, on the rare occasions when I needed to place people in patronage positions, Lloyd was extremely cooperative.

A few months after I had been elected, Lloyd's father became ill and died. Without realizing the significance of my decision, I decided to go to the funeral. Lloyd was overwhelmed by my attendance and insisted I go to their home and meet his mother. With some trepidation, I went and struck up a warm friendship with Mrs. Rader that lasted until her death in 1976. Whether or not Lloyd had arranged it, Mrs. Rader had my photograph on her piano when I got there and she repeated many complimentary things Lloyd had told her about me.

Vera Adler was Lloyd's secretary and his strong right hand. In her forties, from Choctaw, she was a bright and talented person and sometimes I wondered whether Lloyd told Vera what to do or whether it was the other way around. A whiz at shorthand, she had a court reporter's ability to take down every conversation of consequence in a meeting or interview and reproduce records showing precisely what had been agreed to, frequently preventing disagreements.

Rader and I served as members of the Oklahoma Capitol Improvement Authority. This was the body the legislature had created to build badly-needed state office space. Under Oklahoma law, it was illegal for the state to spend more money than it took in. Considering the austere budgeting condition Howard Edmondson and I both faced, there were no funds to build state offices even though the state was renting space from private owners and even though the office spaces were jammed to the point of impairing productivity. Someone in the Edmondson administration came up with the idea of creating a Capitol Improvement Authority empowered to borrow money from the state treasurer, build needed office buildings, lease the buildings to the state agencies, and use the rent money the state had been paying to property owners to pay off the bonds. While it probably took some winking at the constitution, the Supreme Court held the scheme to be constitutional and the board went into business. By the time I came on the scene, both the Will Rogers and Sequoyah buildings were built and our duties were to fix rents, take care of existing and outstanding contracts, and generally serve as landlords. There were many tense and difficult times, largely because of the intransigence of the attorney general, Charlie Nesbitt. But by and large the work of the Capitol Improvement Authority went smoothly with Rader, Ted Parkinson from the state Board of Public Affairs, and myself as the active participants. Vera Adler took minutes in great detail and frequently made suggestions on her own that were superior to those coming from the regular members. My admiration for Vera was equal to the strong admiration I felt for Lloyd Rader.

An insight into Lloyd Rader and government came when he informed me that a representative of the USDA was coming from Dallas to discuss starting a food stamp program in Oklahoma. Choctaw and Pushmataha counties had been selected by the USDA as pilot counties to switch from commodities to food stamps. The commodity program was under attack because county commissioners who administered the program locally would personally hand out packages of commodities to each recipient. The impression was that the county commissioners were giving the food and other necessities to constituents. This proved to be one of the greatest empire-building arrangements that county and local government had ever seen. In fact, campaign advertisements put out by some county commissioners said that unless these commissioners were reelected, the commodity program would stop. It was true that counties did put out a small amount of money for warehousing and transporting commodities, but the food was provided by federal funds.

Lloyd informed me he did not want to see the food stamp program started. He felt the cost of administering stamps would be excessive, that abuses would be serious, and that Oklahoma was better off staying with the commodity arrangements in spite of their obvious shortcomings. I knew little about either stamps or commodities except for the bad press and while I argued with him for a time, I finally realized Lloyd had made up his mind and that I probably was powerless to do anything to change it. I agreed to oppose the food stamp program when the federal officials came to see us. At this point, Lloyd gave me a valuable lesson in government operation. "No, that's not the way to do it," he said. "If you oppose the food stamp program, this official will go to the newspapers and put out statements making it sound as if you are heartless and against the poor. A better approach is to insist the program be made so fat that the feds will not accept it and therefore we can make it look like they are the ones who are heartless and against the poor."

The federal proposition was that if a family was entitled to one hundred dollars worth of food stamps, they could purchase these stamps for twenty-five dollars. Lloyd's suggestion was that we contend this was too hard on poor people and that we say that the hundred dollars worth of food stamps should be purchased for five dollars. He was convinced that the federal officials would not agree to these terms and that Oklahoma would not have a food stamp program at least for the immediate future. During the meeting the next day, I turned the matter over to Lloyd except for the key point that we felt the price tag was too high. The federal official was astounded at our reaction and promised to go back and take it up with higher authorities. We never heard from her again.

My relationship with Rader has to be looked upon as one of the key reasons for whatever successes I had as governor. He provided the funds which made it possible for me to have a realistic program the first two years I was in office, he supervised the transition of the mentally retarded program from one that was a disaster to one that served families better, and he helped me successfully shepherd many bills through the legislature that otherwise would have been doomed. In addition, he was cooperative in matters of joint concern and served as kind of a father confessor when I needed knowledge about individuals. He had a deeper and broader understanding of government operations than anyone else I ever worked with. I came to have almost unlimited admiration for his ability to get things done.

In the 1960s, Oklahoma had a long ballot. Some twenty-six state officials were elected at the time I was elected governor. These people varied in ability and dedication to duty from the sublime to the ridiculous. One of the most able and dedicated among the lot was Dr. Oliver

Hodge, who had served twenty years as State Superintendent of Public Instruction. It wasn't long after I was elected that I became aware of Dr. Hodge's ability and high character. I decided that rather than try to work with Furman Phillips and the Oklahoma Education Association that had so violently opposed me during the campaign, I would conduct matters relating to education through the Office of the State Superintendent and Dr. Hodge. I announced this at a news conference and received a virulent attack from Phillips. I later learned that Dr. Hodge did not care much for Furman Phillips either and that he was delighted with my decision. He felt, properly, that the people of Oklahoma spoke when they chose the state superintendent and that Phillips represented only one segment of those concerned with the state's education needs.

While I served on several boards and commissions with Dr. Hodge, our most regular and important association was as members of the School Land Commission. Under the law, the governor was chairman of the commission but traditionally, the state superintendent served in this capacity and I was pleased to have Dr. Hodge continue. Income from rent of the 800,000 acres of farm lands the commission controlled, bonuses and royalties received for oil leases, interest received on school land loans, and bonds the commission held were available to assist in paying for the operation of the state's school system.

Soon after election, Dr. Hodge came to see me and told me the director of the commission, put in office at the insistence of Governor Edmondson, was incompetent. He recommended I begin to look for a replacement. He told me he was not concerned about the politics of a new director, he simply wanted someone who was honest and cooperative, someone who could deal effectively with the lessees and the legislature, and someone who knew enough about land to make intelligent decisions. I recommended the appointment of Bill Sharp, a farmer-rancher from Nowata County who had on two occasions run for Congress against Ed Edmondson. Dr. Hodge persuaded others on the commission to approve Bill and he was installed.

The operation of the School Land Commission was one of the most successful activities of my administration. We cleaned up operation of the agency, brought about more realistic leasing policies and rates for the land that we owned, and generally carried on a thoroughly competent and honest administration. Dr. Hodge was pleased with the additional revenue the schools received and also with the fact that he could look with pride at the operation which many times during his long tenure had been run in a shabby fashion.

As a result of our association, Dr. Hodge and I became close personal friends and on occasion he felt free to give me advice. One of these occasions was after the legislature had passed a bill giving Oklahoma's teachers a $1,000-a-year pay increase when there was not one penny available in the treasury to pay the costs. Hodge suggested I sign the bill and then turn down the tax increase that would have to follow to meet the demands of the raise. I could not understand this reasoning. If I had signed the pay raise bill I would have felt honor-bound to sign a tax bill. I felt forced to veto the bill which promised the raise. The teachers were furious when I vetoed the bill; nine hundred or more came to the governor's office to protest. However, I believe that generally people across the state agreed with my position. Dr. Hodge apparently heard only from teachers. I had made the pledge during my campaign that I was determined to keep: "No New Taxes." The goal was to eliminate waste in government, reducing costs to taxpayers, thereby making Oklahoma a more attractive place for new industry. Had I signed the pay raise and the tax increase which would have followed, I would have broken my pledge.

When I first addressed a joint session of the legislature, I felt it necessary to lay down some ground rules so we could work together effectively. One statement I made was on the futility and counter-productivity of holding grudges. At the same time there was need for legislators to realize that I was not so gullible that I could be lied to time after time. I said that the rule would be, "Forgive, but remember." It has proven to be a useful policy ever since.

J.D. McCarty was a member of the Oklahoma House of Representatives in 1947 when I was also a member. He was a fairly new, young legislator and referred to himself as a member of the "knot hole gang" — a term he and others in his group used to indicate they were on the outside looking in. Over the years, J.D. became the Oklahoma prototype of the worst kind of politician. As Speaker of the House, he became loud, fat, power-mad, and heavy-handed in his dealing with those over whom he could exert either influence or authority. After my election, I realized it was essential for me to get along with both President of the Senate Roy Boecher and J.D. McCarty, Speaker of the House. Within a week after the election, I arranged breakfast with Boecher and McCarty where I invited them to make suggestions for the budget and the legislative program. They both declined to make suggestions, saying they were legislators and Democrats and they felt I should develop my own proposals without any effort to work cooperatively. They pledged they would be helpful passing legislation they felt was good for the state but that I need not take their concerns or desires under consideration in preparing my own package of legislation.

Since the governor's race had been run on basically one issue, "no new taxes," little thought had been given to preparing a legislative program. It came as somewhat of a shock when I discovered the legislative leadership expected me to present a package of proposals. One was quickly patched together for presentation to the legislature but it received little attention, which is probably what it deserved. I believed the governor's job was to be the state's chief administration officer, not to propose new legislation. I felt that was the job of the legislature, though obviously it was a shared responsibility and I was negligent in not being better prepared.

The breakfasts with Boecher and McCarty continued infrequently through much of the first legislative session. There were also meetings with both men, together and individually, often in J.D.'s suite in the old Biltmore Hotel, sometimes in restaurants near the capitol, and on occasion in my office. When we were together our relationship was outwardly cordial and there was never a time I could not call J.D. and talk with him in confidence and with candor. The relationship with Senator Boecher was even better, bordering on personal warmth.

J.D. McCarty's control over the House of Representatives was absolute. Anytime he took the rostrum and pointed his thumbs upwards, the matter under consideration passed with a sizable majority. Anytime he made the opposite gesture, thumbs down, the measure failed. In dealing with the state Senate, it was necessary to deal with a majority of the forty-four members. In dealing with the House, there was no point in dealing with anyone except J.D. Frequently, J.D. would become incensed at some action or inaction on my part. On these occasions, he was an easy mark for reporters and television cameramen. They would go to his office either voluntarily or at his summons and receive or produce a McCarty tirade. His televised attacks on me were generally vitriolic and verbose and the more he talked, the more agitated he became. As his wrath and the decibels increased, J.D. would shake his head, causing his heavy jowls to tremble in a particularly ominous way.

He was a wonderful public political enemy. Often, without knowing what had happened in the Speaker's office, I would go to a news conference and be confronted with the fact that the Speaker had that very hour launched another assault against me. So far as I could, I made the most modest possible rejoinder to try to turn away the wrath. The result was that during the six o'clock news there was a sharp contrast between the governor's calm appearance and the Speaker's tantrums. As the months went on, I realized that if the governor needed an enemy, J.D. was perfectly cast for the part. The contrast between J.D. and myself was an asset and probably contributed much to whatever political success I had in retaining public support as governor.

The fact is, however, that J.D. was by far the more powerful person in Oklahoma government during the first two years I was in office. He was in the same class as Lloyd Rader. He had the House of Representatives totally under his control, was highly regarded by many business interests in the state, and had a better understanding of government than I had at that time. J.D. had some qualities I admired and tried to utilize. He was extremely sympathetic toward the problems of the mentally retarded and the physically handicapped. He was the godfather of Central State Mental Hospital in Norman and could work closely with Lloyd Rader.

In 1964, Senator Roy Boecher declined to run again for Senate President Pro Tempore. A bitter contest developed between Senator Clem McSpadden and Senator Leroy McClendon for the Senate presidency. McClendon was backed by southeastern Oklahoma members, including powerful Senator Gene Stipe. J.D. chose to get involved in this Senate contest. His apparent plan was to place his choice in the Senate presidency and in this way control both houses. He had not been able to do this with Roy Boecher, making it possible for me to help head off many legislative propositions I felt were unwise. When the votes were counted, McSpadden won, and the relationship between him and McCarty was thereafter extremely sour. This was to the governor's advantage because it was possible to play McSpadden against McCarty and secure the legislative compromises which often were essential.

The one time these two got together was when the Oklahoma Education Association and supporters of higher education convinced the legislature to pass a resolution calling for a statewide vote on a proposition to raise the state sales tax from two to three percent. Both McSpadden and McCarty went all out to secure votes for this proposition. I never understood why the two old pros would put their heads on the chopping block over such an obviously unpopular proposition. The referendum went down by a sizable majority and both legislators' power was damaged. The loss may have contributed to McSpadden's defeat later when he ran for governor. It also eroded McCarty's support in the legislature, though it certainly did not keep him from being king of the mountain in the 1965 session.

The defeat of the sales tax proposition increased the bitterness between McCarty and McSpadden. McSpadden felt he had been conned by McCarty and felt even more unkindly toward the Speaker than previously. In 1966, an undertaker from Capitol Hill named Vondel Smith came to my office and announced that Oklahoma County Republican Chairman Al Snipes had convinced Vondel to run against J.D. While his chances were not good, I did what I could to support his election, including raising a sizable amount of campaign money. Vondel proved to be an aggressive and effective campaigner.

On the night of the election, my family and I were guests of Amber and Bill Robinson. One of the first election return announcements was that J.D. had been defeated. That was a happy moment in my political life. It reassured me of the effectiveness of the elective process and the judgment of rank-and-file voters. Apparently, when given a choice, they were willing to vote out their powerful representative and take a chance on an untried person even though they knew he could not serve their selfish interests as well as J.D. had.

Soon after his defeat, J.D. became the object of an Internal Revenue Service investigation. He was accused of failing to report certain income. Primarily, the case involved $12,000 a Chamber of Commerce had turned over to J.D. This and perhaps other sums were made available to him so he could use them to influence members of the House. Stories had circulated for a long time that any member who had financial difficulties could go to J.D. to get bills paid, get out of scrapes, or receive other kinds of favors. The Chamber of Commerce appeared to have been using J.D. to gain control over the legislature so that propositions important to it would receive favorable action. J.D. was found guilty and sentenced to serve time in a federal prison in Texas. At the time, an F.B.I. agent told me that the life expectancy of a powerful public official convicted and jailed for a crime was less than seven years. It proved to be true in this case. J.D. served several months before he was paroled. He came back to Oklahoma City and quietly went into the insurance business.

After I was elected to the U.S. Senate, I was asked to help secure a full pardon for J.D. While I did not have direct responsibility for pardoning, I opposed the idea because I still considered J.D. a sinister and potentially dangerous political power in the state. Also, the five years normally required for pardon consideration had not run, and it would have been awkward to have participated in such action. In 1973, I was again approached to recommend this pardon and again I declined. As far as I am concerned, keeping J.D. McCarty out of active political roles may be one of the best things the Internal Revenue Service ever did for Oklahoma.

Prior to my election, Senator Roy Boecher had been elected by the Democratic members of the state Senate as President Pro Tempore. Once I became governor, I worked much more with Boecher than with McCarty and had more success with the Senate than with the House. Boecher was especially supportive in my efforts to unearmark the $11 million of sales tax which we put into the mental retardation and other funds. He was not strong for welfare and his county was not one of the low income areas, so it was easy for him to be supportive. Without Senator Boecher's support I doubt we could have succeeded. Time after time Roy was helpful. He made it possible for me to get control of the State Board of Agriculture so we could install a new president and a new administrator of that agency. He helped me pass many bills through the Senate, assisted with appropriation matters, and was frequently in my office to advise me about one matter or another. My dependence upon him grew stronger and stronger.

One day late in the first legislative session, after I had benefitted from numerous Boecher favors, the senator invited me to have breakfast with him and a friend at the Ramada Inn. The invitation seemed somewhat mysterious but I had no choice but to accept. The other guest turned out to be Quentin Little, a wealthy Ardmore oil man who was strongly supportive of the O.U. football team. He had been a member of the O.U. Board of Regents appointed by Governor Raymond Gary. Quentin had been removed from the board by Governor Howard Edmondson and was not someone I even remotely would have considered for an appointment to the O.U. Board. He was not well educated and did not seem to have a genuine interest in education. He was interested in football and supported the team generously. During breakfast, both Boecher and Little expressed a great desire for me to put Quentin back on the Board of Regents. They were emphatic about what they considered to be the injustice done to Little by former Governor Edmondson. Serving again on the O.U. Board would remove a blemish on his career that Little felt was hurting his reputation.

Senator Boecher had me in a box. He had helped in extraordinary ways to assure the success of my administration and championed my position in many legislative battles, so he had me in his debt. I talked to Dr. George Cross, president of O.U. While Cross was not enthusiastic, he did agree to Little's service on the board and the appointment was made. It received much criticism in the newspapers and was generally described as a Bellmon payoff for Raymond Gary. The fact was that I had declined to appoint Little when Gary had recommended it earlier. It was because I felt indebted to Roy Boecher that I got myself in a position where I had to agree. The experience made me doubly wary of accepting favors or becoming close to anyone with power in the legislative arena.

Al Nichols, Democratic state senator of Wewoka, had served Oklahoma government as long as any person in state history. He was a strong and highly partisan Democrat but I came to have both respect and affection for Al. His was not a forceful personality. In fact, he was mild and reticent, spoke infrequently, and with some difficulty. However, once you gained Al's friendship, he was both loyal and loquacious. When problems developed in the legislature that Al felt I needed to know about, he would come to my office. We had many friendly and thoroughly entertaining conversations. Towards the end of the term, Al came to see me one day and told me he had informed his Democratic colleagues that in his judgment I was "dumb—dumb like a fox" and that the Democrats had created a "political Frankenstein" in allowing me to be elected and to complete my term with some degree of success. He was trying to be complimentary.

Al Nichols was also perhaps the best living raconteur concerning a former governor, the legendary "Alfalfa Bill" Murray. In Oklahoma's fairly brief history we have produced a few really colorful political figures. Of these, Bill Murray is by far the most flamboyant. He served as a member of the Oklahoma Constitutional Convention; he was elected governor in the depths of the Depression and performed this arduous duty under the most difficult circumstances; he became a national figure when he ran as a Democrat for the presidency. He remained throughout his life a person of modest means and, though somewhat uncouth and controversial, was never touched in any way by scandal.

When I was in the legislature, Bill had written a small book about the proposed partition of Palestine. It seemed like an interesting souvenir. When Bill came on the floor of the House selling his book for a dollar a copy, I told him I would take one if he would autograph it. The old man sat down in my seat and with great flourish wrote his name. He shaded each letter so that the signature was truly a work of art. As he handed me the signed copy of his book, he said, "Son, there was a time when that signature could save a man's life." He was referring to a governor's power to commute the death sentence. At that moment, I had no thought that at some point in the future I would be able to make the same statement. After buying the book, I took out my billfold and found that I had only a ten dollar bill. I gave him the ten dollar bill whereupon Bill said, "Fine, I'll give you nine more books." And he did.

When Bill Murray had run for governor, Al Nichols was a prominent member of the state Senate. Another member of the Senate, Tom Anglin, of Holdenville, was also running. Since Al and Tom lived in adjoining counties, Al supported Tom in the primary and runoff. Anglin lost. After Murray was nominated, Nichols realized he needed to repair his fences and form a working relationship with the soon-to-be governor. He got up his courage, requested an appointment with the governor-elect and timidly went into his presence. As their meeting began, Al explained, "Now Governor, I am not going to lie to you. I was not for you in the primary and I was not for you in the runoff. I had another candidate, but my candidate has lost and you won. I am now going to be in the Senate and you are going to be governor and I want to work with you. You can count on me to help you every time you are right."

At this point, Bill Murray cleared his throat with a great "hrrummph" and said, "Hell, Senator, I don't need your help when I'm right." There is a great deal of political truth in that conclusion.

Roy Schoeb was a successful automobile dealer and farmer who lived north of Cherokee on the Salt Fork River. Roy was active in the Republican party in northwestern Oklahoma and one of those I leaned on hardest in getting the party organized in his section of the state. In 1962, Roy filed for the state Senate and was elected. We had run our campaigns closely together in Alfalfa and Major counties and our relationship was very good. When Roy was sworn into the Senate he exhibited the same "take-over" tendencies he had used successfully in both business and agriculture. He came regularly to the governor's office with a variety of suggestions and criticisms and wanted far more responsibility and participation than is normal for members of the legislature. The situation between Roy and myself grew increasingly tense.

It came to a head following the controversy over the election of a Republican state chairman. He came to my office and proceeded to recite for me several blunders which he felt I had made as governor, concluding that my performance in office up to that time had demonstrated my lack of capacity to handle the job. He further stated that, as the state's first Republican governor, a great deal depended upon my performance and that my success could only be assured if I would change the way the office was being operated. His solution to my alleged incompetence was that I should appoint a board of directors that he volunteered to head. This board would be made up of seven members chosen by me with Roy's concurrence. It would be called in for consultation every time I had a difficult decision to make. At the moment Roy made the suggestion, I looked upon it as comical. However, after he left, I realized the huge insult he had paid me. I was burned up and from that point on there was very little communication between the senator and myself. After his first term, his district was reapportioned and he lost his seat. During my second campaign for the U.S. Senate, I called on Roy, who was then in his seventies, and our relationship was restored to a far more cordial basis.

Frequently when I went to Tulsa to attend meetings, I would be accosted by one of the most interesting and unusual characters I've ever met. His name was Akos Ludasay. He was an elderly Hungarian refugee who had come to the United States following the 1954 Hungarian revolution. Apparently Akos had been a brilliant scientist in his home country, but somewhere along the line his mind had slipped. He now prided himself in being an artist as well as a designer of moon rocket ships. Akos's appearance was anything but striking. He was always poorly dressed, unshaven, had many missing teeth, and spoke with a heavy accent at great speed and voracity. The result was that he sprayed saliva into the face of whomever he was addressing. Often when I was in Tulsa shaking hands with well-wishers who came to speak to me, Akos Ludasay would elbow his way through the group and come to the head of the line. He would carry a recently completed painting wrapped in butcher paper and tied with binder twine. Speaking and spraying, he would unwrap the painting, hold it up for me to admire, ask me to buy it from him (usually for $35) and then when I refused, ask me to take it to the mansion, hang it on the wall, and see if I could not develop an attachment for it.

Akos owned some artistic talent. The subjects he painted were frequently offbeat. He once did a painting called "While George Washington Waters His Horse, Necking Occurs." The painting was attractive. It showed a man dressed in a blue military uniform, sitting on a horse with the horse's head down drinking water from a stream. Obviously, this was "While George Washington Waters His Horse." The "Necking Occurs" part only became obvious when the painting was turned upside down. What appeared to be clouds when the painting was upright turned out to be a couple embracing. Akos presented me with many paintings and I never bought any of them. He often attached the ribbons he had won at art shows and sometimes attached the empty tubes of paints he had used in creating his masterpieces.

Also, from time to time Akos would present me with an intricate drawing of a space ship. This drawing would cover as many as ten sheets of typing paper taped together. The entire space would be covered with intricate formulas and drawings which were absolutely mind-boggling. I have no idea whether they made engineering or scientific sense but they were certainly a subject of bewilderment and astonishment for all who saw them. Akos sometimes attached the empty ink bottles and even the ink cartons to the drawings when he gave them to me.

Over the years, I accumulated many Akos Ludasay paintings and when it was time to leave the mansion we were in a quandary as to what to do with them. We did not care to present them to the O.S.U. library and give the impression that we had deliberately collected such an oddball assembly of art. On the other hand, they had been a source of amusement to those few who had seen them. We finally decided to simply leave them in the attic of the mansion and let someone else worry about the problem. I don't know what happened to them, but they were gone by the time we moved back into the governor's mansion in 1987. I am a little sorry we didn't arrange to put them into proper hands, though I have no idea where that might have been. I never saw Akos again after my first term as governor. Perhaps he began showering his favors upon another lucky politico.

After I had served in the governor's office for a few months, Irvin Bollenbach began to talk to me about the possibility of coming to his ranch near Kingfisher for opening day of dove season. Growing up, I had never really felt any desire to shoot dove or quail. In fact, my mother always considered both dove and quail songbirds so I felt protective of them. However, Irvin finally convinced me I should come to his ranch for opening day of dove season. To my surprise, when I arrived, there were several prominent business leaders present, including publisher Ed Gaylord, who was also getting his first taste of the pleasures of dove hunting.

I was taken about five miles northwest of Kingfisher and stationed near a field where hundreds of doves were feeding. The only shotgun I owned was an old L.C. Smith field grade double-barreled twelve-gauge. I thought it was quite a good shotgun but the rest of those in the party of some fifteen people made fun of my old blunderbuss. My assigned position was near a fence. The rest of the group stationed themselves nearby to watch the fun as I tried to bring down the fast-flying, elusive birds. The doves were flying high and fast that day and they seemed to me to be hard to hit. But there were lots of them and after an hour of heavy shooting, I had seventeen birds on the ground. My old shotgun got so hot from the rapid fire that it was sometimes difficult to hold. Irvin and the other hunters were surprised at my success. They also had a lot of fun with me since, unbeknownst to me, there was a bag limit of twelve. The day established my marksmanship with Irvin and Ed Gaylord. The hunting experience, plus the dinner and card game that followed, enabled me to become good friends with Ed. This friendship proved to be pleasant and valuable to me as the years went on.

Each year, Irvin invited neighbors, family members, and friends for opening day of both dove and quail seasons. His guests usually included Ed Gaylord and several officers of the Oklahoma Publishing Company. Also in attendance would be Don Kennedy of OG&E; Chuck Vose of First National Bank; Ed Joullian of Mustang Fuel Company; Dr. Rainey Williams, an Oklahoma City physician; and Dr. Burge Greene, a relative, of Stilwell. Opening days were always pleasant experiences. They usually began with hunters gathered at the Bollenbach home in Kingfisher. We would be dispatched to whatever hunting site Irvin had selected for us. Lunch was served at a cabin on the ranch. After the hunt, we would return to the home where refreshments were served and birds were dressed and bagged. Eloise would serve one of her delicious home-cooked meals or the group would go to a local steak house. Both at home in Kingfisher and at the cabin on the ranch, Irvin kept player pianos. He owned a large selection of old songs. On almost every occasion, the program for the day would include a half-hour session with Irvin at the player piano accompanied by group singing.

When in 1967 the Grand National Quail Hunt was organized, Irvin agreed to make his ranch available for the first hunt. He divided the ranch into about twenty hunting areas and assigned a group of hunters with their dog handlers to each tract. The Grand National guests included many people prominent in business, entertainment, sports, and government. A large bonfire was lighted in front of the cabin. Bales of straw were positioned so that guests could be seated while having dinner. It was the kind of outdoor experience many of the guests had never enjoyed and the day certainly gave a good impression of Oklahoma friendship and hospitality to those who participated. The purpose of the Grand National was to help attract leaders into the state, show them a better side of Oklahoma than the "Grapes of Wrath" image. We felt if these people could see Oklahoma as it really was and get to know Oklahomans on a first-name basis, it might attract new business to our state. Once Irvin had shown how it could be done, it was fairly easy to get other landowners to host similar events.

One of my acts as governor was to help create the Oklahoma Aeronautical Commission. The first person I requested to serve on the commission was Irvin Bollenbach. He accepted on the condition that none of the resources of the agency be used to improve the Kingfisher airport, which he owned. The aeronautical commission came to be a highly successful agency and provided guidance and financial support for dozens of smaller airports in the state. Irvin was the commission's moving force from the first.

There are some who criticize politicians for appointing good friends to government positions. In my judgment, these decisions are totally defensible. It is only natural for a politician to want people he can trust in positions of responsibility. In government, loyalty is perhaps as important an element as any. Unfortunately, many highly competent and well-experienced people do not have this essential quality. If a politician fills the spaces he must fill only with professional people who may or may not be attuned to the political atmosphere in which government must be run, the politician can never be sure his flanks are guarded. By putting in people he can trust, he can forget those jobs and concentrate on the balance of his responsibilities. In the final analysis, politics is people, people of all kinds: rich and poor, smart and dumb, honest and dishonest, good and bad. A successful politician has the instinctive ability to see through pretense and to understand the character and motives of others. In this way, dedicated, qualified people can be fitted into positions they are prepared to fill and mismatches can be avoided.

Those who speak of political science do a great disservice to the political process. It is not a science but an art in the same way that mixing form and color to create a landscape is an art. Bob Kerr called political talent "the rarest gift of God." I believe he was correct.

All things considered, serving as governor is a wonderfully exciting, satisfying experience. Governors are where the action is. They can make good things happen. They can make a difference for better or worse. Doors are open to them and their families. They are accepted and welcomed wherever they go, and they go to many interesting places and meet fascinating people, many of whom become life-long friends. There are tough days in a governor's life, but most of the memories are of the good days and fine people who abound.

Two-Term Senator

senator and the president exchange quips at the time Henry invited Nixon to the dedication of the -McLellan Navigation Channel.

NG PAGE, ABOVE: New York Senator Jim Buckley, Bellmon, Michigan Senator Bob Griffin and National blican Chairman George Bush.

NG PAGE, BELOW: Henry held this lunch in the Senate Dining Room to introduce former Secretary of the sury and presidential hopeful John Connally to Tennessee Senator Howard Baker, whom Bellmon hoped ally would consider as a running mate. Russell Long is also with them.

TOP: During the Senate years, Shirley became an active member of the Senate Wives Red Cross Chapter, w hosted The First Lady's Luncheon each year. Here she guides First Lady Pat Nixon and Judy Agnew, wife vice president, through the maze of Senate wives.

BOTTOM: On tour with Alaska Senator Ted Stevens on the island of Yap.

t a meeting with President
Nixon in the Oval Office,
oined by, from left,
Secretary of Interior John
Texas Senator John
cretary of Agriculture Cliff
d White House
nal Liaison Clark
r.

1959, as Noble County
chairman, Henry was
Washington to lunch with
ke Eisenhower and to visit
President Richard Nixon.
irley are pictured here with

Senator Edmund Muskie, chairman of the Senate Budget Committee and Bellmon, ranking minority mem
the new budget process on Meet the Press. Bellmon developed an abiding respect for his Democratic colleag

Nixon and Company

"Less Brilliance, More Wisdom"

The first time I met Richard Nixon was at a fund-raiser in the Skirvin Tower Ballroom in Oklahoma City while he was vice president. It was 1958 and I was serving as Noble County Republican chairman. Suffering from laryngitis, the vice president gave a few opening remarks and turned the major portion of his talk over to his wife, Pat, who handled the assignment well. As the Nixons were leaving the hall, they happened to come down the aisle where I was seated and I had the opportunity to stand and shake hands with both. My impression of Richard Nixon at that time was not particularly good. He seemed soft, indecisive, and weak.

My next association with Nixon came during the presidential race of 1960 and, again, was somewhat negative. During the Republican National Convention in Chicago, where Nixon was nominated to be the Republican candidate for president by a large majority, Nixon's campaign manager called a meeting in his hotel suite of all fifty Republican state chairmen. Many of us were seated on the floor with our backs against the wall. Nixon's chairman went around the room asking us one by one to give our preferences as to whom we wanted for vice president. Many names were mentioned, including Jerry Ford, Thurston Morton, Barry Goldwater, and others. Not one person mentioned the name of Henry Cabot Lodge. After the meeting, as we were leaving the hotel, a newsboy in the lobby was hawking newspapers with the headlines "Nixon Picks Lodge." I was immediately angered by the realization that the meeting in the chairman's suite had been totally cosmetic, that the decision on Lodge had already been made, and that a crude effort had been made to make the state chairmen feel we were having input into the selection process. I deeply resented what I considered to be a transparent political trick and felt let down and disenchanted with the whole process as well as with the candidate.

As Republican State Chairman, vigorously involved in trying to build an organization in all counties of the state, I believed our support of Nixon was the chief selling point. This was particularly true after the Democratic convention nominated John F. Kennedy, who was philosophically unacceptable in our state. We already had succeeded in getting our organization up and running in many counties where Republicans had not previously been organized. I became increasingly confident that Richard Nixon would do extremely well in Oklahoma and perhaps the organization we put together for him would be beneficial to the party for years to come.

Sometime during the summer, I was contacted by Peter Flanagan, then a Democrat in charge of "Volunteers for Nixon," about the establishment of a Nixon volunteer organization in Oklahoma. I explained to Flanagan that such a group was not needed and that it would syphon away party leaders, workers, and contributors. We needed to build the regular party and I opposed establishing this competing and totally temporary organization. Subsequently, other conversations took place between Flanagan and myself. Finally they became bitter exchanges with Flanagan insisting that my resistance was going to cost Nixon the chance to win Oklahoma and perhaps the election. I was equally firm that the regular organization could carry the state handsomely for Nixon. Finally, late in September, without my agreement, a Volunteers for Nixon organization was established. By that time the regular Republican organization was in place and functioning. Also, our campaign budget had been raised and we were in such good shape that the Nixon volunteer organization made little impact. In fact, the regular party used it as a dumping place for the misfits and oddballs who always are drawn to a political campaign headquarters.

At the time of the 1960 campaign, I was badly pressed for money. In my travels as Republican State Chairman, I normally stayed in the cheapest hotels I could find. One of these was the Hudson Hotel in Oklahoma City where it was possible to get a room with a community bath down the hall for two dollars a night. As could be expected, the clientele of the Hudson Hotel was not exactly drawn from the country club set. On the night of the Kennedy-Nixon debate, I was staying in the

Hudson. Since there was no television in the room, I went down to the lobby to watch the broadcast. There were perhaps twenty people there. They were of the income level of people who would stay in a two-dollar-a-night hotel. None of them was aware that I was the Republican State Chairman and therefore vitally interested in their comments about the debate. My own expectations had been that Richard Nixon would absolutely demolish Jack Kennedy. As the debate began, I was appalled at Nixon's appearance and the weak showing he made. Also, the negative comments of people around the room made me realize that blue-collar people were turned on by Kennedy's performance. Until that time I had been supremely confident that Richard Nixon would be elected president. After his showing on the debate, I was much concerned and went to bed feeling he really had his work cut out for him. Also, I made up my mind that if I ever was involved in such a debate, I would take time to be prepared and refreshed for the appearance.

One personally pleasing moment in the 1960 campaign occurred when Nixon came to Oklahoma to attend a meeting and reception in the Municipal Auditorium. Shirley and I noticed our smallest daughter, Ann, who was seven, was missing. Later we found she had maneuvered herself into the group where Nixon was standing and asked him to pose for a photograph. He agreed and we still have the picture of Richard Nixon standing with his arm around Ann, both of them beaming.

Nixon carried Oklahoma with a sixty-two percent majority, the third highest of any state in the Union. The day after the election, Peter Flanagan called to congratulate me and closed by saying he wished the country had more stubborn state chairmen who stood their ground and fought the battle in the way they felt would have been most effective. If that had been the case, he said, Nixon would have won the presidency rather than losing narrowly. Peter Flanagan and I struck up a lasting friendship. Partially as a result of our building an organization around Nixon's candidacy, Republicans captured the Oklahoma governorship in both 1962 and 1966. We elected an attorney general, a supreme court justice, and a secretary of labor. Also, we more than doubled our strength in the House and Senate, and gained considerably in registration, although registered Republicans were still very much in the minority.

On election night 1962, while elated with my own election as governor, I was totally dismayed to find that Nixon had lost the governor's race in California. His infamous news conference following this defeat also distressed me a great deal. I felt that surely here was the political end of a person I had come to respect, who seemed to have developed greatly since I had first met him. In 1966, Nixon made a visit to Oklahoma where he campaigned on behalf of our Republican ticket, especially the gubernatorial candidate Dewey Bartlett. He was warmly received by a respectful crowd and it was obvious he was back on the campaign trail.

After the 1966 election and before I left the governor's office, I took a group of Oklahoma industrial leaders and newly elected Governor Bartlett to New York, as well as to other cities, to renew contacts with corporate executives who had shown an interest in investing in Oklahoma. While we were in New York, I took time to call on attorney Richard Nixon with the intent of suggesting to him that he not seek the presidency again. I felt he should step aside and make room for a new face who could run in 1968 without the handicap of two defeats. Several in the group accompanied me to Nixon's law office including Ed Matthews, who was serving as the state's coordinator in Washington, and Drew Mason, my administrative assistant. These men knew what was on my mind when we went in and they must have been dumbfounded when I wound up suggesting to Nixon that he run and that I would help him.

The reason for my quick change of mind was that Nixon seemed to have changed. He was vigorous, highly animated, and exuded self-confidence. It appeared to me that he had been in the shadow of President Eisenhower and not his own man as vice president. Then he had suffered two political defeats which further undermined his confidence in himself. Now, however, he seemed to have come into his own. Four years of success in the big leagues of the legal profession and as the author of two books had restored his confidence. I became convinced he might succeed in another try for the presidency. It was obvious he had made up his mind to make the race and it appeared to me that there was nothing I could do to dissuade him. Also, thinking politically, I realized that if he did run he would get the nomination; I suppose it was a show of cowardice but I did not care to be in a position of opposing him in case he wanted to make a second try for the nomination.

In April 1967, after leaving the governor's office in January, I received a phone call from Peter Flanagan who told me that a small group had organized in New York for the purpose of laying the groundwork and launching the campaign to help Richard Nixon seek the presidency in 1968. Flanagan asked me to go to New York and meet with the group to give them whatever counsel I could as to how the campaign should be run in the central and southwestern sections of the country. Once or twice each month from then until August I met with the Committee in New York City. Others who regularly or occasionally attended included Jerry Milbank of the Borden Milk Company, Richard Kleindeinst of Arizona, Fred LaRue of Mississippi, and John Whitaker, John Mitchell, Tom Evans, and John Sears of the Nixon law firm. I was told that Bob Haldeman and John Erlichman had met with the Committee prior to my joining but they never attended a meeting while I was there.

By the time I joined the Committee, the group had already acquired the services of a Dr. Parkinson of California who was being paid $75,000 per year to serve as campaign manager. Repeatedly when we met, Parkinson brought out his organizational books and charts showing the great plans he was making for the campaign. When asked about actions he was taking or personnel he was recruiting to fill various slots, he repeatedly asked for more time. He gave one excuse after another as to why the necessary personnel were not in place. By July it was obvious that Parkinson was not going to be able to handle the campaign manager's job. The principal reason seemed to be that he was an unknown outsider who did not have access to governors, members of Congress, or party leaders which he needed in order to get the necessary commitments. It was decided that he needed to be replaced.

A problem arose because one of Richard Nixon's main difficulties in the past had been his inability to surround himself with the people he needed. Also, he had been widely criticized, especially in 1960, for being a "take-charge" person who could not delegate authority and who wanted to make every decision on his own. This was looked upon as a weakness since as president he would need to attract capable people and delegate responsibility. For this reason, he and the Committee were reluctant to replace Parkinson and make it appear that here was "the same old Nixon" at work again. It was at about this time that Parkinson's wife became ill in California and an exploratory operation revealed she was suffering from terminal cancer. Upon receipt of this news, Parkinson immediately resigned from the Committee to go home and be with his wife.

That summer Shirley and I took our three daughters for a week's stay at a Presbyterian family camp, Ghost Ranch, in New Mexico. Ghost Ranch is a relatively remote and rustic camp where the telephone service was bad. While I was there, I received a telephone call from Peter Flanagan. The connection was so bad that I could barely hear him. I told him that I would be leaving the camp the next day and that I would call him as quickly as I could get into an area where the phone service was better. By this time I had already launched my campaign for the United States Senate. Several organizational meetings had been held and several others were planned for August and the remainder of the fall. My intent was to move around the state re-establishing contact and developing an organization for the 1968 Senate campaign. When we left Ghost Ranch and as soon as I could find a satisfactory telephone, I called Flanagan. His message was that Parkinson had left, that the Committee had considered available prospects for his replacement, and had decided that they wanted me to become the national Nixon campaign chairman. I told Flanagan that was impossible since I had already launched my campaign for Senate and it would be difficult to beat incumbent Mike Monroney even under the best conditions. I needed to be in the state full time until the campaign was over.

Flanagan was not satisfied with my reaction but as I recall he did not argue too much. A day or two after I got home, I began holding the meetings which had been set. At Wetumka, we were having an organizational meeting in a restaurant when a waitress handed me a note that I was wanted on the phone. It was Richard Nixon, who personally asked me to take time out from my Senate campaign and go to Washington to be national chairman of the Nixon Election Committee. Under the circumstances, I found it impossible to refuse. I interrupted my Senate campaign in mid-August and went to Washington. I agreed to stay until a permanent chairman could be found and was given assurance this would not take longer than November. Shirley and I had already planned to take a trip abroad in November in behalf of the Williams Pipeline Company for which I was serving as a member of the board of directors.

Arriving in Washington, I found the reason I'd been selected to take Parkinson's place was that former Kansas Congressman Bob Ellsworth, who was serving as behind-the-scenes manager of the campaign, was looked upon as being too liberal. Also, because of his primary race against Senator Jim Pearson in Kansas, Ellsworth was not particularly popular among many of the Republican members of the Senate with whom Nixon needed to establish contact. So, the arrangement which developed was that, while I was the front person for the campaign, Bob Ellsworth was the operational head. He did most of the decision-making and was most closely in contact with the candidate and the financial power structure underwriting campaign activities. My job was to move around Washington and the country trying to line up as many political leaders as possible and get them committed before the New Hampshire primary or state conventions were held. I called on many governors, many members of the House and Senate, and had considerable contact with state chairmen and members of the National Committee. As a former governor and as a former state chairman, my entree was good. I was generally well received wherever I went. However, I found most political leaders unwilling to commit themselves so early in the process to a presidential candidate with a record of two losses.

A large press conference was held in Washington at the time my appointment as national chairman was announced. John Sears and Bob Ellsworth, who were both highly effective in their respective positions in the campaign, spent a day trying to prepare me for this ordeal. Sears was truly a walking encyclopedia so far as Republican personalities and party conflicts were concerned. Ellsworth loved intrigue and was skillful in dealing with the media and the political establishment. I went before the cameras and met the newsmen with great fear and trembling. To my amazement, the group treated me cordially and even kindly, perhaps out of pity, and as far as I know the conference went well. Nixon later called and thanked me for what I had done, saying it was pleasant for him to have a campaign manager who was speaking out plainly in his favor and not apologizing, the way previous campaign chairmen had seemed to do on many occasions.

After George Romney announced his candidacy for president, I held a second news conference. This time the questions were more pointed and the reporters were much more aggressive. I said that "George Romney could not handle the issues." This statement was carried in a news story and when Ray Bliss, Republican national chairman, read it, he was infuriated. Ray came to see me and bawled me out thoroughly. He said he was dedicated to keeping the party together and holding down attacks by one Republican presidential contender against another. I explained that I did not feel I'd made an attack on Romney. I had simply stated what I saw as a plain fact. But Bliss was adamant.

Nixon distrusted Bliss. He was convinced that Bliss was solidly in Romney's corner, not neutral as a party chairman should be. I had no knowledge that this was the case and did not agree. I had known Bliss for a long time and felt he was playing it straight. I never convinced Nixon of this even though I arranged a meeting in New York where the two of them sat down together. Neither man's attitude toward the other was changed during that meeting. After Nixon's nomination, Bliss was replaced. Nixon felt he needed a spokesman who would defend the Republican candidate and the Republican president. Neither was Nixon convinced, as I feel he should have been, that organizational politics, where Ray Bliss was a master, are important.

I strongly feel that Bliss' removal was a tragedy for the president and for the party; that had Nixon left Bliss in as Republican national chairman the strength of the party would have been much greater in succeeding years and that Nixon might have gained support in Congress in 1970 and 1972. In addition, I am convinced that Ray Bliss's counsel in the 1972 campaign might have prevented some of the stupid and amateurish pranks which led to the Watergate scandal and the undoing of Richard Nixon as president.

One of the first assignments I undertook as Richard Nixon's campaign manager was to visit President Eisenhower and get some indication from him about how he felt about supporting Nixon. At the time there was a large number of other well-known and well-qualified potential Republican candidates. Bob Ellsworth and I made an appointment with the former president in his office in Gettysburg. We were driven to the meeting by George Revitz, son of the owner of Alban Towers, where I was staying, in the large Cadillac the family owned. We drove from Washington to Gettysburg on a sparkling fall morning. Bob and I, who had not known each other well before I came to Washington to join the campaign, welcomed the chance to get better acquainted. We thoroughly enjoyed the trip.

We arrived in Gettysburg a bit early and spent several minutes in a restaurant waiting for the appointed hour. Both of us were apprehensive because, although we considered our mission serious, we expected President Eisenhower would look upon us as bothersome intruders and give us curt treatment. At the appointed time, Bob Ellsworth and I went across the quiet street from the restaurant to the upper floor of the two-story building where Eisenhower had his office. We were received at the first floor by a Secret Service man and a male assistant to the former president. Promptly at the appointed time, we were taken up the flight of stairs to Eisenhower's office where he greeted us warmly. We were joined at the landing by a man who was working with the president on his memoirs and helping with speeches.

President Eisenhower took Bob and me into his office. It soon became obvious that he was delighted to see us. Almost as soon as we were seated, he opened the middle drawer of his desk and took out a glossy photograph which he obviously kept handy for frequent viewing. The General passed the photograph to Bob and me for our examination and began to explain what it was about. The photograph was taken during the second Eisenhower-Nixon inauguration ceremonies. It showed President Eisenhower and Mamie on the right with Dick and Pat Nixon on the left. To the right of Mamie Eisenhower was David Eisenhower and to the left of Pat Nixon was Julie Nixon. These two young people were leaning forward, looking steadfastly at each other. President Eisenhower chuckled as he showed us the photograph and said that it is obvious "these two young people have had their eyes on each other for a long, long time." Only a very short time before, announcement of the engagement of Julie and David had been made public and this obviously pleased the former president a great deal.

Our conversation with Eisenhower went on for no less than an hour and a half. He seemed like a man hungry to talk politics and may even have been a little lonely for visitors. At our suggestion, he discussed each of the various prospective Republican presidential candidates. He said that in order to be a good president, an individual needs to have "executive experience." He felt this experience could be achieved through military service, industrial management, service in the executive branch of the federal government, or through the experience as governor of a state. He did not seem to feel that experience in the legislative branch alone was enough to properly qualify an individual to become president of the United States. When it came down to talking about specific individuals, he very pointedly eliminated all except Richard Nixon.

He felt George Romney was not going to control his compulsion to expound upon every subject that came up. (Shortly after that Romney made his famous statement that he had been "brainwashed" on Vietnam. As a result, his candidacy rapidly began to fade.) Eisenhower seemed to have deep misgivings regarding the prospect of electing Nelson Rockefeller. He did not state exactly why he felt this way but events proved him right. He seemed to feel that Chuck Percy of Illinois was very much a comer in the political arena, but questioned his grasp of national affairs and his lack of acquaintance with leaders of the country, which he would need in order to serve as our nation's chief executive. Roughly the same sort of comments were made about Ronald Reagan, who was then governor of California. President Eisenhower obviously regarded Reagan as an attractive person and a great crowd-pleaser, but he doubted his service as governor and his brief experience in the political world were adequate to qualify him for the responsibilities of the White House. Of all the other candidates discussed, the president seemed to have the highest regard for Bill Scranton, except he felt Scranton had badly garbled his attempt to be nominated at the 1964 convention. The president felt Scranton would not again seek public office for personal and family reasons, and again his opinion was borne out by subsequent events.

In spite of the president's obvious preference for Richard Nixon, there was no way we could get him to agree to say anything publicly. In fact, Ellsworth and I both felt it was the better part of valor not to press him at that time. However, we did leave the meeting feeling that when Eisenhower thought it best he would give Nixon a public boost and that in the meantime we could call upon him for counsel and advice on a private basis. Over the early months of the campaign, as far as I know, President Eisenhower did very little to help Nixon, though he may have done more than I know, since I left the campaign after the New Hampshire primary. At any rate, he did not in any way damage Nixon's prospects, and I really feel he was personally delighted when Nixon was nominated.

Before I had gone to Washington to join the Nixon campaign, Gertrude Kennedy of Oklahoma City had asked me if I was going to see

Eisenhower. The Kennedys and Eisenhowers were good personal friends. I told her that more than likely I would be in contact with the president. I thought Mrs. Kennedy wanted to send greetings or some personal message. Instead, she told me she wanted me to ask him why in the world he had appointed Earl Warren to be chief justice of the Supreme Court. At the time, I doubted I would have the opportunity to or would feel comfortable raising the question. At Gettysburg, our conversation with the president went on so long and became so warm and informal that finally my courage was raised to the point that I brought up the conversation with Mrs. Kennedy and asked him point-blank why he had made the Warren appointment.

The story Eisenhower told was that after he became president, he found that many prominent lawyers felt the reputation and regard of the people for the Supreme Court had fallen to an all-time low. Therefore, it was recommended that he be extremely careful in making his appointments to fill vacancies that occurred on the Supreme Court bench. He was advised to make a great effort to appoint justices with prestige, good judgment, and reputation, so that the status of the Court could be improved. When the first vacancy occurred, President Eisenhower called in the attorney general and told him to scour the country to identify the best legal minds and come up with the one man the profession felt would add stature and quality to the Court.

According to the president, the attorney general made this investigation and after about thirty days came in and recommended the appointment of Governor Earl Warren of California. The president said he had never considered Mr. Warren, that he had made absolutely no promises to Mr. Warren, that he owed Mr. Warren no political debt of any kind, but that he selected him because respected legal professionals felt he would make an outstanding justice. They felt he would help bring the Court back into the place of honor it had once held. After explaining how it happened, the president looked at Bob Ellsworth and me and said very candidly, "You know, it is the worst damn mistake I ever made."

The conference in his office in Gettysburg is the last time I saw President Eisenhower. He was obviously a man very much at peace with the world, plainly enjoying his work and his life, and vitally concerned with political events, the progress of our country, and achieving peace in the world.

Drew Mason, who had been my administrative assistant, and Helen Lawson, who had been his secretary, had been recruited by Flanagan to be in charge of direct mail fund raising long before I joined the Nixon campaign committee. By the time I arrived in Washington, Drew and Helen had underway a thoroughly effective direct mail fund solicitation campaign. Their effort kept the campaign treasury from going bankrupt time after time. In fact, campaign treasurer Maurice Stans leaned so heavily on Drew for finances during this period that Drew was frequently unable to pay the postage needed to carry on the campaign in what he felt was a realistic and effective way. Had Maury given Drew access to the funding he needed, perhaps an even greater part of the campaign funds could have come from direct solicitations by mail. As it was, Drew did keep the campaign from going broke and deserves great credit for the job he did. The charge that the early Nixon for President Campaign was funded by wealthy contributors is totally false. The support came in hundreds of sacks of mail in $5, $10, and $20 checks and currency. A $500 contribution was cause for celebration! When the campaign was over, the direct mail firm had advanced some $40,000 for postage, which Maurice Stans refused to pay. It took much effort on my part to see that this account finally was settled fairly. I considered it a sad commentary on the part of those who handled Nixon's finances that they were reluctant almost to the point of dishonesty in settling up with this direct mail organization.

During the early days after I arrived in Washington, Maury Stans invited my staff, my family, and me to a safari party. Stans was an avid big game hunter. We spent the evening looking at his trophies and viewing a movie made during a recent hunting trip to Chad. While Maury was making his comments, some of the stuffed animals, including a large tiger, came tumbling down on his back. It was somewhat symbolic of what was later to happen to him, though the later attack came not from wild animals, but a different type of predator. The Watergate tragedy caught Maury in an unfair way. His operation of Nixon campaign finances had taken place under the old, lax rules. After that campaign, much-needed changes in the rules were made by Congress. But it was wrong to condemn someone for doing what had long been accepted and legal.

During some of the Watergate hearings or trials, I remember a statement Maury made: "Give me back my good name." It would be necessary to know Maurice Stans to understand the importance he attached to that statement. Here was a person who had made a lifetime of successful and honorable dealings, caught in the quicksand of politics, his reputation destroyed. He had come into politics solely to try to make way for better government and had acted according to the rules of the game at the time. Following his trial and prior to his sentencing, I was contacted to write a letter as a character witness for Maury. I was delighted to do so and hope it had some part in moderating the sentence the judge handed down.

About this time, Maury came to Oklahoma to attend the Grand National Quail Hunt. He and I were assigned to the same team and spent a pleasant day on a ranch near Waynoka hunting together. The quail were difficult to find, but it was one of those exhilarating, clear, fall days when it is a pure delight just to be outdoors and alive. Our greatest experience of the afternoon was coming upon a flock of some 250 wild turkeys. This was a great sight for anyone, but a particular thrill for Maury who, as far as I know, had never seen anything like that before.

One of the firm impressions I have of Richard Nixon is that he was absolutely disinterested in detail. I had expected him to live up to his reputation of being a take-charge guy. The fact was that he had absolutely no interest in what was going on in his campaign organization. All his efforts and energies seemed to be devoted toward travel, conversations with intellectuals, columnists, and journalists, and studying, speaking, and writing about the "big issues." For instance, John Whitaker, who handled Nixon's schedule and the advance work, met with our committee from the beginning and had a vital role in the campaign. Repeatedly, John would arrange with Nixon to attend planning meetings, sometimes in the New York headquarters and sometimes in the Nixon apartment on Park Avenue. When we met in the Nixons's apartment we normally had dinner and sometimes Pat would be there. Also his Cuban aide was always present.

Time after time we would meet with Nixon after having screened the speaking invitations down to no more than a dozen. We would explain what we felt could be accomplished in each of these appearances and suggest that the candidate choose the occasions he felt were most suited to his purpose. Generally after an hour or more of discussing the matter, we realized that Nixon was not going to make a decision and we would go away and make the selections ourselves. The same kind of conversations took place regarding staffing. We were badly in need of a respected, accomplished, experienced journalist to handle the news and public relations side of the campaign. On different occasions we prepared lists of individuals we thought could handle this duty and might be available for the job. Frequently, Nixon would talk over these matters with us but he would never choose the person he felt could do the job best. As a result, the campaign drifted along for many months without a press secretary. Finally, after I left the campaign in March, Herb Klein more or less attached himself to Nixon in this capacity and carried on that function during the balance of the campaign and into the new administration.

Nixon showed by his inattention and indifference to routine decision-making that he was no administrator. I therefore came to the conclusion that if he was elected he would need to bring into his administration a truly top executive who could make decisions, give attention to detail, and not let small matters pile up until they became overwhelming. I had enough experience in the governor's office in Oklahoma to know that the kind of decision-making Nixon seemed to abhor was really the most essential function of a chief executive. Unless Nixon was fully supported in this area, the likelihood of trouble seemed great.

As time approached for me to leave the Nixon campaign and return to Oklahoma to actively begin organizing and campaigning for the Senate, I again saw how difficult it was for Nixon to make a decision. I told him several months ahead of time that I was going to leave and hoped that he would go ahead and make plans for my successor so the campaign could move ahead without interruption. To my knowledge, he never chose anyone to take my place as national campaign chairman. It seemed that increasingly Dick Kleindeinst and John Mitchell moved into the vacuum in the organization, but I don't believe there was a time when Richard Nixon said "I pick you, John, to run my campaign." It may have happened after I left, but to my knowledge at the time I finally quit working with the Nixon Committee no real successor had been formally appointed.

The next several months were spent in my own endeavors in Oklahoma and resulted in my election to the U.S. Senate. About twenty days after Nixon's inaugural, a group of early supporters, dubbed by Nixon "the early birds," was invited to the White House for dinner. He identified us as the members of Congress or elected officials who had worked openly for him prior to his presidential primary victory in New Hampshire. Nixon told the first Early Bird meeting that he wanted to be not just a good, but a great president. He wanted to make us all proud of him.

The most vivid memory of that evening is the way President Nixon seemed to have been affected by his three weeks in the White House. I had seen the man many times and observed him under many conditions but I had never seen him so gloriously happy and vibrant and animated as he was that evening. He was relaxed, confident, and seemed to feel totally in command. He showed by his actions, words, and demeanor that he was in no way awed by the presidency. He took us on a personal tour, not only to the rooms normally seen by visitors to the White House, but to the personal living quarters as well. When we walked past a piano, he said "This is a piano that Harry Truman used to play." Then we went on to another part of the president's quarters. When we came back by the piano, Nixon sat down and played the "Missouri Waltz" to everybody's great surprise and pleasure. He also took us into a small room by the Lincoln bedroom which he said he was having fixed up as his own private working office. The room probably wasn't any bigger than fourteen by fourteen feet and it had only a couple of chairs and a desk. It also had a wood-burning fireplace which was burning brightly. It created a warm and pleasant surrounding for the president to do his most serious work.

During my years in the Senate, my contacts with President Nixon were as a member of one group or another. He called me only on two occasions. Once when we were having a birthday party at the farm, he called to wish me a happy birthday. He called about 5:30 p.m.; the crowd had left about four. Any political advantage he may have intended was lost because of bad timing since there was no one there when the call came through. Also, on the day I announced that I was going to run for re-election to the Senate, he called me in Oklahoma and told me how pleased he was with my decision. He volunteered to come to the state to help me campaign. That promise was promptly announced at a news conference and it later came back to haunt me when the president got into such serious trouble over Watergate.

From time to time, the president would have members of Congress down to the White House in groups of about twenty to talk about farm legislation or to discuss with us his latest feelings about Vietnam or on occasion to talk about energy programs. I was in a dozen or so of those meetings over the five years that he was in the White House. It seemed like in those meetings there were so many people, most of them senior to me, always competing to be heard. It was tough to get a word in unless you more or less ran over someone else. Also, President Nixon seemed to have a tendency to want to do most of the talking. I've been to meetings that would last an hour or an hour and a half and I would estimate that President Nixon talked at least eighty percent of the time.

Over the years, he seemed to develop a feeling that he had to be the star of the show. When we met he wanted to impress us with how much he knew rather than give us a chance to talk about the problems as we saw them or to give whatever information we might have that could have been helpful in working out a solution. This attitude of showing his knowledge and dominating the situation became one hallmark of the Nixon administration. To me it was a sign of growing insecurity. I believe Nixon's desire to dominate the situation influenced him heavily in his selection of staff. The people he placed around him were mostly inexperienced, young, obviously highly motivated, and intelligent people. In my judgment, the president would have been better served with less brilliance and more wisdom. None of the Nixon staffers seemed to have the stature required to stand up to the president or to deal with him on anything like an equal basis. In all the meetings I attended I never saw anyone openly disagree with the president. It was always "Yes, Mr. President. That's right, Mr. President. I agree, Mr. President."

On one occasion in August of 1970, I became deeply concerned that the president's staff was not serving him well. I talked the matter over with Senator Howard Baker and Senator Bob Dole. I suggested that we get an appointment with the president to discuss the matter and they agreed. I arranged a time with Rose Mary Wood and the three of us went to the White House. The president received us promptly at the appointed time and we spent about forty-five minutes with him in the Oval Office with only the four of us present. We told him that we felt his staff was not doing a good job, particularly in his dealings with Congress. Several members of the House were running for the Senate or for governor and it was obvious that not all of them would be elected. We suggested that after the election he choose a person in whom he had confidence and who was well regarded by members of the Congress and that this person be brought into his official family as Congressional liaison.

To our surprise, the president was readily receptive to our suggestion and after we made our point, he called in Bob Finch. Finch had recently left his post as secretary of Health, Education and Welfare and was on the president's staff as a counselor. Nixon told Finch he was convinced that the White House was not doing an adequate job in dealing with Congress. He wanted Finch to watch the election outcomes and find former members of Congress who could be added to the staff when the elections were over. The upshot of it was that Clark McGregor was brought in. It seemed to me Clark tried very hard to do the job, but he never got anywhere. Whether or not Nixon followed up to see how well McGregor was doing is hard to say. McGregor stayed at the White House for several months. After he left things went back to the status quo.

Meanwhile, the Watergate matter got progressively worse. Earlier, when President Nixon had volunteered to come to Oklahoma to help me campaign for reelection, I had welcomed his help. By January 1974, it became obvious that President Nixon's presence in Oklahoma on my behalf was not exactly going to be a great asset. I was in a box. If Nixon came to campaign, I would be hurt. If he didn't come, I would be hurt. I began to figure a way to bring the president to Oklahoma in a non-political role without going back on the promise he had made me in public. It was going to be awkward if people knew that I rebuffed the president. In thinking over possible ways in which we could capitalize on his promise, I remembered that four years earlier, Dr. Bob Kamm, president of Oklahoma State University, had urged President Nixon to make the commencement address at O.S.U. So in February, I called and reminded the president through Rose Mary Wood that he had agreed to come to Oklahoma to campaign for me. I told her that the place he could do me the most good would be at the O.S.U. commencement.

In mid-April, President Nixon agreed to come to O.S.U. By the time he got there the Watergate matter had become so notorious that there was much national interest about whether he could go to a college campus and make an appearance without a great deal of unpleasantness. I talked to Dr. Kamm and told him that if he was concerned or if the student body was going to resent President Nixon's appearance we could probably get the event cancelled. Dr. Kamm hung tight. He said that he still wanted the president on the campus and was convinced the event would go off without any unseemly incident. Also the decision was made that no political people would participate, and that the only elected official to be on the speakers' stand would be the president. Dr. Kamm would introduce the president, who would make his commencement address and be free to leave.

The arrangements were made for Air Force One to land at Vance Air Force Base in Enid. Shirley and I rode together with the president and his party to Stillwater and back to Enid in the presidential helicopter. We then rode back to Washington in Air Force One. Nixon was absolutely elated and delighted with the way he had been received. We sat in the president's cabin after he had eaten his dinner and talked for about an hour and a half. The worst thing about the trip was that an Oklahoma congressman became a little inebriated and got in a back-slapping mood with the president. He sat for at least fifteen minutes with his hand on the president's knee making one kind of pronouncement after another — many totally unrelated to the matters that were being discussed. Oklahoma Senator Dewey Bartlett and Ann also rode with Nixon back to Washington. We talked at some length about how universities like Oklahoma State never seem to get a fair share in the division of federal research funds. President Nixon assured us that he was going to try to straighten the matter out. He said that he could see no point in granting the bulk of federal research funds to "our enemies" while the institutions which tended to be friendly were left out.

He said, and I agreed, that it is obvious that the institutions that get the grants can get the research staff. There was no magic about whether the research is done on the east coast or the west coast or in the midwest. He felt that probably we could get better research if the projects could be moved into universities in the heart of the country and he assured us that he was going to take steps to see that was done.

By the next month, tensions on Capitol Hill were mounting. There was no longer any doubt that the Nixon presidency was coming to an end. The only remaining questions were when and how. Around 4 p.m. Thursday, August 8, Rose Mary Wood, personal secretary to the president, called and invited me to a meeting of the early birds. The meeting was to be at 6 p.m. in the Cabinet Room of the White House. Though Rose Mary gave no details, I knew instinctively that the Nixon presidency would soon be history. Shortly before 6 p.m., about twenty-five of us gathered in the Cabinet Room to await the president. There was none of the usual banter; in fact there was little talk of any kind. A feeling of foreboding permeated the atmosphere.

We expected Nixon to come out of the door leading into the Oval Office. Instead, he came in from the main hallway and caught everyone by surprise. We all applauded as noisily as we could. The president did not hesitate or shake hands or speak with anyone. He went immediately to the one high-backed chair at the center of the large oval table and signaled for us to sit down. The president dropped his head and we all sat in embarrassed silence for what seemed like a long time. Nixon then raised his head, looked around, and started to speak in a very high voice. It took him a full minute to get control of himself.

Everyone was thoroughly uncomfortable. We did not know what to expect. I was apprehensive about his imminent appearance on national television — scheduled to occur in less than an hour. Then he seemed to steady himself. He began by saying this was the group he always knew he could count on no matter how difficult the issue we faced. He told us he felt it was our solid support in Congress that made it possible for him to make some of the difficult decisions he had made. He felt that with our support the Nixon administration had achieved a satisfactory settlement of the Vietnam war. This in turn had made it possible for him to undertake his initiative to open the door to China.

Then he talked at great length about the mental processes he had gone through leading to the decision he planned to announce to the nation later in the evening. He said that had he decided to stay on he knew he could count on this group and he felt there were others. He had determined that there were probably thirty-four or thirty-five members of the Senate who wanted to stay with him and after they had heard both sides of the case probably would vote against his removal from office. He said he was convinced the House was going to impeach him; there was no question in his mind about that.

He said the problem was that the country had already gone through almost a year and a half of uncertainties related to Watergate and was deeply divided on the matter. Congress was dividing its attention between the problems of the country and Watergate. And while up to now he had been able to focus his attention on his official duties and at the same time defend himself, he could no longer do so. He feared that from now until the matter was finally settled, Watergate was going to take the full attention of the Senate and full attention of the president. In his opinion, a Senate trial would take a minimum of four months and most likely six. He felt the problems we had at home and abroad would not allow the country to go through a long period of uncertainty while a removal trial was being held and a decision was being reached. Some national or international crisis was certain. He particularly talked about upcoming trouble in the Middle East and the fact that the Israelis were being very difficult. The Syrians were being re-armed by the Russians. He was concerned there would be another outbreak of war. Also, he was concerned that a long period of uncertainty might destroy detente with the Russians and cause them to become adventuresome again.

As much as it hurt him to do so, he said, and as much as he wanted to stay on in the presidency and finish the job he had started, he had decided, over the objections of his family, to resign. He was going to announce his decision when he went on television in less than an hour. After making complimentary comments about Vice President Gerald Ford, he said he hoped we would back the new president the way we had backed him because Ford was going to have difficult decisions to make. He talked for some time about what he felt were the accomplishments of his administration in foreign affairs and domestically. He seemed to be telling us he was pleased with his record, confident it would stand the test of history. He said he was not ashamed and those of us who backed him could be proud of what had been accomplished.

No one but the president spoke. He paused once or twice but mostly the words poured out rapidly and with great intensity. Everyone was totally engrossed in what was being said. After he finished, he again dropped his head and there was a long silence. He then looked up and said "I am having difficulty finding words to say what is in my mind." Then he choked up. His voice broke and he said, "I hope I haven't let you down." At that point he got up and very quickly left the room. It was obvious that he was sobbing. Many others in the room also shed tears.

No other elected U. S. president had ever resigned. We wondered what would happen to the country and its world leadership role, already shaken by the Vietnam war experience. More immediately, our concern was whether or not Nixon could keep his composure when he appeared on television in half an hour. Members of the White House staff took us into the theater to a table laden with food and beverages. Three television sets were available. Most of us stayed at the White House to see and hear the public announcement. Those in the room were sad that the president was leaving, but we knew it was inevitable. At the same time, we felt he had gotten a raw deal; that he had done a good job and that he should have been given a chance to finish his term. There was not bitterness — only sadness. No one was angry with the president. No one in the room felt he had let them down.

Richard Nixon made another trip to Oklahoma in 1981 when he came to speak at the "Welcome Home, Shirley and Henry" homecoming party which some friends in Enid arranged for us. Doug McKeever, who was dinner chairman, arranged through Bryce Harlow for the ex-president's appearance. As far as I know, this was the first public appearance Richard Nixon had made since his resignation. The dinner attracted a turn-away crowd. Richard Nixon was at his best and the crowd loved it. He signed hundreds of autographs before, during, and after dinner and insisted that I co-sign. He made a totally extemporaneous, note-free speech on his favorite subject — foreign affairs. He seemed to glory in being back among friendly people and reluctant to see the evening end.

The next morning on his trip back to Oklahoma City to catch his plane to New York, he insisted that his driver go thirty miles out of the way to visit the Oklahoma State University campus. He seemed to want to relive the happy time he spent there making the commencement speech during the travail that led to his resignation.

Years later, in 1989, after my second election as governor, I had occasion to be in New York and had dinner with Pete and Brigette Flanagan at their home. Pete told me he thought Nixon would appreciate a visit at his office in New Jersey. The next day, I made the short trip to the Nixon office in New Jersey where he and a small staff were working on the latest Nixon book. We spent the better part of an hour reminiscing and he gave me a copy of a case he had tried before the U.S. Supreme Court during his days as a practicing attorney. The president seemed to enjoy the stature he had achieved as an elder statesman. Much of our conversation dealt with foreign relations, which continued to be his main interest.

The visit with Nixon brought back many memories of other contacts I'd had with him over the years. My impression is that he has a brilliant mind and genuinely wanted to be of public service. He aspired to be a great president and had a highly significant salutary effect on the United States' role on the world scene. His opening the door to China was probably a stroke of brilliance which only he, as a confirmed anti-Communist, could have made at the time. His success with China put the Soviet Union on the defensive and probably contributed to the United States' ultimate victory in the cold war.

On the negative side, Nixon's big problems seemed to be a lack of interest in administration, a propensity toward doing expedient things, and an inability or unwillingness to identify and attract individuals with mature leadership and strong character into his immediate official family. The presidency is simply too big a job for any one individual. Success in the White House depends upon a strong team and ultimately, I believe, the inability to create such a team led to Watergate and President Nixon's resignation. Nevertheless, I have a high regard for the man and feel that history will treat him kindly.

The Senator

"Compared to the Governor's Job, Service in the U.S. Senate is about as Exciting as Watching a Stump Rot"

Prior to my involvement in the Nixon for President campaign, at the conclusion of the four years in the governor's office, our family moved back to our still-new home on the farm. The house had been completed shortly before the governor's campaign began and, except for weekends and holidays, we had not really lived there. Pat was a freshman at OSU. Gail and Ann re-entered the Billings Public School. I was happy to be back on the farm and out of the political limelight.

Again, as when I returned from the Marine Corps, I faced the loss of a regular income. Wheat harvest was several months away, so no income from farming could be expected until mid-summer. A wealthy and friendly Oklahoma City businessman came to the rescue. He invited me to become a part-time fund-raiser for the Oklahoma Medical Research Foundation (OMRF), a job which provided a livable stipend. I travelled the state, making calls on individuals, relatives, and other prospective OMRF contributors with only moderate success. I was pleased when, late in the summer, my role in the Nixon campaign developed and I could quit the fund-raising job.

Toward the end of the first governor's term, Shirley became interested in using the state bird, the scissortail flycatcher, as decoration for women's dresses. After the term, she established a small dressmaking business in our farm home where she and several neighbor women skillfully sewed dresses with appliques on them that were sold through dress shops all across Oklahoma. This business outgrew our house and finally Shirley moved it to Billings and enlarged her work force. She also began making career clothes for banks, restaurants, and even nightclubs. The business continued after we moved to Washington, though it was difficult to operate it from afar.

Late in my first term as governor, I became acquainted with R.D. Hull, of Tulsa, who invented the Zebco fishing reel. I had gone to Tulsa to participate in the dedication of the new Zebco plant that had been purchased by the Brunswick Company. As I was leaving, R.D. Hull showed large containers of gears made of powdered metal which were used in assembling the fishing reels. He said that the company was having problems getting delivery on the gears since the only sources were in the Great Lakes area. The companies which made the gears also produced parts for automobile companies and when they had a large order for automobile parts, they hesitated to interrupt the production line to produce the smaller gears needed for fishing reels. Mr. Hull requested that I try to find an Oklahoma investor who would get into the powdered metal gear-producing business. An attempt was made through the Oklahoma Department of Commerce, but no one was interested. Shortly after I left the governor's office, I discussed the possibility of putting in a plant to build the gears with a friend, Bill Rush, who had recently sold his propane business in Billings. Bill and I visited the Zebco plant in Tulsa then went to Chicago, located a small powdered metal production plant in the garage of a local citizen, found out what equipment and materials were needed, and proceeded to begin the development of Rush Metals on the promise of receiving a gear contract from Zebco. The powdered metal process was relatively new in our part of the world. In fact, there was no plant operating between St. Louis and the west coast.

Using as much money as Bill Rush felt he could put into the operation, plus money I received from sale of one quarter section of land, we still needed to borrow about $120,000. We went to the local banker, who agreed to let us have his limit, about $20,000, and sent us to Fourth National in Tulsa, his correspondent bank. They took the matter under advisement and invited us to come back a week later when they told us they would make the loan provided we built our plant in Tulsa. We had planned to build the factory in Billings, largely to provide work for local citizens who needed jobs due to the closing of a small refinery and removal of the Champlin pipeline crew from town.

After the turndown by the Fourth National Bank, we went to National Bank of Tulsa where, based on our order for Zebco gears, Mark Tower made us the loan we needed. We were in business. Unfortunately, the loan began to come due in six months. Before we could get the plant in operation and make any income, we had used all our money. Luckily, I had become acquainted with Jack Stevens, an investment banker from Little Rock, who visited our plant, liked what he saw, and made us a six-year loan of adequate size to put us in business in a proper way and keep us going until the plant became profitable. I owned a third interest in Rush Metals for nine years. During that time, I received no income from the investment, though when I sold out to the majority owner I received about ten times what I had invested initially. The plant is still in operation. It has enlarged over the years and employs about sixty people from the Billings area.

As governor, I was frequently irritated with U.S. Senator Mike Monroney's proclivity for dabbling in state matters. He seemed eager to embarrass me so it was impossible to work with him. Over the years, Monroney had become highly enamored with the Washington scene and gave the impression of having lost touch with our state. He seemed vulnerable to replacement.

My decision to oppose Monroney for the Senate came at the time a Monroney appointee, with the senator's apparent approval, undertook to embarrass me because of the Farmer's Home Administration loan Shirley and I had made in 1958 to build our farm home. We had been completely eligible for this loan but under the FHA regulations, after I was elected governor the loan should have been paid off more promptly. I was eager to pay it off and arrangements had been made at the time the Monroney criticism and publicity occurred. Monroney's conduct seemed petty and partisan. I concluded that Oklahomans deserved better, that he needed to be replaced, and that he could be defeated. I decided to become a candidate for U.S. senator.

My first campaign encounter with Monroney came at a joint meeting sponsored by the Associated Press Editors of Oklahoma at Western Hills Lodge. Monroney's conduct startled me. He was the incumbent and I was the challenger. In a normal campaign, he would have left the burden of attack to the challenger. However, exactly the opposite took place. Monroney blistered me and I was thoroughly shocked. Apparently he felt he was going to devastate me and make me run from him. This did not happen. I carefully prepared myself for our next joint appearance. I was ready for his assault and when our encounter on statewide television before the Oklahoma City Jaycees was over, Monroney had had his fill. Never again did he accept a joint appearance and our campaign was carried on at arm's length.

The 1968 campaign against Monroney was the easiest of the four state-wide races I made. After our second joint appearance, I felt I was in control of the situation and that victory was reasonably certain. In Stillwater, we held a campaign meeting in a private home and many university faculty attended. During the question and answer period, one of the professors asked, "Can you cope?" Whether it was intended as an insult, I wasn't certain, but I took it as such. The notion that a former governor might not be able to cope with the duties of U.S. senator never occurred to me. I resented the professor's apparent snobbery. The campaign effort was fairly relaxed. Unlike the senator, who had duties in Washington, I had full time to give to the campaign and we were never under any financial constraints. While many feel, and election results show that congressional incumbency is an advantageous position, it can also be a burden if the challenger applies himself properly. The incumbent has a responsibility to be in Washington to discharge duties of the office and travel back and forth is tiring so the candidate is rarely in top form. The challenger is always on the scene, always in position to be in good form and always more current on developing local attitudes. Also, the incumbent has a record to defend and some actions are certain to be vulnerable to attack. Since the incumbency is somewhat of a burden, I have no objection to incumbents using some of the emoluments of their office in campaign activities: a reasonable and responsible use of the frank, use of some staff time in campaign activities, and whatever use of the media the incumbent can make to forward the cause.

Our 1968 campaign was well-organized and well-financed. We had the issues going our way and the advantage of being able to devote our full efforts to campaign activities. Monroney was uneasy, insecure, and apparently resigned to defeat almost from the beginning. He was past sixty-five and sensitive about his age. On the Fourth of July, the town of Crescent holds a celebration that draws a large crowd from surrounding counties. Monroney arrived at the event early. He was dressed in youthful-looking clothing he must have purchased at a college campus store. He made a great show of his supposed youthful appearance and vigor. As the local newspaper publisher, who was also Monroney's campaign manager, began to introduce Monroney, the senator started jogging across the baseball diamond to the truck where the microphone and loud speakers were mounted. Monroney seemed to wilt as he reached the steps. The newspaper publisher concluded his remarks by introducing Monroney as "Oklahoma's senior citizen" instead of Oklahoman's senior senator. This mistake occurred at least four times during the campaign and seemed to devastate Monroney.

We won the election by 55,000 votes. Monroney had been chairman of the Senate Commerce Subcommittee on Aviation and on election night he made his concession statement in aviation terms. He took his defeat in good grace: "We have come in a little short of the runway and will therefore not reach our destination." In Washington, Monroney did not accept his defeat with such good form. There was no effort on his part to bring about an orderly transfer of responsibility from his Senate office to ours. He gave me no counsel nor did he transfer caseloads to our office.

My twelve years in the U.S. Senate were filled with frustrations. After having been pretty much my own boss in the farming business for over twenty years and in the governor's office for four years, going to the U.S. Senate where I was one member of a hundred-member committee — and a very junior minority member at that — was a real letdown. The time seemed to drag. I felt like I was being herded around. Control of my time was in the hands of others. Members were slaves to the buzzer system. Most of the decisions we made seemed trivial. Frequently, we rushed to the Senate floor with no idea what we would vote on and once we found out, had only a few seconds to make a decision. As a place for debate and thoughtful contemplation, the U.S. Senate was a complete bust. Compared to the responsibility, work load, and excitement of the four years as governor, serving in the U.S. Senate initially seemed about as exciting as watching a stump rot.

In the 1960s, newly elected U.S. senators were nobodies. They wound up with the smallest, least convenient offices, the dullest committee assignments, and sat at the foot of the class wherever they went. (Things have changed since then with better offices following construction of the Hart building and some relaxation of the seniority system which gives new members at least one major committee assignment and more staff support.) I did have a slight advantage because of credits given for former service — in my case, my years as governor. I was somewhat rankled to find that new senators who had served as members of the House of Representatives received more credits than former governors. I considered the position of governor to be far more important than serving as one of the 435 members of the House. This quirk of circumstance put me one rank behind former Congressman Bob Dole of Kansas. As time went on this came to be something of a problem.

Shirley and I did not want to live in Washington, D.C. proper. Traffic was congested, crime was rampant, air and water were polluted, buildings were discolored from soot, and the climate was dull. Even though I'd spent many pleasant weekends in Washington during the period I was stationed with the Marines in Quantico, Virginia, in the 1940s, and even though we had taken the girls to Washington on a trip in the 1950s, none of us felt comfortable there. Ann was still in high school. To get her into a quality public school and to get out of the city, we rented a house in Mantua Hills, near Fairfax. She attended W.T. Woodson High School. We feared that, coming from the small school at Billings, she would be at a disadvantage when thrown into a large student body of over three thousand. The opposite proved to be the case. Ann was graduated near the top of her class. Pat and Gail were in college. Gail went one semester to George Mason University in Fairfax, found the experience intolerable, and next semester joined her sister at Oklahoma State University in Stillwater.

Drew and Janet Mason had bought a home eight blocks away and Helen Lawson lived in an apartment nearby, so there was a bit of an Oklahoma community in our locality. The Masons were the closest friends we had. Shirley and Janet were frequently together and we often went there for dinner or for card games. In the beginning, several of us, including Drew, Helen, and Carl Williams, carpooled. By leaving as early as 6:30 a.m. we could make it to Washington in less than an hour. If we waited until seven, it frequently would take an hour and a half or sometimes longer. The car pool arrangement and the long drive to Fairfax proved to be unsatisfactory. Frequently, I needed to stay for evening meetings and this meant that other members of the car pool would have to spend their time needlessly around the office.

After Ann finished high school, Shirley and I bought a home in Alexandria, only a twenty-five-minute drive from the capitol. This made things a little better so far as Shirley and I were concerned. Shirley began to acclimate to Washington life, mostly through her participation in an International Club and the Senate wives Red Cross group that met weekly to make clothing for hospital use. Using the expertise she had gained in her own garment-making business, she helped reorganize the Senate wives into a far more efficient sewing group and vastly expanded the output of hospital garments.

Among Shirley's special Senate friends were Ann Stevens, the wife of Ted Stevens, senator from Alaska, and Phyllis Moss, wife of Senator Ted Moss of Utah. These three women decided to go into the business of remodeling rundown Capitol Hill townhouses and putting them back on the market. As they gained experience and confidence, they undertook the project of converting an abandoned office building and grocery store into a condominium complex. This project entailed borrowing a fairly large amount of money, working with the District of Columbia government to acquire the needed permits, receiving clearances from the Capitol Hill Historical Preservation Society, and engaging the services of many craftsmen. The women put their hearts and souls into the project, even doing some of the manual labor, as well as decorating and finishing the condominiums. The project was an organizational and architectural success, but a downturn in the market kept it from being much more than break-even investment. Tragically, Ann Stevens lost her life in a plane accident in Alaska soon after that project was completed.

During our years in Washington, Shirley became interested in working with stained glass. She became quite accomplished to the point that she developed her own designs and made many colorful additions to our farm home. On one occasion, she prepared three stained glass windows to use in the entry hall of our farm home. She was encouraged by some of her friends to enter them in a Washington craft show. To do so, it was necessary to put a price on the articles. Since she did not want to sell them, she set the price very high, but to her amazement, all three sold before the end of the first day.

After the Senate campaign, Drew became my administrative assistant and Helen Lawson served as my secretary. Our Senate office was small and cramped. Because there were one hundred senators and ninety-nine available office suites, it was necessary for two new senators to share one office. As luck would have it, Senator Ted Stevens, also newly elected, and I were each assigned one-half an office which formerly had been occupied by a senator from California. Under this arrangement Ted and I saw a great deal of each other and came to be good friends. Our careers in the Senate followed fairly parallel paths and we served together on committees and worked harmoniously on several projects. Drew did an excellent job of organizing and conducting the affairs of the office from the administrative side. Most of our staff were either brought from the governor's office or were recruited from among our campaign workers.

In staffing, we made a serious mistake. We felt that the Senate job would be similar to the governor's work, so we did not seek the services of the thoughtful specialists needed in a legislative office. Instead, we tried to rearrange our staff. Because of the congested quarters, we decided soon after my election to return the staff case workers who dealt with constituent problems to our spacious offices in Oklahoma. These were the individuals who handled problems related to Social Security, military, welfare, U.S.D.A, immigration, and other government agencies. Offices were set up in both Oklahoma City and Tulsa and we transferred a number of our people back to Oklahoma. Through use of the federal telephone system, communication between the offices was constant and adequate. Agencies and constituents often were not aware of where calls originated.

Following my election to the Senate, I contacted Peter Flanagan, who headed Nixon's transition team with John Mitchell and Dick Kleindienst, screening applicants for cabinet posts and other high positions in the administration. I expected to use my earlier connection with President-elect Nixon to have some input into the formation of his cabinet, but I got nowhere. I couldn't believe that after what I considered to be a substantial sacrifice toward Nixon's election, I had absolutely no entree with this group. I had identified two or three people in Oklahoma who I thought would make suitable members of the cabinet or top agency administrators. I submitted their names and resumes both by letter and by telephone but was unable to get them considered. I couldn't even arrange interviews. The same thing happened generally with the recommendations I made for lesser positions. One case demonstrates how things were being run. It had to do with a professor from Oklahoma University who had not been active in the Nixon presidential campaign. The professor contacted me with the information that he, on his own, had arranged an appointment with Secretary of Interior designate Wally Hickel. The professor wanted to know if I wanted to accompany him for an interview. I couldn't believe that after all the difficulty I had in getting my candidates considered for various appointments, this novice, out of the blue, had gotten himself set up to be considered for an important job in the Department of Interior. To see how things were done, I agreed to go with him to a meeting with Secretary Wally Hickle in the Shoreham Hotel. To my amazement, Hickle *was* considering the professor to become his scientific advisor and later the professor got the job.

It seemed incredible to me that the Nixon administration was operating in such a way that the advice of loyal campaign workers and members of the Senate was not even considered before positions of such magnitude were filled. Apparently, political considerations were given absolutely no thought. If every Republican senator was being treated in the same cavalier manner, it meant rough going for future Nixon legislative proposals. Once in Washington, I thought I would be in good position with the White House. But, while conditions with the White House were very friendly, it was difficult to turn those connections into activities that benefited the state of Oklahoma. Nixon seemed contemptuous of those who worked closely with him during the campaign. Many of the people I knew were not that close to "the boss" once he was in the White House.

Peter Flanagan was made a special assistant but did not seem to have much access to or rapport with the president. On one occasion, I was in frequent contact with Pete to try to get an Australian route for American Airlines. American operates a major maintenance base in Tulsa and as a result I developed a close working relationship with George Spaeter who at that time was CEO of American Airlines. American was interested in being chosen by the president to operate the newly available route to Australia. On different occasions George came to Washington and frequently dropped by to explain the difficulties he was having in winning the route he so coveted. Finally one day, in desperation, George asked me if it would be proper to come to Washington with a suitcase full of cash and distribute it around to people in decision-making positions. I told him that would be the worst thing he could do. After many months, American did get the Australian route, which it operated unprofitably for less than a year.

John Sears, the Nixon political guru with whom I had developed a friendship during the presidential campaign, was given a small office in the Executive Office Building, where he seemed to have no particular responsibility. I talked to him frequently when matters came up that required a direct line to the president, but it soon came home to me that John was not in good standing with top White House staffers. Before John left the staff in frustration and returned to the practice of law, I brought one matter to his attention. The national business agent of the Teamsters Union was from Cushing, Oklahoma. This man started as a driver for a truck line in Cushing and wound up in the powerful union position in the St. Louis headquarters. One of his acquaintances was Bud Massey, my good friend from Cushing. The Teamster official called Bud Massey and asked him to get a message through me to the president regarding Jimmy Hoffa, the former Teamster president, who at that time was serving a prison term. Hoffa was incarcerated in a maximum security facility and the union wanted him transferred to a minimum security facility in Pennsylvania. The message was that if the president could arrange this transfer, the union would make a $300,000 contribution to the Republican Party or the Nixon campaign fund.

When the message was first conveyed by Bud to me, I simply ignored it and allowed the matter to drop. I felt it probably was not a legitimate contact, that the matter was not the sort of thing I wanted to get involved in, and that it was unlikely any responsible Teamster official would use such a circuitous route to make a serious contact. A few days went by and I received a second call from Bud Massey on the same subject. I discussed the matter at length with Bud and expressed my reservations, which Bud shared. After an additional passage of time, Bud called a third time and felt I should make contact with the White House and convey the message so that at least the Nixon group would know what was going on. I contacted John Sears, who I felt was as good a political operator as anyone in the White House. By then the ante was $600,000 and the proposition suggested not Hoffa's transfer but his parole. An appointment with John was arranged and I laid the whole story before him. He was neither overwhelmed nor appalled by the information and I didn't think he took it seriously. I reported to Bud Massey that the message had been conveyed and I heard nothing further. I was startled a few months later when Hoffa was released from prison and allowed to return to his home. I have no idea whether any contribution from the Teamsters to the Republicans or the Nixon campaign took place or whether Sears relayed the information to other individuals. In any event, the union did appear to get what it wanted and I have always been curious about the circumstances surrounding the Hoffa parole.

When the Nixon welfare reform bill, which came to be known as H.R.1, was being prepared, Oklahoma welfare director Lloyd Rader came to see me and suggested that of all the people in the United States no group was more knowledgeable about welfare problems and programs than the state directors of various state welfare departments. I agreed. Rader suggested that these individuals were anxious to work with the Nixon administration in developing a new welfare program. They understood the shortcomings in the existing system and volunteered to put together a delegation of officers of the welfare directors group, including the state director from California, who they felt had the confidence of President Nixon. They asked me to get them an appointment with John Ehrlichman, who was at that time domestic counselor to the president. I called the White House and got the appointment. On the scheduled day, I went with this group of state welfare directors to the White House to see Ehrlichman. We sat waiting for an hour in his outer office. Ehrlichman refused to see us. Finally, Clark McGregor came and talked to us for a few minutes. These powerful individuals who had come from all over the country to volunteer their services to the Nixon administration went away totally rebuffed and angry. I could not believe that Ehrlichman could be so inept as to offend this group that probably represented as much knowledge and political clout on welfare matters as any group in the country.

Soon after we moved to Washington we were invited to a dinner party at the home of Illinois Senator Everett Dirksen. At that time he was minority leader of the Senate and was truly a Washington institution. Shirley and I went with mild apprehension, but the Dirksens proved to be extremely hospitable, warm people. They had many guests that night, including Bryce Harlow, a presidential counsellor from Oklahoma whom we knew well. There were several others we had known in various activities connected with the Nixon presidential campaign and governors' conferences. After a few minutes, we felt right at home. By some strange quirk of circumstance, we wound up sitting at a table for four with John and Martha Mitchell. Martha was trying her dead-level best to be the center of attention. She was extremely giddy and very little she said made any sense. As we were leaving the Dirksen residence we walked out with Howard and Joy Baker, the Dirksens' daughter and son-in-law. As we went to our cars, the Mitchells passed and Howard said, "That woman will cause a lot of trouble in this town before this administration is over." How right he was!

The evening at the Dirksens was one of the highlights of our Washington experiences. Their home near Herndon, Virginia, was probably an hour and a half's drive from Washington, though in Everett's case that was no big problem because, as minority leader, he was furnished a car and a driver. The old senator could read or nap as he travelled. An avid gardener who specialized in growing marigolds, Dirksen showed us fruit trees and a garden that he tended personally. I envied and admired him for having chosen to live in such a rural setting. Everett Dirksen stands at the head of my list of interesting political personalities. Once, I arranged for a shipment of fresh Oklahoma strawberries from Stilwell to be brought to Washington for distribution to members of the Senate. Several Oklahoma visitors were in the city at the time the strawberries arrived and went with me when I took the first two boxes to Senator Dirksen's office. The Senate photographer accompanied us. Each time Senator Dirksen lined up to have his picture taken, he ran his hand through his thinning gray hair to give it a rumpled and uncombed appearance, his trademark.

A controversy erupted in the Senate over an amendment offered by Dick Schweiker that would give the Government Accounting Office authority to do a thorough job of auditing defense expenditures. I felt that Schweiker was on the right track, largely because of excesses that had grown out of the C5A airplane cost overrun controversy. I was immediately set upon by many of the "hawks" in the Senate, including Everett Dirksen. Everett came striding across from his seat to my place on the back row, seemingly intent on making me change my mind. I think the old man was genuinely startled when I refused to bend to his persuasion. After a few moments, he went back to his seat and never brought up the subject again. I never knew whether or not he was displeased or pleased with the fact that I stood my ground.

During debates on the Senate floor, Everett had the ability to prevail over an opponent though he might not get the votes he needed to win the battle. He had an endless store of pertinent anecdotes which seemed to pop into his consciousness at the crucial time and which helped him immensely in his debating efforts. Even though he was only minority leader, during those months before his death, he dominated the Senate and it was never the same without him. It's difficult to know whether, if Everett Dirksen had lived longer, he might have prevented or moderated some of the excesses of the Nixon administration. He was a great favorite of President Nixon's and it is my feeling that, had he been around, he would have sensed the problems that were developing in the White House and helped President Nixon take timely corrective action.

As a freshman senator, I was unable to secure the committee assignments I most wanted, though I was fortunate in gaining a seat on the Interior Committee. The other committees I was assigned were Labor and Public Welfare, where I had little interest, and District of Columbia, where I had no interest at all. I had hoped for assignment to Foreign Relations, Finance, or Appropriations. I quickly learned that these were the choice committees reserved for the senior senators, many of whom served on more than one of these powerful committees. The Labor and Public Welfare Committee was chaired by Senator Ralph Yarbrough of Texas. At our first meeting, Yarbrough looked around the room, spotted me, and very pointedly made the statement that every senator needed to be on guard against defeat at election time because it was a source of great concern when an outstanding senator like Mike Monroney could be replaced by a Republican unknown. He obviously didn't think I was qualified to serve in Senator Monroney's place on his committee. Yarbrough's attitude toward me never changed.

It was with no reluctance that upon the death of Senator Dirksen a few months later I gave up membership on the Labor and Public Welfare Committee and filled an opening which developed on the Agriculture Committee. This put me on two committees that had great importance to the state of Oklahoma. Interior handled energy legislation as well as Indian Affairs. On the Agriculture Committee I hoped to make my mark and in some ways I succeeded in doing so. I sat one seat down from Bob Dole, who represented Kansas, a heavily agricultural state. Dole had been involved with farm legislation on the House side. He was not trained in agriculture and had no farm experience, but, as a farm state senator, service on the Ag committee was important to him.

Chairman of the Agriculture Committee was Herman Talmadge of Georgia. Herman was a colorful senior senator. From the beginning we got along well. He seemed to be most interested in tobacco legislation, though basically he was a competent and fair chairman. He sat at the head of a long table in our committee room with Democrats arranged by seniority on his right and Republicans on the left. Herman liked to chew tobacco and kept a spittoon beside his right foot. During committee hearings, witnesses sat next to Herman on the right. They were frequently shocked the first time our chairman aimed a stream of tobacco juice at his spittoon. As far as I know Herman never missed the spittoon or splattered a witness' shoe, but it could have happened.

One evening when the Senate was staying in late, Susie Thompson, one of my secretaries, stayed in the office for a couple of extra hours so we could catch up on the mail. After we'd finished the mail, I invited Susie to have dinner with me in the Senate dining room. As we walked into the dining room, I noticed that it was vacant except for a table where Senator Herman Talmadge was seated alone. He stood up and invited us to share the table with him. We accepted. Since Herman had already ordered his food, it arrived ahead of our dinner and Herman went ahead and ate. After he finished eating, he reached in his coat pocket, took out a long, black cigar, and, being the thoughtful southern gentleman that he was, turned to Susie and said, "Do you mind if I smoke?"

To my astonishment, Susie said, "Yes I do." Whereupon, Herman stuck the cigar back in his pocket and the conversation at the table died. After a few minutes, Herman reached in his pocket, took out the cigar, turned away from Susie, lit the cigar, and blew smoke in the opposite direction. So much for Southern chivalry.

Herman arranged for our Ag Committee meetings to begin early so other Senate business would not interfere. We often started at 7 a.m. when we were working on farm legislation and were through with our meeting by nine so that members avoided the usual conflicts. Most committees started at ten and frequently several were going on at the same time so it was impossible for senators to be at all the places they were needed. It was not unusual for a member to have five committee or subcommittee meetings scheduled at the same time. The common practice was for the senator to choose the most important meeting to attend personally and assign staff members to monitor the others. Senators would be summoned when needed for voting. The scheduling conflicts caused senators to miss the discussions and debates on many issues so it was necessary to rely upon staff advice when summoned to vote.

On many matters before the Agriculture Committee, I had experience which I could share and had significant input on farm legislation on different occasions. Having spent years in the wheat and cattle business, I understood the operation of farm programs and could convince others when changes needed to be made. Farm legislation was significantly improved during the twelve years I was in Washington despite the fact that it's difficult to develop workable farm bills when the United States is the only country seriously trying to balance world food supply and demand. Two of the ideas I managed to get incorporated in the farm program were "target price" legislation and the "farmer-owned reserve." The notion of target price came about because high commodity price support levels in the U.S. encourage other grain-exporting nations to grow extra grain and market it at prices slightly below the U.S. support price. This had cost the United States a large share of its export markets.

It was believed to be in the national interest for the U.S. to encourage sufficient production of agricultural products to assure an adequate and dependable domestic food supply plus an abundance for export. It also was considered to be in the national interest to build a floor under farm prices so that if export markets failed to develop, producers would not be economically devastated by the resulting crash in prices which could lead to future food shortages. The problem is that if farmers are to be at the mercy of foreign government policies, then the only way they can continue to produce food abundance is for our government to share the risks. On several occasions, U.S. foreign policy has mandated grain export embargoes, causing U.S. prices to drop. The target price concept provides insurance to producers against political manipulation of the market and to consumers for stable food supply and cost.

The target price idea was simple. The cash costs of producing basic commodities are calculated by the U.S. Department of Agriculture. This becomes the target price. No costs are included for land or labor. The target price is not intended to be profitable to farmers — only a safety net. If the market price is below the target price, a direct payment is made from the U.S. Treasury to farmers based on quantities produced. This lets farm commodity prices float up or down with world prices and takes away the incentive for other countries to overproduce. I worked out the target price idea with Senator Milt Young of North Dakota, another farmer, and it was readily accepted by the Senate, the House, and the administration. It is some satisfaction that this concept is still a part of farm legislation, having survived the test of more than twenty years.

The farmer-owned reserve came as a result of the rapid increase in grain prices that followed huge purchases of U.S. grain by Russia in the early 1970s. At that time, most of the grain surpluses in the country were owned by the U.S. Department of Agriculture. When the USDA chose to do so, they could easily manipulate prices by simply announcing they were going to dump grain on the market. The market would drop immediately, whether sales were made or not. This happened frequently during the time Secretary Freeman was in office and it was something grain farmers wanted stopped. The fact is that cheap food is popular with consumers, who vastly outnumber producers. Cheap food is good politics for most members of Congress — never mind that cheap food means shortages and high prices in the long run. The idea behind the farmer-owned reserve is that it is in the national interest to have a dependable supply of food for domestic use or export. To avoid market manipulation by government for political purposes, producers would retain ownership and control of grain reserves and not be forced to put grain on the market until demand causes price levels to rise. The way the grain market works, it is not wise for anyone to own extra grain when the new harvest begins and prices drop. Therefore, most producers and marketing organizations try to sell all the grain between harvests. The idea of the farmer-owned reserve was to give the nation a protected supply of grain in case of a crop failure in a major producing country and use the reserve only to avoid another run-up of world prices like the one in the mid-70s after the Russian grain deal.

Another change that came as a result of my work on the agriculture committee had to do with the export of grain under a program called PL480. This program authorizes the secretary of agriculture to export grain under favorable conditions to developing countries that face a food shortage. Unfortunately, secretaries of agriculture are also subject to political pressure and sometimes have been known to dump surplus grain on foreign countries to strengthen U.S. grain prices, particularly during an election year. One such event happened at a time when I made a trip to Bangladesh to observe our foreign aid program in operation. Even though the Bangladesh grain farmers had harvested their best crop in years, and even though their warehouses, called "go-downs," were full, the USDA made a decision to send them 250,000 bushels of un-needed and unwanted grain. During the time I was in Bangladesh, different officials raised the issue of why our government was dumping grain on them. Having the grain dumped on the market would further depress prices the Bangladesh farmers would receive and, in addition, much of the U.S. grain would spoil since there was no place to store it and keep it dry during the monsoon.

When I returned to the United States, I inserted an amendment into the Foreign Aid Bill which makes it necessary for the secretary of agriculture to make two findings before grain exports under PL480 could occur. First, the secretary had to determine that there was adequate and suitable storage to prevent waste of American grain when it arrived in a foreign country, and secondly, the secretary had to determine that the export of U.S. grain to a foreign country would not depress local prices and therefore damage the capacity of local people to produce their own food. These came to be known as the "Bellmon amendments."

Another change I was able to make in farm legislation had to do with an irritating problem relating to wheat grading. Over the years the practice of classifying wheat according to "dark hard vitreous" (DHV) qualities had developed. This meant that a grain grader was required to visually inspect grain and classify the kernels that were dark, hard, and vitreous and the other kernels referred to as "yellow berry." These were subjective judgments that had nothing whatsoever to do with food value of the grain. It was possible by chemical analysis to determine the moisture content, the protein percentage, the ash, and even the baking qualities of the wheat protein. But the DHV was an imprecise, subjective grading technique that was often used to force down the price farmers received for grain that had been rained on after it was ripe. The grain merchants also opposed DHV grading since each government grader who inspected the grain would place a different DHV value on any shipment. Repeated efforts were made to get the USDA to quit classifying grain by DHV appearance. U.S.D.A. bureaucrats consistently refused. In the markup of the agriculture appropriation bill I inserted a prohibition against use of any funds for grading grain by DHV standards. This ended the practice, and as far as I know it has never been brought back.

It took several years before I achieved sufficient seniority to be appointed to conference committees to write the final versions of the Ag bill, but toward the end of my service on the Ag committee I was selected. Conference committees are where the action is in Congress. The conferences on agriculture legislation were spirited, though not as lengthy or as heated as the later conferences on budget resolutions. The main differences that needed to be resolved in the farm bills were issues having to do with the levels of price supports or target prices, the conflicts between different commodity groups, the conflicts between various farm organizations and their different philosophies, and of course the perennial arguments as to whether or not the U.S. government should be subsidizing and supporting the production of tobacco. On this last point I was strongly opposed to the use of federal funds to encourage tobacco production in light of the overwhelming evidence connecting tobacco use with lung cancer.

One of the things I hoped to achieve in the U.S. Senate was expansion in the export of American beef, especially to Japan. Farm programs were keeping fifty million acres of American farm land idle at a cost of about $4.5 billion a year to the U.S. Treasury. This seemed a great waste of resources when the world's need for food, especially protein, was growing. Also, this idle land was a serious economic depressant on the levels of prosperity in every American farm community. It was as if a factory producing goods the world vitally needed was being forced by government regulation to operate at sixty percent capacity while many of its workers and much of its equipment stood idle. One product which makes effective use of our land resources and which has a ready market abroad is choice beef. It takes far more land to produce a ton of beef than it does to produce a ton of grain. Also, American consumers were using roughly eighty pounds of beef per capita per year; the Japanese used only five pounds per capita per year. The low consumption was due to beef import controls imposed by the Japanese government. The country is so small and crowded that it can never support a large beef-breeding industry. The Japanese people like beef and pay high prices for the limited supply available. So Japan, which is a highly prosperous industrial nation, was a likely outlet for millions of pounds of American beef each year.

We needed a means of getting around Japanese import restrictions. A trip to Japan was arranged through Drew's friendship with a Korean man named Ki Soo Chin. Ki Soo came to our office, made my acquaintance, and when he found I was interested in going to Japan, he took charge. I do not know to this day how he worked it out or who paid the expenses. I am confident that Ki Soo worked with the Korean Embassy and used his contacts there to get airplane tickets as well as the funds for expenses in Japan and Korea. Drew, Ki Soo, California Congressman Bob Mathias, and I flew from Washington to Tokyo. Ki Soo, who was involved in the export business, made the appointments I needed with ministers in the government with whom I discussed the prospects of shipping American beef to Japan. Ki Soo also arranged a meeting with a Japanese businessman introduced as Machii. I was not impressed when we first met. But Ki Soo arranged for a dinner at Machii's apartment. It was one of the most impressive occasions I have experienced.

Machii's living quarters were on the tenth floor of an apartment building he owned in downtown Tokyo. As we left the elevator and walked towards the apartment entrance, I noticed what appeared to be a lifesize Japanese doll arrangement at the end of the hall. As we reached the entry, the dolls began to move. They were Machii, his wife, and their children, and this was their way of greeting us. The evening got more and more fascinating. Machii, who did not speak English, showed us his collection of rare antique artifacts and oriental art. Our guide pointed out that the collection was worth approximately $15 million. At the appropriate time, his wife and children retired and Machii took us into the formal dining room for dinner. I was struck by the furnishings and architecture of the room. The teakwood table was a large, eight-inch-thick square with a handsome floral arrangement and fountain in the center, flowing with water drawn from a large pool filled with tropical fish. The food was exquisite, with a main course of sukiyaki steak. Machii and I spent much of the evening talking about beef and the tremendous opportunity open to Japan for increased consumption of this needed food product. Machii owned sizable tracts of land about eighty miles from Tokyo and was in the process of developing residential areas. He felt there was room and opportunity to build a large cattle feedlot and was interested in buying lightweight feeder calves in the U.S. and shipping them by air to Tokyo to be fed on his farm for sale in the area. He also owned twenty nightclubs and restaurants in Tokyo and part of his plan was to market his beef through these establishments.

Ki Soo later told me that Machii was not Japanese, but Korean; that his Korean name was Chung. He had been brought to Japan as a slave laborer by his Japanese army captors during World War II. There were 300,000 young Korean nationals in Japan, brought there during the Japanese occupation of Korea, and they were deeply resentful of their Japanese captors. When General McArthur came to Tokyo and undertook to establish democratic processes, he found that his efforts were being thwarted by a communist underground. According to Ki Soo, a colonel on MacArthur's staff decided to ask Machii to take charge of dealing with the problem, because he was considered the most influential. When a trouble-maker was identified, Machii would be given the individual's name, and that person would not be heard from again. Often after the disappearance of a Japanese communist, whatever property that person owned wound up under Machii's ownership. As a result, Machii emerged as a fabulously wealthy person, considered to be one of the richest people in Japan. His holdings include several businesses and apartment buildings, a shipping line, oil and gas property in the United States, and a home in Los Angeles.

After a few days in Japan, arrangements were made for Machii, Congressman Mathias, and our group to go to Seoul, Korea, to check into the possibility of cattle-feeding in that country. In Korea, we had the same access to high government officials and our conversations about beef went smoothly. In short order, an arrangement was worked out for a shipment of American cattle to be sent by air from the U.S. to Korea. A cattle-feeding lot using imported U.S. feed grain would be constructed at a site thirty miles from Seoul. Marketing of the Korean beef in Japan would be simple, due to the large trade imbalance between Korea and Japan. A Japanese reluctance to allow American beef into Japan could be overcome, officials felt, if the beef originated in Korea. Japan seemed eager to allow the Koreans to send anything they produced to Japan. It was reported that the Japanese were buying several millions of dollars worth of Korean seaweed each year and dumping it back in the ocean because they had no use for it. The act of buying the seaweed lessened the strain between the two nations.

A shipment of 350 feeder calves was sent from Tinker Air Force Base in Oklahoma City to Seoul. There the animals were fattened successfully and the beef marketed according to an agreement worked out between the Feed Grain Council in the U.S. and the governments of Korea and Japan. Plans were made for further beef feeding, but at that time prices of American cattle soared to such levels that shipment of feeder calves from this country to Japan became uneconomical. Local cattle were then used to stock the feed lot. The experiment proved to be a source of valuable information and has helped with the introduction of cattle feeding into other Asian countries.

Just as prospects for increased beef consumption by Asians were growing brighter, the price of Arab oil soared and each country was forced to seriously restrict the production or importation of beef because available foreign exchange was needed to buy oil. Beef was a luxury item the Japanese felt their people could get along without. Our well-made plans were wrecked. As for Machii, when we were in Seoul, he undertook to entertain us at one of his nightclubs. We were seated around a table on the floor and the serving girls joined us. As the evening wore on, to my surprise, it became apparent that these girls were available for more services than putting food on the table. I left early.

Back in Tokyo, I paid a last call on Machii at his office. He was not present, but his assistant was there. As Congressman Mathias and I were taking our leave, the man handed each of us a small box. The man expressed Machii's regrets that he could not be there to say goodbye and asked that these gifts be presented to our wives. The small boxes were wrapped in paper marked "Mikimoto Pearls." I put the box in my pocket, expecting it was a set of earrings or some other trinket. When I got home, I handed the unopened box to Shirley and she unwrapped it. I heard her give a startled cry and turned to look. She was holding an exquisite string of pearls. We took them to our local jeweler in Perry to have them appraised. A day or two later he called to tell us he had taken them to an expert who said they were cultured pearls valued at close to $2,000. I was stunned. The act of casually giving such an expensive gift was completely foreign to my experience. Machii ultimately decided against going into the cattle feeding business and I have heard nothing from him since.

While Cliff Hardin was secretary of agriculture, we became good friends. We saw each other frequently on social occasions as well as at Ag Committee meetings. At one point, he was invited to open a trade fair in Kinshasha, the capitol of the African Congo, now called Zaire. It was his mission to help promote contacts and commerce between the people and governments of Zaire and the United States. Senator Miller of Iowa had planned to go along, but he was a candidate for reelection and decided at the last minute he should not make the trip. Shirley and I were invited by Secretary Hardin to go. With only two or three days to prepare, we had our shots and joined the group.

We flew to Rabat, Morocco, where we were domiciled in an American-style hotel and assigned an automobile and driver. The first evening Shirley and I called for our car and told the driver we wanted to see Morocco, not as tourists but as local citizens see the city. Among other places, the driver took us to the "common man's" bazaar, frequented not by tourists or the high income citizens in the city, but by common people. The bazaar stretched along both sides of a street for several blocks and we spent three hours wandering from one shop to another. Merchants lived above their shops and produced their wares in a back room with a shop open to the street. A considerable number dealt in food, much of it from other bazaars where wealthier buyers had already taken what they needed. The goods were shop-worn and reduced in price. About 11:30 that night, as merchants realized closing time was approaching, they began culling the stale and spoiled bakery goods, fruits, and vegetables. This garbage was thrown into the gutter. As this was done, dozens of beggars appeared from nowhere. As fast as the merchants threw away food, the beggars collected it and devoured it or put it in containers. The reason for their haste soon became evident. A large garbage truck appeared at one end of the street and workmen began to shovel up the garbage and throw it in the truck. The beggars were crudely knocked out of the way or moved ahead. It was a heart-breaking scene. The mob of beggars was made up of the very old, the blind, the crippled; some were obviously mentally retarded and some were young children — orphans who had difficulty competing for the food. The workmen had no patience with the beggars, who knew to stay out of their way or suffer harm. Merchants at the bazaar paid little or no attention other than to make sure no beggar came into the shops to steal.

When I hear complaints about America's various welfare programs, I remember this experience of what happens in a society where there is no provision to take care of the less fortunate. There is no question that the American welfare program allows abuses, but there is also no question that our society would be seriously brutalized if no provision were made to help families when members are disabled or aged and cannot care for themselves. In a poor society, an American-type program is out of the question, but the plight of under-privileged citizens impoverishes a nation in ways far beyond simple economics.

One afternoon, guides drove us about 125 miles out of Rabat to a river valley where large acreages were devoted to growing grain, sunflowers, and fruit crops. The grain crop had grown very tall and fallen over. We watched an ancient combine try to harvest the downed and tangled mass of straw and grain. About one-third of the grain was being left on the ground because the combine could not pick it up or because it was carried with the damp straw out the back of the combine onto the ground. The land was fertile, alluvial soil and, given proper management and efficient equipment, could have produced at least double the amount of crop being harvested.

In Zaire we stayed in Kinshasha, the capitol city, which had a population in excess of a million people. It was a primitive place. The evening of our arrival, the local police arrested a band of seven "thieves." The next morning at sunup the entire band was put before a firing squad. The executions were broadcast and rebroadcast on national television. There had been no trial. As likely as not the "thieves" were political opponents of the government. That afternoon, Secretary Hardin had an audience with President Mobutu at the "palace" in Kinshasha. It was a modest, one-story, open building. Congressional members of our party waited in an outdoor reception area while Secretary Hardin and official members of the delegation went in to see the president. Several of us walked around and discovered that the palace was located in the center of the city zoo. Large numbers of wild animals and birds were housed in quarters much like their native habitat. Many people wandered freely about the zoo and over the palace grounds. There was no evidence of security. Close by was another open building with a thatched roof where the president went for meetings with elected officials. The complex was built along the banks of the Congo River, which was over a mile wide at that point and was said to carry more water than all the rivers of the U.S. put together.

While wandering around the grounds, we came upon a dapper, solitary figure wearing a leopard skin military hat and carrying a walking stick with a carved handle. We had no idea who he was but realized he was considerably different from the others. He was walking at a rapid pace, totally unaccompanied even though there were large numbers of people in the park. When we returned to the waiting room, Secretary Hardin was ready to leave and confirmed that the person we had seen was President Mobutu. It struck me as extraordinary that the president of a country could order seven "thieves" put to death without a trial and the same day feel safe to stroll among the people with no body guards and apparently without any thought of personal danger.

Another day, we were taken on a tour of Kinshasha University. It was closed as a result of a rather remarkable set of circumstances. Some months before, President Mobutu's mother had died. In her honor and memory, the president had declared a week of national mourning. To the university students, most on full government-paid scholarships, the week of mourning seemed excessive. They scheduled a mock funeral in which several hundred students, dressed in mourning garb, sobbed, and marched around a make-believe casket located near the flagpole on campus. Upon hearing of their act of disrespect, the president immediately inducted the entire student body of the university into the military. They were not given arms with which they might have rebelled, but were assigned details like cleaning out barns and stables and making garbage collections at various installations. The faculty was similarly inducted and the entire university was closed.

We also visited the president's farm, some forty miles from the city. It was, in effect, the country's agricultural experiment station. The president had ordered that the meeting place for Congress be constructed at this location. Apparently, the president felt that members of Congress would devote more time to business and be less distracted if Congress met at a site well removed from the capitol city. In addition to a meeting area, banquet rooms, and office spaces, each member of the legislature was provided with an apartment, making it unnecessary for members to leave the area. The agricultural research work at the farm was being carried on by a group of Nationalist Chinese from Taiwan. They had taken wasteland and turned it into one of the most productive agriculture areas I have ever seen. There were several hundred acres of rolling, sandy land devoted to the production of pineapple, various vegetables, and rice. The experiment stations showed how productive African land could become under improved management.

Zaire's problems are related to its type of government and to a lack of incentive for outside capitol to invest. Zaire, which is three-fifths as large as the United States east of the Mississippi, has only two thousand miles of highways. Transportation is mainly by boat on the Congo River system or by air.

At the trade fair, about forty American business interests were represented. Next to the Belgians, who had colonized the Congo and occupied the country for many years, Americans had more businesses there than any other nation. There were many types of American food products, pre-fabricated houses, equipment, photographic supplies, and a wide range of other products on display. I had taken along several samples of wheat, soybeans, corn, and peanut products which I attempted to interest different exhibitors in marketing. I also met with the minister of agriculture who told me a story about their past experiences trying to import American food. One shipment of bulgur wheat had been sent over in bulk for use by the military. When it was received, it was heavily adulterated with sand and was inedible. Somewhere along the way, a thief had taken much of the grain and substituted sand. Obviously, the U.S. cannot expect customers to reorder when the product arrives in such condition. Also, government officials complained that under our PL-480 food aid programs, food was often made available to a country but then no effort was made to develop commercial sources for the same type of product. When government funds were cut off, the product people had come to depend on would suddenly disappear. This official felt it would be far better if we arranged for commercial sale of products distributed through PL-480 so that the products would still be available even when conditions in the country made PL-480 funding no longer necessary.

In Liberia, we visited a rubber plantation operated by Firestone. We drove through almost totally underdeveloped areas but upon arriving at the plantation, the situation changed. There were thousands and thousands of acres of carefully manicured land planted to rubber trees. It was an example of the enormous potential Africa holds for future development. Latex gathered from trees was processed into a semi-finished product before it was exported. The area was remote and self-sufficient, with stores, clinics, residences, schools, and basic services needed to support a population. Each worker had complete authority for a certain number of trees. In season, the workers pruned the trees, controlled weeds, tapped the trees, and delivered the latex to the collection center. Pay for rubber workers was considerably higher than incomes for those outside the company. According to company officials, there was a long waiting list of people wanting to work on the rubber plantation.

On the way back, our guide pointed out efforts the native population was making to produce rubber. They were tapping native rubber trees scattered throughout the jungle but were making little progress. Our driver told us that Firestone purchased all the rubber that natives produced. This was far better than having the rubber purchased by government officials because the Americans were "much more honest," the driver told us. I questioned the driver closely but he persistently maintained that dishonesty was so rampant among Liberian officials that the Firestone people were more to be trusted and that the natives preferred this arrangement.

Since our twenty-fifth wedding anniversary was approaching, I talked to an official in the embassy in Monrovia about buying a rough diamond to have made into a ring for Shirley. The man was intrigued by the possibility and arranged for me to call on a local diamond merchant. While Liberia does not produce diamonds, it is a center for black market diamond merchants from the Ivory Coast and other territories where taxes are higher. This "merchant" was actually a smuggler who operated from Monrovia as a contact for a European diamond cutting house.

We climbed four steep, narrow flights of stairs in a nondescript building on the main street. We knocked and a young man with red hair came to the door, raised a window blind, peered out, and allowed us to enter. His quarters were extremely bare — two chairs and a small table covered with linoleum. After a few preliminaries, he began to bring diamonds wrapped in heavy oil paper for us to inspect. He would bring out a bundle, unwrap it, and spread the diamonds so we could examine them one by one. Many packages contained dozens of diamonds, which looked like pieces of broken brown bottles. It was impossible for an untrained person to have any concept of what the diamond would be like once it had been cut and polished. The merchant examined any diamond that interested me to see if desirable qualities were present.

After an hour of searching through one bundle of diamonds after another, the merchant finally told me he felt it was a serious mistake for a person who wanted only one diamond to buy an uncut stone. No matter how carefully the stone was selected, it was impossible to know whether or not unseen flaws would show up during the polishing or whether the stone might break apart and have to be reduced to several smaller ones. A dealer would come out okay on the average, but to take a chance on just one stone was foolhardy. After we had been with the dealer for an hour or so, he told us he wanted to show us something special. He went into his living quarters and brought back a well-wrapped, extra large uncut stone. He said this was a special prize that local diamond merchants had been competing for over a several week period. He had only that day bought the stone for $75,000 and was very proud of his purchase. I was astounded to see such wealth unprotected in such a bare and vulnerable place. I was persuaded by the wisdom of his advice about not buying a single diamond and left without making a purchase.

While the rest of the group visited an American-financed irrigation and flood control project, I flew to Rome. I was trying to find a way to export feeder calves to Italy, which at that time was importing cattle from European Common Market countries as well as from Bulgaria, Yugoslavia, and Romania. In Italy, I was escorted by the U.S. agricultural attache who drove me to Milan and then to a farm near Verona. The farm was operated by a friend of the attache's and was located in the fertile Po Valley which produces corn, wheat, and fruits of many kinds. The land resembles the American corn belt.

Our host, Giorgio Rossonalgia, was an interesting man. A small-time hill country farmer, his health had failed when one of his lungs collapsed. Realizing he could no longer do the hard physical work he had done before to earn a living, he told his wife he was going to sell his property, take the money, and travel to the U.S. where he would tour and look at American agriculture while recovering from his illness. He moved his family in with relatives and followed his plan. He visited U.S. dairies, cattle feeding operations, poultry farms, and toured the corn belt. He was astounded by the openess of Americans and by their readiness to share knowledge. He received what he regarded as a university education. He then approached American international lending institutions and arranged for needed capital. Upon returning to Italy, he forsook the mountainous region where he had been living and acquired land in the Po Valley. Using American capital, technology, and equipment, he put in one of the most modern poultry operations in the world. His poultry buildings housed some 250,000 layers. The feed for his chickens was delivered by conveyor belts. Similar belts brought eggs back to the processing room where workers tested their purity with electronic equipment and packaged them into cartons for shipping. Poultry manure was scattered over the land where corn was planted.

This farmer had a large cattle barn where about 1,000 head of young bulls were being fed on slatted floors over a lagoon. Above the bulls was a grid of electrically-charged wires to keep them from riding each other. Feed for the bulls was silage Giorgio produced on his own land blended with soybean meal which he imported from the U.S. Rossonalgia had become a wealthy person. The family home was a refurbished ancient castle. It was alongside a burned-out silk mill Allied bombers had destroyed during World War II that was being used as a stable for forty thoroughbred horses. Between the stable and the castle, the family had put in a swimming pool.

The family car was a Mercedes, which Giorgio loved to drive at high speeds. On one occasion, he took his family, the attache, and me into Verona for a sightseeing tour and dinner. The speedometer showed us traveling 200 kilometers an hour. I made mention of this high speed, hoping to get him to slow down before we all got our necks broken. He pointed out to me that there was no speed limit and therefore driving fast was okay! Rossonalgia turned out to be a political conservative deeply concerned that the communist movement would bring down the government and result in the same kinds of economic policies that had devastated other countries, including the Balkan states where he bought cattle and conducted business.

We ate dinner in Verona at an outdoor restaurant and Rossonalgia selected some choice Italian dishes for us, including veal. Later I was shown a veal feeding operation. Most of the veal from the feedlot was sent to Germany, France, and England. The less desirable cuts were consumed in Italy, where veal was the preferred meat. But Italian consumers were growing accustomed to choice-fed beef which American-style feedlots would produce.

Using the facts furnished by our Ag attache, I felt Italy could become a purchaser of at least three million head of American feeder calves each year. But my efforts to develop cattle shipments between the U.S. and Italy ran into an unexpected problem. U.S. cattle carry organisms which can cause a disease called blue tongue. It causes practically no difficulty under American conditions, but it was claimed cattle from the U.S. would give the disease to the Italian livestock, which had no resistance to it. Therefore, the Italian government prohibited the importation of live cattle from the U.S. Whether this claim was a ploy to evade competition from U.S. cattle imports could not be determined.

When Secretary Hardin decided to leave the Nixon cabinet and go to work for Ralston Purina, I was interested in seeing that he was replaced by a well-qualified secretary. I talked to Bryce Harlow in the White House on this subject. Bryce later called and asked to have breakfast to discuss the secretary's position. I had no idea what he had in mind and was thoroughly surprised when during the breakfast he told me he had been authorized by President Nixon to offer me the appointment as secretary of agriculture. This offer raised serious questions in my mind. Having recently been elected to a six-year term in the Senate, I felt guilty about walking away from the job when my term was less than half over. My replacement would likely have been a Democrat and I was not sure Oklahoma Republicans who had spent a large sum of money in my election would take kindly to this development. Also, the salaries of cabinet members had been increased to $60,000 at the same time Senate salaries had been increased from $30,000 to $42,500. I wondered whether or not I would be eligible to be appointed and called Bryce and raised the matter with him. Bryce took it up with White House lawyers who concluded the only way I could be appointed secretary of agriculture would be to have Congress pass a special bill reducing the salary back to the level where it had been before Congress acted.

I discussed the matter with several people, including Senator Abe Ribbicoff of Connecticut. Abe had served as secretary of health, education, and welfare in President Kennedy's cabinet. Abe's advice was that becoming a cabinet officer was a great frustration for a senator and former governor. Cabinet officers must be team players, he said, and willing to conform their own views to the views of the president. Senators and governors are in position to make their own decisions and follow the course of action they choose. Cabinet officers don't have that freedom. Based largely on Abe's advice, I decided to remain in the Senate. Bryce told me that since I was not interested, the position would likely go to Earl Butz. He was dean of agriculture at Purdue and a former assistant to the secretary of agriculture under President Eisenhower. He had learned how the bureaucracy operated and established himself as an effective spokesman for farmers and ranchers. He had the reputation of being an eloquent speaker who Bryce and, apparently, the president felt would do a fine job in behalf of both the administration and producers.

The Butz nomination was opposed by many, due to his service as a member of the boards of directors of several large agri-business corporations. The concern was that he would be tempted to represent corporations, not farmers. The Senate Ag committee was divided about his confirmation almost fifty-fifty. His name was sent from committee to the full Senate by one vote, with me voting for him. Chairman Talmadge and ranking Republican Senator Carl Curtis of Nebraska both voted against the Butz nomination. On the Senate floor, after more debate, Butz was finally confirmed by a substantial margin. Once in office, he went overboard to prove he was an advocate for farmers and ranchers, not a tool of agri-business. He became an eloquent speaker and one of the best crowd-pleasers in the Nixon administration. By 1974 Butz was very popular with farmers. Early in that year I invited him to Oklahoma to address the Oklahoma Press Association meeting, another meeting in Tulsa, and a fund-raising event in my behalf. Butz made a great hit at the fund-raiser where several hundred people paid $100 a plate to hear him.

My relationship with Butz began to cool rapidly when the Senate undertook to write a new farm bill, the concept of which Butz opposed. He was sold on the Ezra Taft Benson theory that the best farm program was no program at all. Also, his ideas of agriculture were permanently fixed in his boyhood days on a subsistence-style Indiana farm. He demonstrated no concept of production agriculture or of the risk of growing food under current world market conditions. When Senator Young and I came up with the target price concept and had it written into the farm bill, Butz opposed it vigorously. When the program went through the Ag committee and the Senate without serious opposition and also cleared the House, Butz gradually moderated his position until he finally was agreeable to the bill, provided we set the target prices at low levels and did not build in a cost-of-living escalator. The bill finally was worked out and President Nixon signed it. Amazingly, soon after the bill was passed, Butz became one of its ardent supporters and at times appeared to be taking credit for having originated the idea. He began to push the target price concept for the peanut program and later for rice as well. Butz made public statements opposing embargoes on soybean exports, cotton seed, and, later, on wheat. Either he was ignored or took a different position in the cabinet meetings because export embargoes were put in place. The effect on U.S. farm prices was devastating. As a result of the price drops, farmers turned strongly against the Republican administration.

I became increasingly convinced that Secretary Butz was an opportunist, whose economic philosophy and understanding of agricultural production were far too narrow for the position he held. This became particularly obvious and painful when Butz successfully urged the veto of a new farm bill that would have updated target prices. He never seemed to understand the hazardous financial condition American food producers faced. In order for this nation to continue to have an abundance of food, there must be both the incentive and the means for producers to continue their efforts at efficient production. If farmers and ranchers do not have available the funds for purchasing fertilizer and other inputs, the food supply for this nation's people and our customers abroad will be seriously impaired. Perhaps I made a mistake in not accepting the offer Bryce Harlow made. On the other hand, being a member of the Nixon cabinet when Watergate broke would almost certainly have brought my political demise. There was no point in brooding over the matter for as has been said, "of all sad tales of tongue or pen, the saddest is this, 'It might have been.'"

In Washington, I soon discovered that Oklahoma Welfare Director Lloyd Rader had as many problems and as many projects with Congress and the federal administration as with the Oklahoma state legislature. Because I was on better terms with Rader than Governor Bartlett or other members of the Oklahoma legislative delegation, our Senate office became his Washington home away from home. Carl Williams, who had been my state budget officer, joined my Washington Senate staff, and he and Lloyd had something going continually. Every Rader problem quickly escalated into a crisis, so that I spent a great deal of time trying to work out welfare hang-ups between Lloyd Rader and federal authorities. Time after time, Lloyd berated the Nixon administration for firing all the older, experienced HEW administrators and replacing them with new people who had little concept of how state welfare programs operated and no empathy with those the programs were intended to serve. As time went on, I came to agree with Rader and deeply resented the people Nixon brought into HEW. In particular, problems developed in maintaining federal support for the mentally retarded. I had been close to this program for many years and was extremely agitated when federal regulations were issued establishing unrealistic criteria for state institutions to meet in order to qualify for federal funds. The federal government seemed to intend these regulations to be impossible to comply with so that federal funds could be withdrawn. At Lloyd's suggestion and with his authorship, I introduced an amendment into a Social Security bill which gave legislative sanction to the federal support which Rader had won by administrative action. This amendment was passed, but in writing the regulations to put the amendment into effect, HEW managed to provide grounds for withholding funds except under specific and almost impossible circumstances. A fight went on for over three years until the regulations were finally modified and Lloyd Rader had won again.

Lloyd wanted to bring about a closer working relationship between the Oklahoma University Medical School, Veterans Hospital, Children's Hospital, and the Oklahoma Medical Research Foundation. These institutions were located adjacent to each other and shared services but were financed and governed separately. While governor, I helped get the Oklahoma Health Sciences Center started, and these four institutions are the backbone of the system. But Rader felt closer coordination was needed. On his own and without much help from the governor, legislature, or anyone else, Lloyd managed to accumulate funds to rebuild the old children's hospital and, in his words, "make it the finest children's hospital on the face of the earth."

Lloyd brought Dan Macer, administrator of the VA Hospital, to my office in Washington. They explained that the Everett Tower, part of the Oklahoma Medical school, had been overbuilt. The original plan had been for this hospital to have six hundred beds. During construction, funds ran short so the hospital had been completed with fewer than four hundred beds while it had kitchen, operating rooms, laboratories, and other facilities to take care of a much larger population. Across the street, the VA Hospital badly needed access to the kinds of facilities under-utilized at Everett Tower. Macer and Rader came up with a plan to build an overhead corridor across Thirteenth Street to physically connect the VA Hospital and Everett Tower. Their plan would have made possible the sharing of facilities by all three institutions. The potential economic savings were considerable.

I made an on-sight inspection and concluded the scheme was sound and went to work on the VA officials in Washington to gain their consent. Once they approved, a meeting was scheduled in Speaker Carl Albert's Washington office at which Macer, Rader, Governor David Hall, the head of the VA, members of the Oklahoma delegation, and others were present. To my absolute amazement, even though he had originally expressed his support for the idea, Governor Hall stood up in the meeting and said it was too soon to proceed and that he wanted a study made. This derailed the whole idea since nothing could be done without the governor's support. We discovered later that some of the veterans orga-nizations had gotten in touch with Governor Hall, who was soon to run for reelection, and convinced him the scheme was not popular with veterans. Rader felt betrayed and was furious. So was I. The Hall flip-flop made us both look foolish to federal officials.

In the meantime, Rader continued with construction of the Children's Hospital and we did move ahead with the corridor plan later. After Governor Hall's defeat by David Boren, the connecting link was finally built and closer cooperation between the medical institutions became a reality. During the time Lloyd Rader was focusing his attention on rebuilding Children's Hospital and other buildings in the medical com-plex, he decided to renovate an existing four-story structure and turn it into offices for the faculty at the medical center. He arranged for his carpentry crew to thoroughly remodel the interior of the building and divide it into suites of offices. The carpenters had finished their work and the painting crew was busy in the building. Cleta Detherage, a legislator from Norman, drove by the building and felt it might be suitable for housing prison inmates who came to the medical complex for treatment.

She made such a suggestion in a statement on the House floor during a debate. When Mr. Rader heard of Cleta's suggestion, he was extremely angry. He did not like the idea of prisoners being housed at "his" medical complex even though they were ill and in need of treatment. To avoid this eventuality, he immediately contracted with a demolition crew to destroy the building. It was somewhat of a surprise to the painting crew that was still working in one end of the building when the wrecking ball started knocking down the opposite end. The next Monday morning when Cleta Detherage drove past where the building had been, she was amazed to find it gone.

One of the first calls I received after my election to the U.S. Senate was from Doug McKeever who told me that Judge Chandler of the federal court for western Oklahoma wanted to talk to me. I had no idea what the judge had on his mind. I had never met him, though I certainly had heard a great deal about him, most of it unflattering. Judge Chandler had long been the most controversial judge to serve on the federal bench in Oklahoma. At one point, the tenth circuit in Denver had gone so far as to withhold cases from him. This action was dealt with in a Supreme Court suit in which Judge Chandler claimed that, in effect, the tenth circuit had impeached him and that the constitution provided that only Congress could take such action. Judge Chandler won that case. I arranged an appointment with the Judge. He was in his late sixties and still had the appearance of great physical vigor and mental alertness. He said he wanted to resign from active duty on the bench, but the controversy surrounding him had besmirched his name and he could not resign unless action was taken to restore his reputation. He proposed to resign on two conditions: that I arrange for him to be appointed to the Appellate Court in the District of Columbia, and that I arrange the appointment of Doug McKeever as his successor.

The judge's conditions were an affront to me. There is no provision for a federal judge to choose his successor and any judge who had his controversial background would not be confirmed by the U.S. Senate for a position on the D.C. Court of Appeals. Over the months, I discussed with the judge various means of obtaining his resignation. These conversations involved Attorney General John Mitchell and especially Deputy Attorney General Richard Kleindienst. They were both eager to proceed with the resignation but clearly could not go along with Judge Chandler's unreasonable conditions.

The Washington lawyer who had won the judge's case before the Supreme Court was the Republican national committeeman for the District of Columbia. He became a regular visitor in my office and we tried to work out arrangements with Judge Murrow, who had become the administrative officer of the U.S. Court of the Judiciary. Murrow was one of those Judge Chandler disliked and mistrusted most and Murrow's appointment to the Court of the Judiciary made discussions with Judge Chandler even more difficult. Complicated negotiations went on for years and finally Judge Chandler agreed to accept appointment to the Franklin D. Roosevelt Memorial Commission. This was a nothing position but Judge Chandler became convinced it would be a sufficient face-saving appointment. When the judge's resignation was finally received, to my astonishment, he had attached another condition requiring the promotion of his secretary and other members of his staff and stipulating the full use of his quarters for as long as he desired. These conditions made it impossible for the Justice Department to accept the resignation and the whole arrangement fell through. I discovered he had tried to work similar deals with Mike Monroney and these also had never culminated.

Meanwhile, Dewey Bartlett had been elected to the U.S. Senate, so Judge Chandler took his ideas to Bartlett and began to try to work out some arrangement with him. I explained to Dewey at great length all that had transpired in this matter. We decided that at the first opportunity we both would confront Judge Chandler and tell him to his face there would be no deals and no further negotiations and that when he was ready to resign, all that was required was that he submit his letter to the president. On the day the appointment with Judge Chandler was arranged, Dewey and I happened to be on the Senate floor together. We returned to my office, where Judge Chandler was waiting, and both of us went after him. Dewey told him in as straight and strong language as he could what the situation was. The judge blanched and stuttered and tried quickly to figure out another devious proposition. But neither Dewey or I would hear any more of it. He left the office and that was the last I ever saw of him. Since I had filled all the federal patronage positions in Oklahoma, Dewey and I worked out an agreement that the first vacancy for U.S. judgeship would be his to fill. This was also explained to Judge Chandler

When he did ultimately resign, he was replaced by Judge Ralph Thompson, Dewey's nominee.

Judge Chandler had one of the most undisciplined minds of anyone I ever encountered. On the desk in his chambers he kept a pencil holder full of probably fifty newly-sharpened yellow pencils. Also on his desk he kept a stack of yellow legal pads. As quickly as a conversation began, he would take one pencil after another and doodle page after page of concentric circles. I once discussed the judge with Dale Cook. As Assistant U.S. District Attorney, Dale had frequently been in his court. Cook recalled that Judge Chandler had been appointed over Justice department objections at the insistence of former Senator Elmer Thomas. Apparently Thomas owed Judge Chandler some favor for the work he had done in Thomas's campaign. After he was nominated, the American Bar Association and the F.B.I. both refused him clearance, and the matter hung fire for a considerable time until Thomas could build pressure in the Justice Department which caused them to yield and give Judge Chandler the green light. After he was sworn in as judge, the first dozen or so of his decisions were reversed one after another by the Tenth Circuit Court. The judge decided he would allow no more of his cases to come to trial. From that point on it was almost impossible for litigants to get him to set their cases for trial. Rather, he procrastinated and browbeat contestants until they were willing to settle out of court. At the time he was appointed, he was a young and inexperienced attorney. After the first series of reversals, he seemed to suffer from an immense inferiority complex. He did not possess either the qualifications or the character normally found in a federal judge.

Judge Chandler's case caused me to do a great deal of thinking about finding some method of removing incompetent judges from the federal bench. After all is said and done, I am convinced the present system is as good as can be devised. Federal judges need the security of the lifetime tenure in order to make the sometimes difficult and unpopular decisions they are called to make under the U.S. constitution. If the time ever comes when judges must stand for reconfirmation or be subject to political pressures, the possibility of obtaining justice in the U.S. courts will be significantly diminished. Therefore, I believe the system can afford to suffer the handicap of an occasional Judge Chandler better than it could bear up under the political pressures which might build up in times of social stress if the position of federal judge were made less secure.

While serving as national chairman in 1972, George Bush came to my office one day and asked if I was planning to run again for the Senate. My first term was ending and, apparently, the rumor had reached him that I might not run for reelection. George was concerned that I stay in. He told me that President Nixon was in far more trouble than any of us realized and was certain to need all the friends he had in the Senate. George made me promise that before I made a decision, I would talk it over with him and that I would not make any public announcements against running until he had a chance to discuss it with me further. A week or so later, I went to his office and we had another talk about the Senate race. He told me he was going to have the president call me. That evening I flew back to Oklahoma and the next day, President Nixon called. He also hoped I would run again and that I would announce my intentions at an early date. After that conversation, I talked to Ferrold Hammock, who was looking after the farm, about whether or not he would be willing to continue to run the farm for another six years. He agreed and within a day or two I held a press conference in Oklahoma City in which I announced I would seek another term in the Senate.

As time approached for the 1972 presidential campaign, I realized we should have someone in Oklahoma actively involved in the activities of that election. This would give us a chance to observe the effectiveness of the various campaign workers and help us prepare the organization for my 1974 reelection effort. I discussed this matter with Drew Mason, told him that we should find the right person and get him involved in the '72 campaign and give him the responsibility for laying the foundation for 1974. A short time afterward, Drew came to my office, told me that he had found the person and identified the person as himself.

Drew's decision to return to Oklahoma was a considerable shock to me. I felt that he was totally oriented and acclimated to the Washington scene, that he was doing a fine job and enjoying his work. I had no thought that he would want to return to Oklahoma. Whether he made this decision as a service to me and at a sacrifice to himself, I do not know, but it was his choice. This decision may very well have resulted in the margin needed in my narrow reelection. In such a close campaign, there is no way to really know. The same statement could be made about many individuals and decisions.

Drew's return to Oklahoma put him in a position of managing our state office operation. Since he knew he would be in Oklahoma for at least two years, he and Janet purchased a home in the Edmond area. I was frequently an overnight guest at their home and Drew and Janet often hosted social events for members of the staff or those engaged in political activities. In the 1974 campaign, Drew insisted upon and was given the title of campaign manager. In that campaign, it proved impossible to find a person with proper credentials to take the title of finance chairman, so in effect, Drew filled that position as well. It is entirely due to Drew's efforts that the financing of the 1974 campaign was possible. He used the direct mail experience and talents he had developed earlier in the Nixon presidential campaign and, in addition, put together many fund-raising dinners involving Washington personalities. This method was used early in the campaign to generate funds. In addition, he was extremely persuasive in working with the National Republican Senatorial committee which contributed heavily to the campaign. In total, the 1974 campaign used more than $700,000. We tried to be careful to avoid using government-paid employees or other government services in the campaign. The cost of the campaign could have been held down had we not put Drew and other staff members on our campaign payroll and had we utilized our Washington staff in campaign activities, as other members often did.

School integration, which was one of the greatest controversies of my Senate career, was a major factor in the 1974 campaign. The school issue had been particularly troublesome in the Senate because Senator Jesse Helms and a few other Southern senators rarely missed an opportunity to propose an "anti-busing amendment" in every appropriations bill or other vehicle which was appropriate. In every case, I voted to let integration continue and was roundly criticized by newspaper editorials, particularly in the *Daily Oklahoman*. It was an issue that wouldn't die. The anti-busing quarrel grew extremely intense, especially in Oklahoma City, where a federal judge had ordered cross-town busing to accomplish integration which the school board had not been able or willing to accomplish otherwise. Busing became such an explosive issue that one city council candidate acquired a yellow school bus, parked it at busy shopping malls and intersections, and provided baseball bats and sledge-hammers for people to use to beat on the bus. He was elected. In the 1974 campaign I was to be opposed by former Congressman Ed Edmondson, who initially favored integration but changed his position in my race and came out strongly against busing.

The 1974 campaign proved to be, by far, the most difficult statewide campaign of my career. It was clearly an uphill fight from the beginning; early polls showed me behind by thirteen percent. Matters were not helped by several blunders made by President Ford. At that time, the whole country was turned off by politics. The Watergate scandals had soured many previously enthusiastic Republicans who had felt that our party was clean and above much of the corruption they had seen in Oklahoma state government under Democratic administrations. It now looked as if both Republican and Democrat politicians were the same tainted breed. Also, there were a great many difficulties besetting the state. Besides the busing issue, there were economic problems. Cattle prices were so low that many growers faced bankruptcy. The economic condition of rural voters upon whom I heavily depended was bad and getting worse. With the electorate's anti-government attitude, volunteers were hard to recruit and motivate. I was handicapped in building a campaign organization because I had to spend most of my time in Washington.

Ed Edmondson was a worthy opponent. He had run against Dewey Bartlett and was well known throughout the state. Articulate and energetic, he was a more talented and vigorous campaigner than Monroney had been. He also had the advantage of overwhelming Democratic registration and twenty-two years of service in the House of Representatives. Another handicap was the fact that Doc Jordan's advertising agency had now become quite large. Since Jordan could not give his full time to my campaign, he assigned a young woman to be the account executive. She tried hard, but there was not the same working relationship which Jordan and I had enjoyed in previous years, and nothing in our advertising campaign really sparkled. Perhaps the fault was more mine than the agency's but all the way around, the 1974 political advertising campaign did no credit to either of us. Altogether, the lack of Jordan's personal involvement, the handicap of Watergate and the Nixon and Ford administrations, the economic difficulties, the generally sour attitude voters had toward government, the negative campaign which Edmondson ran, and my own somewhat less than all-out enthusiasm for the Senate made the 1974 Senate campaign an experience that I would just as soon forget.

At the time Edmondson filed for the Senate, I looked forward to a gentlemanly campaign. I felt there was good rapport between Ed and myself and that the campaign would come off on a basis of "may the best man win." How wrong I was. My first campaign experience with Edmondson came at a meeting with the cable television group in Oklahoma City. Candidates for both governor and U.S. Senate were included. I was prepared for the event but was shocked at the fierce personal attack Edmonson made on me. It was obvious he was not going to carry on a campaign based on issues but had made up his mind to go after me personally and be as destructive as he could. I decided that Ed, who had acquired the services of Marty Haun, the state's leading Democratic campaign consultant, was determined not to be accused of the same low-key campaign he had carried on unsuccessfully in the U.S. Senate race against Dewey Bartlett. This time he seemed to be going all-out to convince voters that I was unqualified for the job. He had accepted the old philosophy that voters vote against rather than for candidates. In eight various programs, including television debates, in which we appeared jointly, we never got around to discussing issues. They always degenerated into name-calling contests.

One evening, Channel Eight in Tulsa invited me to appear on its one-hour nightly news program. After arriving, I was surprised to be informed that Ed would also be on the program. Just before we went on the air, I learned we would appear *together*. There was no time or opportunity to make preparation for the unannounced encounter. When Edmondson walked into the studio, I realized he had been tipped off well in advance because he carried a foot-high stack of research on my Senate record. As soon as we went on the air, the television reporter announced he was going to give each of us the opportunity to ask the other questions. From then on, Edmondson dominated the program. Prepared with excerpts of my statements from the Congressional Record, he put me on the defensive and kept me there throughout the program. I was infuriated and felt Channel Eight had double-crossed me by inviting me to this encounter without announcing it would be a joint appearance.

The one light moment in the campaign came when a group of Edmondson supporters stopped to campaign on Main Street in Billings, my hometown. Unknown to the group, Billings is also the home of the Fairchild Center, a large nursing home that cares for mentally retarded adults. Local citizens are accustomed to seeing Fairchild residents hiking together, carrying walking sticks, and talking, gesturing, and shouting. The Edmondson visitors were not prepared for such a sight. When the Fairchild Center residents reached Main Street on their daily walk, the Edmondson campaigners assumed they were about to be attacked by a mob of angry Bellmon supporters. In great haste, they jumped into their automobiles and sped out of town. Thinking to embarrass me, they promptly reported the incident to the media. The embarrassment was theirs when reporters checked and discovered what really happened.

By the time election day came, I realized I was in a fight for my political life, but I felt I would win — narrowly. The polls, including two we had run, showed me losing. But each poll showed we had gained somewhat so that by election day we might well be pulling ahead. I went to the "watch party" with fairly high spirits. As the evening wore on, my high spirits sank. The early lead we built up in Tulsa County eroded until, by early morning, we were barely ahead. In fact, there was one report which showed us more than 1,000 votes behind. I watched Ed make his public appearances. One statement was to the effect that God was on his side. By 5 a.m., when I became exhausted and went to bed, the outcome was unknown, though it appeared we were 2,000 or 3,000 votes ahead. The next day when the count was over, we had won by a scant 3,700 votes. It was difficult to believe I had lost heavily in the rural areas where I had counted on a fairly strong vote. It was equally difficult to understand how I had carried Oklahoma County. Because of the school busing issue, I had expected to lose there, heavily. Oklahoma County may have proved that Edmondson's heavy-handed campaigning methods did not work. He had made a statement during the campaign that I was a "pet coon." This racial slur may have turned the busing issue, which was hurting me badly there, around to some extent. I carried many black precincts.

After the election, I was concerned we would be in for a lengthy, controversial, and costly recount. We called supporters throughout the state to keep watches on the ballot boxes. To my amazement, Ed made the decision not to have a recount, but to challenge the election on the basis of "massive irregularities" which he alleged had occurred in Tulsa

County. The protest was based on the way the Tulsa County election machines were programmed. The fact that the county and state election machinery was totally dominated by Democrats did not matter to him. Also the fact that I had nothing to do with programming voting machines made no difference to my highly partisan opponent.

The Senator, Part Two

"This Is One Vote that Will Make You Proud"

I felt the Edmondson challenge was unfounded and would get nowhere. Yet I confess a high degree of apprehension after evidence had been presented to Judge Byrum in the Tulsa District Court and as the judge began to announce his decision. Judge Byrum was a life-long Democrat and I did not know whether his decision would be made strictly on the evidence or whether he might allow partisan considerations to dominate. The three to five minutes he took to make his statement are some of the longest minutes I have ever endured. He began by stating what seemed to be points in Edmondson's favor. As he went on, I felt he would eventually get around to saying "but" and then would go in my direction. Of course this *finally* happened, but it seemed to take a lifetime for him to announce that conclusion. I later went to the judge's chambers and thanked him for what he had done. He proved to be a warm and understanding person, obviously a man of great strength and courage. Naturally I developed a high regard for him. My confidence in our judicial system also was tremendously enhanced.

Edmondson's appeal was heard before the Oklahoma Supreme Court. It did not carry the same emotional strain for me as in the Tulsa court. I felt Judge Byrum's decision would be upheld. As the questioning went on, it was obvious the court was leaning in my direction, and I was not greatly surprised that its decision was unanimous in my favor. Edmondson's challenge before the U.S. Senate *was* a surprise. I felt that having gone through the Oklahoma courts, which were totally made up of Democrats, Ed should and would accept their decision. I had difficulty taking the Senate challenge seriously and doubted it would receive significant attention.

The fact that a New Hampshire contest between Wyman and Durkin was before the Senate gave Ed an advantage. Chairman of the Rules Committee, Howard Cannon of Nevada, became incensed by the successful efforts of Republicans to filibuster the New Hampshire decision and prevent it from coming to a vote. Republicans felt it was not safe to allow the matter to come before the Senate where Democrats heavily outnumbered Republicans, that partisanship would play the decisive role. They felt there was no choice but to hold out for another election. The New Hampshire matter was finally settled by sending it back to state authorities with instructions to hold a new election. Durkin, the Democrat, won the election. The outcome in New Hampshire, while favorable to Democrats, did nothing to change Howard Cannon's angry feeling toward Republicans. He took the floor of the Senate and made a bitter, partisan attack on Republicans for their conduct in the Wyman-Durkin controversy. The New Hampshire matter proved how difficult it is for Congress to deal with the issue of seating members on the basis of factual information. Those contests generally come down to a partisan vote, regardless of the facts. I became concerned my case also would be decided on a partisan vote and I began to understand why Edmondson had challenged my election before the Senate.

The matter was delayed until the New Hampshire case was settled. This took several months. Afterwards, I had hoped the Edmondson challenge would be dropped quickly and quietly, but this was not to be the case. Even though the facts already had been thoroughly considered in two Oklahoma court cases, the Rules Committee sent investigators to Oklahoma on different occasions and held hearings in Washington. Finally, after a delay of sixteen months, my advisers and I made the decision to force the issue in a vote on the Senate floor. The question was phrased so if we lost, the matter would still be before the Senate and additional work could be done to bring in the votes we needed. Since Republicans were outnumbered thirty-seven to sixty-one, it was necessary for me to talk to several Democrats to see if they could cross party lines and vote in my favor. It hurt my pride and offended my sense of fairness, but I began to lobby for votes. Among those I approached was Senator Jim Eastland of Mississippi. Jim was not a particular friend of mine and I had not served with him on any committees, but he did seem a fair person who was above partisanship. When I approached him with the problem, he immediately agreed to help. When our plan was changed and we decided to approach the matter in a slightly different way, I went back to him to explain the change in plans. Senator Eastland cut me off in mid-sentence. He put his arm around my shoulders and said, "Boy, when I tell you I'm *with* you, I'm *with* you." And he was.

Eastland's attitude was shared by other southern Democratic senators, many of whom voted for me to be seated. Among those I did not approach was Senator Lloyd Benston, Democrat from Texas. Lloyd had been mentioned prominently as a Democratic presidential candidate. He was a wealthy Texan and had always seemed aloof and somewhat unapproachable as far as I was concerned. Among those I counted on was Senator Ed Muskie, with whom I'd worked closely as the ranking member of the Budget Committee. Ed and I had an excellent working relationship and were on good personal terms. I felt I did not need to discuss the matter with him and did not do so. Another prominent Democrat with whom I had a good relationship was Hubert Humphrey. He and I had travelled to Moscow in the dead of winter. In addition, we served on the Ag committee and had participated in joint hearings dealing with rural development. We had a friendly personal relationship, and I felt he was one vote I could count on. When the roll was finally called on the Edmonson-Bellmon controversy, I was formally seated by a single vote. Ed Muskie was not present and Hubert Humphrey voted against me. Hubert explained he had to cast one vote for the party and that he would have been for me the second time around. Baloney! However, to my amazement, Senator Lloyd Benston, with whom I had had no relationship and with whom I had not discussed the matter, contributed the deciding vote. Later, when I became better acquainted with Benston, I asked him why he crossed party lines and voted in favor of seating a Republican. Lloyd told me that during his campaign for the Democratic presidential nomination, he had come to Oklahoma to contact party leaders asking their support. Among those he called upon was Ed Edmondson, who refused to make the desired commitment to Benston. That night while Benston was in his motel room, he turned on the television to watch the ten o'clock news. I was being interviewed and one of the questions asked was which of the Democrats I felt would make the best president. Without hesitation, I said "Lloyd Benston." He told me his vote had paid me back!

Two days after the vote, I was scheduled to catch an airplane at

Washington National airport to make an appearance in Oklahoma. I went rushing through the airport late, as usual, reached the gate with only minutes to spare, passed my ticket to the attendant, and hurried onto the aircraft looking for my seat. To my astonishment, the two persons sitting in adjacent seats were Ed Edmondson and his wife, June. As I put my briefcase in the overhead compartment and started to take my seat, Ed looked up, saw who I was and said, "I wonder what the mathematical probability of this is." That's all that was said between us during our long and tense ride from Washington to Tulsa.

This whole series of events convinced me congressional methods of deciding contested elections needed to be changed, particularly with regard to the provisions in the constitution allowing the House of Representatives to select a president in case no candidate receives a majority in the electoral college. It is almost certain such a selection would be made on a partisan basis. The result could be a president who received fewer popular votes than the loser. I doubt this country could be well or wisely governed by a president who lost in the popular vote then was chosen in the House of Representatives on a partisan basis. Unquestionably, a president who takes office under those circumstances will have problems governing this nation and providing leadership on the world scene.

The long hiatus during which I served in the Senate under a cloud probably reduced my effectiveness to a degree. It definitely soured my attitude toward the partisanship displayed by many members. The lengthy contest added to the alienation I was building up toward the total Washington scene. It's no fun being a second-class senator. Nevertheless, I had to go on. Over four years remained in my term, and I wanted to make the most of it.

My departure from the agriculture committee came about under rather unusual circumstances. When Senator Robert Dole became the ranking member of the agriculture committee, I realized there was little chance Dole would leave the committee because of the importance of agriculture in his home state of Kansas and that he was unlikely ever to be defeated. I was one seat junior to Dole and my becoming chairman or ranking member of the committee was foreclosed as long as we were both in the Senate. After my reelection in 1974, I had the option of becoming the ranking member on the budget committee. To take this position it was necessary to give up one of my other committee assignments. Since the opportunity to serve on the budget committee had arisen out of my service on appropriations, it was necessary I remain on that important committee. The opportunity to become a ranking member was too good to pass up so I forfeited my seat on the Ag committee and became ranking on the budget committee. From that point on, the budget work heavily overshadowed all my Senate activities and kept me from active involvement in developing other legislation.

As the ranking Republican on the budget committee, had I run in 1980 and been reelected, I would have become budget chairman, since Republicans won control of the Senate in 1980. I had strongly disagreed with President Reagan's "supply-side economics" as a member of the budget committee. In fact, I was one of two Republican senators who voted against a Republican-sponsored amendment to the fiscal year 1981 budget resolution that made room for a "supply-side economics" tax cut in 1981. As chairman of the budget committee, I would have faced a Hobson's choice: either go against a newly elected, popular Republican president (which would have been political suicide, especially in Oklahoma), or resign a powerful committee chairman post, or change my position and put aside my own strong belief that supply-side economics would not work. I've always been thankful I did not have to make such a choice.

My assignment to the budget committee brought me into contact with the chairman, Senator Edmund Muskie, a powerful Democrat with whom I had no prior relationship. I stood in considerable awe of Muskie. As a former governor of Maine, a former presidential contender, and one of the most powerful debaters in the Senate, he was not easy for a junior Republican to deal with. Also, he was reputed to own a violent temper. After I was selected ranking Republican member of the budget committee, the first thing I did was to contact Robert Boyd, who had served on my governor's staff and who had moved to Kansas City where he was working as an investment banker. After some arm-twisting, Bob came to Washington at a salary sacrifice and immediately plunged into his duties as minority chief of staff of the Senate budget committee. One of our first actions was to schedule a session with Senator Muskie.

I approached the meeting in a state of fear and trembling. I wanted agreement on the conditions controlling committee operations to assist in establishing an effective and lasting budget process. I told Senator Muskie I felt as a ranking minority member I should be allowed to select one-third of the staff, that our staff needed satisfactory quarters equivalent to those used by the majority, and that I should have a voice in choosing witnesses and access to research funds in case they were needed by the minority members. Also, I suggested to Senator Muskie that we fight our battles in committee and that once the committee agreed on a position and developed a resolution, that, regardless of our position on the issue in committee, we should both defend the budget committee's position when the resolution reached the Senate floor. To my surprise, Senator Muskie readily agreed to all my proposals. I was amazed at how reasonable and pleasant Senator Muskie was as our working relationship began. He had a reputation of being something of a tyrant with staff and I had often seen him verbally destroy members who opposed him during debate on the Senate floor. He was an extremely eloquent and skilled debater, and possessed perhaps the loudest voice of any of the one hundred senators.

The budget process started on shaky ground. It was looked upon by other powerful committee chairmen such as Russell Long, chairman of the finance committee, and John McClellan, chairman of the appropriations committee, as an intrusion onto their turf. Until the budget committee was established there was no place in Congress where matters relating to both spending and revenue came together so intelligent decisions could be made. It was largely due to the strength, energy, and dedication of Senator Muskie that the budget process survived the initial phase. Muskie was dedicated to making the process work. Never once did he depart from our agreements. He was a man of his word and he made me keep my end of the bargain. As chairman of the budget committee, Ed Muskie was looked upon by Republicans as a liberal. But those of us who worked with him closely and observed his leadership soon became convinced that while Muskie may have been liberal on social issues, he was probably the most financially responsible and fiscally conservative member of the Senate. Perhaps his attitude had been shaped by his service as governor, but for whatever reason, he was anything but a big spender.

Muskie's famous, or infamous, temper proved no problem. He seemed to know when and how to use it as an effective debating device. Even when he appeared most agitated in floor or committee debate, he would make a quiet aside remark to me that let me know he was in full control of his wit, his words, and his actions. He was always considerate — even kind — to me and I came to respect him as ally and friend. Given more time, I believe he would have made a great Secretary of State.

My work was made easier because of the philosophical inclinations of three Democratic budget committee members: Senator Sam Nunn of Georgia, Senator Fritz Hollings of South Carolina, and Senator Lawton Chiles of Florida. These three frequently joined the six Republicans to make a majority on committee votes. Even though Senator Muskie might argue vigorously for his position and lose when the committee voted, once a position was adopted he would support the budget committee resolution with all his vigor and eloquence when it was brought to the Senate floor. During one period, Muskie was immobilized due to a back problem. His chief of staff, John McAvoy, Bob Boyd, and I went to the Muskie home on occasion to transact budget committee business. I have never seen a staff member abused more viciously than John was at the hands of Senator Muskie. During one particularly bitter tirade from the senator, John wrote a note and handed it to Boyd. The note said, "Is $55,000 a year enough to put up with this?" I never understood why Muskie was so easy for other senators to work with, yet so tough and even mean to the staff who served him to the best of their ability.

In budget committee work there was a sharp contrast between the way Senate Republicans operated and the way House Republicans functioned. On the House side, under their ranking member, Delbert Latta of Ohio, most Republican members refused to be a constructive part of the process and simply voted no. To get the budget resolution through the House budget committee, it was necessary for the committee chairman, Congressman Brock Adams from Washington state, to draft a resolution with generous spending for social programs and low spending for defense.

The House resolution always was heavy on social spending and the Senate resolution was heavy on defense spending. Thus, when the House and Senate conferences were held, we were at loggerheads as we endeavored to work out a middle ground and produce a resolution that could win a majority of votes in both the House and Senate. On one occasion I went to Congressman John Rhoades, Republican leader of the House, to try to get him to persuade Latta and the House Republicans to take a more constructive role. Rhoades explained that the House Republicans were determined to use the budget process and budget resolutions as a way to win Republican control of the House of Representatives. Therefore they were not going to participate in a positive way. The irony of it is that four years later the Republicans won control of the *Senate* and were not even close to winning control of the House. So much for political connivance.

Senator Muskie continued as chairman of the budget committee until he resigned to become Secretary of State during the last six months of the Carter administration. His position was taken by Senator Fritz Hollings of South Carolina. Senator Hollings and I continued the same compatible relationship which had existed earlier. Fritz was a strong party person but he was philosophically conservative and had a pro-business and pro-defense bent which made it easy for us to work together. I went so far as to make a small contribution to Fritz's campaign when he tried to win the Democratic presidential nomination in 1984.

As a member of the appropriations committee, I served on the subcommittee that handled White House funds. This brought me into an interesting relationship with Vice President Nelson Rockefeller and his wife Happy. Arrangements had been made for the vice president to take over a dwelling on Massachusetts Avenue which was located on the Naval Observatory grounds. It had been used as a home by numerous admirals. Congress felt it was more appropriately suited as the official residence for the vice president. The building was reported to be more than one hundred years old, and while it was stately and well-built, it lacked many of the modern necessities such as air-conditioning. A study was made and it was determined that, largely due to the thickness of the walls and the fact that major structural changes would have to be made, the cost of installing air-conditioning was something in the range of $180,000. Nelson contacted me and asked that this sum be provided so the house could be made more livable and useful for official functions. There were many members of the appropriations committee who felt that spending $180,000 simply to air-condition an existing dwelling was an extravagance. It took some effort on my part to get the appropriation approved. Nevertheless, the bill was passed and became law and the air-conditioning was accomplished. A few months later, Shirley and I, along with several other guests, were invited to the newly refurbished home for vice presidents. Happy was a warm, personable woman and it was obvious she appreciated the work Congress had done to make their home more livable. She took me in tow and showed me many changes they had made, including the fact that the air-conditioning vent for the master bedroom dumped cold air directly on the spot where they tried to sleep on their $35,000 bed. In order to direct the air in a different direction, Nelson had climbed up and taped a hand towel over the vent.

The passage in 1975 of the Pearson-Benston Amendment, whereby the Senate, for the first time in history, took a step toward decontrol of natural gas, throws a little light on how the Senate operates. My involvement started by accident when I happened to be on a Senate subway car with Russell Long, Chairman of the Senate finance committee. Russell was widely regarded as a leader of the southern block and was particularly respected in legislation dealing with taxation or financial matters.

During our brief ride, Russell mentioned that with the upcoming vote on gas deregulation it would be wise for members who were knowledgeable in the energy area to get together to develop a plan of action. I agreed, but the ride ended before more was accomplished. Concerned that Russell would not follow up on the thought, I contacted his colleague from Louisiana, Senator Bennett Johnston, and recounted the conversation. Johnston agreed to such a meeting and we immediately called Long and worked out a time and place. Johnston invited Democratic senators and I invited Republicans.

Fifteen members, seven Republicans and eight Democrats, showed up for the session. A strategy was developed whereby there would be an initial offering of a gas deregulation bill which all agreed would never pass. But it would give senators from consumer states something to vote against. We agreed the Pearson-Benston Amendment would then be offered. Long wanted to insert language establishing a ceiling on natural gas based on the BTU value of "new oil." I strongly opposed this move because I felt we had the votes to pass the Pearson-Benston Amendment and if we allowed the establishment of the ceiling, no matter how realistic it now appeared, it would be difficult to remove a few years hence if it became unrealistic. We would be back in the same position of imbalance between costs of different energy forms that was responsible for the growing gas shortage. Other members were divided, but the decision was made to go without the Long proposal. Members of the group agreed to contact senators with whom they had influence and convince them to vote for the Pearson-Benston Amendment. It was further agreed another amendment would follow in case we failed.

The day before the vote, a second meeting was held and a nose-count indicated we had sufficient votes to win. That afternoon, there was considerable debate between supporters of decontrol and Senator Hollings, who loudly proclaimed the advantage of controls and whose oratory was demeaning toward those who felt the time had come to let market forces operate. The vote on total decontrol failed decisively. Then, at 3 p.m. the next day, the vote on the Pearson-Benston Amendment took place. We won, forty-five to fifty with two members pairing to allow absent members to be counted. It was a decisive and historic victory.

When the subject of ratifying the Panama Canal treaties to transfer control of the canal to the government of Panama was first brought before the Senate, I had little interest in the matter. It seemed the canal was operating satisfactorily and my attitude was "if it ain't broke don't fix it."

At about this time my colleague from Oklahoma, Senator Dewey Bartlett, became seriously ill with lung cancer. He quickly made arrangements to go to Sloan-Kettering in New York for radical lung surgery. I went with a group of his friends from the Senate to Dewey's home the night before he left for New York. We prayed for his recovery and as we left, I gave him a book to read while he was recuperating. Upon his return to the Senate in January 1978, he thanked me for the book and asked if I had read *Path Between the Seas* by David McCollough. I told him I had not and he said he would like to get the book for me. He hoped I would take time to read it because his reading of that volume had made him see for the first time there was a need for change in our arrangement with Panama regarding the canal.

I was surprised to hear Dewey Bartlett, who was against treaty ratification, indicate there was some legitimate reason for a new agreement with Panama. A few days later Dewey brought me the copy of *Path Between the Seas* and I read it with fascination. It told about the events leading to the building of the canal, the difficulties encountered in its construction, and the sacrifices made by the thousands of indigenous and imported laborers who did most of the work. The book ends when the canal opened for navigation in 1914 at the beginning of World War I. The book, of course, had nothing to say about the treaties, but it gave many insights into the reasons Panamanians and other Latin Americans resented the U.S. domination of the Canal Zone. Without saying so, it made a strong case for renegotiation of the treaties which had been written seventy-five years earlier and which no Panamanian government had ratified. I was especially impressed with the record of intrigue that had taken place between Secretary of State John Hay, President Teddy Roosevelt, and the Frenchman Phillippe Berena Verilla. It was easy to understand why the Panamanians might feel the U. S. had taken unfair advantage of their country while it was in its infancy, and it was easy to understand the long-standing agitation to get the U. S. out of Panama. Also, it was plain to see why many U.S. presidents, beginning with Eisenhower, had advocated new treaties to help improve U.S. relations with Panama and other Central and Latin American countries. The existing treaty called for a minimal annual rent payment to Panama allowing U.S. use of the Canal Zone. It gave the U.S. government sovereignty over the Canal Zone. Full control and operational responsibility for the Panama Canal were U.S. rights. Toll fees were set by the U.S. government, which retained the earnings. Most years the canal had been operated at a loss to the U.S. Treasury. The new treaties provided that control of the Canal Zone and operation of the canal would move to Panama by the year 2000 with the U.S. retaining certain military base rights in the area.

After reading *Path Between the Seas*, I became intensely interested in the canal debate. I read many of the papers relating to the canal and was particularly impressed by the supportive position taken by the chairman of the United Fruit Company, the U.S. firm that used the canal most regularly. As time for debate about ratification of the treaties grew closer, the load of mail to our office became abnormally heavy. Bob Haught, my administrative assistant, arranged for a young man named Martin James to join our staff to deal primarily with the treaty question. I think Bob acted more out of kindness than necessity, but I was glad to have Martin's assistance in dealing with the mail and, later on, keeping track of the debate as various issues arose. It was apparent early on that the Panamanian question had been made the *cause celebre* of self-styled conservative groups from all parts of the country. We received many letters at our farm home from different so-called conservative organizations making serious and inaccurate charges against the terms of the treaties as well as impugning the integrity of the negotiators and supporters of ratification. In practically all the letters there was a plea for money. It became plain the Panama Canal Treaty controversy — like gun control, abortion, school busing, and other emotional issues — was being used for the monetary gain of some of its most vocal detractors. Among the groups heard from most often were various elements of the John Birch Society. Since I had been at odds with their group since early in my term as governor, I found their involvement particularly repugnant. I had openly and successfully opposed their efforts to take over the Oklahoma Republican party and was dubious of any position taken by the John Birch Society.

As the time for final debate on the new treaty drew near, I asked Martin James for an update on the amount of mail we had received pro and con. He told me we had received about 9,000 letters and the mail was running ninety-five percent against the treaties. It was difficult for me to believe there was not a more balanced view of the treaties among Oklahoma citizens. In an attempt to get at the true attitude of Oklahomans, we included a Panama Canal question on the newsletter/questionnaire that went out in February. The responses to that letter were something like ninety percent against and ten percent in favor. Even this return did not satisfy me, so I requested that members of our staff in Oklahoma conduct an informal telephone poll to see if they could get an indication of how the ordinary citizen who is not sufficiently motivated to return a questionnaire or write a letter felt on the matter.

In preparing the telephone questionnaire, I followed the advice of Senator Howard Baker who told me he and Senator Byrd of West Virginia had drafted two amendments, one of which gave U.S. ships the right to go to the head of the line in time of war. The other gave the U.S. the right to take whatever action was necessary to keep the Canal open and in operation. Our staff people were instructed in asking their questions to first simply say they were calling for Senator Bellmon and wanted to know how the respondents felt about the Panama Canal Treaties. Then they were to ask how they would feel if the Baker/Byrd amendments were adopted. The interesting thing about the poll was that even though the Panama Canal controversy had been receiving headline attention in Oklahoma for several weeks, a third of those called had no opinion about the Canal issue. To those who did have an opinion, we explained the Baker and Byrd amendments and asked their position on the treaty if the amendments were adopted. Half of those called became pro-treaty and half were against.

When I went to meetings in Oklahoma during this time, I made it standard practice to bring up the Canal question and ask members of the group how they stood on the treaties. It seemed to make little difference whether it was a Chamber of Commerce meeting or a Republican fundraiser, a meeting of farmers or any other group. The answers were always the same: the vast majority of people, usually ninety percent or more, were anti-treaty. There were three exceptions: a Chamber of Commerce meeting in Bartlesville, a meeting with a group of health care deliverers in Oklahoma City, and a collegiate Young Republican event in Stillwater. At the Bartlesville meeting, twenty-five percent were pro-treaty, and at the Oklahoma City medical group and at Stillwater there was an almost even split. There could be little doubt those who were active in the Republican party and in most other organized groups were heavily against the treaties. There *was* a question as to how important the ordinary rank-and-file citizen felt the treaty issue was.

One of the issues I asked Martin to settle for me was how important the Canal was to our country. He brought forth studies showing it cost about thirty cents more to ship a bushel of wheat around the tip of South America than it cost to send the same commodity through the Canal en route to Japan. The extra cost of sending the same bushel of wheat overland from Oklahoma to a West Coast port en route to Japan was about thirty-six cents. Also, Martin provided figures showing that most of the U. S. Navy, with the exception of large aircraft carriers and supertankers, used the Canal.

As the debate progressed and the day for voting came closer, I was called several times by Assistant Secretary of State Doug Bennett. Prior to his appointment by President Carter, Doug had been the majority staff director of the budget committee where he and I had become good friends. Doug made no effort to twist my arm but made it plain from the beginning that the Carter administration, which put its full weight behind ratification of the treaty, felt the treaty vote was going to be close and offered to give me any information I needed to make the decision. Doug told me I was one of five undecided senators and my vote might very well determine the outcome. Also, he offered me the opportunity to go to Panama for a first-hand look. I had hoped to make the trip during Christmas recess but one event after another interfered and I was never able to join a group that went to Panama.

During the time Bert Lance had served as director of the Office of Management and Budget, I had become acquainted with his administrative assistant — a young man named Herky Harris. Herky and I got along well so I was not too surprised when, about two weeks before the vote was scheduled, he began to call to inquire about my feelings on the treaty question. About a week or ten days before the vote was scheduled, a White House staff member called our office and invited me to a meeting with President Carter. Since I had always regarded an invitation to the White House a "command performance," I readily agreed to go. Later in the day, I began to think about the matter and wondered if I was to be a member of a group or if the meeting was between myself and the president. Early on the day the meeting was to be held, I called White House lobbyist Frank Moore, who told me the president and I would be alone. I told Frank I thought he was doing me an injustice to invite me down and put me in the position of seeming to be "hot boxed" and influenced by the president. I told him I felt the decision was one I needed to make strictly on my own and asked that I be taken off the president's schedule. Frank agreed and I did not talk to President Carter either personally or by phone at any time prior to the treaty vote.

During an earlier meeting at the White House, which I attended in company with other Republicans, the president had given each of us an opportunity to bring up a subject we felt needed his attention. I jumped at the opportunity to talk about control of natural salt pollution in the Arkansas and Red Rivers. I asked him point-blank if the Carter administration was to have a "no new start" attitude toward water development projects. The president had seemed to flare at this pointed reference to his "hit list" of water projects that had caused so much controversy in 1977. He very curtly but candidly stated it was not the policy of the Carter administration to have "no new starts" but rather to insist that water projects that were funded be meritorious and sound economic investments for the country. It was necessary for any new water project to have a favorable cost-benefit ratio. This was good enough for me because I felt certain both the Red and Arkansas chloride control projects were highly meritorious and would have attractive cost-benefit ratios. This discussion would come up again at a crucial time during Canal vote discussions.

A few weeks before the vote, my Oklahoma Senate colleague Dewey Bartlett had announced he was not going to seek reelection. It occurred to me that since Dewey had given a great many years to public service as a state senator, governor, and U. S. senator, that prior to his leaving the Senate, his friends in the state should do something to honor him. During the Easter recess, I went to see several of our mutual friends. Interestingly, in almost every case, as soon as the discussion of the proposed Bartlett event was over, the people I was calling on brought up the Canal treaty question. Dean McGee, CEO of Kerr-McGee oil company, was adamant the treaty not be ratified. His company was building a soda ash plant in California and anticipated shipping their product from California through the Canal to markets on the East Coast. Dean took the position that if President Torrejos took over the Canal and raised the toll, even if the Canal continued to operate, it would damage the profitability of the Kerr-McGee chemical plant in California.

Perhaps the most adamant opponent of the treaty was Ed Gaylord. I had high respect for him as a businessman and especially for his position as publisher of the *Daily Oklahoman* and *Times*, the state's largest newspapers. When I went to see Ed, he listened closely while I discussed the Bartlett event and readily agreed to be supportive. He was obviously a great admirer of Dewey Bartlett and wanted to take charge of the fund-raising activities for the Oklahoma City area. As soon as we had completed our discussion of the event, Ed lit into me over the Panama Canal question. He had served for a year and a half in Panama during World War II and had a good deal of firsthand information about the Canal and its operation. In addition, he had recently bought a full page ad in the *Wall Street Journal* to call attention to the seventy-fifth birthday of the Oklahoma Publishing Company. At the center of his ad, a copy of which he gave me, were three editorials opposing treaty ratification. In addition to the *Wall Street Journal* ad, he also gave me an envelope filled with literature on the question. I promised him I would read it on the airplane on the way back to Washington, which I later attempted to do. To my amazement, I found the literature was practically all from the John Birch Society or its affiliates. It was the same sort of highly emotional hate mail we had been receiving at the farm and in our various Senate offices.

One evening during the time the debate over the canal treaties was at its greatest intensity, the Gaylords invited Shirley and me to dinner at their home. Shirley was seated at a table with Ed and I was seated at a table with his wife, Thelma. After dinner, we were the last couple to leave. As we said goodbye, Ed took me by the elbow and guided me into his bedroom. He showed me a closet filled with drawers for his socks and handkerchiefs and underclothes. When he opened the door there were two photographs attached to the inside of the door. One was of Dewey Bartlett and the other was a campaign photograph of me, Shirley, and our girls waving from a wheat field.

He told me, "I just want you to know, these are my two favorite politicians."

I don't think he was trying to pressure me in any way, but it was a kind gesture by which he was trying to tell me he valued our friendship, no matter what our differences were on political issues.

About this time, I had a conversation with Bob Ellsworth. Bob had been a Congressman from Kansas who had worked as the executive director of the 1968 Nixon presidential campaign when I was national chairman. Bob came to see me in his capacity as president of a shipping company making regular use of the Panama Canal. Bob's position was that if the treaties were not ratified, the likely scenario would be that Panamanian President Torrejos would station snipers along the Canal route to shoot a few sailors. From the shippers' standpoint, Bob maintained the Canal would then be effectively closed because no company could require its sailors to sail through the combat zone the Canal would become. He claimed our military would be forced to hunt down the snipers. Then a lengthy and costly civil war would follow and during the whole time the Canal could not be used by commercial ships.

Following my discussion with Bob Ellsworth, I had the opportunity to talk at some length with Major General Parfaitt, military governor of Panama, who was in Washington to testify before one of the Senate committees. I asked General Parfaitt two questions: first, if we turned down the treaty did he feel there would be a civil war in the Canal Zone? He answered yes. Then I asked him if civil war did come in the Canal Zone, could he as the senior military officer in charge maintain order, protect U.S. citizens, and keep the canal in operation? General Parfaitt hedged on the second question. He said there was no question that, with the military power of the United States, if he was given sufficient troops and equipment as well as full authority, he could handle any civil war that President Torrejos might start. However, he said, there was no way he could successfully sustain an anti-guerilla activity in Panama if the politicians in Washington were continually criticizing and making speeches against the distasteful and costly military actions his troops would be forced to take. He felt U.S. troops would require political support and not political condemnation if they were asked day after day, month after month to risk their lives in the jungles or on the streets and alleys of Panama.

But military will or might is not the real question, he said. The real question, the general said, is political will, the same issue we confronted in Vietnam; that is, how long the U.S. public would support a U.S. military operation which was costing heavily in American lives and money. A guerilla war probably would result in the Canal being closed with much loss of life and much property damage. General Parfaitt reiterated that the real question was political, and, he said, "You're the politician, I'm not." In reflecting on the matter, it seemed that so soon after Vietnam the American public would not support an extended military operation in Panama that was costly in both lives and tax dollars. Treaty ratification would remove a major anti-American weapon our detractors in Latin American were using to stir up U.S. opposition. Throughout our history the United States had never tried to hold territory adversely. The people of Panama had voted in a plebiscite by a margin of about two to one in favor of treaty ratification.

By this time, the debate on the question was getting into the final days. I had many discussions with people on both sides of the issue. Perhaps the most persuasive opponent of the treaties was Senator Bob Griffin of Michigan. His seat was directly behind mine on the Senate floor. I had a high regard for Bob and read the statement he made in opposition to the treaties with great interest. He was a member of the foreign relations committee, had participated actively in the hearings on the Panama question, and had voted against reporting the treaties to the Senate floor. He had written a persuasive argument on his independent views of the Panama Canal question which was printed in the committee report. His conclusion was that it was necessary for us to work out a new relationship with Panama, but that the treaties before us were "fatally flawed."

During this time I also talked with Utah Senator Paul Laxalt at considerable length. He was one of the leaders of the anti-treaty group and was by far more reasonable than my seatmate, Jesse Helms. Senators Strom Thurmond and Orrin Hatch and many of the other members were so worked up over the question that intelligent discussion was impossible. Paul made no effort to twist my arm, but we did talk about the treaties several times.

Feelings among my Senate staff members about the Panama Canal treaties were especially high. They were almost unanimous in opposition. Their attitudes probably were influenced by the barrage of mail and phone calls our office was receiving as well as by editorials in the *Daily Oklahoman.* Every staff member knew the political damage a yes vote on treaty ratification would cause. The most outspoken opponent was Don Ferrell, whose brother was a career army officer stationed in Panama.

During the final days of the debate, Herky Harris called from the Office of Management and Budget asking if I had made up my mind. I told him I had not. Within a few hours, the clippings from Oklahoma came in and among those put on my desk was an editorial from the *Tulsa World* that claimed I had made a deal with the Carter administration to trade my vote for their approval of funding for the Arkansas-Red River chloride control projects. I asked my secretary, Cathy Buchanan, to get Jim McIntyre, director of OMB, on the phone and proceeded to read the editorial to him in totality. Cathy sat in the office and listened.

My pitch to Jim was that I had not made a decision but if I did vote for the treaties I was going to pay an extremely high political price in the state. I told him the *Daily Oklahoman,* our largest paper, had been editorializing heavily against the treaties and that our mail was heavily in opposition. I also told him the Arkansas-Red River chloride control projects were terribly important to our state and if I did finally decide to vote for the treaties then I wanted some assurance the Arkansas-Red River Project would get fair consideration by his office and by President Carter. McIntyre told me he would take the matter up with Carter. Within a day or two, Jim called back and asked if I had made up my mind. I told him I had not. He stated that he had talked the chloride control matter over with President Carter and I could be assured the administration would look kindly upon the Arkansas-Red River chloride control project. Jim had already agreed to come to Oklahoma for a first-hand look at these large Corps of Engineers water developments and environmental improvement projects. He assured me he would keep the schedule he had previously set.

Following the conversations with Harris and McIntyre, I went to Oklahoma for a weekend of fence-mending meetings. On the way back to Washington, I slept most of the way to Chicago. When we left Chicago, the plane was full and the person sitting next to me was a huge man who filled the center seat to overflowing. His presence made me so uncomfortable I could not go back to sleep. Partly because I realized I had to make a decision on the Panama Canal matter in two or three days and partially to help make the time go faster, I took a legal pad from my briefcase and started to write a statement on the Canal question. It was my intention to write arguments both for and against the ratification and then make my decision. I do not know why, but I started out on the pro side and by the time I had finished that part of my statement, our plane was letting down for the landing in Washington and I had almost completely convinced myself the pro side was the right side. I never wrote an anti-treaty statement.

The next evening, Monday, Shirley and I made our weekly visit to the grocery store after I came home from the Senate session. As we walked along between the boxes and containers, she asked me how I was going to vote on the treaty. I asked her how she would vote if she were in my place. She said she did not know.

The next morning, Tuesday, I got up about 3:30 and put the finishing touches on the statement that had been in my briefcase all day Monday. I particularly referred to historical documents printed in a book called *We the States*. It was published by the Virginia Commission on Constitutional Government chaired by James J. Kilpatrick. The book was copyrighted in 1964 and had been sent to me while I served as governor. The primary purpose of the book seemed to be to make a case against federal intervention into state affairs. Ironically, a portion of the book is dedicated to trying to make a case against the integration of schools. Over the years I have found the book to be a good compilation of many of our nation's founding documents. I found it helpful in this case.

When I got to the office that morning, I suggested to Cathy that she, Bob Haught, and press secretary Andrew Tevington take whatever time was necessary to go to our small "hideaway" office in the Capitol (which I rarely used) to type and edit my statement. I told them the statement put me in a position of voting for the treaties. They were not too surprised. Also, I suggested to Andrew that we schedule a news conference for 9 a.m. Thursday, the day set for the vote.

Late in the afternoon on Tuesday, I called Minority Leader Howard Baker and told him how I was going to vote. I suggested he be discreet in putting out the word, because I was not particularly interested in helping get any of the Democratic members off the hook any more than could be avoided. Baker told me, "This is one vote that will make you proud the rest of your life."

I also called Jim McIntyre and told him about my decision so that he could give the message to President Carter if he chose.

On Thursday morning, I called Claudia Quam of the Oklahoma staff at home and told her what I was going to say at the news conference. I suggested she call our other state offices and do her best to prepare them for the avalanche of critical calls certain to follow. I believe Claudia was disappointed, although perhaps her reaction was due to her dread of the abuse she and others on the staff would take over the next several days. Before going to the news conference to make my decision public, I hesitated several minutes deciding whether or not to call Ed Gaylord. I concluded the call would do no good. It would only further infuriate him. His public position was too strong to be altered by a phone call.

Thursday, the news conference seemed to go fairly well. I went from the news room to the Senate floor where I got time and read my statement in full. Ironically, both Howard Baker and Bob Griffin were present on the floor at the time and both heard everything I had to say.

In part, I said:

> This decision cannot be made by a simple accounting of the pros and cons in the treaties themselves. Instead, the decision must be based on American principles — those great ideals upon which our Nation stands. . . .
>
> Consider another part of our Declaration of Independence: "We hold these truths to be self-evident, that all men are created equal, that they are endowed by their Creator with certain unalienable rights . . . that whenever any form of government becomes destructive of these ends, it is the right of the people to alter or abolish it. . . .

Those words, "the right of the people to alter," if applied to all people, if exported to Panama as we have chosen to export our other ideals to that country and the rest of the world, would appear to strongly support the updating of our relationship with Panama. They further make untenable, and in fact repulsive, the often heard argument that Panamanians should not be given full rights and responsibility for running their own country or managing their own resources, including the resource of geography. . . .

As a combat veteran, I probably take more seriously than most the responsibilities governments have for actions which may lead to the sending of young men into combat of whatever kind. Having had this experience on many occasions, I feel that such actions should only be taken for the most serious of reasons — those relating to the defense of our country or the maintenance of our basic principles and ideals. If these treaties are not ratified and guerilla warfare results in Panama, I am afraid that American servicemen and their families will have a difficult time maintaining a strong fighting spirit when the purpose for their sacrifice is basically commercial. It is difficult to develop a rallying cry around the concept of "Whip the Panamanians and keep cheap freight.". . .

Can the Panamanians successfully operate, maintain, and defend the canal after the year 2000? . . . The mere asking of this question is an affront to Panama. History is replete with examples of peoples rising to the challenge when given the opportunity. There is no reason to believe that Panamanian citizens are born with inferior morals, intellects, or mechanical aptitudes . . . given the opportunity, Panamanians will prove to be fully capable and even more solicitous of the continued successful, independent operation of the Panama Canal than we have been. . . .

The Senator from Oklahoma is a veteran of World War II and was involved in several landings in the Pacific, including Iwo Jima. It pained me at first when it was learned that Iwo Jima and Okinawa, which American fighting men won at heavy cost, were to be returned to Japan. My own personal opposition was intense. We won it. We own it. Let us keep it. But why? As a symbol and perhaps as an irritant to our former enemies? . . . On reflection, these seemed grossly unworthy reasons.

There are other symbols more important to our national pride and stature than occupying territory outside our national boundaries: the symbol of fair play, the symbol of equality — including equal rights among nations — the symbol that the United States desires to deal with other nations as we would have other nations deal with us . . .

To me, the word 'republican' means that while I was elected to represent the views of the people of Oklahoma, I was also chosen to devote my time to gaining a knowledge and full understanding of both the short- and long-range effects of the questions which come before the Senate and to cast my vote in accordance with the best judgment I can make. Two years before the founding of our Nation, Edmund Burke explained the duty of an elected representative succinctly: "Your representative owes you, not his industry only, but his judgment; and he betrays, instead of serving you, if he sacrifices it to your opinion."

The treaties are not perfect. Government rarely achieves perfection. Bob Griffin probably was right in much of the criticism he made. However, the negotiation of these treaties was achieved over the span of many years. They are probably the best agreement that could be worked out under the circumstances.

The vote was sixty-eight to thirty-two. Howard Baker and I were the only Southern Republicans who voted in favor of ratification.

I had not fully foreseen the bitter reaction of Ed Gaylord and the *Daily Oklahoman*. I was crucified by its editorials. They even went so far as to call me a traitor and a Benedict Arnold, something I strongly resent. I had written a letter to Ed on the energy question. This letter arrived in his office after his editorial condemnation of me had been printed. He then wrote back to me on the Canal question. That letter arrived at our farm and I looked upon it as something of a peace offering. I carefully dictated a reply, resulting in Ed's inviting me to come to his office for a conversation. We met for breakfast at the Skirvin Hotel in Oklahoma City. Our meeting was cordial; he kidded me about being a hard-headed Dutchman and gave me another package of material opposing the treaties. He said he hoped I would read it and change my mind. I had picked a batch of asparagus from our farm before I left that morning and gave it to Ed as my contribution to our renewed relationship.

In the weeks following the vote on the first treaty, there were two meetings I attended where the crowd stood and applauded at the mention of my vote on the Canal question. One of these meetings was at the First Presbyterian Church in Oklahoma City where I spoke on food and hunger issues. The other was at the Equal Rights Amendment conference in Tulsa where a large number of people, especially from Bartlesville, came up and commented favorably on my vote. Again there was a standing ovation at mention of the Canal vote. Several people at the ERA meeting pointed out that they were Republicans. A few said they previously had been on the other side, but as time had gone on they had changed their positions and now favored ratification.

Some things that happened disturbed me a great deal. One is the seemingly highly prevalent attitude that I did a sinful thing because I did not vote as the majority of my constituents wanted. I cannot accept the theory that a member of Congress should be elected and then make decisions based on the number of letters and phone calls received on any given issue. It was plain in the Panama Canal case that a concerted effort was made by the opponents to generate mail and phone calls. And while I would readily agree that the majority of Oklahomans opposed the ratification of the treaties, the balance between pros and cons is far different than a simple count of the mail and calls would indicate. I remain committed to the proposition that it is the duty of a legislator to get the facts on issues and then follow the course which is determined to be in the public interest. It is a perversion of the public trust for an elected official to act against the public interest in order to retain office. Legislators who claim to always do their constituents' will are in effect trying to follow rather than lead. Mass confusion is the natural result, since majorities often change directions as understanding of issues improves.

Another thing that disturbs me is the seeming fixation in both the state and national media that some kind of deal was made between the president and those who voted for the treaties. I am highly doubtful deals were made. The chloride control projects in Oklahoma were not funded. A change in policy took away the power-related benefits. Without these, the benefit-to-cost ratio was grossly unfavorable.

Perhaps the aspect that troubles me most about the Canal question was that it would have been totally against the American character to engage in a lengthy guerilla military action over Panama. There is no record of our ever having forced a continuing U.S. presence on unwilling citizens of another country. I believe we would have found it highly distasteful and ultimately unsuccessful had we undertaken a military action to maintain control of the Panama Canal. Meanwhile, a U.S.-Panamanian war certainly would have soured further our country's relationships throughout Latin America. It was my feeling that Panamanians deserve the right to manage their own resources and it is in the U.S.'s interest to give them a chance to do so. I believe these treaties will succeed in keeping the canal in operation.

Years later, in 1990, I sent Secretary of State James Baker a copy of a news article reporting the spread of elected governments throughout Latin America and asked if he felt there was a connection with the growth of representative governments and ratification of the Panama Canal treaties. The *New York Times* article, dated March 18, 1990, said: "In the last year Latin America has gone through a surprising transformation, quiet compared with Eastern Europe's but profound nonetheless. . . . In Brazil, as in Chile, Nicaragua, Costa Rica and Honduras, recent elections have ended with the victory of center-right presidents who believe in the market economy, popular suffrage and all the other values that the United States holds dear."

I wrote Secretary Baker: "My vote on the Panama Canal treaties was cast in the belief that ratification would improve the climate for democracy in Latin America as well as remove a major barrier to improved relations between those countries and the U.S. I am curious to know whether you feel these representative governments would have been put in power if the Panama Canal Treaty had been rejected."

Secretary Baker replied in part: "Many analysts believe the Treaties did in fact remove an important obstacle to productive dialogue between the United States and Latin America and helped change Latin American perceptions about the U.S. commitment to democracy and the possibilities for cooperation with the United States."

This administration's strong and consistent support for the Treaties was an important factor in the *inability* of the Noriega regime to mobilize popular feeling against the United States during the recent crisis, and our unequivocal pro-Treaty stance also stood us in good stead throughout Latin America. Protecting the integrity of the Treaties and assisting Panamanians to restore democracy were both essential objectives in our decision to intervene in Panama in December 1989.

As I recall, there were serious, substantive arguments made on both sides of the debate over Treaty ratification. You voted your conscience, and now the Treaties are the law of the land. They have proven effective in protecting the national interests of both the United States and Panama. To the extent that they provide a mutually acceptable framework within which the United States and Panama can work to safeguard their interests in the Canal, they contribute to stability on the Isthmus and thus assist Panamanians in building a prosperous and democratic Panama.

Soon after arriving in Washington as a freshman senator, I chanced to meet up with Alex Adwan, an old friend from Oklahoma who was working as a reporter for the *Tulsa World*. Alex had covered the state capitol when I was governor and was then serving as the *World*'s Washington correspondent. Alex volunteered to take me on a tour of the capitol and I gladly consented to be his guest. Our tour took us through the press room, past the pay office, to the Senate dining room, and we wound up standing in the press gallery looking down at the empty seats on the Senate floor. Alex looked at me and said, "You're going to be proud to be associated with the other ninety-nine members who serve here. The people of the country have used good judgement when they selected the members of the United States Senate."

As time went on, I became more and more convinced of the accuracy of Alex's statement, but twelve years in the Senate were enough for me. When the time came to decide on running for a third term, the decision was easy. My first Senate term had not filled me with ardor for Washington. The second term was worse. The long Edmondson election controversy, the frustrations and the work overload which came with serving on three important committees (Budget, Appropriations, and Energy), the growing dissatisfaction of maintaining two homes and a money-losing farming business, the heavy travel schedule, the artificiality and transitory nature of Washington life, and the frustrations of not controlling my own time made me long for a return to life in Oklahoma. In addition, I had no desire to grow old and incompetent yet psychologically dependent upon political office. Perhaps I lacked the ego, the sense of self-importance which is needed to face the constant battering a legislator takes from angry and disappointed special interests. There may be a legislative and a distinctly different executive mindset. If so, I fall into the latter category. The machinations and circuitous maneuverings which attend the legislative process did not intrigue me.

At the same time, I could see that I was arriving as a respected member of the Senate. The work and success of the Budget Committee was attracting attention. I was invited to appear on national television interview shows and was frequently included in the small group invited by the leadership to develop strategy on ways to deal with upcoming legislation. Could I have been reelected? I believe so. There was no Democratic opponent on the horizon of the stature of Ed Edmondson, Mike Monroney, or Bill Atkinson. I knew of no strong Republican planning a primary challenge. The Panama vote would have been a problem but hardly as difficult as the busing issue of the 1974 campaign. Later events bore this out. In 1986, when I ran for governor again, the Panama Canal Treaty issue came up frequently — even after a long lapse of time. There were many who probably cast their votes against me because of my stand. But I was elected by a comfortable margin in a four-way race with two self-proclaimed conservative Republicans running as independents. Apparently, if there ever was a ninety-five percent disapproval of the treaties among Oklahoma citizens, many either changed their minds or forgave the vote on the basis that I acted in what I considered to be the national interest.

It was a singular honor to have been elected again to statewide office after taking what were considered unpopular stands on highly emotional issues. This shows a high degree of understanding and tolerance on the part of Oklahoma voters. It is a lesson which should not be lost on present and future officeholders as they face new issues and new controversies. It was with few regrets that, in December 1980, Shirley and I loaded our personal belongings into a rented U-Haul truck and trailer and made the two-day trip from Virginia to Oklahoma. We were accompanied on the trip by Rudy Abramson, a writer for the *Los Angeles Times*, who rode in the truck cab with us and wrote a story about my leaving the Senate. We spent hours in pleasant reminiscing about the years in Washington and I felt thoroughly debriefed by the time we arrived at the farm

Governor Again

While living in Washington, Shirley designed and made stained glass windows, including the Bellmon brand and the Oklahoma state seal that were installed at the farm home near Billings.

President Ronald
_n came to
_boma to campaign
_enry in his bid for
_vernor's office. The
_n to run at this
_ his life took a lot
_l-searching.

_: First Lady
_y Reagan and
_ura Bush, wife of
_e president, greet
_y at a Red Cross
_Lady's Luncheon
_shington after
_'s retirement from
_nate.

Shirley holds the Bible as Henry takes the oath of office from Judge Bob Lavender and makes history again a
person to be reelected governor of Oklahoma after having been out of office. Below, in a public ceremony at M
School in Tulsa, Bellmon, surrounded by school children, supporters and opponents of House Bill 1017, sign
reaching and controversial Education Reform Act into effect. It was one of the happiest days of his political c

d term as governor would be Henry's final tour of elected public service duty — and in Bellmon style, it would
y or quiet. Indeed, it would be a final lesson in Bellmon leadership: determine where the public interests lie and
it direction, irrespective of temporary swings in public opinion.

Henry makes remarks at a party on t[...]
of the governor's mansion.
BELOW: A fisherman from childhood,[...]
shows off red snapper caught off the c[...]
Alabama at a National Governor's
Conference during his last term.

The Troubleshooter

"It is Impossible for a Ruler to be Omnipotent and Sane"

Prior to leaving the Senate and returning to Oklahoma, I undertook to enlarge the farming operation so there would be work for the two men who had been running the farm as well as myself. This involved buying about 1,250 acres of grassland located twenty-five miles east of our home farm. The tract we purchased was a beautiful piece of land. It had excellent, deep soil, beautiful stands of tall grass, a mile and a half of Arkansas River frontage, a few deep canyons which were ideal sites for clear water lakes, many springs which ran all year long, sufficient timber to shelter a large herd of deer as well as a sizable flock of wild turkeys and many coveys of quail, acres of plum thickets, many wild blackberry bushes, and hundreds of redbud and pecan trees. Going there to work was like taking a short vacation.

The land had once been a part of the 101 Ranch. Next it made up the central section of the Bar L, which was later divided into thousand-acre plots so that each of the rancher's seven children could have his or her own unit. The plan was to utilize bermuda grass on the home place to maintain a cow herd of 500 head and use bluestem grass on the new place to summer and fatten the yearlings after they had been wintered on wheat pasture. To increase the grazing capacity on the new place, I cleared some of the brush and replanted the better areas to bermuda grass. The land purchase and improvements stretched our financial resources to the limit. In the year when the U.S.D.A.'s PIC program was announced, feed grain prices soared and feeder cattle prices dropped through the floor. We suffered a loss of some $60,000 and had great difficulty meeting our interest payments on the land. We were $25,000 short of getting the interest fully paid before it came due again. Rather than being a source of new income, the expansion proved to be a major financial drain.

Running both places put strain on our labor as well, but we operated the ranch for six years, at which point I decided to run for governor. In the meantime, I took several outside jobs to provide income. Had I understood the earning capabilities of an ex-senator, I probably would not have been so eager to expand the farming operation. As I was leaving office, I discovered I was highly employable at universities, where I could teach, and by different businesses that offered me positions on their boards of directors. Unfortunately, several of the companies that contacted me were involved in the energy business. Under Securities and Exchange Commission regulations, it was improper for a director to serve on the board of more than one energy company. I chose to re-affiliate myself with the Williams Companies in Tulsa, partly because of my previous experience with them and partly because, in addition to other enterprises, they were the nation's largest fertilizer company. I felt my knowledge of agriculture would be of some value to them. The association proved to be pleasant for me and, I hope, beneficial to the company.

I elected also to join the board of United Funds, a mutual fund located in Kansas City. The fund managed over $5 billion of resources for investors and I felt my work on the Senate budget committee, which had given me some understanding of economic forces and trends, might be helpful. I believe it was. For many months I served as a commentator for KOCO television in Oklahoma City. Along with these activities, I was approached about joining the staff of four universities: Oklahoma City University, Oklahoma State University, Central State University, and Oklahoma University. At one time or another, I was able to accept all the invitations and taught at each of the universities.

The most satisfactory university relationship was at Central State University where I taught two classes, one on state administration and one on the U.S. Congress. Both were night classes and were composed of young adults who had returned to school to complete their education after several years in the workplace. They were serious students with a good grasp of the importance of government, so many lively discussions took place in class. The least satisfactory teaching experience was at Oklahoma State University where I served as a "floating" lecturer for various freshman political science classes. These were large classes of students who were taking political science as a required course and who had little interest in the subject. That experience caused me to wonder about the wisdom of forcing college students into classes where they are not interested in the subject matter.

My relationship with OU began when President Bill Banowsky contacted me about the possibility of raising private funds to create a "Bellmon Chair in Public Service" at the university. I agreed. Banowsky agreed to raise $1 million. At the time, Banowsky was riding high and was widely looked upon as a political comer in the state. He undertook the fund-raising and enjoyed considerable success, though he did not reach the million dollar objective. Once the chair was established, I was contacted about filling it and did so. At Oklahoma University I taught the same two classes I'd been teaching at Central State, but to younger students. Classes were also larger and while they were, I believe, mutually satisfactory, the lively discussions which had occurred at Central State seemed difficult to generate at OU. Nevertheless, it was on the whole a satisfactory experience and one I would like to repeat.

During an energy policy meeting at the Oklahoma University campus, I was approached by Dr. Bill Talley, head of the RAM Group, about joining his organization. In subsequent discussions, I learned that the RAM Group was managing a large portfolio of oil and gas properties which had been taken over by the FDIC as a result of the failure of the Penn Square Bank in Oklahoma City and other banks. In his relationship with the FDIC, Dr. Talley had become convinced that there was an opportunity for his organization to apply the expertise they had gained through their dealings with federal agencies to the agricultural credit crisis which was rapidly developing. Hundreds, probably thousands, of farmers and ranchers were in danger of losing their land because debt had grown to the point that it exceeded the value of the collateral with which it was secured. Talley had the notion that private funds could be raised to take over loans from the Federal Land Bank at true market value and save the government the legal costs, ill will, and political repercussions which would follow extensive foreclosure proceedings against farmers.

I joined the RAM Group both because the income was attractive and because I genuinely believed that a privately financed and operated farm land rescue plan could be developed. It seemed to me to be unlikely that

Congress would provide funds to allow delinquent farm and ranch owners to keep their land; if the government helped one such operator it would need to help all. Several months were spent in discussion with Wall Street investment bankers, insurance executives, and other major sources of capital as well as with various Federal Land Bank officials. No workable farm loan program materialized and Congress did provide funds to keep the federal farm credit system afloat.

While attending a Williams Board meeting in Denver, I received a call from Oklahoma Governor George Nigh. At first I thought the Williams directors were playing one of their practical jokes and declined to take the call. After some moments of jocular horseplay, I decided the call must be for real and went to my room where I could talk to the governor in private.

Governor Nigh explained that Lloyd Rader, who had been director of the Department of Human Services since its infancy some thirty-one years before, had decided to retire. The governor was looking for a new director who could bring order to the state's largest agency, which had grown to be almost one-half of state government and was difficult to manage. He asked if I would be interested in the job. At first I thought the idea was completely ridiculous. The notion of a former Republican governor and former U.S. senator joining a Democratic administration in what was potentially the state's most explosive political position was at first illogical. Nevertheless, I agreed to think the proposition over and discuss the matter with the governor directly when I returned to Oklahoma City.

I certainly needed help with the farm financial situation. Also, in discussion with the governor, I found he was willing to give me a free hand so I could do the job without political interference. I was the choice of Lloyd Rader with whom I'd worked for many years and who seemed to feel I was the logical person to be his successor. The agency had become involved with several lawsuits and Mr. Rader felt that his good name and career were at risk. Perhaps he felt that at my hands he would be fairly treated.

The Welfare Commission, which sets policy for the Department of Human Resources, agreed to an arrangement in which Bob Fulton, the former minority staff counsel for the Senate Budget Committee, and I would be given two months to review operation of the Department of

Human Services and prepare a report recommending changes we felt were needed. This would provide me the opportunity to gain more current knowledge of the agency and its personnel and be better prepared to take over when Lloyd Rader retired January 1. We also agreed to bring on board Claudia Scribner and Sharon Sharp, who had worked for me in the Senate office, so we would have a small staff to do research and prepare the report. Claudia had joined the Senate staff as a new graduate of Oklahoma State University and over the years, had developed into a trusted confidante. When my second Senate term ended, she continued to assist me with university classes, personal scheduling, and correspondence. The work at DHS put her under great stress but she rose to the challenge and served the state well. She also worked in the governor's campaign and became my executive assistant in the governor's office. Her naturally cautious nature made her the ideal "no man" as well as an effective traffic cop in the governor's office.

Sharon Sharp served as the early morning secretary in my Washington Senate office. We both came in at 7 a.m. and usually had two uninterrupted hours in which we could answer mail, return phone calls, write speeches, and plan the day. Sharon was fast and proficient in her secretarial skills in addition to being a pleasant, loyal person to work with. An avid outdoors woman, she went from Washington to a job at a ski resort in Colorado, then back to Tulsa for a job with an oil company. She was pleased to rejoin me at DHS where she remained until she joined the governor's staff to handle the same duties she had handled so proficiently in Washington. The work at DHS was challenging but Sharon was up to the task. She became secretary to the DHS Commission.

Those early days at DHS were some of the most difficult in my political career. The agency was terribly demoralized. Mr. Rader, now well into his seventies, was still on the scene and totally in control. But he was not functioning with the same alertness and energy which had marked most of his years at the helm. In addition, he was under attack for "Oklahoma shame," a series of events involving the state's juvenile institutions and schools for the mentally retarded. Several legal actions were pending, including claims for over $100 million, many lawsuits contending that Mr. Rader was personally liable for incidents at state institutions. To make matters worse, Mr. Rader was refusing to discuss conditions openly with his commission and reporters. He had limited access to information to a small group of his closest and most trusted associates. Others in the agency felt left out and under attack. There were other complications. One involved the young nurse who had looked after Mr. Rader during a bout with pneumonia and whom he then brought onto the state teaching hospital staff and elevated to a senior management position even though she was far less experienced and less educated than other more senior nurses.

Among those Mr. Rader trusted most implicitly was his long-time personal secretary Vera Adler, who had worked with him during most of the years he brought the welfare department from its infancy to its current status as the state's largest agency with 13,000 employees, 225 clients, and a budget of over $1 billion a year. Fortunately, my relationship with his secretary was excellent. She gave me much good counsel and advised me who in the agency were the most competent officials and could be trusted to give factual and timely information.

Since DHS had taken over the management of the state's teaching hospital complex, Mr. Rader had moved his office to a building in the medical center, where he was overseeing the construction of the latest elements of the $200 million capital improvement. He arranged for me to occupy his former office in the Sequoyah Building, which housed the state DHS headquarters group. Due to the controversies swirling around the agency, Mr. Rader had become extremely distrustful of everyone except a small group of five people who travelled with him whenever he was on the job. He arranged to station one of those confidants in an office overlooking mine and gave him the responsibility of reporting every phone call I made, every visitor I received, and every employee I contacted. Mr. Rader formed the habit of critiquing my efforts to understand the agency and seemed to resent any contacts I had not previously cleared with him. Since it became impossible for us to prepare the report in the DHS offices because of the air of suspicion and mistrust, we made arrangements to open a private office where Claudia, Sharon, Bob, and I could work on the report, often before or after regular office hours. Many private interviews with DHS employees were held there.

Under Mr. Rader, the Department of Human Services had been run as a one-man empire. Little authority had been delegated to other officials. I was dumbfounded when, late in the evening on my first day as director, I was presented with three stacks of papers each about eighteen inches high, to which I was told to affix my signature. Mr. Rader's rule had been that everything that went out of the agency went out over the director's signature. It required some three hours to sit and sign my name to documents, most of which I had no chance to read and the content of which I knew practically nothing about. To my amazement, one of these documents called for the authorization of the purchase of $2 worth of cotton swabs. On another occasion, I was presented with a piece of paper which authorized the manager of one of the state's schools for the mentally retarded to send twenty fat lambs to market. Apparently, this college graduate in animal husbandry needed Mr. Rader's permission before he could market a few hundred dollars worth of sheep. Another document I signed authorized the expenditure of $4,000 to purchase a certain kind of pump. When I asked the person who presented the paper to me what the pump was for, the rather halting explanation was that this device was being installed in a welfare patient so the patient would be able to have an erection. Those decisions, in my judgment, did not need to reach the head of the agency who was totally unqualified to judge their merit.

After this charade had gone on for a couple of days, I called the different departmental managers together and told them that henceforth they were to make their own decisions and sign the documents their departments produced unless some change in policy was involved. I had no desire to attach my name to hundreds of documents each day, the content of which I had no opportunity to explore and understand. I told them if they were not competent to make decisions of this kind, they should turn in their resignations. Also, we established a "management team" and arranged for weekly meetings where policy matters could be discussed. We also set a regular monthly meeting with lower-level managers so they could have some idea of conditions inside the agency and learn about policy changes as they occurred. It was the first time anyone outside Mr. Rader's immediate circle of confidants had had any direct voice in policy-making in the agency.

Rader lived several years after his retirement. There's no question he made substantial contributions on both the state and national scenes in developing laws and means to provide needed social services to less fortunate citizens. Also, there's no question he stayed in his position too long and made many mistakes toward the end. Staying too long in office is a mistake public officials should try to avoid.

As historian Will Durant wrote after studying governments as far back as the Pharaohs, "It is impossible for a ruler to be omnipotent and sane." The earmarking of sales tax provided Mr. Rader a large and constantly growing source of revenue and removed him from the discipline of legislative oversight that the governing and appropriation processes normally require. For all practical purposes he was omnipotent in Oklahoma government for many years. While, during the early days, he made many wise decisions and conducted a complex program in a highly professional manner, towards the end he began to take on an attitude of infallibility. Being a master politician, he was able to curry favor with governors and most members of the legislature, including the leadership, by astutely granting requests and using patronage. As Bob Fulton and I dug into the operation of the DHS, it became ever more apparent that both Mr. Rader and the state of Oklahoma would have been better served had he been required to justify appropriations to the legislature. Rader never bothered to prepare budgets nor did he require his institutional directors to plan the use of funds. When they needed something, they simply asked him for the money, and if Rader wanted the projects to go ahead, he provided the resources. In many cases he substituted his own judgment for that of institution directors. A case in point was at the school for the mentally retarded in Enid where the director wanted to renovate the hospital. Instead, Mr. Rader provided funds for a large farm machinery storage and repair shop.

The job of running the DHS after Mr. Rader's retirement was monumental. The state was in economic decline following the oil and gas boom and bust and revenues were falling rapidly. It became necessary to exhaust every reserve fund we could find, to cut services in many ways, to continually go before legislative committees to request supplemental appropriations, and to reduce grants and benefits.

One of my earliest and most unpopular actions was to close the Whitaker Juvenile Center at Pryor. This center had capacity for more than two hundred juvenile offenders but the law had been changed so that courts no longer sent juveniles to the center. Rather than lay off staff, Mr. Rader had kept the full compliment of workers on the payroll even though the population of juveniles had dropped to less than fifty. A quick analysis of costs showed it was costing the state about $35,000 per year per juvenile to keep the center open. As quickly as this fact was brought to my attention, plans were made to reduce the population to zero so the facility could be closed.

I scheduled a public meeting in Pryor to announce this decision. I have never confronted such a hostile crowd. Ironically, even though several legislators were on hand who had voted for the change in law which brought about the decline in the center's population, they unanimously protested the closing. They were joined by the Chamber of Commerce and civic leaders. There seemed to be much more concern about the impact on the local economy than the wisdom of keeping an unneeded center going at great expense to the taxpayers. It was the Senate fight over closing unneeded military bases all over again.

The vocal local opposition to closing the center was ironic since for years there had been frequent protest over the conduct of the juveniles. Many escaped and stole cars or raided nearby residences to get the means for running away. Regardless of local and legislative opposition, the center was closed. Since then, other uses of the Whitaker facility have been developed so that now the community is much happier with the ongoing programs housed there. It was somewhat gratifying in my race for governor to carry the town of Pryor substantially. Apparently their wrath with me was short-lived. This experience shows again the wisdom of proceeding with needed reforms even in the face of opposition. Public attitudes do change once the facts are understood.

The outcome of federal lawsuits filed while Mr. Rader was director made detention of juveniles legal only in the most severe cases. Other facilities found to be unnecessary were closed. Fortunately, other communities were less agitated than Pryor and other institutions were converted into facilities for the Corrections Department which, with badly overcrowded facilities, was in need of additional capacity.

Inside DHS we found several faithful, dedicated, and experienced executives who were willing to help make long-overdue changes. Arrangements were worked out for Bob Fulton to become director as of July 1 when I needed to move on to other activities.

Another of the jobs I took was serving as the court-appointed receiver for the National Cowboy Hall of Fame and Western Heritage Center. Here another troublesome situation had developed. It appeared that certain high-income directors were being allowed to buy art objects at a nominal price and then loan them to the Cowboy Hall of Fame for display. After a period of time, a friendly licensed appraiser would reappraise the art, giving it a considerably appreciated value. The board members would then donate the art works to the Cowboy Hall of Fame, receiving tax benefits often in excess of the original purchase prices. In addition, the Hall of Fame apparently bought artifacts from certain directors at prices far beyond the real value and sold art objects from the Cowboy Hall of Fame collection to directors at far below their real value. This seemed to be the case with a Remington collection that went to a board member from California. To further complicate matters, board members from California decided that Oklahoma City was the wrong location for the Cowboy Hall of Fame. They seemed to be working with the management to bring about the collapse of the museum in Oklahoma City, apparently planning to move the art properties to a new museum being built in Southern California. After a particularly acrimonious board meeting, several of the protesting board members resigned, leaving this California faction totally in control. I believe this was an extremely short-sighted action by a group of normally responsible community leaders. It was only after a legal action was filed and the court stepped in that the collapse of this fine institution was avoided.

My months as receiver at the Cowboy Hall of Fame consisted of scrambling to find money to pay the bills and placate creditors to keep the museum open and finding ways to reduce costs or increase revenues while the issue of control was dealt with by the courts. To his great credit, Ed Gaylord proved to be an "angel" by providing collateral for loans and also by using his influence to get other financial help. The Cowboy Hall of Fame controversy was not fully resolved until after I resigned to begin the campaign for governor. The resolution came through the efforts of my replacement, a hard-nosed Oklahoma City lawyer who persuaded the court to end the procrastination and take action which permanently placed control of the Hall back in the hands of responsible directors.

Overall, I enjoyed the role as troubleshooter at the Department of Human Services and at the Cowboy Hall of Fame and Western Heritage Center. I found the challenges stimulating and the results gratifying. These experiences would prove excellent preparation for a second term as Oklahoma's governor when the entire state faced troubled times.

Over the years, Peter Flanagan, who had been in the Nixon White House and who now worked on Wall Street, had often invited me hunting. After I left the Senate, I wasn't sure I would be asked to join him on these pleasant occasions, but I was. Pete was a member of a shooting club called Clove Valley in upper New York State. The club had developed an old iron mine near Poughkeepsie into a splendid hunting preserve where some 10,000 mallard ducks were raised each year along with about an equal number of ringneck pheasants. From time to time Peter invited groups of his business and political friends to go shooting with him. Mostly he invited leaders from the business or industrial community but he often included a politician or two as well as dignitaries from foreign countries. I have found that a day in the outdoors in the company of a guide, a well-trained bird dog, and a group of kindred spirits to be a guaranteed formula for creating friendship and making the wheels of commerce or government turn more smoothly. There is no competition — only good-natured commentary about dog work and shots made or missed. Associations and friendships made during hunting trips are invaluable to business and political concerns.

On different occasions Pete and his wife Brigette invited me and sometimes Shirley to spend the night with them at their fine home in White Plains, New York. It was always a pleasant experience to have an evening with the Flanagans and their friends, one of whom was Don Kendall, CEO of Pepsi-Co, who lived nearby.

On one of these occasions after I had left the Senate, Pete and I had been hunting at Clove Valley and had returned to his home where I spent the night. At breakfast the next morning, buckwheat pancakes and honey were served. I commented to Pete how delicious the honey was, which turned out to be the right thing to say since his son Tim was the beekeeper. Pete got up from the table and went down into the cellar where the honey was kept and brought me back a glass quart jar of honey. I knew immediately when he gave it to me that I would never get the honey safely back to Oklahoma but I did not know how to gracefully decline the gift.

A little later, Pete's driver brought the family station wagon to the front door and we loaded my two shotguns, my suitcase, and my jar of honey in the back of the auto. That morning, Pete had a meeting at the Plaza Hotel in New York at 9:30. I had arranged a ten o'clock meeting with Bob Boyd, who was then working at City Bank. The driver let Pete off first at the hotel and then took me to City Bank for my appointment. The City Bank Building is a luxurious skyscraper, awesome to a farm boy from Billings.

The driver pulled up in front of the building and let me out so I could go inside and scout out which elevator I should take to Boyd's office. I came back, took my two shotguns, my suitcase, and my jar of honey out of the back of the station wagon and the driver drove away. The only entry to the bank was through a revolving glass door. I was fearful that in trying to maneuver through the door some accident would happen, and I was right! As I went through the door, the shotgun banged against the side. I relaxed my grip on the jar of honey and it dropped to the floor, breaking into a thousand pieces and splattering honey everywhere.

There was little I could do. I was concerned that if I let the revolving door sweep around, it would spread glass and sticky honey all over the floor. Then all the customers who came through the revolving door would have honey on their shoes and track it through the building. The only solution was to block the door and stand there, holding my suitcase and shotguns until I could attract the attention of a security person and get him to lock the door and open up another entry into the bank. It took several minutes, during which time a long line of curious, would-be bank customers gathered on the sidewalk outside the door looking in at the strange sight of a person with two shotguns and a suitcase blocking entry into New York City's largest bank. Soon their curiosity was overcome by impatience. Finally, a security guard noticed something was wrong, came over, locked the revolving door, and opened an adjacent entry so the people could pour through. Totally embarrassed, I escaped to Bob Boyd's office with my shotguns and luggage, renewed our acquaintance, then flew home to Oklahoma. I have never mentioned the incident to my New York friend Pete Flanagan.

On election day in 1984, Nancy Apgar, Republican state chairman, called me into the state headquarters where we had a long talk. She was greatly concerned about an Oklahoma City evangelist who had been on the presidential campaign trail in Oklahoma making speeches on behalf of Ronald Reagan, the Republican presidential candidate. She was afraid this man, who was articulate and attractive, would succeed in convincing party people he was the most logical Republican candidate for governor of Oklahoma in 1986. Nancy had strong misgivings about the qualifications of the preacher and even stronger questions about his electability. She urged me to show a public interest in the governor's race at that time, which I declined to do for many reasons. As we talked, the idea of starting a "draft Bellmon campaign" emerged. Nancy felt this would give Republican voters the message that there was a viable alternative to the preacher and also would help keep my name alive during the ensuing twelve months before a real gubernatorial campaign began.

It was my thought that, rather than drafting only a candidate for governor, the effort should be to draft a Republican team. This idea got nowhere with Nancy, who felt it needed to be a one-person show. Don Ferrell, my good friend and former staff member, publisher of the *Lincoln County Times at Chandler*, agreed to be chairman of the draft committee. To run the draft on a day-to-day basis for a nominal salary, an arrangement was worked out with Joe Allbaugh. Joe also had been on my Senate staff, then became a professional campaign manager for the Republican National Committee. The draft effort succeeded in both its objectives. Long before the governor's race began to heat up, the preacher encountered financial problems and disappeared from the political scene. The effort was successful in keeping my name before the public. In addition, a considerable sum of money was raised, both in gifts and pledges, so that when time came to actually start a campaign, we were well financed.

Complicated personal financial activities preceded my decision to run for governor in 1986. The problem arose because of the bad economics in the farming business during the decade of the seventies while I was in Washington and after I returned to Oklahoma. I had kept the farm as a safety net in case my political career came to an untimely and disastrous termination. During the years in Washington, I continued to operate it even though each year it showed a financial loss. Land values were rising rapidly, ten to twenty percent per year. It was easy to increase the land loan to cover farm operating losses. I had bought more land because renting is difficult for an absentee farmer. In addition, I was convinced that land prices would continue to rise due to inflation. By the time I came back to Oklahoma in 1981, the farm debt had risen to over $700,000, but there was still sizable equity in the land due to inflation of land prices. With the income from Channel Five, United Funds, Williams Company,

Cowboy Hall of Fame, and RAM, as well as my Senate retirement, funds were ample to not only manage the debt service and keep the farm operation going, but also to begin reducing the loans.

As I considered the possibility of entering the governor's race, it was obvious that I would need to reduce my debt significantly, since my income would virtually stop. To run for office I would have to give up salaries amounting to about four times as much as the governor's pay. Bill Banowsky, then president of Oklahoma University, was very interested in seeing me run for governor. On his own, he discussed my financial bind with an Oklahoma City businessman and outdoorsman who called me and expressed an interest in purchasing the Bar L ranch. An appraisal came in at $85,000 less than the price I was asking, but I agreed to sell at the appraised value, which was all the businessman would pay. At the same time, I discussed selling land near Billings with the trust department of an Oklahoma City bank. Prospective land buyers were brought to look at the farm land. Finally a family trust agreed to acquire 240 acres, provided half the oil royalty was included. The place had oil production and the prospect for additional wells was good. Buyers were also found for a truckstop site along Interstate 35 that I needed to sell.

Over the years, I had been involved in oil production in a small way. The involvement began when a partner and I purchased an abandoned shallow well and equipment for $2,200. The partner took over as operator and managed to bring the well up to the point that it produced two or three barrels of oil a day. The second involvement followed the discovery of another abandoned well which still had casing in place. We put it in production at minimal cost and it, too, produced two to three barrels a day. Since I was receiving both royalty and working interest income from the wells, the oil checks were of some significance, as much as $500 to $700 a month.

When I came back from the Senate, the 1980 oil boom was at its height. Shortly after my return, I was approached by an Oklahoma City operator who wanted to lease 480 acres of mineral rights I owned so he could drill several wells as part of a large oil development program he had underway. Of course I was delighted to lease to him and arranged to take up to a one-eighth operating interest in the properties. Five wells were drilled rapidly without adequate tests to determine what the production would be. It was necessary to borrow money to pay my share of drilling and completion costs. The bank most aggressive in making oil loans was Penn Square in Oklahoma City. I ultimately borrowed $180,000 from Penn Square Bank to participate in nine wells operated by two separate companies. A few of the wells proved to be profitable but several should never have been drilled. When the Penn Square Bank failed, it was necessary for me to move the loan. First National in Oklahoma City took it over, then First National also failed and I had to sell the properties to pay off the bank. By this time I was preparing to run for governor. A wealthy Oklahoma City oil man and philanthropist took over the properties at their independently appraised value. I believe that over time they have proved to be a sound investment for him.

Working out my personal financial problems took months of careful thought, figuring and refiguring, and endless negotiations with bankers, lawyers, and businessmen. It was stressful and at times I was so angry with the process I considered walking away from politics. Getting my financial house in order so I could make the governor's race required the sale of property I wanted to keep. The sales were all at fair market price based upon independent appraisals. None of those who purchased property from me ever asked for or received favors of any kind. They never challenged decisions I made as governor or tried to benefit in any way from my service as the state's chief executive officer.

Those who involve themselves in elective office should understand they are expected to serve at a financial sacrifice. There is small recognition that government salaries are low and that those who devote their lives to public service have little opportunity to build financial reserves. My advice to potential candidates is build a sound financial base first and avoid speculative enterprises that can go sour. There is a need for a public official to feel secure so difficult, unpopular stands can be taken in the public interest. Without a degree of financial security, the need to live on income from elective office may dominate the official's thinking during the decision-making process.

While resolving my finances, work at the Cowboy Hall of Fame and RAM group gave me plenty to do and also provided convenient reasons to delay announcing a formal decision on whether or not I would become a candidate for governor. To be ready in case I decided to run, contact was made with Vice President George Bush to arrange a date for a fund-raiser in Oklahoma City. The date selected was June 27, which appeared to allow plenty of time to work out my finances.

On the day in early June selected for the announcement of my candidacy, we held a news conference at the farm. A sizable group of former staff members was invited and most of them found it possible to attend. The news conference began outdoors on the patio and was proceeding nicely until rain began to fall. We then moved the news conference inside the house, which required the television people to rearrange their lighting and get cameras set up again. By the time we got started again, the rain had become a downpour with much lightning and strong winds. The news conference went on for another forty minutes before questions were exhausted, then when reporters tried to leave, it was raining so hard they could not get back to their vehicles without being drenched. Some reporters stayed in the house with the staff people to wait out the storm, and everyone seemed to enjoy the conversation. In all, six inches of rain fell that afternoon. Luckily, it rained so hard the roads were packed down and everyone got back to the highway without getting stuck in the mud.

I had insisted on holding the announcement news conference at the farm because I wanted reporters to see and understand that the Bellmons were normal country folks. I was concerned that twelve years in the U.S. Senate might have given the false impression that we were somehow changed. I knew full well becoming a candidate meant living in a fish bowl again and I felt that bringing reporters to our farm home was a good way to begin our renewed relationship.

The campaign organization was shaping up reasonably well. Joe Allbaugh was campaign director and Don Ferrell campaign chairman. Again, Drew Mason ran the money-raising operation. Attorney Burns Hargis was Oklahoma County finance chairman, Travis Freeman was Tulsa County chairman, and Jim Barnes of MAPCO was Tulsa County finance chairman. Claudia Scribner did scheduling and looked after my personal interests with her usual dedication and competence. On balance it was a good crew, mostly people we had worked with before, and everyone worked together well. There was a large group of volunteers who were faithful about helping at headquarters by handling mailings and other matters that require much man- and woman-power.

It is only natural for campaign organization workers to become staff members, once the candidate is elected. It's wise for a candidate to be careful in selecting campaign staff since after election they make up the backbone of the administration. Once in office, a governor especially needs to have access to a reservoir of talented, dedicated people because one of the greatest responsibilities of the office is to make appointments to agencies, boards, and commissions. An effective media candidate may be a failure as a governor due to lack of opportunity to know and evaluate potential appointees which a person-to-person campaign provides.

My involvement in the Cowboy Hall of Fame controversy kept me from actively campaigning for governor for several months. This proved to be a disadvantage since I did not have the opportunity to travel extensively over the state as I normally would have. I could not establish the contacts or make the acquaintances which would have been valuable in selecting individuals to serve on the numerous boards and commissions which the governor must fill.

Shirley and I made weekly swings of about three days' duration into different quadrants of the state. Television, radio, and newspaper advertisements accompanied each of these swings. We did not resurrect the two-party-tea-parties although we did something not too dissimilar in the counties where it was possible to schedule meetings in private homes. Shirley designed a collar made from the leftover Bellmon Belle material that had been in our basement since 1974. Some of the younger women made "jams" out of this material and from their old Bellmon Belle dresses.

One troubling aspect about the campaign was that Freckles Little and Jerry Brown, both Republicans, filed as Independents. Both were great detractors, largely because of their dislike of my vote on the Panama Canal Treaties. What developed was a four-way race for governor with three candidates — one Democrat and two Independents — gunning for me. The two Republicans who turned Independent obviously had no thought of winning. They were "spoilers" planning to be as destructive of my candidacy as possible.

On the Democratic side, David Walters, whom I had known slightly through our relationship at DHS, filed to oppose Attorney General Mike Turpen in the Democratic primary. Initially, Walters was practically unknown outside Oklahoma City and some western towns. He proved to be young, bright, and articulate and he received significant financial backing. Much of the backing came through multiple mortgages placed on his already heavily mortgaged home. When these transactions became public, it produced an outcry from Mike Turpen, who lost in a runoff after a late deluge of television advertising by Walters. Turpen and Walters continued feuding past the general election with a considerable amount of Turpen support coming to my assistance. I again benefitted from the bitterness between Democrat contenders, just as I had in 1962.

During the general election campaign, the League of Women Voters invited Walters and myself to debate. The biggest issue in the campaign was Walters's multiple mortgages. This appeared to be a transparent evasion of legal limits on campaign contributions and had become the subject of a lawsuit by Turpen. Since the loans were the subject of a lawsuit, I was advised not to discuss the matter in the campaign. If I agreed to a debate without bringing up the multiple mortgage issue, it would look like the illegal loans weren't important. For that reason I declined the invitation to debate.

Walters put on a chicken suit, came to our headquarters, and paraded around saying I was afraid of him. A few days later he took information from the public record of my sale of the Bar L ranch and put together some charts, showing how land values had jumped up when I sold my land and how they went down after the sale. Since he'd come to our headquarters, I went, uninvited, to his news conference where he was going to disclose these "financial irregularities." I sat there and listened to a Walters aide go through his "disclosures." When the reporters asked me about it I was able to denounce his charges as wildly inaccurate. I've always felt that was one of the turning points in the campaign.

The election outcome was close. I won by 26,000 votes with the two Independents (Republicans) receiving almost 73,000 votes, most of which would normally have been mine. The spoilers reduced the margin but failed to change the final outcome of the election. The campaign had been thoroughly unpleasant. The Walters approach was totally negative. Fortunately, after so many years of public service, my standing with voters was solid. They even accepted my votes on the Panama Canal Treaty. It was an honor and a vindication to be elected. Even Ed Gaylord supported me!

Governor Again

"If You Don't Shoot Any Cartridges, You Won't Get Any Partridges"

A fter the campaign ended, as governor-elect for my second term, I found activity sped up rather than slowed down. I had to deal immediately with the selection of staff members, planning for the inaugural, development of a legislative program, the next state budget, and the selection of a cabinet that the legislature had recently mandated. Letters had to be written to campaign workers and volunteers as well as contributors. There was also a rash of invitations for public appearances and calls on legislative leaders with whom a working relationship needed to be established.

Since the state's economy was in a state of serious recession and citizen moral was low, plans were made to turn the inaugural ceremony into a celebration of the beginning of the state's recovery. Three inaugural parties were held with great enthusiasm and obvious pleasure on the part of the several thousand guests who attended. Unlike my first inaugural, this event in 1987 occurred on a warm, bright, sunny January day, a good omen for the new administration. Governor Nigh, with whom I'd worked as a member of his administration, and his wife Donna were gracious in the transfer of authority, meeting with Shirley and me on different occasions and easing the transition. He was affiliating with Central State University and asked to take much of the furniture and appointments from the governor's office to help decorate the office of the George Nigh Institute which he was to head. This arrangement was worked out with the legislature and was satisfactory to me except it left the office of governor somewhat barren for many months until the vocational-technical schools completed building the desk and tables I was to use in the governor's office for the next four years. The tables were made from cured walnut lumber cut from trees on our farm in Noble

County. When they were finally delivered, the furniture was well made and a delight to use and show to visitors.

When we moved into the office, I was surprised to find the plan and decor had remained unchanged since before my previous term some twenty years earlier. During the interim, the space had been expanded to include the area formerly used by the secretary of state as well as an adjacent office called suite 210. In addition, the Nigh administration had placed several desks in the long hallway leading to the governor's office and probably due to the tight financial straits which had prevailed in recent years, the entire suite of offices had a generally down-at-the-heels appearance. Drew Mason, who became my chief of staff, inspired us to undertake a major office renovation plan under the guidance of volunteer architects and interior designers using funds from private sources. The renovation took more than a year and generated considerable confusion, but the result was gratifying. The office remodeling project was entered in a national competition by the American Society of Interior Designers and won first prize.

One of the first calls I made immediately after I was elected was on House Speaker Jim Barker, a Democrat, with whom I'd been somewhat acquainted during my service as director of the Department of Human Services. Due to the rough time I'd had in the previous term with Speaker J.D. McCarty, I had misgivings about my relationship with Barker. Unlike boisterous, overbearing McCarty, however, Barker was a mild-mannered, modest, almost retiring, man. After we talked cordially for several minutes and discussed our mutual objectives, he opened a manilla folder on his desk and showed me clippings from the *Muskogee Phoenix*, his hometown newspaper. They were political advertisements which had been run by my opponent, David Walters, during the general election. For whatever reason, Walters had run ads attacking Speaker Barker in his own hometown! Barker was understandably appalled at this affront from a member of his own party. After I had read the ads, he asked me what I thought of them. Of course I expressed my incredulity. At that point, he told me, in what I believe was complete honesty, that he had crossed party lines and voted for me in the general election. This was the beginning of a friendly and productive working relationship between myself and Speaker Barker.

Barker had created a leadership team of five individuals who had the reputation of controlling the House of Representatives with an iron hand. The most visible and powerful of the group was Representative Guy Davis, House majority leader, who had many of the characteristics of a J.D. McCarty. Davis was large, boisterous, crude in his handling of people, and the champion in use of pork projects to achieve legislative goals. The overbearing manner of Davis was finally to be the undoing of the Barker speakership.

I also made an early call on Senator Rodger Randle, president pro tem of the Senate. Randle was from Tulsa County, an area which I had carried heavily. To my surprise, he proved to be almost as friendly and low-key as Barker. Because of divisions along rural-urban lines among Democrats in the Senate, Randle's position was considered to be somewhat tenuous and it was obvious he was not going to lead from a position of great power. Another senator with whom I established early contact was Bob Cullison of Tulsa County, leader of the more progressive, urban Democratic members of the Senate. He would succeed Randle as president pro tem. Also, I reestablished contact with Senator Gene Stipe, leader of the rural elements of the Senate. Stipe was a colorful man sometimes referred to derisively as the Prince of Darkness. I had worked with him in my earlier term, and through the years, we'd maintained a relationship that bordered on personal friendship.

As a Republican governor, I was fortunate in the choices House and Senate Republicans had made in minority leaders. The Senate chose Jerry Smith of Tulsa and the House selected Walter Hill from Turpin. These gentlemen proved to be extremely level-headed and courageous in positions they took in supporting the administration's efforts to reform state government and provide the revenue needed to maintain government services at a satisfactory level. Their leadership was in strong contrast to the those who would be chosen for the 1989 and 1990 sessions. Then, Republicans selected leaders who not only refused to lead but often seemed to get great satisfaction in taking positions or making statements embarrassing to their Republican governor.

The voters of Oklahoma had elected Robert S. Kerr III to be lieutenant governor. Kerr was a member of the Democratic party, which obviously was going to make it difficult for us to collaborate closely since it would not further his political aims for him to be seen to be on good terms with a Republican and I couldn't confide in an office-holder from another party. Nevertheless, we tried to develop a common working relationship and succeeded in many ways. The lieutenant governor agreed to serve as the state's representative on international trade missions, work in tourism development, and serve as host for out-of-state groups that came through on economic development missions. Under the law, he also served on several state boards including the School Land Commission, State Insurance Fund Board, and the State Board of Equalization. Kerr proved to be somewhat indifferent to many of his responsibilities and seemed most interested in furthering his political career, which he attempted to do in the 1990 election when he ran unsuccessfully for Congress in the Third District.

The second time around, we were fortunate that more than half our staff would be composed of former staff members. These included all the key positions. I was gratified that so many who had worked with me in other capacities were ready to leave other jobs and be associated with the new Bellmon administration. Drew Mason became chief of staff and Joe Allbaugh took on the responsibility for overseeing appointments and Senate liaison. I was fortunate in getting the services of Andrew Tevington as the governor's chief counsel. Andrew had worked on the U.S. Senate staff in Washington as press secretary, had returned to Oklahoma, earned his law degree, worked as a lobbyist for a time, and willingly joined the staff when invited. He proved to be an outstanding legal counsel with fine political instincts and unbounded courage and energy. One of the earliest and most fortunate cabinet choices was the appointment of OU Professor Alexander Holmes as state finance director. Lex had gained a reputation as an authority on many aspects of state and local government and was well known to several legislators. Andrew and Lex made an excellent team working on legislation, though both of them came to be somewhat controversial as a result of legislative opposition to various proposals. They were the point men of the administration and took much of the heat that otherwise would have been directed toward the governor.

The formation of a cabinet was particularly important since Oklahoma government had never before used the cabinet system. In previous administrations, contacts had been made directly between the governor and nearly 200 agency and commission heads. Except for key agencies and in cases of crisis, the agencies were on their own, run by directors hired by boards or commissions. Theoretically, boards or commissions made up of lay people set policy. As a practical matter, most directors tell boards only what the directors want them to know. Street-wise directors can therefore run the agencies as little czars. The cabinet system promised to bring order and closer coordination, provided qualified and astute people were chosen as secretaries. Great care was used in making cabinet selections and only trusted, experienced, and dedicated individuals were appointed.

The principle champions of the cabinet system had been Senator Rodger Randle and former Governor George Nigh. The legislators had gone along, not knowing the next governor would be a Republican. Now the legislators were skeptical about the wisdom of this arrangement. Despite the fact that we were fortunate in the choice of individuals who accepted cabinet positions, the Senate refused to confirm the cabinet except for a couple of members who were not only cabinet officers but departmental directors as well. The cabinet would serve without confirmation for three years before the Senate finally accepted their own creation and gave it the blessing of formal confirmation.

One of the biggest shocks to follow the election was the discovery that the state was facing an enormous fiscal deficit. During the oil boom years, income from the severance tax as well as petroleum-related increases in sales, income, and excise taxes had boosted state income handsomely. Taxes had been reduced a dozen times. As the oil boom played out and revenues dropped, the legislature and governor had drained all the state reserve accounts in a successful effort to postpone a significant tax increase. This left the new governor and the new legislature with the responsibility of finding a way to make up some $350,000,000 or seventeen percent in revenue shortfalls. This would become the central focus of the first legislative session and the source of heated controversies for many months. Other major problems were serious prison overcrowding, the partisan makeup of the state tax commission, and the fact that revenue shortages had made it impossible for the state to match some $200,000,000 of available federal highway funds.

In an effort to bring business expertise to state government and to fully define the changes which needed to be made, various study groups composed of public officials and private citizens were created. Many of their recommendations would be incorporated in the legislative proposals and new budget to be presented to the legislature the day after the inauguration. Due to a resignation, Lex Holmes was placed on the payroll early and immediately began preparation of the fiscal year 1988 budget on a crash basis. We had a scant thirty days to complete this task before the document was due at the printers.

It was a challenge for us to get as many facts as we could, make the most realistic revenue projections possible in light of the uncertain economic conditions, and find ways of cutting unnecessary government spending in as many areas as we could identify. Some of these included highly sensitive proposals such as removing the state from the business of running nursing homes for veterans (at a cost nearly triple the cost of privately-provided nursing care), eliminating one of the state's three medical schools, closing the under-utilized dental school, eliminating one institution of higher education, and eliminating the $5 million cost of supporting an unsuccessful program to encourage doctors to practice in rural areas. Many, many millions of dollars in savings were possible. None of the cuts would be approved by the legislature, however; pressure groups would succeed in protecting the status quo.

Probably the most difficult problem we had was to come up with a package of tax increases that would generate the necessary revenues to keep a satisfactory level of state services and at the same time not abort the state's economic recovery. The proposal I delivered to the joint session of the House and Senate on the day following my inauguration stirred enormous controversy. It included a number of proposals for saving tax dollars but even so, it was necessary also to propose the state's largest-ever tax increase. It was obvious from the beginning that the legislature would insist on a thorough overhaul of the governor's proposals, yet it was important for the state's chief executive to take the lead in establishing the need for more revenue.

Following the practice which had been established by the Nigh administration, regular Tuesday morning breakfasts were held with the House and Senate leadership teams. With a Republican governor, it was necessary to bring in minority leaders from both the House and Senate. Since the Barker leadership team included five people, Senate Democrats felt they needed to bring in an equal number and these, added to the minority legislative leaders, gave us a group of twenty, far too many for an effective or confidential decision-making process. Much as I tried to talk the president pro tem and the speaker out of the notion of bringing along such large groups, they insisted it was all or nothing. In addition, several Republicans bore grudges for what they considered to be slights from previous years when the Democrats were in total control. (Democrats controlled each house of the legislature by roughly two to one.) Republican legislators seemed determined to get even now that they had a Republican governor. These breakfasts generated much heat and very little light. Finally, after a few weeks, it became apparent that they were a total waste of time for all concerned, and the breakfasts were discontinued. From that point on, I had to meet with individual groups separately and try to work out agreements as the need arose.

After it became clear that our first package of tax proposals was going nowhere, Lex Holmes and I put together a second package and offered it to the House and Senate. Privately, the speaker told me he liked my leadership style. He said that when I realized the first package wouldn't fly I didn't hesitate to come up with a second one that he thought had a better chance of winning approval.

A little later, Speaker Barker asked for an appointment and when he arrived, he brought with him his five-member leadership team. By now we were all acquainted and on nominally good terms. The speaker explained that, while I probably did not realize what had happened since my previous term, what he called "special projects" had come to be a major part of the legislative process. Special projects included such things as lights for local baseball fields, paving of local streets, support for local activities like watermelon festivals, rattlesnake hunts, Indian cultural events, and anything else local members thought was important for their hometowns. Barker explained these were tools he and his leadership team had to use if they were to deliver the necessary number of votes to pass the tax package. Without giving the matter much thought, I quickly agreed to go along with the special projects practice. It occurred to me that it was going to be tough enough to get votes we had to have to pass the tax bill and keep state government from being paralyzed, and that this was not the time to launch into a major reform of the pork legislation which the legislators liked to refer to as special projects. The agreement was reached that the governor would approve the special projects bill which the House and Senate would send after an acceptable tax measure had been passed and signed into law.

The result was that one commitment after another was made to win votes needed to pass the tax bill. As soon as one legislator discovered a fellow member had made a deal, another deal became necessary. Millions of tax dollars were promised. A great many of these special projects went to districts represented by House Democratic leaders who would have voted for the tax bill in any event. They were simply using the tax fight as a way of securing questionable projects that otherwise would not have been funded. Using pork projects to bribe legislators to do the job they were elected to do was wasteful, self-defeating, and caused legislation to be considered on a "what's in it for me" basis rather than on merit. Finally, I made up my mind to put an end to this pork parade. This would not be easy because there were many Republican members of the legislature who also were getting their pieces of pork. The total bill for the projects probably came to somewhere between $15,000,000 and $20,000,000, depending upon what was classified as pork. At one point, Speaker Barker told me he was fed up with the whole special project business since he had demands for more than $50,000,000 of pork projects.

The final vote on the tax bill, which was the main focal point of the first session, appeared to be very close. Speaker Barker invited me to come to his office and watch the tally as votes were cast. From time to time, different members were sent in for me to talk to and different agreements were reached. To my knowledge, every one of those was kept meticulously. When it came time for the vote, Speaker Barker switched on his inner-office communication system and I watched as the votes were electronically recorded. The minute the count reached the number needed to pass the bill, the speaker terminated the roll call and announced the outcome. There was great jubilation among legislative leaders as well as among members of the governor's staff and cabinet. Had we not succeeded in raising new revenues, state government services, including schools, colleges, prisons, health services, welfare, and highways, would have had to be cut by at least seventeen percent. Hundreds of millions of federal matching funds would have been lost. Though more money could and should have been saved, cuts of this magnitude were simply impossible.

When the '88 session began, I told the new speaker, Steve Lewis, who had been chairman of the House appropriations committee, that the time for ending the pork business had come; I was not going to participate in that process any longer. Not only was this an unconstitutional waste of tax dollars, but by using pork, the leadership had an enormous club to use over their members in passing unworthy legislation. When Attorney General Robert Henry held that the "special legislation" was unconstitutional, it was a great help to us in bringing this intolerable perversion of the legislative process to an end.

In 1988, until I took my position on abolishing pork, things had been going well between the Republican governor and the Democratic leaders of the House and Senate. As soon as this new "no pork" policy became known, my relationship with the House and Senate soured dramatically and the session, which had been headed for early adjournment, went the full length of time allowed by law. Very little in the way of needed legislation was accomplished, but I vetoed all pork legislation that reached my desk, and the vetoes were sustained. Even though the House and Senate procrastinated for many weeks, accomplishing little, all appropriation bills were held back until late in the night after the new fiscal year began. Starting about midnight, the voluminous documents began arriving in the governor's office. Apparently the plan was to hide pork projects and other questionable actions in the language on the assumption that time would not permit careful examination of the new laws. The ploy failed to work. Lex Holmes, Andrew Tevington, and their assistants worked all night going over the bills and taking out objectionable features by using the governor's line-item veto. Even so, state government operated illegally for several hours since no legally appropriated funds were available to be spent.

The experience showed how irresponsible a legislature could be in attempting to achieve its goals. As a result, petitions were circulated setting a date and time certain for the beginning and end of the legislative session. When the question was voted on by the citizens it was approved overwhelmingly. A constitutional requirement for orderly adjournment of the legislature thirty days before the end of the fiscal year ended much of the connivance.

During the 1987 session, I had been contacted on more than one occasion by the Bush organization and asked to serve as state chairman for George Bush's presidential campaign. I had declined to become involved until the legislative session was over. After the session ended, I accepted the Bush for President campaign chairmanship. Fortunately, U.S. Senator Don Nickles agreed to release one of his top administrative assistants, Clinton Key, to serve as campaign director and this took most of the burden of the campaign off my shoulders.

Of the people I have known in politics and government, the two for whose personal abilities and attributes I have the greatest respect and admiration are Peter Flanagan and George Bush. Strangely, both are Yankees, come from wealthy families, and have had all the advantages wealth and position can provide. In short, they come from backgrounds as different from mine as can be imagined, but they both possess immense native ability. Both George and Barbara Bush are among the warmest people I have come to know in political activities.

I had first heard of George Bush, who was active in Texas politics, when John Tower was achieving success in his Senate race. I was active in Oklahoma Republican party affairs and met George during this period. Early on, I felt he had the possibility of becoming vice president and president, provided he got the breaks. When George made his race for the Senate in Texas, I was governor of Oklahoma. He invited me to Houston to help with the campaign. I eagerly went and did what I could, which wasn't much. His method of campaigning was not greatly different from my own. His meetings were mostly low key, the crowds were warm and enthusiastic, and George took the same personal approach I had used in Oklahoma. My friends in Texas told me that had John Connally stayed out of it, George probably would have been elected United States Senator at the time Lloyd Benston was first elected. Had he won, it's questionable he would ever have become president.

George's selection as Republican national chairman in 1971 pleased me. On different occasions, he and I had conversations about what the national committee should and should not be doing, but I am not certain George paid much attention to my admonitions. I doubted he was getting the support he needed from those in the White House to make changes. The Nixon years were the greatest opportunity the Republicans had since the Depression to build for the future. This all went out the window due to the lack of interest on the part of the president's staff and the problems of Watergate.

Over the years, George and I became good friends. In Washington, I was his guest at the small, informal meetings he hosted at the Alibi Club. George would assemble a small group of friends, usually about twenty, around the large old cypress wood table in the club for a meal of fresh spinach salad and steamed oysters and an evening of enlightening, lively conversation. George Bush could put together a guest list of people who were both convivial and articulate. He created an atmosphere which encouraged discussion to flow freely and openly. These were evenings with a purpose. Usually, he invited a principal guest: on one occasion, Arthur Burns; on another, Hermann Kahn; and on other occasions, leaders of the energy industry who tried to inform the non-energy guests of impending problems.

After the door to China had been opened, President Nixon appointed George Bush to be the first U.S. envoy to the People's Republic. When George and Barbara came back to the United States for their first visit after having spent time in China, Shirley and I were among their guests at a small dinner party at the Chevy Chase Country Club. That evening, George spent considerable time talking about his experiences in China and giving the group general insights into the relationship between our two countries. Again, it was a pleasant social occasion that produced much valuable information.

When President Ford chose George to be director of the CIA, I was appalled. I considered George one of the most likely prospects for the vice presidential nomination and felt that the CIA job would make him unelectable because of the scars he would receive. Gaining a reputation as the nation's chief spy would be no help in a future campaign. I felt he was too valuable an asset to the party and the country to be wasted in the CIA slot. At the time President Ford made this nomination, he also nominated Elliot Richardson to be secretary of commerce. I felt he should have reversed these two spots since Bush's previous service as Republican national chairman gave him a partisan identity which would hurt him at the CIA. Elliot Richardson, who was looked upon as "Mr. Clean," could have gone to the CIA with no stigma. Also, I felt the public image of Elliot Richardson was such that he stood a much better chance than George of surviving the experience at the CIA. After the nomination was sent to the Senate, I called George and talked the matter over with him. I told him I felt he was being wronged by the president by being asked to take the assignment. He strongly disagreed. He said he wanted the CIA position and felt he could render a real service as director. He asked me not only to vote for his confirmation but to campaign among other members to make sure he got the appointment, which I did. George was confirmed and served at the CIA effectively. The agency recovered lost public respect and professionalism. However, there seemed to be a major problem in that George was not as close to the president as he needed to be. He reported to President Ford through General Scowcroft. This made it difficult for George to get information to and from the president in an ungarbled form, and I believe it was a disservice to both Ford and Bush.

When I was offered membership in the Oklahoma Hall of Fame, George Bush agreed to come to Oklahoma and read the citation at the ceremony. He also agreed to be the guest speaker for the annual College Leadership Seminar I hosted that year. In 1979 he came to Oklahoma as a candidate for president. I was invited to a private meeting with party leaders where he spoke. It was a small meeting—probably not more than fifteen people—and I was stunned at the poor appearance George made. He attempted to position himself to the right of Ronald Reagan, which was a political impossibility. He seemed to realize that in Oklahoma, Republican leadership was solidly in the Reagan camp and he was making an effort to win them over. It was futile and he got nowhere in Oklahoma as a presidential candidate that year. As Ronald Reagan's running mate, George did no harm to the ticket though it's questionable if he won Reagan much additional support. Not many people vote for a president because of his running mate and George probably was as good a choice as Reagan could have made.

Following the 1980 election, I returned to Oklahoma and was no longer directly involved in political activity. However, on occasion when I was in Washington, D.C., I would drop by to see Vice President Bush in the White House. We had friendly and open conversations; obviously he was very content with his role as Reagan's understudy. On one occasion in 1986, I went to see George to tell him I hoped he was making preparations to run for president after Reagan concluded his second term. If he planned to make the race, I felt it was time to begin putting some distance between himself and Ronald Reagan. He needed to stake out his own positions and I wanted him to become his own man. He objected strongly to the idea and finally said that even if he wanted to, it would be impossible because, "I love the man too much." That seemed to settle the matter as far as George was concerned.

When Bush began to actively seek the presidency, he came to Oklahoma and asked me to be his campaign manager. This was soon after my election as governor when I was deeply embroiled in controversy with the legislature over trying to resolve the state's growing financial crisis. I told George I had too much to do right then but would consider the matter when the legislature adjourned. Senator Bob Dole of Kansas also asked me to join his campaign as chairman of the Oklahoma Dole for President Committee. Bob even went so far as to arrange for his wife, Liddy, to come to Oklahoma where we had a pleasant lunch in the governor's office and discussed the presidential campaign. As much as I admired Bob as a senator and Liddy as a charming person, I did not feel that Bob was temperamentally or professionally as qualified to be president as George Bush. Bob Dole's entire experience had been in the legislative branch. I was not certain he could make the transition to the executive side. As politely as possible, I told them so. The contest between George Bush and Bob Dole created mild strains in the governor's office. I had given members of the staff total freedom to back whomever they wished, and Drew Mason chose to become a leader in the Dole camp.

As far as I know, George made no effort to get anyone else to serve as his campaign manager and when the legislative session ended, I proudly accepted the title. During the campaign, I was invited to go to Kennebunkport, Maine, where I met with candidate Bush and five other governors in an all-day session discussing state-related issues and how the campaign would be run. I flew to Boston, was met by one of George's campaign assistants, and spent the night in one of the beachfront lodges near the Bush home. The next morning, George called and arranged for Governor Garry Carruthers of New Mexico, his wife Cathy, and me to come to the Bush compound early for an ocean fishing trip.

It was a beautiful spring morning and we arrived about 9:30 to find George in a very relaxed and convivial mood. He invited us to go with him to fish for "blues" in a cigarette boat — long, deep-sided, narrow, powerful, and very fast in the water. At the appointed time, George backed the boat away from the dock and we headed out to sea. At that time, some columnists insisted on referring to George as a wimp and frequently brought up what they called the wimp factor, but anyone in the boat with George Bush that morning would have known that this man didn't have a wimpy bone in his body. The seas were far from calm, but George opened the throttle all the way and raced out hitting only the tops of the waves as he left the trailing Secret Service boat in his wake. He told of an earlier fishing excursion during which his guest, a prominent news reporter, became so violently ill he required medical attention.

When we reached the place George thought the blues might be biting, he rigged our fishing gear and, guided by George's occasional advice, we trolled for an hour and a half. Unfortunately, the blues were not running and we had no success. As lunchtime approached, George suggested we give up our fishing expedition. On the return trip, he took us on a cruise around some of the smaller islands, showed us where seals were sunning themselves and managed to get some of the animals to plunge into the water. Again, he skippered the boat at high speeds and frightened me more than a little. It was as if he was reliving his days as an eighteen-year-old airplane pilot, totally in command of the situation, showing off. As we finished our cruise, we approached the dock at a very high speed. I was absolutely certain he was going to crash head-on into the granite slabs where the boats anchored. At the last moment, he cut the throttle and the boat coasted safely and smoothly to its proper resting place. I've never been more relieved to be safely back on land.

The rest of the day was spent in conversation and in conviviality. We were served New- England-style seafood with fresh roasting ears and fresh fruit. What must have been the entire Bush clan gathered for the event, and it was obvious there was a great deal of warmth between the generations. While I'd known Barbara and George Bush before, this was my first exposure to the Bush family, a tightly-knit group who plainly enjoyed their lives together at the Bush compound. After lunch, the governors and the vice president gathered in the living room where George and Barbara explained how they had rebuilt their house following a devastating storm. We launched into discussions about issues which likely would arise in the presidential campaign and how they affected our various states. I'm not sure how much George gained from the conversation but he seemed vitally interested in developing an active working relationship between the presidency and the governors to deal with federal and state interests.

During the campaign, George came to Oklahoma on different occasions, mostly for fund-raising events. The entire party structure of the state was largely supportive of George and fund raising was not a great problem. However, the state's economy was seriously injured as a result of the oil crash and funds did not flow as freely as they had in the Reagan election. Usually I met George at the airport and took advantage of the opportunity to discuss the growing federal deficit. He did not seem to be much concerned with the rapid growth in the federal debt which had occurred during the Reagan administrations.

On one of his campaign visits, I met him at the airport in Tulsa. The limousine took us into the city for an appearance and a fund-raiser. When we returned to the airport, George spotted a 1937 Ford Highway Patrol car, one of the first the state had used. He had the limo stop, got in the old patrol car and took it for a short drive. He said it brought back fond memories since he had used a similar auto in Texas after World War II.

The appearances George made in Oklahoma were not particularly noteworthy. He seemed to be simply another candidate searching for ways to position himself in the best possible light and shy away from controversial issues. On Super Tuesday, Bush won every state in the South including Oklahoma and for all practical purposes locked up the nomination. I was relieved but not surprised at the outcome. His speech at the New Orleans Convention was Bush at his best as far as the Oklahoma delegation was concerned. It seemed that for the first time he was beginning to set a course for the future and become his own person again. However, I was appalled when he made his "read my lips: no new taxes" statement. My admonitions about the danger of the growing federal debt had fallen on deaf ears. I strongly felt he would be unable to keep this pledge and would be hurt when he changed positions.

Because of the lack of support for Michael Dukakis in Oklahoma, I didn't expect George Bush to come to the state to campaign, but he chose to do so. I went to the airport again and rode with him in his car to the rally on the courthouse steps in Oklahoma City. During our visit, we talked about different issues — mostly about the need for the next president and Congress to confront the huge federal deficit. I asked him as a favor to leave out of his speech any planned critical reference to the American Civil Liberties Union. He laughed and said his criticism of the ACLU was a line that always got a good crowd reaction. Three members of my cabinet were active ACLU members and reporters were having a lot of fun with the issue. I felt there was no need to raise it again in my own backyard. He searched through his speech cards and took out the ACLU reference.

The campaign basically went well for George Bush. He took advantage of the prosperous years most of the nation had experienced during the Reagan administration. Also, he reflected the anti-crime mood of the country as well as the renewed national pride and international prestige. These issues are important to Oklahoma's patriotic citizenry. Bush won in Oklahoma as well as all other Southern states. After the election, I was invited to two meetings at the White House where the formation of the new administration was discussed. Plans were made to clear appointments of Oklahomans with a small committee of campaign leaders. Again, as with the Nixon White House, the staff principally was made up of eager, bright former campaign workers with little experience in government. An attempt was made to have two Oklahoma Bush supporters considered for cabinet positions. As was the case twenty years earlier following the Nixon election, I was unable even to arrange interviews. It is amazing how quickly a newly elected president's staff takes charge and how little past loyalties and service mean.

A major rupture with the White House staff, including John Sununu, came over his veto of two Oklahomans who were nominated for sub-cabinet posts. Both were well qualified to fill vacancies and were selected by department heads. Opposition came from ultra-conservative Republican senators and the White House yielded to the pressure. I felt betrayed and was furious. Even a direct telephone conversation with President Bush did no good. The same was true when I called President Bush to ask him to make a telephone call to an Oklahoma Republican state senator to request help in the passage of House Bill 1017, the Education Reform and Funding Act. Bush was trying to establish himself as the education president and Oklahoma was the first state to undertake to pass a major education reform and funding bill. It seemed logical for an education president to make one phone call that would position him and the national party behind action, not empty rhetoric, on education. Again, Chief of Staff Sununu intervened and the phone call was never made.

After passage of the 1990 farm bill, I was approached by a USDA official about serving on the newly created Rural Development Task

Force and agreed to be appointed. Shortly after, I received a four-page form from the White House staff inquiring if I had ever done anything that could be considered controversial. Somewhat irritated, I replied that I had served as the George Bush for President state chairman which was very controversial with Senator Bob Dole. I heard nothing further about the appointment. How someone could serve as governor and U.S. senator and not be involved in controversy is hard to understand. Later, Shirley and I were invited by President Bush to be members of a small team of U.S. observers who travelled to Bulgaria to watch the election, the first in forty-five years.

Several activities we undertook early in the administration were worthy projects. Neal McCaleb, secretary of transportation, developed a program called "Don't Lay That Trash on Oklahoma," stressing the importance of keeping our highways free of trash and debris. Part of the program required enlisting the services of volunteers who were willing to adopt two-mile stretches of highway and clean them four times a year. This project was launched with a public advertising campaign, funded by state agencies. Shirley made a popular television ad in which a baritone voice was dubbed in while she mouthed the campaign slogan. The program proved to be eminently successful with some 28,000 volunteers signing on. State highway litter was reduced by forty-seven percent.

Another project we undertook was the creation of four additional state turnpikes. No new miles had been added to the turnpike system since the Cimarron had been built fifteen years earlier. The system was in strong financial condition, easily able to handle the debt service on additional bonds. It was obvious that the state's highway network and the state's economy could use the infusion of several hundred millions of outside dollars and the thousands of jobs that would be created. Therefore, a plan was worked out to build four new sections of turnpikes in different parts of the state. This received legislative approval only after considerable controversy because of the insistence by legislators in south central Oklahoma that a four-lane road from I-35 east through Ada to Henryetta or Okemah be a part of the package. Fortunately, the language was written to provide considerable flexibility. After some delay, bonds were sold and all four roads were built.

Probably the most controversial decision and perhaps the biggest mistake of the administration was to join in the competition for selection as the site for the federally-supported super-conducting super-collider. Because of the short time available before a proposal had to be submitted, we undertook to commit the state to this project without receiving appropriate legislative approval. This matter was held over my head throughout the entire first session of the legislature and was a matter of great concern and embarrassment. As a part of the effort to develop the Oklahoma proposal for the collider, we put together a commission of prominent Oklahoma scientists, educators, and business leaders. Breene Kerr, a prominent Oklahoma City businessman, philanthropist, and son of former U.S. Senator Robert Kerr, accepted the position as chairman of this group and served with great dedication and skill. He made a significant personal financial contribution to complete the work on the Oklahoma proposal, and largely due to his efforts, a highly professional proposal was produced in record time. Oklahoma did not succeed in winning the competition or even in making the short list. However, in the process, the state identified the weakness which kept it from being a more serious contender in this competition: the need for greater emphasis on education. It became clear that university research needed more support. This finding became the impetus for creation and funding of academic and research chairs at the universities and ultimately led to the special session which resulted in the passage of House Bill 1017.

When I took office, the Oklahoma prison system had recently been released from supervision of the federal courts where it had been placed due to overcrowding. To hold down the prison population, the legislature had passed a cap law under which sentences were reduced when the inmate population exceeded capacity and prisoners were released early without supervision. Led by Pardon and Parole Board Director Ray Page, we began an aggressive program of evaluating inmates for early release under supervision. In this way, prison overcrowding was held to tolerable levels with a minimum of criminal activities by parolees. The federal courts did not intervene, though prison population exceeded capacity by over 2,000 inmates, even after 2,100 new beds were added to the correction system. Several prisoner work camps were established to help alleviate inmate idleness and to provide low-cost labor to towns and state agencies. These became so popular that host communities requested many additional camps.

During our first legislative session, a strong and ultimately successful effort was made to bring bipartisan, professional administration to the state tax commission. Even though it meant tying state government in knots for several days, we struggled with the Senate leaders to break the patronage stranglehold the Senate had held on the tax commission since statehood. A bipartisan tax commission was created along with authority to select an administrator to run the agency. A C.P.A. was hired as director. He modernized procedures and ran the agency in such a way that public criticism was virtually eliminated. Former Democratic opponents became convinced that the change was needed.

While much of Shirley's time during the first governor's term had been devoted to taking care of the needs of our three daughters, in the second term, she was free to involve herself in many activities. When we returned to Oklahoma after twelve years in Washington, Shirley's interests in stained glass and other handicrafts led her to hold a bazaar and crafts show at our farm home. To my great surprise, more than a dozen artisans displayed their handiwork at the first bazaar, attended by several hundred people. Thousands of dollars in sales were made. In each of the next five years, the bazaar grew rapidly until, on the last year before my reelection as governor, almost one thousand people came to look and buy. During the time the last farmhouse bazaar was held I was running for governor and interrupted the campaign to help out. Unfortunately, the day of the bazaar fell during a week when our area received a record twenty inches of rainfall. Our yard and pasture were so muddy that cars could not be parked there, so we arranged for a van to shuttle the visitors from the roadside, where they could park their cars, to our house. Unfortunately, many of the visitors had to walk through the mud and rain. We were afraid it would destroy the interest in the bazaar. The next year the event was renamed "First Lady's Bazaar" and moved to the Harn Museum grounds in Oklahoma City where it was held in tents. Over the four years we were in the governor's office, the number of artisans displaying their wares increased to one hundred; yearly attendance grew to over three thousand.

Shirley's experience with the bazaars convinced her there are many home-based businesses, mostly run by women who are attempting to supplement the family income. In many cases these entrepreneurs are in need of business counseling. This conviction led Shirley to work with extension agents at Oklahoma State University to conduct home-based business conferences in all sections of the state. The conferences were well attended and much-needed information and guidance were provided. During President Bush's education conference in Williamsburg, Virginia, Barbara Bush heard Shirley tell about home-based business development. Barbara invited Shirley and the home extension leaders from OSU to the White House to discuss their activities with reporters from the national media. Several news stories were written as a result.

Shirley worked on the "Don't Lay That Trash on Oklahoma" program as well as other efforts to beautify highways, including promoting the planting of wildflowers and the production of wildflower seed by prison inmates. She also undertook a complete renovation of the first floor of the governor's mansion. She located and supervised the reinstallation of leaded glass cabinet doors and entry doors in the library, then supervised the restoration of the wood and tile floors on the first floor of the mansion and remodeled the kitchen. For her efforts, the state Historical Society selected her for its George Shirk award.

Shirley worked from an office on the second floor of the mansion. One day not long after we had moved in and during the time she was getting herself organized, a group of women were having lunch on the third floor. Doors to the bedrooms, sitting room, and the office were closed. But a few of the more curious women decided to give themselves an unguided tour. Shirley heard them in our bedroom, then in the sitting room, which is next to the office. She feared they also were going to open the office door and since she was not fittingly dressed or prepared to have them pop in on her, she ducked into a closet in the office. They *did* open the office door, commented on the state of the confusion on her desk, and left. Shirley, who gets claustrophobia, suddenly panicked at the thought that she might not be able to get out of the closet. Finally, when the women had gone upstairs, she tried the closet door and was relieved to find she could open it from the inside.

From her experience with home-based businesses, Shirley and a friend developed a line of dolls called the "First Lady's Collection." These were displayed at the Dallas gift market in the summer of 1990, where orders for more than three thousand were taken. This put Shirley and her partner in the position of starting into the doll production business on a crash basis. She now operates a doll-making business from a former hardware store building in Billings.

With the doll business, she has truly come into her own. She is a woman with a focus and the determination to see it through. It has nothing to do with her children or her husband. It is hers. Shirley's role is an important one. She helped raise three daughters who are members of the generation of women whose choices are unlimited, while her generation was caught in the transition between traditional roles and nontraditional ones. It wasn't always easy, but Shirley has made that transition. She raised a family and was a political wife in a time when it was still important to be a traditional political wife. Then, she became one of the those in her generation to break out of those roles. I have always been proud of her, but never more than I am today.

Until the 1990-91 school year, Oklahoma teachers' salaries were among the lowest in the country — lower than salaries paid in similar private-sector jobs. Beginning teachers were paid $15,060. Even so, due to other demands for money, when the legislative session in 1989 was concluded, we had failed to provide funds for any significant improvement in teacher salaries. After the session, I talked with Representative Glen Johnson, chairman of the House appropriations committee, and mentioned this fact to him. He agreed that, although we had done some things to improve higher education, we had not done well enough by primary and secondary education. Soon after the session, I attended a meeting of the Republican Teachers Association. I went there expecting to be warmly received, but have never encountered a more hostile group. They were furious at their low level of compensation, shortage of funds for textbooks and supplies, and at the lack of significant progress in education funding throughout their careers. They felt educators were doing a good job in Oklahoma but were not receiving the compensation or the support they deserved.

I went away from the meeting thoroughly shaken up. If this "friendly" group was so hostile, it was obvious that the Oklahoma education situation was becoming explosive. In thinking about and discussing the matter with state finance authorities in subsequent weeks, it became clear that the 1990 legislative session would again be short of money. In addition, legislators would be thoroughly occupied with reelection campaigns and in no mood to raise taxes. I wanted to make the thrust of my 1990 program improvement and preservation of the state's environment. These issues, plus a major education funding and reform bill, would simply have been too much of an undertaking for the regular session of the legislature. About this time the Oklahoma Education Association announced its plans for an initiative petition drive calling for a special session to deal with education issues. It was obvious that such a petition had little chance of going anywhere because by the time it was circulated, had cleared the Secretary of State, had received the approval of the Supreme Court, and had been put on the ballot, the regular 1990 session would already be history. The OEA plan was probably aimed at quieting restive members, but it did start my thinking seriously about a special session to deal exclusively with education issues and it gave impetus to that course of action.

At a cabinet meeting, I brought up the idea of a special session to deal exclusively with education reform and funding. To my surprise, the suggestion received almost immediate and unanimous support from cabinet officers. After that meeting, discussions were held with State Finance Director Dr. Lex Holmes, Chief of Staff Andrew Tevington, Secretary of Education Sandy Garrett, and a few others about getting legislation ready for introduction at a special session. Then, we set the date of August 14 for the special session and began a furious effort inside our office to draw up the proposed legislation. Knowing that it was unlikely that the legislature would vote the major tax increase to properly fund education in Oklahoma, we decided we would not ask for a tax measure but for a vote of the people on a proposition which would have eliminated the household personal property tax, the tax on small farms and small businesses, and the tax on the first $500,000 of property value of large businesses, with the remainder being distributed statewide. The sales tax rate would be *reduced* from four percent to three percent. Revenue lost by lowering the taxes plus $280 million of new money would be raised by extending the sales tax to cover services, except those related to health care. The net result would have been an increase of about $280,000,000 in revenues for education. From this amount, each teacher would receive a $5,000 pay raise and the balance would be available for a variety of education reforms.

Admittedly, the plan was put together quickly and not enough attention was given to the package of reforms we were recommending. We felt details would be added to the legislation as it moved through the House and Senate. The major reform we recommended gave parents the right to enroll students in the public school they felt would provide the best opportunity for an education so long as the receiving school agreed to the transfer. In my mind, raising teacher salaries to competitive levels so we could attract and hold our best teachers was the biggest reform of all. The decision was made not to discuss the upcoming special session with any of the legislative leaders, since the leaders, who had only recently finished the shortened session required by the constitutional amendment which I had sponsored, would now be unwilling to bring the House and Senate back into session so soon. If we discussed the matter with them then called the session over their objections, it was likely they would quickly adjourn and nothing would be accomplished. On the other hand, if I, a Republican governor, called the session and the Democratic leadership refused to take it seriously, the educators would be very angry with the Democratic leadership. This was not likely to happen since the OEA is considered to be a major part of the Democratic power base in Oklahoma. Speaker Steve Lewis was considering becoming a candidate for governor and needed the support of educators.

These assumptions proved to be accurate. When it was first announced, the special session was highly unpopular — not only with the Democratic leadership but among the membership of the House and Senate as well. Republican leaders were incensed. Their reaction was "call the damn thing off." This was borne out dramatically when only one member, a Republican, would agree to introduce my education bill. Without even the courtesy of hearings, the House voted ninety-six to one against approving my education package. Most members felt they would then adjourn and go home.

Perhaps it was due to Speaker Lewis's leadership skills, his personal political ambitions, or a fundamental mistake that adjournment did not happen. Rather, the speaker brought out his own education proposal, which included a $350,000,000 tax increase and a great expansion of the reforms we had recommended. The Lewis Plan included many reforms which apparently had been under consideration by staff prior to the calling of the special session. The effect of the Lewis action was to give vigorous life to the special session education reform idea and insure that action would be taken to improve education in Oklahoma. I was delighted. I felt that much of the speaker's proposal had an excellent chance of passing the House and that if it did, the Senate would not allow the program to die on its doorstep.

After the introduction of the Lewis proposal and the defeat of my plan, Task Force 2000 was brought up in a meeting between the House and Senate leadership and myself. Task Force 2000 had been authorized by an act of the 1989 session. It called for the creation of a twenty-seven-member study commission to look into needed changes so the state could better educate its citizens for the next century. Neither the speaker nor the president pro tempore nor I had taken the Task Force 2000 resolution seriously. None of the appointments had been made. It was decided that we should immediately make these appointments and give Task Force 2000 the responsibility of examining the needs of Oklahoma education and making recommendations as to how these needs could be met. This was done and Task Force 2000 began meeting. The special session recessed from August until October to give the task force time to do its job. Considerable thought went into selecting the chairman of Task Force 2000. There were two names that came to mind immediately. One was George Bragg and the other was George Singer — both Tulsa business leaders. On checking into George Bragg's background, we found that none of his children had attended public schools, whereas the entire Singer family were products of the Tulsa Public School system. For that reason, George Singer was selected. On the one hand, Singer turned out to be a wise choice since he was a man of great intellect, boundless energy, and enormous drive. On the other hand, once the education bill was developed, he came to be regarded as arrogant and was not as effective as he might have been in helping secure passage.

Task Force 2000 worked tirelessly during the eight weeks it was given to hold hearings, bring in education authorities from around the country, listen to ideas from various legislators, parents, teachers, businessmen and education leaders, and examine the financial needs of Oklahoma's educational system. Their report and recommendations were published in a timely way and were available for guidance to the legislature when it came back into session on November 6, 1989. The education proposal became House Bill 1017, and recommendations by Task Force 2000 were its backbone. It was first considered by the House; hearings by the House education committee and the mark-up of the bill required the better part of a week, during which some seventy amendments were considered and many of the proposed reforms were deleted.

Speaker Lewis and I met and concluded that the best plan was to get the bill through the House in whatever form possible, get it through the Senate, and write the legislation in a conference committee. Lewis was determined that the bill not die in the House because senators were enjoying the difficulty the speaker was having in getting the votes to pass it. He wanted the Senate to get its full share of the political controversy.

To get the bill through the House required the support of several Republicans. Most Republican representatives were frightened by the notion of voting for a major tax increase. Many of them had run for office on a no-new-tax pledge. All of them felt they would be seriously criticized if they voted for higher taxes even as part of an education reform package. One by one, we convinced Republican House members to support the bill. The final move was mine when I met with three House members from Tulsa. These men were all concerned that needed reforms would not be in the bill when it cleared the conference committee and came up for final passage. They felt it would be simply a huge tax increase when it came back for final action. I assured them that they would have a hand in deciding whether the bill contained the reforms which we all agreed were essential, and if it didn't, I would veto the bill. This seemed to give them the assurance they needed and we received eight Republican votes when the bill came up for final action and passed fifty-five to forty-six. The vote on the emergency clause, which would put the plan into operation immediately, was two short when two freshmen Republicans failed to keep their promises. On a second vote, the exact number needed attached the emergency.

After the House passed the bill, the Senate seemed to realize that it had to get serious about education issues. We were fortunate on the Senate side to have Bernice Shedrick as the chairman of the education committee. Senator Shedrick represented the Stillwater district where Oklahoma State University is located. She realized, as did some others, that solving the needs of primary and secondary education would make it easier to deal with the pressing needs of higher education. Senator Shedrick held extensive hearings and spent a week in mark-up of the House-approved bill. Fortunately, on the Senate side there was much interest in reform and many of the Task Force 2000 recommendations — plus several others which members of the Senate supported — were put back in the bill. Senate Republicans participated actively in the mark-up process and several of their amendments were included in the committee-approved bill.

After the Senate education committee had acted, I began the process of trying to secure Republican senators' votes. This proved to be much more difficult than was the case on the House side. On the House side, Representative Joe Heaton was minority leader and was not in favor of the bill. But he was willing to let his members act individually and independently. On the Senate side, the minority leader was Jerry Pierce of Bartlesville. Pierce was determined to hold the Senate Republicans together as a block in opposition to the bill. He told me face-to-face that the only amendment he would allow to be made on the floor was an amendment taking out all the new money, which was the same as killing the bill. He was not willing to allow the bill to be amended in any other way. Without some Republican Senate votes it was impossible to make progress.

The Christmas season was now approaching. The legislature went into recess for two weeks during the holidays. Soon after the recess began, the Tulsa Republican Senate delegation held a news conference in Tulsa. When I read the report of the news conference I was astounded because the Tulsa Republicans took the position that if the Senate Democrats would allow five reforms to be added, they would vote as a group for the bill. Senator Smith was quoted in the *Tulsa World* as saying the Republicans wanted the bill to have five reform issues: mandatory consolidation, open transfers between districts, a $1,500 raise for all teachers, merit pay for teachers, and removal of teacher tenure. No mention was made of changing the level of funding. Upon reading this news account, I realized that Jerry Pierce did not have his delegation locked up behind his amendment to take out the money. I immediately scheduled a breakfast meeting in Tulsa with the five Republican senators and discussed the matter with them. They agreed that the statement in the newspaper was accurate and if the five amendments could be agreed to, they would support the bill.

From that meeting I went to Bartlesville and had lunch with Senator Pierce. I reminded him that during his campaign he had invited me to Bartlesville to help him raise money for his campaign and that I had gone there under some difficulty. I told him that I had come to his support when he needed it, but I was not going to ask him to come to my support.

Rather, I asked him to get out of the way and let me work with the Republican members of the Senate individually as I'd done on the House side and I felt he agreed. At least he did not disagree.

Following that meeting, I scheduled a dinner at the governor's house on the night before the session was to reconvene. To that dinner I invited Senator Charley Ford of Tulsa and Senator Gary Gardenhire of Norman as well as President Pro Tem Bob Cullison and Senator Herb Rozell who represented the area near Tahlequah. Also present were Secretary of Education Sandy Garrett and Superintendent of Public Instruction Gerald Hoeltzel. I had asked Hoeltzel to prepare a proposal for funding voluntary consolidation which had been discussed in Tulsa as well as Bartlesville and at a luncheon with Senator Gardenhire.

At dinner, discussion went round and round for a couple of hours. It was obvious from the kinds of objections they raised that Senators Ford and Gardenhire were trying to find ways of avoiding the issue. Senator Rozell, who was most impacted by consolidation, appeared willing to see some of his rural schools consolidate, provided it was done on a voluntary basis. Senator Gardenhire proposed taking $25,000,000 out of the Rainy Day Fund to help consolidating districts build needed new facilities, purchase needed equipment, and/or pay "severance" to administrators or teachers who lost their jobs in the consolidation process. This seemed to please Senator Rozell and gave the Republicans the victory they wanted on the consolidation issue. It was planned that the consolidation would reduce the number of school districts from 250 to 150 districts. Many districts knew they were going to be merged or consolidated since it would be impossible for them to meet new curriculum standards.

After the dinner, Senator Cullison and I talked about how to proceed. He decided to bring HB 1017 to the floor, which was done the next day. During floor action, each of the Republican amendments was accepted and I felt the matter was settled. In our discussions, the subject of money had been raised. We had modified the proposal to provide a $5,000 increase in beginning teachers' pay with other salary schedules to be adjusted accordingly. The Republican position had been that they would support whatever tax increase was required to pay the cost. To my amazement, the Republicans, after having been successful in all their amendments, proposed cutting the revenue package from $230,000,000 to about $120,000,000 by taking out the half-cent increase in sales tax. This was totally unacceptable both to me and legislative leaders since it would make it impossible to pay the $5,000 salary increase to which I felt we'd agreed.

A series of heated and lengthy meetings followed. It appeared that only two Republicans — Senators Gardenhire and Olin Branstetter — would support the bill as it stood. Ford, who was the leader of the Tulsa group, was determined to cut back on the money. He wanted to send the bill to conference where the exact costs would be worked out and then agree to raise whatever money was required. I tried to convince him that $230,000,000 would not be adequate in any event since it would take $200,000,000 to pay a $5,000 pay raise to the state's 40,000 teachers and that the other reforms would certainly cost more than $30,000,000. Senator Ford remained adamant, as did other Republican senators.

Again, political dynamics came into play. One was the fact that Senator Ford had lost his 1988 race for minority leader. He felt the loss was due to his support of the previous tax increase and was determined to hold out against a second tax increase. Senator Frank Rhodes of Tulsa was being challenged by Democratic Representative Kevin Easley in his upcoming race for reelection. Rhodes wanted to position himself to the right of Easley and he felt this could be accomplished by opposing HB 1017. Easley had voted for the education bill on the House side. To me Rhodes' position made no sense since both Tulsa newspapers as well as most business leaders in Tulsa supported 1017 vigorously. Another problem was with Senator Jerry Smith, who we felt was almost a sure vote for the education package. Smith had been minority leader when we passed the tax bill in 1987 and had shown true leadership qualities in that contest. The problem was that Senator Smith planned to become a Republican candidate for governor. He did not want to vote for a second major tax increase and further alienate conservatives. Senator Ged Wright's problem was that he felt the business leaders of Tulsa had lobbied him in a rough and insulting fashion during public meetings. Even though he liked the bill and particularly the reforms that were in it, he was determined to get even by withholding his support. Senator Don Rubottom, a freshman member, was full of ideas. While he claimed to support education, his comments made it clear he had no intention of voting for any bill that could conceivably be passed. One of the problems may have been that the Rubottom children were being "home schooled." The senator's real interest in improving the public school system was not evident.

On the day the Senate took up the bill, I was scheduled to go to Detroit for meetings with executives of the Ford and General Motors corporations. These companies operate large facilities in Oklahoma and both were considering major investments in updating the technology of their factories. We delayed the departure as long as possible and I spent the time talking to various members of the Senate, hoping to be able to bring out the five Republican votes that Senator Cullison felt he needed to pass the bill. I could come up with only two votes, even though we talked with and cajoled every remotely winnable Republican.

On the trip to Detroit with me were Secretary of Commerce Don Paulson; Ed Martin, general manager of the *Daily Oklahoman*; and Bill Durrett, CEO of American Fidelity Insurance Company. At our meeting with Ford officials, I asked what we could do to help improve the economic climate for the company factory in Tulsa. Without a moment's hesitation, the reply came: "Improve your schools." I looked at Ed Martin and he had obviously gotten the message. On the way back from Detroit, I suggested to Ed that if the *Daily Oklahoman*, which had been lukewarm towards the whole education reform proposition, was now convinced that the bill contained the necessary reforms, it would be very helpful if they could let this be known. He agreed the bill included the reforms they wanted. I suggested we have a breakfast at the governor's house on Monday morning before the Senate convened and he agreed to come and bring Jim Standard who is in charge of the editorial page. We invited Senator Kay Dudley, Senator Tom Cole, and Senator Howard Hendrick, all of the Oklahoma City area, as well as Joe Heaton. Joe was invited because, as Republican House minority leader, if he understood that the *Daily Oklahoman* was now behind this proposition, he might be more helpful when the bill came back from conference. Ed Martin was far less forthright at the breakfast than he had been on the plane. In conversations I had held with the editorial board of the *Oklahoman*, publisher Ed Gaylord had indicated that the paper might take a moderate position. In one meeting, he concluded by saying, "Hell, I know education needs more money. Just don't waste it." However, for reasons I don't understand, the *Daily Oklahoman* became increasingly strident in its opposition to 1017 in both editorial comment and news coverage.

Partially compensating for the opposition from the state's largest newspaper, strong support developed from a consortium of more than a dozen statewide organizations. The consortium was led by the Oklahoma State Chamber of Commerce and included farm groups, labor groups, educational groups, economic developers, and professional organizations. Also, much of the electronic media and the Tulsa newspapers were favorable to the bill.

By the time the House was to vote on the conference committee report, the *Daily Oklahoman* was publishing front page editorials regularly attacking the education bill for its many assumed deficiencies and threatening the political demise of legislators who voted for the proposal. This made it difficult to hold the Republicans who had voted for HB 1017 when the bill cleared the House the first time. It was necessary to secure new commitments to win approval of the conference report.

The passage of 1017 was not too difficult but gaining the two-thirds majority necessary to attach the emergency clause and make the bill effective immediately appeared to be impossible. The Oklahoma constitution provides that when a bill is passed without the emergency attached, the law does not become law for ninety days during which time citizens may circulate petitions calling for a vote on the issue. If the petition receives the required number of signatures the bill does not become law until approved by a statewide vote. The House and Senate leadership and I had agreed that under no circumstances would 1017 be sent to the governor unless the emergency was attached. We knew that the 90,000 signatures needed to put the matter to a vote of the people could easily be secured. This would put school funding in limbo for several months or years while the matter was reviewed by the courts, appeals were decided, and the issue was finally voted on by the people. There was slim chance that a bill of over 150 pages containing a major tax increase would be read and understood. If the vote came after the bill had been in operation for a year or more and voters could see the results from education improvements in action and understand that the impact of the tax increases was relatively mild, 1017 would have a better chance of surviving.

The first break came when former Senator Garrison of Bartlesville called to tell me that Representative Jim Dunlap of Dewey had sent word that he would vote for the emergency. He wanted his decision kept absolutely secret until the vote was cast. This was good news but of course the information had to be shared with the speaker so he would know what the vote count was. Somehow, during the day, the information got back to Dunlap that I had told the speaker how Dunlap would vote and Dunlap was furious. He then changed his position and said he would no longer vote for the emergency. Many discussions went on to try to get him back on board but we were not successful.

Representative Karroll Rhoads of Ada was a vote we desperately needed. A Republican, he represented Pontotoc County, a strongly Democratic area, and had been elected under extraordinary circumstances. The incumbent legislator had been defeated in a primary after being arrested on a drunk driving charge. The Democratic nominee was not a well-respected or well-known candidate and Rhoads was able to win in the general election. Rhoads was an attractive young businessman who was well regarded. He was elected as a Republican in spite of heavy Democratic registration. At the same time, he recognized that his situation was somewhat tenuous and felt that voting for any tax bill would bring an end to his political career. However, Ada is the home of Southeastern State University and a considerable university constituency realized that solving the common school funding problem would make it easier for funds to be made available to higher education. Using this argument, I got Rhoads to agree to vote for the emergency. He made the commitment in the presence of Speaker Lewis. It's easy to imagine how dismayed and disappointed we both were when, during the roll call on the emergency, Rhodes went back on his word. The same thing happened with Dunlap and the tally came up two votes short.

Representative Bill Brewster had chosen that particular day to announce his candidacy for Congress in the third district. About 10 p.m., the House leadership received word that a plane carrying two of the Brewster children and two campaign supporters was missing. At the time of the recess at midnight, no one knew whether the outcome of the Brewster family crisis would be tragedy or thanksgiving. By morning, no word of the missing plane had been received and it was known it could not still be in the air. An intensive search began and legislative activity was put on hold. The weather was overcast so that search for the missing aircraft was virtually stalled until the weather improved. Many resources of the state were activated to help in the search. At the same time, privately owned planes from in and out of state as well as some federal resources were brought in.

On Saturday, I went to Ardmore, where the missing plane was likely to be found. A report from the Federal Aviation Authority in Ft. Worth indicated the plane had last been seen on radar as it attempted to make a landing at the Ardmore airport. The pilot of the missing plane had not filed a flight plan, so his route was not known and the search had to cover a wide area. On Sunday, the search continued, using National Guard helicopters, Civil Aeronautics and civilian aircraft, ground searches by the Highway Patrol and National Guard. Hundreds of volunteers walked the countryside. Late on Sunday afternoon, a farmer near Coalgate went out to feed her cows and found the crashed airplane only a quarter of a mile from her home. There were no survivors.

The Brewster tragedy totally stalled legislative work for a week. No effort was made to line up other votes until after the funeral and after time enough had lapsed to allow Bill Brewster to feel he could come back to cast his vote. Once the session was reconvened, efforts were made again to line up the votes of Dunlap and Rhoads. Again, in the presence of the speaker and the governor, Rhoads fervently promised that the next time we needed his vote he would be there. In the meantime, Tom Manar, a Democrat from Hinton, came in with a problem dealing with the state banking commissioner. The problem was easily resolved and Manar decided he would change and vote for the emergency on the education bill. Representative Bill Veitch, a Republican of Tulsa who had been the lone vote for the education proposition I had put forward, decided for reasons of his own to cast his vote for the emergency even though he had voted against it the first time around. This gave us two extra votes, assuming Dunlap and Rhoads kept their promises.

On the basis of these commitments and with the understanding that Brewster would be present for the vote, Speaker Lewis called for another vote on the emergency clause. At the same time, Representative Rick Williamson of Tulsa had an emergency in his family when a member was hospitalized for surgery. We sent a plane to Tulsa where it stood by to bring Williamson from the hospital to Oklahoma City to cast his vote.

The vote had to be kept open for several hours while Brewster made the 120-mile drive from Marietta. In the meantime, four Republicans withheld their votes until Brewster arrived. When Brewster finally came into the chamber and cast his vote for the emergency, three Republicans voted aye and, again, Rep. Rhoads voted no. The emergency was attached with exactly the required number of votes.

The action on House Bill 1017 then moved to the Senate where the proposition initially passed rather easily with no Republican votes. Senator Branstetter of Ponca City was in the chamber but did not vote either way. Apparently, he did not want to be the only Republican voting yes, though he plainly favored the bill. After the Senate had approved the measure, the push began to try to get the two-thirds vote needed for the emergency.

In something of a paradox, the Republican senators in the Oklahoma City area were fearful of voting for the emergency because of the violent opposition being expressed regularly by the *Daily Oklahoman*. At the same time in Tulsa, both the *Tribune* and the *World* newspapers, as well as prominent business leaders, were so strongly for the education reform bill and had criticized Republican hold-outs so vigorously that senators were angered and refused to vote for the proposition, though some of them claimed to favor it in principle. It was a curious set of circumstances to find newspapers in one town blamed for being too strongly in favor and in the other town for being too strongly in opposition. These seemed lame excuses to vote against something that most senators knew needed to be done.

Of the Democrats who voted against the question, several readily agreed to vote for the emergency, but Senator Branstetter was the only Republican who came around. After many hours of discussion with every Republican who seemed at all approachable, there was still no movement. In fact, it got to the place that members were refusing to talk to me. At this point, I went to the fourth and fifth floors of the state capitol and buttonholed members in their offices. Several terse, unpleasant exchanges occurred. The most likely Republican hold-out was Senator Gardenhire of Norman, where Oklahoma University is located. He had voted for the proposition the first time it cleared the Senate and we were counting heavily on his staying with us when the conference committee report came back for a vote. However, during the interim, Gardenhire had been offended by something attributed to a member of the governor's staff and refused to vote for the proposition even though he said he favored it. Senator Tom Cole, a former Republican state chairman, appeared to be actively solidifying votes against House Bill 1017. Cole, a very partisan man, felt Republicans could gain major political advantage by opposing 1017 and the tax increase it included — even though portions of his district were highly involved in education. Philosophically, Cole said he supported educational reforms, but he felt using the measure to make Republican legislative gains was smart politics. He cited public opinion polls which he maintained proved his point.

Early in April, Senator Jerry Smith of Tulsa came to the office and proposed a new package of revenues and reforms to break the stalemate over House Bill 1017. Republicans had previously insisted that the revenue package not include the sales tax and therefore, that the total amount raised be less than $150 million. The Smith proposal was that the total amount of revenue raised be in the range of $200 million and that new revenues be only from income tax and corporate tax increases.

Based on the conversations with Senator Smith, I asked State Finance Director Lex Holmes to put together a new set of income tax tables which would generate in the range of $185 million. This, added to the corporate tax increase, would provide roughly $200 million of new funds for education. This was done and I furnished the information to Smith who seemed impressed since the additional income tax per citizen was relatively small.

Also, fearing that the negotiations were finally going to break down and come to naught, I asked Lex to make a summary of all the available dollars that could possibly be appropriated for education in case HB 1017 finally failed to receive the votes necessary to attach the emergency clause. The state finance office quickly produced a chart showing the amount of money available from rainy day funds, growth revenues, and the so-called five percent money, which had accumulated at the end of the fiscal year due to the fact that revenues were exceeding certification levels. The tables showed that by calling a special session in mid-July after the end of the fiscal year the legislature could appropriate $254,000,000 of what amounted to "one-time money" for education. This would truly create a crisis for the next governor and the next legislature because these funds would not be available again. Educational spending would have been raised to a level at which it could not be sustained except through a tax increase which the next legislature would be under great pressure to pass. While use of these one-time monies would solve the immediate education crisis, it would create a trap for the next governor and the next legislature and force a tax increase.

Negotiations between the governor's office and different Republican senators went on through the middle two weeks of April. From time to time, there seemed to be some movement among different members towards accepting the $200,000,000 figure — provided additional reforms were included. The difficulty was in finding reforms which members would accept. Some were very concerned that 1017 be amended to include parental choice of schools; some were concerned that the timeframe for consolidation be shortened; some were concerned that the teacher tenure provision in 1017 was too weak. Of course all were concerned about the amount and source of revenue. It seemed impossible to get a package together that the three to five votes needed could agree to without losing other votes. On a Thursday evening, I was asked to come to the fourth floor rotunda for a live interview on KJRH television in Tulsa. As the interview progressed, Senator Gardenhire happened to walk by. When the interview was over, he asked me to come back to the Senate lounge for a visit, which, of course, I was glad to do. When I reached the lounge, Senator Smith was there and the three of us had a lengthy conversation about what might be done.

It was obvious both of these Republican members were coming closer to agreeing that 1017 needed to pass in some form. It was finally agreed we would meet the next day, Friday, in Tulsa and that Senator Bernest Cain, an Oklahoma City Democrat, and Senate President Pro Tempore Cullison should be invited to join us.

A meeting in the Westin Hotel was arranged at which Senator Cullison and Senator Cain, Democrats, met with Republican Senators Smith and Gardenhire and myself. The conversations went on for about three hours and when it was over it was my understanding that the $200,000,000 package of revenues, including income and corporate tax, and a reform package which included shortening the consolidation timeframe and a parental choice program involving grades kindergarten through six, plus the dependent districts, would be agreed to.

While we were meeting in Tulsa, Kyle Dahlem, head of OEA, announced that on Monday teachers from all across the state would begin demonstrating at the state capitol. This development was a complete and unwelcome surprise. I was fearful that a teacher demonstration would generate a negative reaction from both the public and from undecided legislators. I called the OEA president and asked her to call the demonstration off. Her reply was that they had gone too far to stop. The matter was out of her hands.

On Monday when the session began, to my amazement, Gardenhire and Smith announced that Senator Charles Ford had become the principal negotiator for the Republicans. Ford was perhaps the most negative, abrasive, and recalcitrant of the Tulsa Five. Bringing him into the negotiations virtually assured that no agreement could be reached. Meanwhile, thousands of teachers, students, board of education members, and parents began assembling in the capitol building and marching on the capitol grounds. When Ford approached Senator Cullison with the Republican proposal, I was not present but the information I received was that Cullison was infuriated. It was not anything like the agreement discussed in Tulsa on the previous Friday. In addition to more reforms, the proposal cut the amount of money from $200,000,000 to less than $150,000,000. Obviously, the plan would not solve Oklahoma's education problems and Cullison could not sell such a package to the Democratic caucus.

On Tuesday, the educator demonstrations continued. In fact, numbers grew in spite of rain. It was becoming obvious that there was great support for education reform and improved funding not only among educators and business leaders but among the population at large. One television station announced the results of a "scientific" telephone poll conducted by a neutral out-of-state firm. Statewide, four hundred respondents voted eighty-two percent in favor of teacher salary increases. The same voters favored passage of House Bill 1017 by a margin of two to one. So much for Senator Cole's polls. If polls could be believed, citizens had changed their minds.

Early on Wednesday morning, I telephoned Senator Cullison in his Senate office. He invited me to come up immediately, which I did. I took with me the information I'd received from Lex Holmes earlier showing the amount of one-time funds which could be made available to support education in case 1017 finally failed to pass with the emergency. Both of us agreed that working out anything like a reasonable agreement with the Republicans was unlikely since Senator Ford had entered the picture as negotiator.

At first Senator Cullison seemed favorably inclined toward calling a special session to appropriate the one-time money for support of education if we could not get the votes to attach the emergency to HB 1017. Use of the money clearly would have made possible immediate major salary increases for teachers as well as providing funds for textbooks and an enriched educational program. Senator Cullison knew I wasn't bluffing because I had already called more special sessions than any other governor in Oklahoma history. He knew the special session would occur at the time the legislators would be running for reelection. Also, he knew that Democratic refusal to spend available funds for education as recommended by a Republican governor was politically unthinkable. He understood that use of this money would create a crisis for the next governor and the next legislature. After discussing the situation for a few moments, the light suddenly dawned on Senator Cullison that I would not be the next governor, since I had much earlier announced I would not seek reelection. Also, Speaker Lewis, who was a candidate for governor, was unlikely to be involved either. Looking at me, he said, "Damn you. You'll be gone next year and Lewis is not likely to be here. I'll be the only one around."

While I have no idea what went through Senator Cullison's mind, who he talked to, or what he did, I do know that on Wednesday even more thousands of demonstrators arrived at the capitol, marching again in the rain, and that sometime during the afternoon, the Democratic senators began to caucus. On Thursday the caucus continued for over six hours. The meeting became extremely tense as Senate leaders pressed hold-out members to vote for the emergency. Some members became highly emotional and tears were shed. Some felt they were committing political suicide. By mid-afternoon information reached our office that the Democrats had hammered out an agreement, that they were going back into session. We immediately switched on the speaker phones to listen to the floor debate.

It was obvious from listening to the debate that a deal had been struck. The debate was restrained and unimpassioned. Both Republicans and Democrats seemed to be in a highly conciliatory mood. Around 5 p.m. the vote was called with the exact number, thirty-three, voting for the emergency. Senator Branstetter was the lone Republican to vote yes.

A companion bill was also approved which provided exemption from the sales tax on groceries for families with incomes below $12,000 a year. This apparently was the concession made to the five Democrats who changed their votes on the emergency and made it possible for the bill to reach the governor's desk.

There was great rejoicing in the governor's office when the roll was called and the bill with the emergency passed. Immediately, we began planning for a celebration to mark the signing of House Bill 1017, which had been nine months in development and enactment. Friday night, April 20, I was scheduled to attend a meeting of the Oklahoma Education Association, where they had planned to give me the OEA Friend of Education award. The meeting turned out to be a celebration. The educators felt their participation in the demonstrations had made the difference in securing the votes to pass 1017. Without question they had a major impact.

My memory went back to my campaign for governor in 1962 when I had been opposed bitterly, and, I felt, unfairly, by the OEA under the leadership of Furman Phillips. After my election I never allowed Phillips to set foot in the governor's office. The National Education Association caused sanctions to be placed against Oklahoma schools because of their alleged poor quality, and this damaged the state's economic progress. In 1965, I was subjected to a demonstration outside the governor's office where some nine hundred teachers came to express their anger after I vetoed a teacher pay raise which the state had no money to honor. The passing of years had certainly made a difference with the OEA. At least on this night, Governor Bellmon was a champion and a friend.

Development and enactment of HB 1017, The Education Reform and Funding Act, had taken nine months. Part of the time was taken up by the work of Task Force 2000. Some time was lost because of the Brewster family tragedy. But much time was spent in endless discussions with Republicans trying to find a package of revenues and reforms to which they could agree. There were times when it seemed the negotiations were going forward in good faith only to have whatever progress had been made lost when Senator Ford or others, who had their own agendas or didn't know when they had made the best deal they could get, reentered the picture. The long time was unfortunate but not in vain since, increasingly, citizens became aware of shortcomings in Oklahoma's existing educational system and gained knowledge of the needed changes. They also became convinced of the direct relationship between an educated work force and economic progress. Problems, court decisions, and events in other states added impetus to the changes needed in Oklahoma.

The final package was not significantly different from that which had emerged from the conference committee. The only significant change was the addition of sales tax credits for low-income families. This will result in reducing education funds by roughly $10,000,000 the first year and about $20,000,000 each year thereafter. It has the salutary effect of making the Oklahoma sales tax slightly less regressive. This change, plus Senator Cullisons's leadership in the Democratic caucus, seemed to be what it took to gain the five Democratic votes needed to pass the emergency and put HB 1017 into effect immediately.

After the passage of House Bill 1017 with the emergency clause attached, I contacted the Senate president pro tempore and the speaker and told them that I would like to have a proper ceremony at a school, preferably in Tulsa, since the community support there was greater than in Oklahoma City. They readily agreed and I asked Linda Sponsler, who ran our Tulsa office, to choose a school. Linda quickly selected Marshall School, which already had been identified to receive a "school of excellence certificate" because of the work they were doing with handicapped children and in gaining parental involvement in school activities. The school is located in an integrated neighborhood, and the principal was highly supportive of education reform as was her husband, the news director for a leading Tulsa radio station. The station had been a strong voice in favor of House Bill 1017. Marshall School was located in the legislative district of Rob Johnson, who had voted for 1017 on the House side. It was also located in the district of Senator Rubottom, one of the bill's most vocal opponents. As far as I was concerned, that was not sufficient reason to look elsewhere.

When word reached legislative members that we were going to hold the signing at Marshall School, we received many negative comments. Black legislators felt we were making a mistake unless we went to an at-risk district. Also, they were vehemently opposed to signing the bill in Senator Rubottom's district. At the same time, many Republicans felt that picking Marshall School was a slap at Rubottom and they were also angry. I called Senator Cullison and his comment was, "You pick the school and we'll be there." As far as I was concerned, that settled it and the signing occurred at Marshall School.

The day of the signing was overcast with rain possible at any moment. This did not seem to dampen the spirit of the event. Colorful balloons and banners were everywhere. The halls of the school were decorated with art work by the students and a festive air was evident throughout the building. We had arranged for the state plane to take the legislative leaders and I travelled by car. I arrived early and visited several classes, including those of multiply handicapped students. At the appointed time, we went outside on the school ground where a platform had been erected along with a table where I was to sit for the formal bill-signing. The Speaker of the House, president pro tem, heads of the House and Senate education committees, and many other legislators were on hand. George Singer, chairman of Task Force 2000, and Joe Williams, president of the state Chamber of Commerce which had been highly visible in its supportive for HB 1017, were also present. Several hundred school patrons turned out. Many classes of children were seated in front of the speakers' platform. The speeches were generally short and well presented with many mutual exchanges of compliments to all involved. It was one of the happiest and most festive occasions of my political career.

Speaker Steve Lewis most accurately summed up events which led to the enactment of HB 1017 when he said, "This bill became law because several people did what they are supposed to do. The governor set the agenda as he is supposed to do. The House of Representatives wrote the tax law as it is supposed to do. The Senate deliberated over the reforms as it is supposed to do. By working together the task was accomplished."

The event was thoroughly covered by news media. I counted ten television cameras and there were many radio stations and newspapers represented. When the time for signing arrived, a cheer went up from the crowd and a feeling of accomplishment and relief swept over me as I'm sure it did the legislative and civic leaders present.

The creation, passage, and signing of House Bill 1017 marked the beginning of an historic change in Oklahoma's education system. In my remarks, I called attention to the fact that the legislature provided educators a tool to give Oklahoma an educational system second-to-none. It was now up to boards of education, administrations, parents, and teachers to deliver excellence in education. I spoke from my heart as

I called the signing of HB 1017 the highlight of my political career.

It will require the passage of some time before an accurate evaluation of the results of House Bill 1017 can be made. The immediate result has been smaller classes, improved curriculum and teaching materials, better teaching conditions, and some improvement in teacher salaries, particularly for beginning teachers. A year and a half after I signed the bill into law Oklahoma citizens voted by a substantial margin in a statewide election to retain HB1017. Oklahomans verified Thomas Jefferson's tenet that "a well-informed citizenry is seldom wrong."

In retrospect, I am mystified by the adamant and unrelenting opposition of Ed Gaylord and the *Daily Oklahoman* to the education bill. As a major booster of state economic development, I can understand his dislike for taxes and for waste in government spending. However, the *Oklahoman's* stance reveals an inability to recognize and accommodate the give and take that is essential to the legislative process. For a Republican governor, faced with a two-to-one-Democratic house and Senate, plus recalcitrant leaders in his own party, compromise is essential if anything is to get done. During the several weeks when the1017 battle was at its hottest, I talked to Ed Gaylord and his editorial writers five times. The last time I went to see Ed was after he had taken an adamant position in opposition. Once more we discussed the need for the bill, but he was unwavering. I didn't leave his office empty handed however. In one of his odd gestures of friendship, he picked up a nice letter opener off his desk and gave it to me. Actually, I'm as mystified by my relationship with Ed Gaylord as anyone else. We are, at once, personal friends and frequent adversaries on issues.

During this second term, Ed and Thelma Gaylord invited Shirley and me to go with them to Nashville a couple of times and once to Colorado Springs. During one trip to Tennessee, the state had just elected a new governor, and since Gaylord is such a major economic power because of his ownership of Opryland, the governor had invited Gaylord to the governor's house for dinner the first night we were there. Ed, Thelma, Shirley, and I went. Governor McWhirter had just returned from visiting the Tennessee National Guard units on active duty in Honduras following a hurricane. After he'd spent the night in Panama, he'd flown home that afternoon. Ed Gaylord, the governor, and I were standing in the living room eating shrimp and talking, as the governor told us about having spent the night in Panama. He said to Ed Gaylord, "You know, we never should have given the Canal away." Ed looked at me and smirked.

We went on talking awhile. It was at the time I had proposed the tax increase. Governor McWhirter said, "I have to work with the Republicans to keep the damn Democrats from forcing a tax increase."

I had proposed as part of my legislative package that Oklahoma legalize greyhound racing, as we had just legalized parimutuel horse racing. Ed Gaylord editorialized vigorously against dog racing even though many producers raise greyhounds in the southwestern part of the state. When I was campaigning, I told them I thought it only fair that they be treated equally with horse breeders. Governor McWhirter was talking about the airport and how it had to be expanded to take care of all the traffic coming to Opryland and that they had turned over the food service to a company out of Buffalo, N.Y.

He said, "I guess you know how they make their money?"

I said no.

He said, with a deep, disapproving voice, "Dog racing."

As soon as we got out of the governor's house, I turned to Ed and said, "You put him up to that." Ed swore he hadn't.

Shortly after HB 1017 was passed, Shirley and I were invited by the Oklahoma Cattleman's Association to the Lazy E Arena, which Eddie Gaylord owns, as guests for the "ranchers' rodeo." We sat with the director and the manager of the cattleman's association. After we'd been there a few minutes, to my total surprise, Ed Gaylord came to the box where we were sitting and visited for a while. As he was leaving, he said, "You and Shirley come join me and Thelma in our box."

While we were visiting with them in their box, Congressman Wes Watkins, who was running for governor, came by. I introduced him to Ed Gaylord. It was the first time the two of them had met. In a light-hearted vein, Wes Watkins peeled off a "Watkins for Governor" sticker and stuck it on the front of Ed Gaylord's jacket. Ed Gaylord immediately took it off and stuck it on the seat of his pants!

Again, just as he had when we were at odds over Panama, it seemed that Ed Gaylord was trying to tell me that our differences over issues didn't change our personal relationship. He needn't have been concerned. That's what Marine Corps boot camp is mostly about. It teaches recruits not to have tender feelings. Recruits are subjected to much unfair and unjustified criticism and are forbidden to react. Psychological pressure is applied to find the recruit's breaking point. If a recruit can't endure abuse, out he goes. I believe boot camp is the best training I ever had as preparation for politics.

During the scrap over the education funding bill I felt that far too many legislators tried to figure out what was good for them personally, rather than taking the position, "I know this is a good bill and even though I know it may cause me some political difficulty, I'm going to vote for what I believe to be in the best interest of my constituents." Over the years, I've seen public attitudes change as issues are better understood. The politician who tries to follow public opinion rather than lead gets left behind. It is, in my judgment, a perversion of the representative form of government for legislators to always put their own reelection concerns ahead of the good of the entity which they are elected to represent. This selfish and short sighted attitude will weaken and could ultimately destroy the representative form of government.

During my first term as governor, I once attended a Republican fundraising event in Oklahoma City where Bill Payne was master of ceremonies. Bill was a Cherokee who became one of Oklahoma's most prominent business and civic leaders, founder of Big Chief Drilling. As a Cherokee, Bill tended to be a man of few words. His introduction of me that day was typically brief. Calling me to the platform, he said, "My slogan is 'If you don't shoot any cartridges you won't get any partridges.' Here's a man who follows that same philosophy."

I found the description flattering, the admonition accurate. And, during my second governor's term, we fired some big cartridges. Many needed changes resulted.

Swan Song

"I'd Do It All Over Again"

Even after forty-four years as a participant and observer, I confess a love for politics and for self-government. Politics is the process that makes self-government possible. Representative government allows the constant adjustment and delivery of public services to meet changing human needs. During a lifetime, a dedicated, talented surgeon, teacher, or engineer may be able to improve the lot of a few hundred or even thousands of people. A gifted politician, by devising the means to construct highways, improve schools, resolve class conflicts, or secure economic justice can better the existence of millions, present and future.

Critics who focus endlessly on the shortcomings and foibles of politicians and practitioners of the art of government seem to expect perfection. In so doing, they undermine public confidence in the political process. Perfection, while an admirable goal, will remain unattainable so long as imperfections persist in human nature. For politics is people and while voters generally do an admirable job of screening out the miscreants, an occasional mistake is unavoidable. On the balance, the process is working well.

Our representative form of government is the best ever devised. The system deserves public respect, understanding, and even admiration because most people in government are dedicated to public service. Citizens need more complete knowledge of how we are being served than is available under the "unless it's bad, it ain't news" media policy. If neglected or mistrusted, U.S. government could get worse, a lot worse. It will change for the better when the people involved change for the better. Like the Marines, our government needs a few — only a few — good people.

My friend Clyde Wheeler says, "The people really want a king—

someone to worship." I hope not. It is my intention, by candidly review-
ing my own career, to remove some of the mystique about politics and
politicians and make the profession more attractive. What really is
needed is a few years of dedicated public service from individuals who
have the rare, God-given political talent Senator Kerr talked about and
a desire to be of public service. My own career has shown that it is not
necessary for an individual to be rich, handsome, eloquent, famous,
brilliant, charismatic, or clairvoyant to be elected and serve in high
political office. What seems to be necessary is a common touch, a closet
free of skeletons, an abundance of energy, the ability to communicate
clearly and directly, a supportive family, and a wealth of friends. A refusal
to be cowed by long odds helps, as does a sense of humility and a *thick
skin.*

Individuals with these attributes need to make themselves available to
the voters and be willing to take the lumps and accept the challenges, the
personal rewards, and the sacrifices, that go with public service. The
personal satisfaction can be great. The financial awards do not compare
with those available in the private sector. If getting rich is your goal, stay
out of politics and government. Politics can be fun if it is looked upon as
combat without real bullets. Outmaneuvering and outsmarting opponents can bring the same sense of accomplishment in office or on the
campaign trail that it does on the battlefield with a lot less risk of life and
limb. If a few good people are motivated to enter the system, I will feel my
efforts in writing this tome have been richly rewarded.

The governor's job is a good job — probably the best job in government. It is where the action is. Unlike federal problems, state problems
are of a size that can be dealt with. The governor is close enough to
explain the options and generally win public acceptance of logical
solutions. Citizens are likely to support distasteful action if they understand the necessity and are willing to pay the reasonable costs of needed
governmental services without borrowing against the future as the federal government increasingly does. There might not be a ninety-five
percent reelection rate of congressional incumbents if taxpayers were
required to pay for all the federal services received as they must pay for
state services.

One day in the final months of my second term as governor comes to
mind. As our plane left Wiley Post airport in Oklahoma City, we flew low

over a new stretch of highway being built by the state highway department along Hefner Road and then over the new John Kilpatrick Turnpike with which it connects. Together, these road jobs represent some $200 million of expenditure of public funds, hundreds of new jobs, and improved driving safety. Neither project would have been possible without leadership by the governor's office. On my recommendation, the legislature enacted a six-cent increase in fuel tax and passed a turnpike authorization bill. The tax was needed to match federal funds, which taxpayers had already paid into the federal treasury and which could not be brought home without state matching funds. Our flight took us to Tulsa, where a meeting was held with the mayor and other members of city government. The discussion there had to do with learning a lesson from our difficulties in acquiring right-of-way for the Creek Nation Turnpike. We talked about making advance right-of-way acquisitions so this same situation would not occur years hence when the road is extended to the east.

The next meeting was with a prominent banker and civic leader to discuss a children's program in which he was greatly interested. The conversation turned to negotiations going on with outside investors attempting to acquire the bank from the FDIC. At noontime, a lunch was held at the new $200 million Kimberly-Clark plant, which came to Oklahoma only after we won a competition with Kansas by the passage of new legislation giving needed tax breaks to the company. Attending the lunch were members of the governor's CEO team, a group of business executives who get together twice a year to provide updates on developments in their fields of endeavor and bring out problems that can and should be addressed by state government. Collectively, the group provides many thousands of jobs and is an active force for economic development in Oklahoma. A tour of the plant and discussion with different workers revealed that the two hundred Kimberly-Clark jobs were good jobs, providing better lives and opportunities for advancement to former aircraft workers, educators, and sales people. Taken together, the day gave a satisfying sense of involvement and accomplishment. Not every day is like that.

During the 1990 governor's campaign, in which I was persona non grata in both Republican and Democratic camps, arrangements were made to bring President Bush to Oklahoma to support the Republican nominee Bill Price. When the president arrived at Tinker Air Base, I was struck by the enormity of Air Force One, the huge new 747 airplane with its dark blue nose, soft blue underbelly, huge, quiet engines, and the U.S. flags painted on the fuselage. I was beginning to savor the majesty of the moment, even beginning to enjoy the feeling of nostalgia that swept over me since I had been through many presidential arrivals in the past and I knew this would be the last one.

The plane was parked, the engines shut down and the steps put in place. Then the door opened and President Bush stepped out with Congressman Mickey Edwards at his side. I was immediately struck by the congressman's presence, because he had strongly opposed President Bush during the presidential primary less than two years earlier and, in recent days, had voted against the president in the crucial deficit-reduction battle. Apparently, the congressman felt that riding in Air Force One, even with a president he opposed, was good politics. The president came down the steps, shook hands with the assembled generals, politicos, and friends, and went immediately to greet a military group, recently returned from Saudi Arabia. They had been assembled for a photographic opportunity with the president. Next, he went through the routine of shaking hands with the crowd assembled in the area roped off for spectators. One small lad was missed. President Bush saw him crying, went back, shook his hand, and gave him a pen imprinted with the presidential seal. The boy hopped up and down for joy.

At this point, the limos with the thick, bulletproof glass and bomb-proof underbellies that had been flown in from Washington were brought into place. A Secret Service agent gave instructions for Senator Don Nickles, candidate Bill Price, and myself to get in the back for the ride with the president to the Cowboy Hall of Fame where a fund-raising reception was underway. As we rode, President Bush kept looking out the window for spectators to whom he could wave. There were none. As we came near the Cowboy Hall of Fame, we saw a line of protestors that police had managed to cordon off roughly a block from the caravan route. As we came into the Cowboy Hall of Fame we passed the place where a presidential photographic opportunity had been arranged for gubernatorial campaign supporters who had "maxed out" with $5,000 contributions.

First in line were publisher Ed and Thelma Gaylord. We shook hands and I moved on to the assembly hall where the crowd was being entertained by a band and emcee-turned-cheerleader. As I looked out across the throng, I saw hardly a face I recognized. There was an obvious generational and philosophical gulf between myself and supporters of the Republican candidate who aspired to take my place and who opposed much of what I had accomplished. The room was hot, the acoustics were terrible, and the crowd was uncomfortably jammed together. After a few minutes, candidate Price and his family came on the platform where he was soon joined by the president, Senator Don Nickles, and Congressman Mickey Edwards. All three of these stalwarts had opposed candidate Bush in his presidential primary campaign two years before.

While President Bush was attempting to establish himself as the education president, candidate Price was campaigning to undo the Education Reform and Funding Act which I'd struggled for nine months to enact. (He would be soundly defeated.) Nickles recently had joined Edwards in voting against the presidential plan to reduce the federal deficit. It seemed odd, but strangely appropriate, that Oklahoma's Republican governor, who had been a longtime friend of George Bush and who had served as the Oklahoma Bush for President campaign chairman, had not been invited to appear with him on the platform. I felt more at home in the crowd of strangers.

The president's speech was a surprise. He said a few nice things about the politicians on the platform with him, mentioned my name favorably, and then launched into a vigorous and almost vicious attack against Democrats. I had read in the morning paper that his deficit-reduction package had been approved with votes of far more Democrats than Republicans. Most of the members of his own party opposed him when the chips were down. The tongue-lashing seemed inappropriate. The hypocrisy and phoniness of politics began to rankle, and the thought struck me that I'd been here too long. It was time to leave, so I did.

My daughter, Pat, and her three-year-old son were spending the night at the governor's mansion. Will and I had a rousing pillow fight and I thought to myself, this is the real world; no phoniness here.

Presbyterians have a tenet which is called predestination. It holds that behind the order in the universe there is a supreme being — the ultimate intellect — God — who is the architect of all creation. It is incomprehensible that such a supreme being would create the cosmos without an ordered plan. The same holds for the affairs of the human race. While we are free to use our wills, our lives are most satisfying when we find our place in God's plan. How do we know? That's where prayer and conscience come in.

Most of my political life, even in the midst of heated controversy, I have felt good about my involvement in politics and government. Sometimes I won; sometimes I lost; but on the balance my sense of accomplishment greatly exceeds the frustrations. The feeling of being where the action is, where problems are solved, where conflicts are resolved, has no equal in my experience. Would I recommend a political career to others? Yes, if the individual has a tough hide and feels driven to enter the fray in order to render a public service. Otherwise, no.

Would I do it again? Without a moment's hesitation, the answer is unequivocally, yes. It's been a good forty-four years. At the same time, I'm glad the phoniness is over for me and my family.